THE BANK OF ENGLAND

The Bank of England

Money, Power and Influence 1694–1994

Edited by

RICHARD ROBERTS
DAVID KYNASTON

OXFORD · CLARENDON PRESS
1995

Oxford University Press, Walton Street, Oxford OX2 6DP

Oxford New York
Athens Auckland Bangkok Bombay
Calcutta Cape Town Dar es Salaam Delhi
Florence Hong Kong Istanbul Karachi
Kuala Lumpur Madras Madrid Melbourne
Mexico City Nairobi Paris Singapore
Taipei Tokyo Toronto
and associated companies in
Berlin Ibadan

Oxford is a trade mark of Oxford University Press

Published in the United States
by Oxford University Press Inc., New York

British Library Cataloguing in Publication Data
Data available

Library of Congress Cataloging in Publication Data
The Bank of England: money, power, and influence 1694–1994 /
edited by Richard Roberts and David Kynaston.
Includes bibliographical references.
1. Bank of England—History. 2. Central banks —England—History.
I. Roberts, Richard, 1952– . II. Kynaston, David.
HG2994.B24 1995 332.1'1'0941—dc20 94–48640
ISBN 0–19–828952–9

1 3 5 7 9 10 8 6 4 2

Set by Hope Services (Abingdon) Ltd.
Printed in Great Britain
on acid-free paper by
Biddles Ltd.
Guildford & King's Lynn

INTRODUCTION

THE history of the Bank of England has been a subject of much scholarly interest. Foremost are the studies by Sir John Clapham (covering 1694 to 1914), Richard Sayers (1891 to 1944), and John Fforde (1941 to 1958). Together they amount to well over two thousand pages. These magisterial official histories by eminent authorities were the product of an enlightened appreciation of the importance of history on the part of the Bank. They constitute a remarkable monument to sponsored scholarship. There is also a considerable, and growing, monograph and academic journal literature on aspects of the Bank's activities that has come into being with the opening of the Bank's archives to outside scholars. Finally, there is a genre of journalistic writing, usually based on interviews with Bank officials and others, that provides a lively picture of the more recent past.

We offer a different approach. Arising from a conference to mark the 300th anniversary of the foundation of the Bank, each essay in this collection takes a long-term perspective on an important dimension of the Bank's activities. Whereas the viewpoint of the official historians is that of the Bank and the world seen through the Bank's eyes, the focus in this collection is the Bank in the context of a set of broad themes. Drawing on the official histories, the wider literature, and the archives, the authors provide conspectual accounts that reflect the most recent scholarship. These accounts—unusually in institutional history—take the story fully up to the present, giving the volume relevance to a larger audience than just other historians. In the final essay, the current Deputy Governor, Rupert Pennant-Rea, offers an authoritative 'inside' perspective on the changes that have been taking place in the Bank and looks ahead to its fourth century.

Since the mid-1980s there has been a marked increase in interest in finance and financial institutions of which financial history has been a beneficiary. Recent years have seen a spate of studies of banks and other financial institutions; the establishment of a bespoke academic journal, *Financial History Review*, in April 1994 was another milestone. The outcome has been substantial advance in the quantity and quality of the historical literature on the City of London and ·international finance. When the editors of this volume began their research in the field a decade or so ago, there were many dark areas to which there was simply no available guide. The situation is now very different. Although much remains to be done (the bullion market, the foreign exchange market, and Lloyd's, for instance, need scholarly attention), it is possible at last to take a synoptic view and to make sophisticated links with political, economic and social history, thereby integrating financial history into the mainstream of historical discourse. These essays represent a step in this direction.

PREFACE

THIS book owes its origins to a historical conference held in July 1994 to mark the Bank of England's tercentenary. An invited audience heard shorter versions of most of the essays included here. The conference was held under the auspices of the Business History Unit of the London School of Economics—munificently hosted by the Bank—and, helped by a distinguished array of chairmen, provided a memorable day for those who attended.

Neither the conference nor this book would have been possible without the generous support of the following: the Corporation of London; the International Monetary Conference; the Worshipful Company of Grocers; and the Mercers' Company. We are indebted to each of them.

There are others whom we would also like to thank, especially at the Bank itself: Christine Turner for compiling the lists of governors, directors and senior permanent officials; Philip Davies for compiling the chronology; John Keyworth for steering us towards the painting on the dust-jacket; Henry Gillett and Elizabeth Ogborn for advice on archival matters; and, last but not least, Geoff Croughton and Chris Bennell for their patience and good humour during the preparations for the conference. The conference administrator was Sonia Copeland, and we are grateful to her and to Terry Gourvish, director of the Business History Unit, for all their hard work.

The Bank of England's tercentenary has coincided with a fundamental evaluation of its status and responsibilities. There are, even more than is usually the case, important lessons to be drawn from the past.

R. R.
D. K.

London, 27 July 1994

CONTENTS

x   *Contents*

LIST OF FIGURES

NOTES ON CONTRIBUTORS

H. V. BOWEN lectures in economic history at the University of Leicester. He specializes in the eighteenth century and is the author of *Revenue and Reform: The Indian Problem in British Politics, 1757–1773*.

SIR ALEC CAIRNCROSS was Economic Adviser to the Government from 1961 to 1964 and Head of the Government Economic Service from 1964 to 1969. His many publications include *Years of Recovery: British Economic Policy 1945–51, Economics and Economic Policy*, and *The British Economy Since 1945*.

P. L. COTTRELL is Professor of Economic History at the University of Leicester and the author of *British Overseas Investment in the Nineteenth Century* and *Industrial Finance, 1830–1914: The Finance and Organisation of English Manufacturing Industry*. He has also written widely on banking history and is co-editor of *Financial History Review*.

ELIZABETH HENNESSY has written twelve corporate histories and is the managing editor of *Central Banking* magazine. Her most recent book, *A Domestic History of the Bank of England, 1930–1960*, was published in 1992.

DAVID KYNASTON is a fellow at the Business History Unit of the London School of Economics. His books include histories of the *Financial Times* and the stockbrokers Cazenove & Co. The first volume of his trilogy on the City of London between 1815 and 1986 was published in 1994.

RUPERT PENNANT-REA was editor of *The Economist* from 1986 to 1993, when he became Deputy Governor of the Bank of England.

ROBERT PRINGLE, editor of *Central Banking*, is the author of *Financial Markets and Governments* (1989) and co-author of *The Central Banks* (1994).

RICHARD ROBERTS lectures in economic history at the University of Sussex. He is the author of *Schroders: Merchants and Bankers* and his four-volume edition of essays on *International Financial Centres* was published in 1994.

1 The Bank of England during the Long Eighteenth Century, 1694–1820

H. V. BOWEN

THE Bank of England during the eighteenth century was not a central bank in the modern sense. By the end of that century the Bank had acquired some of the features of a central bank as now understood, but the Bank had neither been established, nor consciously developed, with central banking functions in mind.[1] Instead, the Bank followed two separate, though overlapping, lines of development which, in their different ways, drew it close to the realm of modern central banking. On the one hand, the Bank became banker to the state and manager of the national debt, while on the other it became, in a commercial sense, one of the City of London's major financial institutions. Such was the hesitant nature of both developments that the characteristics of central banking only emerged slowly as the Bank began to gain the capacity to act as lender of last resort and regulator of financial activity within the economy at large.

There is no consensus among modern historians regarding which of the Bank's various functions were most important during the eighteenth century. The reason for this is partly that the stances adopted by individual historians tend to reflect the particular historiographical context in which the Bank's development is set. Thus, historians working outside the narrow specialization of financial history have emphasized the importance of the relationship between the state and the Bank, not only in terms of the growth of public banking but also with regard to the broader development of the state itself. They have located the Bank at the very heart of the various economic and fiscal processes that contributed to the emergence of Great Britain as a first-rank imperial and military power, supported by unrivalled and sophisticated systems of state bureaucracy and public finance.[2] Indeed, the

---

[1] For the view that the Bank was displaying 'important traces' of all the functions of a modern central bank see E. Victor Morgan, *The Theory and Practice of Central Banking, 1797–1913* (Cambridge, 1943, 2nd imp. 1965), 1. I am most grateful to Professor Philip Cottrell for his enthusiastic discussion of all matters related to banking history. In particular, I would like to thank him for his helpful comments on earlier drafts of this essay.

[2] John Brewer, *The Sinews of Power: War, Money and the English State 1688–1783* (1989); P. G. M. Dickson, *The Financial Revolution in England: A Study in the Development of Public Credit, 1688–1756* (1967).

emphasis within analyses of Britain's rise to imperial greatness has increasingly shifted away from concentration on the process of industrialization towards developments in the service sector. Although this general issue has become, and no doubt will long remain, a matter for debate and controversy, there can be no denying the crucial role played by the Bank of England in allowing the state to mobilize and deploy financial resources on a global scale.[3] As Adam Smith put it in the *Wealth of Nations*, the Bank of England acted 'not only as an ordinary bank, but as a great engine of state'.[4]

Other historians, although not denying the importance of the part played by the Bank in helping to shape and sustain the modern state during times of difficulty and crisis, have argued that by the 1760s this role had become one of less significance when compared with the position adopted by the Bank as an agent of financial change and development in the national economy. The Bank was to an increasing extent, in the words of Dame Lucy Sutherland, the 'institutional centre' of the City[5] and, as such, it helped to determine the pattern and course of economic development in the broadest sense. The Bank stood at the very heart of the nation's credit structure and, after the upheavals of the first two decades of the century, it helped to regulate the course of trade and commerce by acting as an institution with a proven track-record of reliability and soundness. Moreover, by the second half of the century the Bank's general outlook was such that it had begun to take responsibility for ensuring that the effects of financial crisis were minimized through discounting, which served to extend credit beyond its own circle of regular clients.[6] Thus, while a strong case can be made for the Bank's contribution being indispensable to the development of the state, a similar case can be made for its contribution to the growth of the eighteenth-century economy.

This essay seeks to strike a balance between these interpretations of the various roles played by the Bank. In attempting to provide an introductory overview of the period between 1694 and 1820, due recognition is given to the fact that the Bank's development during the eighteenth century represented a broad advance on two different fronts. It was only when these separate lines of development began to meet at a point in the early nineteenth century that the Bank began more clearly to display the characteristics of a central bank.

---

[3] P. J. Cain and A. G. Hopkins, *British Imperialism: Innovation and Expansion, 1688–1914* (1993).

[4] Adam Smith, *An Inquiry into the Nature and Causes of the Wealth of Nations* (1776), ed. R. H. Campbell, A. S. Skinner, and W. B. Todd (Oxford, 1976), i, 320.

[5] Lucy Sutherland, 'The City of London in Eighteenth-Century Politics', in Richard Pares and A. J. P. Taylor (eds.), *Essays Presented to Sir Lewis Namier* (1956), 49.

[6] Michael C. Lovell, 'The Role of the Bank of England as Lender of Last Resort in the Crises of the Eighteenth Century', *Explorations in Entrepreneurial History*, x (1957), 8–21. Lovell argued (p. 17) that when the Bank became the lender of the last resort this was a 'function of much greater significance than its former role as a fiscal arm of the crown'.

War and Crisis: The Pattern of Development

In 1781, as the American War of Independence drew towards a close, Lord
North declared in the House of Commons that the Bank of England 'from
long habit and the usage of many years, was a part of the constitution.' The
Prime Minister then modified this bold and oft-quoted statement a little by
conceding in his next breath that 'if not part of the constitution, at least it
[the Bank] was to all important purposes the public exchequer.' In spite of
this slight but significant shift in his position, North had made a telling
point and few of his contemporaries would have contested his implied
assertion that not only had the Bank of England become a financial institution of the greatest importance, but it now held a central position within
the Hanoverian state. North went on to outline some, but by no means all,
of the Bank's principal early achievements, and he asserted that 'by prudent management, by judicious conduct, wise plans, and exact punctuality,
in establishing its own credit, [it] had contributed very essentially to establish the national credit, a matter equally advantageous to this country both
at home and abroad'. In addition he noted that 'the Bank had from time
to time essentially assisted the public, both on occasions of loans and on
various sudden exigencies'.[7]

Historians of the Bank have largely endorsed the sort of view offered by
Lord North. Few would question its wisdom, if only because North, a
politician who had long taken a deep interest in the nation's financial
affairs, knew what he was talking about. Yet a historiographical approach
which applies the benefit of hindsight to an institution's development runs
the risk of implying, even if unwittingly, that the past is organized along
lines of steady advance or progression. This tends to mask or marginalize
the factors which in reality make the historical process one that is punctuated with crises, setbacks, uncertainties, and pragmatic responses to pressing problems. The history of the Bank provides a good illustration of this
point. There was no smooth, unhindered path to the established position
surveyed by North in the 1780s, but this may appear to have been the case
if one adopts a teleological approach to the history of the Bank. By
approaching the history of the Bank from the beginning of the nineteenth
century and then seeking out trends and developments within a framework
of evolutionary explanation, it is possible to overlook the basic fact that for
much of the eighteenth century, but particularly before the 1760s, the position of the Bank of England was by no means beyond question and its long-
term future was far from secure. The Bank featured prominently on the
political agenda of the day and attitudes towards it played an important

[7] Speech of 13 June 1781 in the Committee of Ways and Means, as reported in William
Cobbett, *Parliamentary History of England from . . . 1066 to . . . 1803* (1806–20), xxii, cols.
517–20.

part in defining positions within contemporary economic and ideological discourse. However indispensable the Bank had become to the smooth running of the nation's evolving financial system, there was no broad consensus which suggested that its continuing existence was necessarily a good and desirable thing.

Uncertainties about the Bank, its role, and its future may be ascribed to a number of factors which quite fundamentally influenced the economic and political context in which it operated during the eighteenth century.[8] Of course, when compared with developments in much of the rest of Europe, public banking took a long time to become established in England. The Bank of England lagged a long way behind the major banks of Holland, Germany, and Sweden. Although this late start was by no means a disadvantage, it reflected the fact that in England there was little broad agreement on, and considerable unease about, the need for a public-banking system. This was not least because in many minds such things were closely identified with republican forms of government. As one pamphleteer remarked in the 1690s, for years 'our more refined politicians assured us that we must never think of settling banks in England without a commonwealth, and this notion became so universal that it was a matter of derision for any one to seem to be of a contrary opinion'.[9]

The uncertainties created by this initial unwillingness to embrace public banking because of constitutional and political fears were then exacerbated by the circumstances which attended the eventual establishment of the Bank in the 1690s. Following much fruitless debate and discussion about the merits of public banks, and after the failure of forerunners such as the Unicorn Bank of Edward Backwell, the Bank of England finally emerged into the troubled and turbulent world of the 1690s. In this sense, the Bank was born out of the immediate need for the newly established monarch, William III, to come to terms with the immense financial strains imposed by extended military conflict in Europe. Although in the short term the Bank fulfilled its immediate task by making funds available to the state, this was not without its problems, as was seen with the suspension during the great recoinage of 1696. Moreover, the circumstances surrounding this conception and difficult birth were seen in some quarters as representing an emergency situation and, in many ways, this continued to define the role played by the Bank during the following century. It matured during a period punctuated by repeated wars and war-related crises.

---

[8] The best general study of the Bank in the 18th century remains Sir John Clapham, *The Bank of England: A History* (Cambridge, 1944). There is also much useful information in W. Marston Acres, *The Bank of England From Within, 1694–1900* (Oxford, 1931), and R. D. Richards, 'The First Fifty Years of the Bank of England (1694–1744)', in J. G. van Dillen (ed.), *History of the Principal Public Banks* (The Hague, 1934; 2nd imp. 1964), 201–72.

[9] *A Brief Account of the Intended Bank of England* (1694), 2. The author of this pamphlet was either Michael Godfrey or William Paterson, both of whom were prominent among the group of projectors whose proposals formed the basis of the Bank's establishment in 1694.

Between 1688 and 1815, England or Britain was involved in seven extended wars, not to mention other military crises such as the abortive Jacobite rebellions of 1715 and 1745 and the numerous small-scale conflicts which occurred in the wider world. In other words, for most of the first 120 years of the Bank's existence the nation was either preparing for war, waging war, or seeking retrenchment after war. It was this continuing element more than any other single factor that defined the Bank's terms of reference and the scope of its different forms of banking activity. This meant that public finance and the institutional mechanisms designed to service the spiralling national debt were forged in an atmosphere of ongoing conflict and crisis.

The Bank's primary role was to help the state with the process of securing and deploying resources. It was, in the words of one modern historian, a 'money-raising machine'.[10] Moreover, because war also often acted as an important agent promoting dislocation and instability within the wider British economy, this meant that, in a commercial context, the Bank was prompted into emergency action as a discounter of bills and lender of last resort as it endeavoured to allay fears and restore confidence within well-established areas of the private business community.[11] Yet, despite the widely acknowledged success it achieved in performing these functions, the very nature of its *modus operandi* was such that the Bank continued to be perceived in some quarters as a short-term expedient measure designed to meet the exceptional demands imposed on the state by continuous warfare.

Late in the century, the political economist Sir John Sinclair remarked that the difficulties of Queen Anne's ministers during the War of the Spanish Succession (1702–13) 'rendered it natural for them to think of making use of this corporation as a resource.'[12] It had indeed become natural for the state to rely on the Bank during such times of need and, as one observer commented in 1705, supporters of the Bank argued that 'the government which is chiefly supplied by them, can scarce expect for the future to be supported without them.'[13] In other words, circumstances had forced government into dependency upon the Bank and, as ministers repeatedly turned to the Bank during times of war, this was reflected in both the timing and the terms of the legislation which effected the six short-term renewals of the Bank's Charter necessary between 1696 and 1781. Indeed, during the eighteenth century the Bank's future was never determined during a period of long-term peace or stability. On several occasions the pressures and demands of hostilities were such that new bargains were struck

[10] S. G. Checkland, *Scottish Banking: A History, 1695–1973* (Glasgow, 1975), 24.

[11] For the part played by the Bank in various, often war-related, 18th-cent. crises see Julian Hoppit, *Risk and Failure in English Business, 1700–1800* (Cambridge, 1987), 125–6, 138–9.

[12] Sir John Sinclair, *The History of the Public Revenue of the British Empire* (2nd edn., 1790), 242.

[13] John Broughton, *Remarks upon the Bank of England, with Regard More Especially to our Trade and Government* (1705), 45.

with the Bank, despite existing agreements having some time to run, with the result that the Charter was always renewed either when the nation was at war or when it was just emerging from it.[14] Ministers had to ensure that they were always in a position to renegotiate the state's agreement with the Bank, and by ensuring that the expiry date of the Charter was never too far distant they were given an effective bargaining counter to use in discussions with the Directors about new agreements. The period of extension never exceeded twenty-nine years and, on each occasion, provision was made for the expiration of the Charter twelve months after a given date. This brought a particular pattern of development to the Bank that was ultimately dependent upon the rhythm of war and peace.

Lord North was forced to concede that, before George Grenville's settlement of 1764, the Bank's relationship with the state had been rather one of 'temporary convenience and accommodation, than of real profit and pecuniary emolument.'[15] This was an important observation because North drew attention to the fact that in 1764 the Bank had for the first time made a direct non-returnable payment of £110,000 to the state in return for an extension of its chartered rights. Before then, all advances to the Treasury took the form of various interest-bearing loans. This stood in marked contrast to the case of the East India Company which had, for example, in 1744 made a substantial donation of £200,000 to the state in return for the confirmation of its commercial privileges. In other words, it seemed to many contemporaries that, while the Bank needed the state as much as the state needed the Bank, the various war-time schemes of arrangement that had been introduced before 1764 had been weighted too heavily in favour of the Bank. As a result, the state had not gained in material terms all that it might have extracted from the relationship. As it was, the repeated renewals of privileges continued to afford plenty of opportunities to a wide range of critics desiring to question and attack the nature of the Bank's status and functions. This only helped to further the impression that its position was somewhat less than secure in the long term.

Suspicion and Hostility: Opposition to the Bank

As late as 1781, when proposals were before the Commons for the renewal of the Bank's Charter, Lord North had to remind the House of the benefits brought to both the public and the Bank by the arrangements introduced over the previous ninety years or so. During the course of a speech which contained a lengthy review of the Bank's origins and history, North sketched out the services provided by the Bank. He declared that he found it hard to believe that 'there was one man living, who, after the long expe-

---

[14] The Bank's charter was prolonged in 1696, 1697, 1713, 1742, 1764, and 1781.
[15] Cobbett, *Parl. Hist.*, xxii, col. 517.

rience of its utility, would deny that it was the duty of Parliament to cement and strengthen the connection and union between the Bank and the public as much as possible.'[16] North received vigorous support from his colleague and fellow financial expert Charles Jenkinson,[17] but the way in which these two senior political figures were obliged to line up four square behind the Bank indicates that there were still those in the House who were far from satisfied with the framework within which the Bank operated. The issue of the extension of the Bank's privileges was of course seized upon by groups such as the Rockingham Whigs with party political axes to grind, but those opposing the terms for the proposed renewal of the Charter were able to draw on several different strands of criticism which had persisted since 1694.

First, the close relationship between the Bank and the state or ministry was deemed to be unhealthy and corrupt and, as one of the three great 'monied companies' in the City (the others being the East India Company and the South Sea Company), the Bank was believed to exert undue influence in high political circles.[18] There was a grain of truth in the charge that the Bank meddled in domestic politics, if only because in 1710 the Bank had tried to prevent Godolphin being dismissed from office by Queen Anne on the grounds that such an action would damage public credit.[19] That this plea failed should have reassured the Bank's critics, but the intervention instead helped to sustain the myth that the Bank's hands were firmly on the levers of political power. As late as 1800 one opposition politician, George Tierney, could claim in the Commons that William Pitt's government was 'the slave of the monied interest.'[20] This charge had become deeply embedded in the 'country' ideology that had developed during the first half of the eighteenth century and it had then been channelled into the radical and Rockinghamite critiques of the establishment that had emerged after 1760.

---

[16] Ibid.

[17] Jenkinson, who had once served as a Lord of the Treasury, spoke of the 'ridiculousness of thinking even of breaking up the present Company, and instituting a new one' and he warned of the 'extreme danger of pulling down a fabric which had stood the test of near ninety years experience.' (ibid. 524).

[18] For the mistrust of the Whig and Tory 'country' opposition towards the Bank and other City institutions during the first half of the 18th cent. see H. T. Dickinson, *Liberty and Property: Political Ideology in Eighteenth-Century Britain* (1977), 170–2, 182. For later hostility towards those operating within the world of finance see H. V. Bowen, '"The Pests of Human Society": Stockbrokers, Jobbers, and Speculators in Mid-Eighteenth-Century Britain', *History*, 78 (1993), 38–53.

[19] Dickson, *Financial Revolution*, 62, 64. Clapham, *Bank*, i, 73–5. For the Bank in City of London politics see Gary Stuart De Krey, *A Fractured Society: The Politics of London in the First Age of Party, 1688–1715* (Oxford, 1985), and, more generally, Sutherland, 'The City of London'.

[20] Speech of 21 Mar. 1800 (Cobbett, *Parl. Hist.*, xxxv, col. 6). Tierney's remarks have to be taken with a large pinch of salt because he was an embittered and hostile political opponent of Pitt, having fought an infamous duel with the Prime Minister in May 1798! Nevertheless, there can be no doubt that this sort of comment always struck a chord with those who questioned the Bank's constitutional and political position.

The Bank was depicted in sinister terms as representing one element within the tangled web of relationships which tied together the state and the City. Governments bestowed favours and privileges upon the Bank in return for assistance during times of crisis, and the monied men who invested in the Bank or directed its operations were widely believed to prosper and profit at the nation's expense during periods of universal hardship and high taxation. As the Rockinghamite MP Sir George Savile put it when he spoke against the renewal of the Charter in 1781, North had depicted the state and the Bank as enjoying a relationship that was closely akin to matrimony and, warming to this theme, he condemned the Prime Minister for speaking 'as if he had been describing a conjugal love, and enlarging upon the affection that subsisted between a man and his wife.'[21]

As part of this criticism of the way in which the Bank stood in relation to the state, some observers developed a second, related, theme by arguing that the Bank's position was an unhealthy one because it enjoyed monopoly status as a public bank. Competition, it was argued, would provide a spur to the Bank and a better deal for the public. While a few commentators clearly troubled North and Jenkinson by whispering about the desirability of abolishing the Bank and replacing it with an entirely new organization, others promoted the idea of establishing a rival bank. In a sense this harked back to the abortive Land Bank scheme of the 1690s, and the idea attracted continuing support not only from disaffected parliamentarians but also from the likes of the well-respected political economist Sir John Sinclair. The state, he declared in his *History of the Public Revenue* of 1790, should always reserve the right to establish a second public bank for the 'consequences of such a rivalship would be of infinite benefit to trade, and productive of many solid advantages to the nation.'[22] Part of the reason for Sinclair adopting this view was that he, like many others, resented the fact that the state did not secure any of the Bank's commercial or transaction profits for its own use. He did, of course, recognize that the Bank provided great service to the state 'in circulating exchequer bills; in facilitating by their notes, great pecuniary transactions; and in maintaining, to a considerable degree, credit both public and private', but he argued that in terms of material benefit the public gained nothing at all from the Bank.

The threat offered to the Bank was not an idle one, particularly in view of the difficulties experienced during the 1790s at the time of the war against France. In 1800, the Governor of the Bank, Samuel Thornton, admitted in the House of Commons that the Directors were seeking an early renewal of the Charter because they had heard that pressure for the establishment of a rival public bank had been mounting in the City. Pamphlets had been written, meetings had been held by interested parties, motions had been made in the House, and this flurry of activity had forced

---

[21] Cobbett, *Parl. Hist.*, xxii, col. 522.   [22] Sinclair, *History of the Public Revenue*, 245.

the Bank into urgent action to defend its position.[23] Over a hundred years after its foundation, the Bank was still having to fight the same battles it had fought during the 1690s.

Public Bank: The 'Great Engine of State'

Whatever critics might say about any shortcomings they perceived in the constitutional or political relationship between the Bank and the state, they could not easily overlook the fact that in practical terms the Bank had become firmly embedded in the financial structure of the nation and the empire. A reshaping of the world of English public banking was not a viable option after the first few years of the Bank's life. Although the development of the Bank was undoubtedly conditioned by the need to meet the short-term demands of war, the various Charter renewals that took place (even though they often bore the hallmarks of hasty *ad hoc* arrangements) can be seen in retrospect to have consolidated its position within a long-term context. Legislation sought repeatedly to remove any doubts about the Bank's status by confirming its 'privilege of exclusive banking' during the term of each Charter. Each renewal served to extend the Bank's capital base, and the original joint-stock subscription of £1,200,000 in 1694 had become £10,780,000 by 1742. At the same time, loans to government had risen more rapidly, so that by 1749 the Bank was owed nearly £11,686,000 by the state. The Bank's paid-up capital remained unchanged until 1781 when a call was made upon stockholders in order to bring the stock more closely in line with the government debt. This saw the Bank's capital increase to £11,642,000, but the government loan moved decisively ahead again in 1816 when, in the aftermath of the Napoleonic wars, an advance of £3,000,000 was taken up at 3 per cent interest.[24] The early growth of the government debt had occurred as the state's long-term borrowing arrangements had moved gradually, albeit in a hesitant fashion, from an initial experimental phase towards a more complicated system in which non-redeemable securities replaced repayable or self-liquidating loans as the bedrock of the national debt.[25] With such a system firmly in place by the 1740s, and secured by Pelham's consolidation of the public finances in the 1750s, the reality of the situation was that, whatever the prevailing political climate might be, the state's repayment of the sizeable loan from the Bank was not possible.

---

[23] Speech of 21 Mar. 1800 (Cobbett, *Parl. Hist.*, xxxv, col. 12).

[24] For details of the growth of the Bank's capital and the government debt see 'Report of the Proceedings of the Commissioners of the National Debt from 1786 to 31 March 1890', *Parliamentary Papers* (1890–1), xlviii, 93 and 'History of the Funded Debt from 1694–1786', ibid. (1898), lii, 67–77.

[25] Dickson, *Financial Revolution*, 243–6.

The nature of the Bank's services to the state went well beyond that of offering long-term credit facilities, and the scope of government-related business undertaken by the Bank widened steadily during the early years of the eighteenth century. Quite simply, the Bank offered an unrivalled range of facilities and expertise to the state and, because of this, it became in effect an extended arm of central government bureaucracy. From its very earliest days, the Bank serviced the needs of the army and the navy by making remittances to overseas spheres of military operations and, from this involvement in the practical affairs of state, the Bank branched out into other areas of government business. As this general trend developed further during the final quarter of the eighteenth century, it marked, in the words of one historian, an 'administrative shift from the Exchequer to the Bank' which allowed clerical work to be carried out with much greater economy and efficiency.[26]

In the realm of short-term credit, the Bank performed a valuable service to the state by discounting the Exchequer tallies that were secured on various branches of the public revenue. Straightforward loans to government were also secured on revenue funds. In the same area of activity, the circulation of Exchequer bills by the Bank began in a major way in 1707 when an issue of £1,500,000 was authorized by the Treasury, and thereafter bills secured on taxes were circulated on a regular basis. In return for this, the Bank received an allowance from the Treasury based on a premium for outstanding bills and it also made a profit on the circulation of the bills. In effect, by 1750 the Bank had been granted, in P. G. M. Dickson's words, a 'quasi-monopoly' over short-term lending to government.[27]

In 1710 the Bank became the receiver of public money for the state lottery and in 1715 it became even more closely involved in the management of the government debt by acting as both receiver and manager of the subscription to the annuity issue of that year. Thereafter, the Bank acted as the manager of government annuities and stock on a regular basis: it took in subscriptions, maintained the ledgers, supervised transfers, and paid out interest. In these important areas of government finance the Bank went on to perform specialist tasks as a matter of routine, so much so that by the 1760s the Bank was managing around 70 per cent of the national debt.[28] In recognition of the services provided, the Treasury paid an allowance to the Bank. This allowance was eventually fixed by statute in 1791 at a rate of £450 per annum per million of capital managed, but previously payments had been made at a variable rate, some taking the form of a salary to the Bank's Cashier and Accountant-General, others a general management allowance to the Bank.[29] Finally, the Bank provided credit and deposit

[26] J. E. D. Binney, *British Public Finance and Administration 1774–92* (Oxford, 1958), 92.
[27] Dickson, *Financial Revolution*, 360. For full details see ibid. 341–92, 415–53.
[28] Clapham, *Bank*, i, 102.
[29] 'Report of the Proceedings ... National Debt', 82–3.

facilities for individual government departments and offices beyond the Exchequer. Direct loans went out to the army, navy, and ordnance, and by the middle of the eighteenth century accounts were held for these three departments as well as for many of the collectors or receivers of different revenues.[30] This took the Bank into the realm of direct management of departmental accounts and balances, but the practice developed in a rather haphazard fashion. It was not until the 1780s that some, but not all, departmental accounts, such as those belonging to the Paymaster-General of the Forces and the Treasurer of the Navy, were formally transferred to the safekeeping of the Bank as part of 'economical reform' measures and an overhaul of government offices.[31] Such actions helped to tie up many loose financial ends within government but, as P. G. M. Dickson observed about developments in the 1750s, it seems that 'as a result of deliberate ministerial policy' they also served to strengthen the Bank's short-term financial position.[32]

All these measures helped to make the Bank the linchpin of the modern bureaucratic state that emerged in Britain after 1688, yet the Bank was much more than the manager of the national debt and banker to the state. The Bank, as Pitt reminded the House of Commons in 1800, was not simply a chartered body dedicated solely to servicing the needs of the state; it was also a private joint-stock commercial organization trading and seeking profit on its own capital resources.[33] Pitt might have added that the Bank also played a key role in currency and the circulation of notes. In these capacities the Bank made itself the corner-stone of the City and of London's financial markets, and, as a prototype quasi-central bank, it had developed a position of great influence well beyond the world of government finance.

Private Bank: Credit and Circulation

By the end of the eighteenth century, informed observers were able to mount a strong case for arguing that the Bank's role as public creditor and manager of the funds no longer represented its most important functions. When, during the financial upheavals preceding the suspension of payments in 1797, Sir Francis Baring campaigned to have the Bank's notes recognized as legal tender, he declared that the most valuable aspect of the Bank's role was that related to 'the general circulation of the country'. This he placed

---

[30] Dickson, *Financial Revolution*, 388–9; Richards, 'First Fifty Years', 247–50.
[31] John Ehrman, *The Younger Pitt: The Years of Acclaim* (1969), 90, 302; Binney, *British Public Finance*, 145–9, 156, 270, 275. For the later tightening up of procedures see Clapham, *Bank*, ii, 46–7.
[32] Dickson, *Financial Revolution*, 390–1.
[33] Speech of 21 Mar. 1800 (Cobbett, *Parl. Hist.*, xxxv, col. 7).

ahead of all government-related business and commercial discounting.[34]
Thirty-five years later, the Governor of the Bank, John Horsley Palmer,
made much the same point when he declared that the chief functions of the
Bank were 'to furnish the paper money with which the public act around
them, and to be a place of safe deposit for the public money, and for the
money of the individuals who prefer a public body like the Bank to private
bankers.'[35] This was a sentiment that would have struck a chord with many
of those who had been instrumental in the creation of the Bank a hundred
years before. Although in a narrow constitutional sense the Bank had
evolved in response to the demands of hard-pressed governments, part of
the initial need to establish the Bank had arisen from a widespread desire
to create a reliable bank of issue and a source of low-interest private credit
for the capital's merchant community.

This question had been brought to the fore during the debates preceding
and surrounding the establishment of the Bank. The author of an influential pamphlet published in 1694 opened his plea for the creation of a Bank
of England by declaring that 'The want of a Bank, or publick fund, for the
convenience and security of great payments, and the better to facilitate the
circulation of money, in and about this great and opulent city, hath in our
time, among other inconveniences, occasion'd much unnecessary credit, to
the loss of several millions, by which trade hath been exceedingly dis-
courag'd and obstructed.'[36] These needs were met under the terms of the
Bank's first Charter, and ten years after the foundation of the Bank a merchant pamphleteer could reflect that 'The power to extend their credit, and
upon so good a foundation as the security of an Act of Parliament is perhaps a more considerable article of their profit than even so great an interest' as the 8 per cent payable by the state on its initial loan of £1.2 million.[37]
The same author conceded that the services the Bank offered were 'chiefly'
the loan finance it had made available to the state, but he pointed out that
when William III's government received its initial loan from the Bank 'it
gave them a power to issue bills of credit equal to that sum, making itself
the security for all those who thus far trusted the Bank'. The net result of
this was that 'by virtue of that privilege, they [the Bank] have a further
power of issuing what further credit of theirs now passes amongst us; and
all this passes currently upon the bottom of public sanction and security.'[38]
From 1709 the Bank was granted a near-monopoly of note issue when an
Act (7 Anne, c.7) of that year was introduced in order to deny partnerships
of more than six individuals the right to 'borrow, owe, or take up any sum
or sums of money on their bills or notes payable at demand, or at any less

---

[34] Sir Francis Baring, *Observations on the Establishment of the Bank of England, and on the Paper Circulation of the Country* (1797), 6–7.
[35] Quoted in Morgan, *Theory and Practice*, 1.
[36] Godfrey or Paterson, *Brief Account*, 1.   [37] Broughton, *Remarks*, 13.
[38] Ibid. 40–2.

time than six months from the borrowing thereof.' Not only did the Act allow the Bank to exercise great influence in this particularly important area of banking activity, but at a time of great political and financial uncertainty in the City this statutory protection also helped to secure the Bank's position against potential rival organizations.

These developments in the realm of note issue helped to give the Bank some of the features that distinguished it from those of its continental counterparts which acted as straightforward deposit and exchange banks. As well as acting as a clearing-house for government paper, the Bank also issued its own notes and offered credit facilities which were in part secured on the sums loaned to the state through the advance of paid-up capital to the Treasury. In this context, the Bank's relationship with the state was a reassuring one for all those who used and received various notes and credit, and contemporaries were able to argue that the Bank 'must be secure apprehension to the contrary' because of the 'great sums they have lent the government upon the faith of a British Parliament which is sufficient to keep them above failure'.[39] This of course helped further to entangle the affairs of state and Bank and it was something Adam Smith remarked upon in 1776 when he observed that 'The stability of the Bank of England is equal to that of the British government.'[40] Yet there were quite definite limits to the support given to the Bank by the state and, while the government's debts to the Bank were secured on revenues, the state did not directly underwrite any of the Bank's own note issues or credit obligations. As has been noted by one banking historian, confidence in the Bank's paper rested entirely on its standing and reputation as a sound commercial organization.[41] This meant that the state and the Bank were in fact separated in an important way by these arrangements. Although the Bank acted as the mechanism by which different forms of government securities were brought before the investing public, the Bank issued its own paper under its own very different terms of (commercial) reference. It was this dual issuing function that so confused foreigners. Baring observed in the 1790s that 'they could not distinguish between paper issued for the sole purpose of circulation, limited in its amount, and under the authority and responsibility of a corporate body absolutely independent, and that which government could issue ad libitum bearing an interest, which rendered it an object for persons to purchase as a productive investment of their capitals.'[42]

Confidence in the Bank as a sound commercial organization rested upon its reputation with London's merchants, since it was from this section of the capital's business community that the Bank drew most of its private customers. As the political economist Sir James Steuart put it in 1767, 'The

---

[39] Malachy Postlethwayt, *The Universal Dictionary of Trade and Commerce* ... (1751), i, 194.

[40] Smith, *Wealth of Nations*, i, 320.   [41] Checkland, *Scottish Banking*, 24.

[42] Baring, *Observations*, 10–11.

ruling principle of this bank, and the ground of their confidence, is mercantile credit.'[43] The accumulation of deposits had allowed the Bank to build up significant levels of bullion reserves and this supported a large volume of notes in circulation. This position had been established early on in the Bank's history, despite the difficulties caused by the suspension of payments in 1696 and the threat posed by rival institutions such as the Land Bank and the 'Old' East India Company, the latter of which attempted to mount a run on the Bank in 1708. The generally sound nature of the Bank was reflected in the price of its stock which stood above par for fifteen of the first twenty years of its life and in the annual dividend payment to stockholders which, apart from 1696 when no payment was made, lay between 7 and 16 per cent during the same period.[44] Thereafter, the Bank's stock remained for the most part quite comfortably above par for the rest of the century, moving within a range of average annual prices between 101 (1762) and 204 (1792).[45] Of course, the close relationship with the state was a source of great comfort to all concerned, but, as Daniel Defoe observed, the London business community also found the Bank to be a reliable and well-ordered institution which serviced their needs in an efficient and speedy manner.[46]

With its position secured in such a way, the Bank was in theory able to engage in a wide range of its own financial activities in the private sector. In practice, however, the Bank remained cautious and careful in its approach to business, and, because of this, private activity made, in Clapham's words, a 'trifling contribution to the divisible income' of the Bank before 1760. Thereafter, private business became much more important, although it was to fall away after 1810.[47] The profile of the Bank's private business remained limited in a geographical sense through a concentration on customers drawn in the main from London.[48] It was also limited through the sort of commercial enterprises with which the Directors sanctioned involvement. In particular, mortgages, personal loans to individuals, and advances to provincial industrial enterprises were avoided as the eighteenth century progressed, even though it is possible to find

[43] Sir James Steuart, *An Inquiry into the Principles of Political Oeconomy* (1767), ed. Andrew S. Skinner (1966), ii, 477.
[44] W. A. Speck, 'Conflict in Society', in Geoffrey Holmes (ed.), *Britain after the Glorious Revolution 1698–1714* (1969), 143.
[45] Philip Mirowski, 'The Rise (and Retreat) of a Market: English Joint-Stock Shares in the Eighteenth Century', *Journal of Economic History*, xli (1981), 569–70. The mean annual share price in the 18th cent. was 129.1.
[46] Daniel Defoe, *A Tour Through the Whole Island of Great Britain* (1724–6), ed. P. Rogers (1971), 310. For details of staff, buildings, and how the Bank's business was conducted at Mercers' Hall, Grocers' Hall, and, after 1734, at Threadneedle Street, see Acres, *Bank of England from Within*, i, *passim*.
[47] J. H. Clapham, 'The Private Business of the Bank of England, 1744–1800', *Economic History Review*, xi (1941), 88–9.
[48] For a profile of the Bank's customers in the late 18th cent. see Clapham, *Bank*, i, 203–10, 215–16.

occasional evidence of transactions such as those related to the provision of credit between 1728 and 1776 to the Company of Copper Miners of England which owned works at Neath and Taibach in South Wales.[49] This was far from typical, however, and regular private business activity increasingly focused on discounting for the London merchant community, making loans to well-established companies, and dealing in bullion. The last activity, while important, was far from lucrative, and annual profit was at times measured in hundreds rather than thousands of pounds.

Assistance to individuals mainly took the form of the discounting of notes and bills and, in practice, the extension of these facilities was restricted to individuals in trade who were resident in London. It was for this reason that the Bank was commonly, and quite correctly, referred to as the 'Bank of London' during the eighteenth century. Profits on this activity were small-scale during the first half of the century and before 1760 annual income from this source never exceeded £20,000.[50] Profits were again limited in the area of operations associated with the provision of loans and overdrafts to a small circle of regular corporate clients, but the accommodation offered to trading companies such as the East India Company, the Hudson's Bay Company, and the South Sea Company (which became little more than a holding company) was such that the Bank can be seen as having played a vital role in the development of British commerce and imperialism. By offering short-term credit facilities and 'running loans', the Bank underwrote British activity in the wider world by helping to oil the metropolitan wheels of corporate finance, and this was particularly the case with the East India Company. Ninety loans totalling almost £8 million were made to the East India Company between 1694 and 1744[51] and at times during the first half of the eighteenth century the Company's annual overdraft repayments to the Bank exceeded £500,000.[52] By the 1760s the Bank was providing regular half-yearly injections of working capital to the Company as a matter of routine. Even during the 1770s, when pressure on resources was such that the Bank was unable to assist the ailing Company and turned down requests for short-term loans, it was still able, indirectly, to come to the rescue. The Bank provided the Treasury with the finance with which the state made over to the Company a £1.4 million loan, as part of Lord North's rescue package and reorganization of East Indian affairs in 1773.[53]

Although its private business activity appears to have been very modest before the 1760s, the sound commercial position and reputation of the

---

[49] R. O. Roberts, 'Financial Developments in Early Modern Wales and the Emergence of the First Banks', *Welsh History Review*, 16 (1993), 301.

[50] Clapham, *Bank*, ii, 14.   [51] Richards, 'First Fifty Years', 253–4.

[52] K. N. Chaudhuri, *The Trading World of Asia and the English East India Company 1660–1760* (Cambridge, 1978), 439.

[53] H. V. Bowen, *Revenue and Reform: The Indian Problem in British Politics, 1757–1773* (Cambridge, 1991), 127–8; Clapham, *Bank*, i, 250–1.

Bank was nevertheless such that by the third quarter of the eighteenth century it had developed the capacity to act as lender of last resort during times of general crisis.[54] As late as 1745 there had been a run on the Bank during the Jacobite rising, but thereafter confidence in the Bank grew to such an extent that financial panic did not lead to such a scramble for bullion occurring again until the 1790s. On the contrary, through the expansion of discounting operations and the extension of credit beyond its normal circle of customers, the Bank was able to limit the extent of business failure during times of financial crisis. Although the Bank had no firm guidelines for determining the regulation of note-issue in the eighteenth century,[55] the reserve ratio (bullion to notes) was permitted to fall as low as 19.7 per cent in 1772, and to an extraordinary 6.9 per cent in 1763. During every crisis between 1763 and 1793 there were significant increases in the volume of paper on discount with the Bank and annual profits on discounting operations rose significantly.[56] This is not to imply, however, that the Bank was indiscriminate in its discounting of notes and bills, or in its extension of credit facilities. The need for care and caution was always uppermost in the minds of the Directors who scrutinized applications for discounts and credit. This was borne out by the fact that the Bank lost only £68,511 on bad paper discounted between 1694 and 1788.[57] Discounting was often limited in attempts to curb excesses in the issue of paper by merchants and other banks and each application for credit was considered on its merits. In 1772, for example, the Bank would not assist the ailing and overextended Ayr Bank on anything other than the harshest of terms, the result being that the Scottish bank eventually collapsed, taking many other firms with it. The general consequences of this action illustrated the extent to which the Bank, through its discretionary restriction of discounting, was beginning, in the words of one historian, to 'apply a restraining hand in the economy'.[58]

From London Bank to National Bank

By the beginning of the nineteenth century the Bank's position was such that it could survive continued political opposition and alarms such as the suspension of cash payments in 1797. It had become a permanent feature within the British state and economy. And yet one crucial issue remained unresolved. This centred on the question of the extent of the Bank's degree of independence and it reflected the fact that, while in some areas of activ-

---

[54] This paragraph is based on Lovell, 'The Role of the Bank'.
[55] J. K. Horsefield, 'The Bank and its Treasure', in T. S. Ashton and R. S. Sayers (eds.), *Papers in English Monetary History* (Oxford, 1953), 51–2.
[56] In 1763/4 the profit was £101,746 and in 1796/7 it was £223,815 (Clapham, *Bank*, ii, 14).
[57] Ibid.   [58] Lovell, 'The Role of the Bank', 17.

ity the Bank retained considerable freedom of action, in others its hands were tied through its close connection with the state. To a large degree this situation had arisen out of the way in which the Bank had developed in two quite different spheres of banking activity. On the one hand, as banker to the state, the Bank was entangled in the web of national finances. It had to respond to the needs of governments during times of war and the general terms of reference in this context were established by ministers who could use both sticks and carrots to get what they wanted from the Bank. The big-stick approach could be used by ministers threatening to review the statutory arrangements for the Bank's operations every time the Charter came up for renewal. This sort of tactic, which was often hinted at rather than used, was made all the more effective because the threat posed by the possible establishment of a rival bank remained a considerable one and it reduced the Directors' scope for manœuvre in negotiations with ministers. Ministers, like Pitt in 1800, could also offer carrots to the Bank in the form of the early renewal of the Charter under favourable terms when the state required considerable advances to fund foreign campaigns.[59] In both of these ways the state continued to exert a considerable controlling influence over the way in which the Bank developed. Yet, on the other hand, the commercial position of the Bank was such that, as a private joint-stock organization, it had established a position of unrivalled influence in the City and the wider economy. Here the Bank acted within its own terms of reference, free to develop business as it wished, and increasingly serving to regulate the ebb and flow of financial and commercial activity through the use of its own discretionary powers and judgement.

The question of exactly where the Bank stood in relation to government in the general context of regulation of the economy was at the heart of the debate that occurred during discussion of the terms under which the Bank would undertake the resumption of cash payments in 1819. Beyond the technical question of how and at what rate payments should be resumed stood the issue of the role the Bank was expected to play by the state in the regulation of note issue and circulation.[60] The Directors of the Bank were quite clear about how they perceived the role of the Bank. In seeking to resist government pressure to force the Bank to resume payments under terms agreed by Parliament, the Directors argued that the 'Ingot Plan' deprived them of any discretionary powers in commercial and monetary transactions. At the same time the Directors argued that 'under the original constitution' it was not for the Bank 'to enter into the general views of policy by which this great empire is to be governed in all its commercial

---

[59] Clapham, *Bank*, ii, 45.

[60] For the general context and detailed discussion of these issues see Boyd Hilton, *Corn, Cash, Commerce: The Economic Policies of the Tory Governments, 1815–30* (Oxford, 1977), 31–66.

and pecuniary transactions'.[61] The Bank was asking for a free hand to determine monetary policy while the Directors were denying that the Bank had any responsibility for the regulation of the nation's financial affairs! The confusions and cross-currents in this general debate were such that ministers joined with the Directors in making contradictory statements over the extent of the Bank's discretion over issue.[62] Things were pushed too far by the Directors when they argued that the Bank's 'peculiar and appropriate duty' was 'the management of the concerns of the banking establishment, as connected with the payment of the interest of the national debt, the lodgements consigned to its care, and the ordinary advances it has been accustomed to make to government.'[63] This disingenuous and very limited view of the Bank's functions made no mention at all of note and bill circulation and it did not acknowledge the Bank's *de facto* position as guardian of the gold standard. Not surprisingly, this provoked a response from exasperated ministers which suggested that the Bank could no longer pretend that it was still established on the narrow lines laid down in 1694. It prompted Peel, who chaired the Commons committee established to review the whole question of the resumption of payments, to make the famous comment that 'the moment has arrived when the nature of the relations between the government and the Bank should be changed'.[64] By this he implied that now was the time to draw together and define clearly the functions of the Bank as both banker to the state and regulator of commercial and monetary activity.

In redefining the Bank's position and securing the resumption of cash payments under the terms framed by the parliamentary committee, ministers not only asserted the state's political control over the Bank,[65] but also advanced the Bank's position significantly towards that of a central bank in a recognizably modern form. The events of 1819 thus held a significance way beyond the technicalities of the resumption of cash payments by the Bank. The state asserted more formal supervision over areas of banking that had previously lain within the jealously guarded realm of private business activity, and this helped to mark an important stage in the Bank's transition from a London bank to a national bank.

[61] The Directors' representations made in the House of Lords on 21 May 1819, in T. C. Hansard, *The Parliamentary Debates from the Year 1803 to the Present Time*, xl, col. 602.

[62] Hilton, *Corn, Cash, Commerce*, 54.

[63] Hansard, *Parliamentary Debates*, xl, col. 602.

[64] Speech of 24 May 1819 (ibid., col. 688).   [65] Hilton, *Corn, Cash, Commerce*, 50.

2 The Bank of England and the Government

DAVID KYNASTON

THIS essay is in five parts.[1] The first (and longest) part traces the shifting balance of power between Bank and government from 1815 to 1988; the second considers some of the attitudes, prejudices, and assumptions that helped to shape the relationship; the third attempts to show some of the ways in which the Bank has sought to influence government economic policy; the fourth deals with the Bank in its role as conscious representative of the interests of the City of London as a whole; and the last part touches on the 'independence' debate that marked the run-up to the Bank's tercentenary.

The Shifting Balance of Power

Lord North may have famously referred to the Bank of England in 1781 as 'from long habit and usage of many years . . . a part of the constitution',[2] yet in the nineteenth century a series of major reform-minded politicians—Huskisson, Peel, Gladstone, and Harcourt—were less complacent. Gladstone, in an undated fragment written towards the end of his life, took a historical line to explain and justify his more critical attitude. He asserted that in the seventeenth century 'the state was justly in ill odour as a fraudulent bankrupt' in its relations with the City and that after the Glorious Revolution of 1688, when 'in order to induce monied men to be lenders' the state 'came forward under the countenance of the Bank as its sponsor', there developed a 'position of subserviency which it became the interest of the Bank and the City to prolong'. And according to Gladstone, in return for 'amicable and accommodating measures towards the government . . . the government itself was not to be a substantive power in matters of

---

[1] I am grateful to Sir Alec Cairncross and Richard Roberts for their comments. This piece owes much to Cairncross's 'The Bank of England: Relationships with the Government, the Civil Service, and Parliament', in Gianni Toniolo (ed.), *Central Banks' Independence in Historical Perspective* (Berlin, 1988).
[2] Sir John Clapham, *The Bank of England: A History* (Cambridge, 1944), i, 103.

finance, but was to leave the money power supreme and unquestioned'.[3] To which, according to this critique, he might have added that the period of almost continuous warfare between 1793 and 1815 had further tilted the balance towards the Bank, as Pitt and his successors looked desperately towards Threadneedle Street for a series of last-ditch funding expediencies. 1815 brought peace and the opportunity for the politicians to begin to redress the balance in relation to what was still a private, profit-making bank that had done extremely well out of the paper money era following the suspension of cash payments in 1797.

The first big battle was fought over the question of whether to return to gold, something that the Bank wanted to delay as long as possible.[4] Huskisson, in the process of becoming the intellectual driving-force behind the Liverpool ministry, in effect spoke for a rising generation of commercially minded middle-class radicals-cum-economic-liberals when in 1818 he argued that one of the great advantages of returning to the gold standard was that it would be so properly regulated from the outset that there could be no possibility of mismanagement let alone greed on the part of the Old Lady. 'The Bank', he assured Liverpool, 'would be the great Steam Engine of the State to keep the Channel of the Circulation always pressing full, and the power of converting its Notes at any time into Gold Bullion at 78s per ounce the Regulator and Index of the Engine, by which the extent of its operations and the sufficiency of the supply would be determined & ascertained'.[5] In May 1819 parliament debated the issue. 'No body of men', Liverpool assured the Lords, 'was ever entrusted with so much power as the Bank of England, or had less abused the power entrusted to them'. However, he went on, 'would Parliament consent to commit to their hands what they certainly would refuse to the sovereign on the throne, controlled by Parliament itself—the power of making money, without any other check or influence to direct them, than their own notions of profit and interest?' Then in the Commons—following a piece of high-class knockabout in which the economist Ricardo rubbished the competence of the 'company of merchants', as he liked to dub the Bank—the vote was taken to return to gold sooner rather than later.[6] The fear that indefinite suspension would give permanent and potentially mischief-making discretion to the Bank over matters of circulation had proved decisive, and in 1821 the restriction period duly ended.

Four years later there occurred arguably the most severe financial crisis of the century—a crisis caused, according to some observers, by Bank of

[3] John Brooke and Mary Sorensen (eds.), *The Prime Ministers' Papers: W. E. Gladstone*, i, *Autobiographica* (1971), 128–9.

[4] Boyd Hilton, *Corn, Cash, Commerce: The Economic Policies of the Tory Governments, 1815–1830* (Oxford, 1977), 31–66, offers a pioneering assessment of this episode.

[5] British Library, Add Ms, 38,271.

[6] T. C. Hansard, *The Parliamentary Debates From the Year 1803 to the Present Time*, xl, cols. 612–13, 672–748, 750–800.

England policy that veered between supine inaction and an over-sharp contraction of credit. After a series of banking failures, a key moment came on 15 December, when the Cabinet gave its sanction to the Bank issuing £1 notes for the first time since the resumption of gold payments, but only on the condition that such issue was 'understood to be strictly temporary'.[7] The next morning the diarist Mrs Arbuthnot and her husband (Joint Secretary of the Treasury) were put in the highly fractious picture by the member of government closest to the City:

Mr Herries told us that such had been the extraordinary demand for gold to supply the country bankers & to meet the general run upon them that the Bank of England was completely drained of its specie & was reduced to 100,000 sovereigns . . . The Bank expects to be obliged to suspend cash payments tomorrow, and they want the Government to step forward to their assistance & order the suspension. Lord Liverpool is unwilling to do this & wishes the Bank to do it upon their own responsibility. By Mr Herries's account there seems to be considerable irritation between the Govt & the Governors of the Bank . . . Such is the detestation in which Mr Huskisson is held in the City that Ld L & Mr Canning did not think it prudent to summon him to London till all the Cabinet were sent for &, in the discussions with the Bank, he is kept out of sight.[8]

Against the background of Nathan Rothschild moving into impressive action to secure gold from France, the Cabinet met that evening and hammered out a political compromise. The central figure was Wellington, who reluctantly accepted the insistent demand of Huskisson and Canning that the Bank must not be allowed to use the crisis as a device for once more going off gold, but convinced his colleagues that Huskisson's notion of depriving the Bank of its charter should it be forced to stop payment was preposterous.[9] The Iron Duke held firm, as Mrs Arbuthnot admiringly recorded: 'He told Lord Liverpool that while there was life there was hope; that there was a chance of the Bank standing & while that chance remained, he wd not despair; that the Government were bound to support them to the very utmost of their power . . . for that their interests were those of the country'.[10] Rothschild gold saved the day, the Bank stood, and in time the gold standard would become an icon of Victorian England.

Instead, public attention now turned towards the less emotive, more esoteric area of how the Bank could function more effectively, above all in terms of an effectively controlled note issue that in practice would operate as a national currency.[11] For a time the Bank itself made the intellectual running, in the person of Horsley Palmer, Deputy Governor and then

[7] British Library, Add Ms, 38,371.

[8] Francis Bamford and the Duke of Wellington (eds.), *The Journal of Mrs Arbuthnot* (1950), i, 426–7.

[9] David Kynaston, *The City of London*, i. *A World of Its Own*, 1815–1890 (1994), 70.

[10] Bamford and Wellington, *Mrs Arbuthnot*, i, 428.

[11] Frank Whitson Fetter, *Development of British Monetary Orthodoxy, 1797–1875* (Cambridge, Mass., 1965), 120–64.

Governor from 1828 to 1833. Unlike most merchants he had a keen interest in monetary questions, and in these years he evolved his own currency principle, by which note circulation would fluctuate in relation to the Bank's holding of specie. It was a principle that in effect sought to further the Bank's independence of government, and in 1832 he cogently enunciated this doctrine to the Bank Charter Committee, so that it became known as the 'Palmer rule'.[12] The Bank's Charter was duly renewed that year, after the City's leading figures had closed ranks around the much-criticized institution. But the rest of the decade proved traumatic for the Bank, featuring not only the financial crisis of 1837 but also two years later, after a severe drain on bullion, the need to turn ignominiously to the Bank of France for a rescue package. By the start of the 1840s two clear schools of thought had crystallized: the 'banking' school led by Palmer that wanted the Bank to have discretionary powers over the volume of currency; and the 'currency' school led by the private banker Samuel Jones Loyd that explicitly refuted such powers, laid the blame for its misfortunes on the Bank of England itself, and called for the rigid separation of the Bank's issuing and banking functions. It was to the latter school that Peel, Prime Minister from 1841, became a convert, as he prepared to put through a fundamental overhaul of the Bank's working practices and its position within the national monetary system. The result, against the wishes of the majority of Bank directors, was the Bank Charter Act of 1844.[13] Its main measures were separation of the Bank's note issue from its banking operations, restrictions on other banks of issue, a fixed ratio between notes and bullion, and a fixed fiduciary issue of £14m. (i.e. the amount of notes that might be issued against securities). Bagehot in *Lombard Street*, almost thirty years on, provided the classic exposition:

By that Act the currency manages itself; the entire working is automatic. The Bank of England plainly does not manage—cannot even be said to manage—the currency any more. And naturally, but rashly, the only reason upon which a public responsibility used to be assigned to the Bank having now clearly come to an end, it was inferred by many that the Bank had no responsibility.[14]

Very rashly, for not only did the Act confer exclusive issuing rights upon the Bank, but in the very narrowness of its remit lay the possibility of a technical mastery over monetary affairs that henceforth few outside critics would be able to challenge.

   Peel's disciple was Gladstone, the financial conscience of the Victorians. By 1854, two years after first becoming Chancellor of the Exchequer, he was displaying what Morley called 'a toughness, stiffness, and sustained anger that greatly astonished Threadneedle Street'.[15] The bone of con-

[12] Kynaston, *City*, 84–5.   [13] Ibid. 126–9.
[14] Walter Bagehot, *Lombard Street: A Description of the Money Market* (1873), 161–2.
[15] John Morley, *The Life of William Ewart Gladstone* (1905; 2 vol. edn.), i, 518.

tention was recondite enough—involving certain well-enshrined conventions allowing the Bank to profit through the timing of payments to it of dividends on the national debt—but for Gladstone the abuse symbolized the continuing existence of 'old corruption' at the heart of the financial system. And though he won this particular battle, thereafter he never forgave the Bank for what he regarded as its obstructive attitude.[16] During the winter of 1860–1, back at the Treasury, he waged another fierce conflict with the Bank, this time over the price paid by government for the management of the public debt, and once again the Bank gave way amidst much thinly veiled animosity. At the same time Gladstone also succeeded, again against Bank opposition, in establishing the Post Office Savings Banks. 'I had an object of first-rate importance', he would recall: namely, 'to provide the minister of finance with a strong financial arm, and to secure his independence of the City by giving him a large and certain command of money'.[17] Resentments lingered. 'At luncheon in the Bank parlour one generally hears grumbles, if not expletives, about Mr G,' noted Edward Hamilton of the Treasury in his diary in 1888. 'One Director said he intended to send Mr G a naive advertisement of an enterprising undertaker, who expressed surprise that people should go on living a life of trouble to themselves and others when they could be comfortably interred for £3.'[18]

Successive late-Victorian Chancellors, whether Liberal or Conservative, were essentially Gladstonian in their approach to the job, as the hard-pressed Bank discovered in the 1890s. Goschen took the opportunity of the renewal of the Charter in 1892 to reduce still further the management charges, prompting Hamilton to describe the Bank as having been 'squeezed'.[19] The following year Hamilton was enjoying a September holiday in Scotland when he received a graphic communication from Goschen's successor, the intemperate Harcourt:

In your absence I have fought a great fight with the dragons of the Bank parlour.

I sent for the Governor [David Powell] who came supported by that valiant champion Deputy Governor Wigram. After some polite beating about the bush we came to close quarters on the rate of interest on Ways & Means advances.

I blandly threw out a ½ per cent above the rate of deficiency advances which at the present discount rates would have been 2½p.c.

The two pundits looked at one another in blank dismay and revealed the fact that they had come with instructions to ask 3½ p.c.; thereupon I poured upon them the vials of my wrath; I showed them that such a rate had never been paid when the Bank Rate was 4%; I asked them with indignation how they dare behave in such a way to a customer who kept an average balance of £5,000,000 in their hands; I told them point blank that nothing would induce me to listen to such an exorbitant demand and I said that it would become my duty to enquire what 'other persons' there were in the City of London who might be ready & willing to accommodate

---

[16] Richard Shannon, *Gladstone, 1809–1865* (1982), 319.
[17] Morley, *Gladstone*, i, 686.   [18] British Library, Add Ms, 48,647.
[19] R. S. Sayers, *The Bank of England, 1891–1944* (Cambridge, 1976), i, 17.

H.M.'s Govt at a reasonable rate. I said I had hitherto been unwilling to open a Govt account elsewhere than at the B. of England but that such demands might make it necessary to look in other quarters for reasonable accommodation. This was quite enough to indicate the proximity of New Court [home of Rothschilds] to Threadneedle St. and they trembled at the notion of the Ch. of the Exch. dealing with Jews less extortionate than themselves. After I had exhibited this bug bear sufficiently I was prepared to dismiss them with the question whether I was to take their proposal as an ultimatum upon which the ferocious Powell hinted that I might write and suggest 3% and they would give it anxious consideration.

These two gentlemen who looked for all the world like the picture of the money lenders at Windsor then retired. The valiant Wigram looked daggers—but used none.

I accordingly wrote a polite note splitting the difference which has been graciously acceded to, they endeavouring to cover their retreat by alleging 'the change in the condition of the money market' as the reason of their climbing down . . .

All this convinces me that the more we deliver ourselves from their hands for extra accommodation beyond deficiency advances the better.[20]

Harcourt's letter thoroughly alarmed Hamilton—'It is an unfortunate occurrence; for I can see that Harcourt would like to break away from the Bank as much as possible; and there is nothing that I should regret more than to see the relations between them and the Government strained'—but within a few days the Chancellor was writing again in as fiery a mood. 'I shall have as little dealings as I can help with these gentlemen in the future . . . We have been made thorough fools of by the Bank this time but it will be our own fault if we allow ourselves to be plundered again by these sharp practitioners.' And as a postscript, he added that next time he really would borrow from Rothschilds '& show up these Bank gentlemen to the public for what they are'.[21]

Harcourt does not seem to have acted on these wild threats, but from the Bank's point of view it could hardly have been worse timing when a few weeks later it emerged that the Chief Cashier, Frank May, had been involved in serious irregularities. Powell and Wigram, who were all for hushing up the matter as much as possible, were summoned to Downing Street and given another piece of Harcourt's mind. Helped by Hamilton they managed to resist the Chancellor's strong impulse to set the Public Prosecutor to work, but the price they paid was assurances that steps had been taken to improve management at the Bank in such a way that nothing of the sort would happen again.[22] 'The great deposit of money which the Government keeps with the Bank, its relation to the State in respect of the management of the Public Debt, its identification through the Issue Department with the currency of the country, in themselves constitute an interest in its manage-

[20] British Library, Add Ms, 48,615 B.

[21] British Library, Add Mss, 48,661, 48,615 B.

[22] The story is told in Hamilton's diary at the British Library (Add Ms, 48,661) and the Harcourt papers in the Bodleian Library (Deps 170, 396).

ment which the Government could not neglect': thus Harcourt, with unusual restraint, informed Powell at the start of 1894, seeking to establish where the ultimate control lay.[23] All things considered, perhaps it was not surprising that the Bank's bicentenary celebrations later that year were strangely muted.

In the end, of course, no Victorian politician was an out-and-out *étatiste*. As Gladstone emphasized to the Commons in 1866, 'nothing could be more inconvenient than the assumption of responsibility by the government in the conduct of the ordinary business of the Bank'.[24] In an age when governments did not pursue economic strategies in any twentieth-century sense, the Bank maintained undisputed control over the nature as well as execution of monetary policy. In particular this took the form of full operational sway over the manipulation of Bank rate, increasingly the means by which it sought to defend the seriously inadequate gold reserve. 'In pre-war days', recalled Sir Otto Niemeyer in 1929, 'a change in bank rate was no more regarded as the business of the Treasury than the colour which the Bank painted its front door'.[25] Niemeyer himself had travelled in career terms from Great George Street to Threadneedle Street, but such a crossover would have been almost inconceivable before 1914. Although Hamilton made weekly visits to the Bank in order to sell Treasury bills, it was then a world of almost entirely separate spheres, a rigid demarcation testified to by the Treasury tradition that, in Niemeyer's words, 'when the Permanent Secretary visited the Bank of England, about once in 12 months, he took a taxi because he was not quite sure where the Bank was'.[26] In October 1903, over a fortnight after he had acquired a new master, Hamilton 'took Austen C. [i.e. Chamberlain] down to the Bank' in order 'to introduce him to the Governors & Directors'.[27] Politicians moved in one sphere, merchants in another (the Governor of the day was Samuel Morley, head of a large textile wholesale business), and save in a crisis rarely the twain met.

The outbreak of war in 1914 was one such crisis, bringing Bank and Treasury closely together—so much so that within a few days of the war starting the Governor, Cunliffe, remarked to Bradbury of the Treasury that so long as the war lasted the Bank 'would have to regard itself as a department of the Treasury'.[28] This patriotic intent, however, did not allow for Cunliffe's domineering tendencies towards successive Chancellors. He got on well with Lloyd George, who was happy to be flattered as the saviour of the City and tended to give Cunliffe considerable leeway over monetary aspects; but it was a different story with McKenna, a competent financier personally. By September 1915 relations between the two men were severely

[23] Anthony Howe, 'From "Old Corruption" to "New Probity": The Bank of England and its Directors in the Age of Reform', *Financial History Review*, 1 (1994), 40.
[24] Hansard, *Parliamentary Debates*, 3rd ser., clxxxiv, col. 717.
[25] PRO, T 176/13.
[26] Sayers, *Bank*, i, 14.
[27] British Library, Add Ms, 48,681.
[28] PRO, T 176/13.

strained. According to Beaverbrook (a bitter enemy of Cunliffe, but usually a reliable source on the inside story), McKenna 'would frequently urge Cunliffe the necessity of providing more bank balances for the government in the United States . . . Cunliffe would reply invariably, "Mr Chancellor, this is a matter of exchange, and the responsibility here lies with me" '.[29] In this dispute Cunliffe enjoyed the valuable backing of Lloyd George, and when in November 1915 the issue was for the time being settled with the establishment of what became known as the London Exchange Committee, it was significant that the Governor was able to control this powerful body almost single-handedly. 1917 was decisive:[30] Cunliffe renewed hostilities against the political arm by waging a fierce campaign against the Treasury over what he complained was interference in questions of exchange. Here he was on reasonably safe ground, but in the summer he miscalculated his strength and brought into the open the mood of revolt that had been brewing in Bonar Law, Chancellor since late 1916. This was over Cunliffe's almost mad attempt to block at a critical stage of the war the government's access to the Bank's gold in Canada, a move which prompted Bonar Law to write angrily to Lloyd George in July that 'the chancellorship is not in commission' and implicitly call on him for his support. This he got, and after a period of resistance Cunliffe was forced to back down. 'So long as I am Governor of the Bank', he wrote to Bonar Law on 12 August, 'I shall do my utmost to work loyally and harmoniously with you and for you as Chancellor of the Exchequer and while I shall continue, if you will allow me, to tender you such advice as I consider it my duty to offer, I fully realise that I must not attempt to impose my views upon you'.[31]

The episode passed into Bank mythology, not least because of Lloyd George's reported threat to 'take over the Bank'.[32] Yet one should not perhaps read too much into it, springing as it essentially did from Cunliffe's personality and possibly Bonar Law's cussed streak; and though as an assertion of political authority in the monetary sphere it does represent a certain landmark, there was for a while yet no diminution of Bank influence over the detailed conduct of monetary affairs. Indeed, addressing his Committee of Treasury barely a fortnight after his letter of apology, Cunliffe's tone remained palpably defiant: 'The Governor said that as he was to see the Chancellor this afternoon, he would take the opportunity of pointing out the position to him as it would probably mean a rise in the Bank Rate before long. He did not propose now or at any time to obtain the Chancellor's special sanction in regard to such changes as might be con-

---

[29] Lord Beaverbrook, *Politicans and the War, 1914–1916* (1928), 153.

[30] Sayers, *Bank*, i, 99–109, provides the most authoritative account of the quarrel between Cunliffe and Bonar Law.

[31] David Kynaston, *The Chancellor of the Exchequer* (Lavenham, 1980), 138–9; Sayers, *Bank*, i, 107.

[32] Sayers, *Bank*, i, 105.

templated in the Bank Rate.'[33] And when, a year later, Bonar Law urged Cunliffe's successor, Cokayne, to lower Bank rate, Cokayne flatly refused and Bonar Law gave way.[34]

It proved, however, a misleading portent, for the inter-war years fundamentally shifted the balance of power away from the Bank. Early honours, in the charged circumstances of 1919–20, were about even: twice the Bank managed to secure rises in Bank rate, from 5 to 6 and then from 6 to 7 per cent. But when in July 1920 Norman, recently installed as Governor, pushed for a rise from 7 to 8 per cent, Austen Chamberlain successfully resisted.[35] Over the next few months he continued to resist, so that by November an exasperated Norman was writing to him: 'When I call to mind your remark to my predecessor (that an independent Rise in the Bank Rate would be an unfriendly act); when I remember our continuing desire for higher rates ever since last July and indeed long before it, and your continuing unwillingness to consent, owing to political reasons ... I wonder what (in the spirit as well as in the letter) is the meaning of "political pressure".'[36] But in the long run, however much Norman may have wished otherwise, there was no avoiding the politicization of Bank rate, the price of money now being seen as impinging directly on levels of unemployment, housing policy, and economic policy in general.

In the short term, as it happened, Norman and the Bank enjoyed an illusory Indian summer. Bank rate went down steadily in 1921 and 1922; even when it rose in 1923 it did not go above 4 per cent either then or in 1924, and a series of Chancellors (no fewer than six between 1921 and 1924) did not question the Bank's right to determine Bank rate policy. 1925 abruptly ended the spell. Churchill—uneasy anyway about his reluctant acquiescence in Bank, Treasury, and general banking orthodoxy over the return to gold—allowed Norman to increase the rate from 4 to 5 per cent in March, but was extremely unhappy that the rise owed everything to the external situation and nothing to the internal.[37] Briefly the rate came down to 4 per cent during the second half of the year, but by the beginning of December, with gold flowing out of London, Norman saw no alternative to another hike. A memorandum by Leith-Ross of the Treasury, dated 3 December, takes up the story:

The Governor of the Bank called at the Treasury on the 2nd December about 7.15 p.m., and informed me that there was every probability that the Bank Rate would be increased ... The matter had not yet been definitely decided ...

I reported this to the Chancellor on the following morning and he at once telephoned to the Governor expressing his concern at the news. He told the Governor

---

[33] Bank of England Archive, G15/7.

[34] Susan Howson, 'The Origins of Dear Money, 1919–20', *Economic History Review*, 2nd ser., 27 (1974).

[35] Ibid.

[36] Sir Henry Clay, *Lord Norman* (1957), 292.

[37] Sayers, *Bank*, i, 145–6.

that if the rate were raised he would have to inform the House that it had been done without his being consulted and against his wishes. It was not fair to the Exchequer that action should be taken which affected all its affairs without an opportunity being given to him to consider it. He expressed an earnest request that action should be deferred at any rate for a week, to enable this to be done.[38]

The next day Norman wrote defiantly to Churchill—'I can now only await the statement which you threaten to make in the House of Commons, but I may say that I believe your action to be unprecedented'—and in the event not only did the rise go ahead but Churchill stayed publicly quiet.[39] Nevertheless, the episode, which had been clumsily handled by Norman, made crystal clear that henceforth there was no possibility of Bank rate policy operating in a comfortably ring-fenced political vacuum. In 1926 Norman tacitly conceded as much when he told the Royal Commission on Indian Currency and Finance that, though he looked upon the Bank as 'having the unique right to offer advice and to press such advice even to the point of "nagging" ', that advice was 'always of course subject to the supreme authority of Government'.[40]

The events of 1929 confirmed the underlying reality. After a Bank rate rise early in the year, imposed by Norman upon an inevitably reluctant Churchill, had earned the Bank widespread flak on account of its unemployment implications,[41] there was hammered out later in the year a compact between Norman and the new Labour Chancellor, Snowden. A Bank memorandum of 4 September recorded the two men's conversation:

The Governor said that his was the technical and financial side—the Chancellor's was the political and fiscal side. On this basis the Chancellor must now leave the Bank Rate to the Governor, to which the Chancellor agreed, stipulating that the Governor should see him next week; the Governor promising that he would not this autumn put up the Bank Rate for fun but only when it was essential.[42]

Put another way, Bank rate decisions may still formally have remained with the Governor, but there was now an acceptance on both sides that the political context was all important. And granted that, only an idealist would have expected the last word not to rest with the politicians.

In a perverse way, the humiliating decision to go off gold in 1931 marked the Bank's last hurrah, with the decision being taken unilaterally on the night of 18 September in the absence of Snowden, who on being informed could do no other than comply.[43] Nevertheless, the implications of the decision went all the other way. In the words of Norman, addressing the governors of the Empire's central banks in 1937: 'When the Gold Standard was

---

[38] PRO, T 176/13.   [39] Bank of England Archive, G15/7.
[40] Sir Theodore Gregory, 'The "Norman Conquest" Reconsidered', *Lloyds Bank Review* (Oct. 1957), 4.
[41] PRO, T 176/13.   [42] Bank of England Archive, G15/7.
[43] Philip Williamson, *National Crisis and National Government: British Politics, the Economy and Empire, 1926–1932* (Cambridge, 1992), 413.

abandoned, there took place an immediate redistribution of authority and responsibility, which deprived the Bank of some of its essential functions. Foreign Exchange became a Treasury matter.' And though Norman went on to assert that in the management of the Exchange Equalisation Account, established in 1932, 'we are given an extraordinarily free hand', he did not deny that it was the Treasury which determined the rate of exchange that should be upheld at any given time.[44] Moreover, 1932 also saw, with the help of that year's major debt conversion, the introduction of the conscious cheap money policy, after a decisive section within the Treasury had come round to the policy's virtues and drafted the memorandum that enabled Neville Chamberlain to impose it upon the relevant Cabinet committee early in the year.[45] Thus from June 1932 until shortly before the outbreak of war, Bank rate remained at a highly political 2 per cent. Norman reluctantly accepted the changed situation; and when in August 1939, following a severe drain on the reserves and with war imminent, Bank rate did go up, being doubled to 4 per cent, Norman took the opportunity, unprecedented for a Governor, to have it put on record that 'the step was taken at the request of the Chancellor'.[46] It was a disclaimer that eloquently revealed Norman's awareness that in practice only a weak Chancellor (which, as it happened, Simon was) would now allow Bank rate to be changed without being in genuine agreement himself. An internal memorandum on Bank–government relations, drafted by the Bank two years into the war, calmly accepted the facts of life: 'The Government, through the Treasury, seeks continuously the advice of the Bank, both on technical and wider questions, but retains undivided responsibility for major questions of policy'. And though the memorandum added that 'the Bank remains the confidential adviser and the administrative agent', there was no pretence that Bank independence went beyond what was operationally necessary— essentially in the markets—in order to give adequate weight to Bank advice.[47]

It was an operational independence that the Bank was determined to retain as it fought a rearguard action with the new Labour government over the exact terms of its nationalization in 1946. Catto, Norman's successor, succeeded probably beyond his expectations: the Bank kept its essential institutional autonomy, quite unlike that of a government department; governors were to be appointed for a fixed term of years and could not be dismissed; and the Treasury failed to secure the power to issue directives to the clearing banks, effectively putting it at the mercy of the Bank's mediation.[48] 'If ever there was anything done for show, not for effect, this is it',

[44] Clay, *Norman*, 437.
[45] Susan Howson, *Domestic Monetary Management in Britain, 1919–38* (Cambridge, 1975), 86–9.
[46] Sayers, *Bank*, ii, 573.   [47] Bank of England Archive, G15/7.
[48] John Fforde, *The Bank of England and Public Policy, 1941–1958* (Cambridge, 1992), 4–30, gives by far the fullest account of nationalization.

Robert Hall of the Economic Section reflected with some bitterness two years after the event.[49] It is tempting to argue that Dalton, out of a mixture of ignorance and over-confidence, blew it on behalf of the New Jerusalem; but at least equally sustainable is the view that Dalton and his Treasury advisers were perfectly happy with the Bank–government relationship as it had evolved over the previous twenty years and that the purpose of nationalization was essentially symbolic.[50] 'They try to pretend it is the same place', Norman remarked poignantly of his former colleagues a few weeks after nationalization had taken effect, but perhaps they did not have to try so hard.[51]

Even so, while all concerned knew that the last word on policy continued to rest with the government, what the 1946 Act was strangely silent about—perhaps reflecting almost a decade and a half of virtually static Bank rate—was the detailed execution of monetary policy. For a few years this deficiency mattered little, the strong instinct of Labour ministers being to consign monetary policy to the dark ages of Montagu Norman; but by 1949 the situation began to change, as the new Governor, Cobbold, consciously sought to restore the traditional importance of monetary policy as in turn the way of enhancing the Bank's own post-nationalization stature, not least within the City.[52] For two years he found himself beating on a closed door, but the change of government in 1951 led directly to, in Butler's own retrospective words, a 'return to the pre-war use of a flexible monetary policy'.[53] Over the next few years Cobbold applied the policy in such a way as almost to squeeze out the Treasury, certainly below the very top level.[54] It was a strategy that depended entirely on the monetary policy itself working, which it more or less did until the débâcle of 1955, when the Bank failed to deliver the credit squeeze that Butler had been promised and that had enabled him to adopt a tax-cutting pre-election budget. The almost direct upshot was the Radcliffe Committee on the Working of the Monetary System, set up in 1957 and reporting two years later. The report, deliberately low-key in tone, disavowed any notion of the Bank—however answerable to the Chancellor of the day and subordinate to his sometimes different priorities—enjoying a monopoly of monetary matters. It called instead for 'a constant co-operation, strategic and tactical, between the central bank on the one hand and those responsible for alternative or supplementary measures, essentially the Treasury and the Board of Trade, on the other'. Furthermore, monetary policy 'cannot be envisaged as a form of economic strategy which pursues its own independent objectives'. Rather, 'it is a part of the country's economic policy as a whole and must be

---

[49] Alec Cairncross (ed.), *The Robert Hall Diaries, 1947–53* (1989), 38.

[50] The latter view is cogently expressed by Susan Howson, *British Monetary Policy, 1945–51* (Oxford, 1993), 325.

[51] Fforde, *Bank*, 30.   [52] Howson, *British Monetary Policy*, 8–9.

[53] Lord Butler, *The Art of the Possible* (1971), 158.   [54] Fforde, *Bank*, 611–12.

planned as such'.[55] In effect, while in no way denying the Bank a necessary measure of independence, Radcliffe put the Bank back into what was rapidly turning into the corporatist pack.

Within that pack, and against the background of a post-Radcliffe conventional wisdom that downgraded the importance of monetary policy, the Bank struggled to punch its weight during the 1960s and first half of the 1970s. When, on the evening of 24 November 1964, Cromer had his celebrated meeting of minds with the newly elected Wilson—the former demanding a complete volte-face in government social and economic policy in order to restore confidence to the holders of sterling, the latter threatening to go to the country in defence of his government's constitutional rights—the most convincing explanation for this ill-judged manœuvre is that it reflected a frustration on the Bank's part of being increasingly 'out of the loop' in the economic policy-making process as a whole.[56] It was a frustration, it should be emphasized, that was more than a few weeks old: over the previous two years Cromer had been still less able to apply a brake to Maudling's expansionary instincts.[57] Cromer's successor, O'Brien, was to prove equally ineffective in preventing the next Tory dash for growth, the so-called Barber Boom of the early 1970s.[58] It was a boom that, inadvertently, led directly to the climactic of the mid-1970s and the renaissance of monetary policy. In the short term that renaissance undoubtedly strengthened the Bank's hand, not least because of the skilful efforts of O'Brien's successor, Richardson, to occupy the intellectual high ground and develop policies for 'practical monetarism'.[59] In the longer term, though, the reassertion of monetary policy proved a less gratifying process for the Bank. This was partly because the Treasury as an institution assumed a responsibility for monetary strategy it had never before enjoyed, at the same time acquiring a novel familiarity with the workings of the money and foreign exchange markets; partly because of personal discord in the early 1980s between Richardson and Thatcher, the latter a zealous rather than practical monetarist; and partly because of the presence through much of the 1980s of a Chancellor, Lawson, not only long-serving but also possessed of a rare intellectual self-confidence.[60] 'The traditional role of the Bank as

[55] Committee on the Working of the Monetary System, *Report*, Cmnd. 827 (1959), para. 767.

[56] Harold Wilson, *The Labour Government, 1964–1970: A Personal Record* (1971), 37–8; Michael Moran, 'Power, Policy and the City of London', in Roger King (ed.), *Capital and Politics* (1983), 55.

[57] Keith Middlemas, *Power, Competition and the State*, ii. *Threats to the Postwar Settlement: Britain, 1961–74* (Basingstoke, 1990), 82–5.

[58] Ibid., 345.

[59] Stephen Fay, *Portrait of an Old Lady: Turmoil at the Bank of England* (1987), 78–83; Keith Middlemas, *Power, Competition and the State*, iii. *The End of the Postwar Era: Britain since 1974* (Basingstoke, 1991), 142.

[60] William Plowden, 'The Treasury: Continuity and Change', *Contemporary Record*, 2 (Autumn 1988); Fay, *Portrait*, 114–27; William Keegan, *Mr Lawson's Gamble* (1989).

a voice to advise and warn government has been reduced', noted the
Financial Times in January 1988 on the occasion of Leigh-Pemberton's
reappointment for a second term as Governor, 'and its utterings now come
more from the wings than from centre stage'. The *FT* added that 'the
Bank's function has become limited to the more technical one of administering policy in the markets'.[61] Almost a century and a half on from the
Bank Charter Act, it was a non-discretionary role of which Peel and his
most famous disciple would have approved.

Attitudes, Prejudices, and Assumptions

The traditional culture of the Bank was solid, unimaginative, and mercantile. It was also deeply resistant to change. Hamilton of the Treasury dined
at Threadneedle Street in November 1891:

I had talk with sundry Directors about the Chancellor of the Exchequer's currency
scheme ... Notwithstanding that the measure has the cordial approval of the
Governor himself, the majority of the Court appears to be very lukewarm about it,
if not hostile to it. It is a case of 'laissez nous faire'. 'We have got on well enough
up till now, why not leave us alone?'[62]

A culture in which duty was valued above opportunity, and the integrity of
sterling above everything; not much changed in the next seventy years. It
was a continuity cemented by the long governorships of Norman (twenty-
four years) and Cobbold (twelve years), the latter in a very real sense
Norman's man. When on a Sunday evening in September 1949, just before
the announcement of devaluation, Cobbold addressed the Court, it might
have been his master's voice. After noting that devaluation was a regret-
table recognition of a state of affairs, never a solution, he went on: 'The
one essential thing—and this I repeat and underline—is that devaluation
can be done once but can and must not even be in question a second time
unless there have been major events such as a world war in the intervening
period.'[63] Eighteen years later, with no world war intervening, the pound
was again devalued; and long afterwards, one of the Bank's Executive
Directors at the time would recall how devaluation this second time round
was 'certainly seen' as 'an act of default in relation to the sterling holders'.[64]
It was in many ways a rather insular culture, born partly out of an intense
loyalty. To call oneself 'a Servant of this House' was no idle phrase; on first
meeting Moreau at the Bank of France in 1926, Norman avowed that 'the
Bank of England is my only mistress. I think only of her and I have dedicated my life to her.'[65] A fascinated witness to this culture was Benn, who
took lunch with O'Brien early in 1970:

[61] *Financial Times*, 29 Jan. 1988.   [62] British Library, Add Ms, 48,656.
[63] Fforde, *Bank*, 300.
[64] Sir Jasper Hollom, quoted in *Contemporary Record*, 1 (Winter 1988), 47.
[65] Gregory, 'Norman Conquest', 3.

I have never been to the Bank of England before and one really did have to go through about five great iron gates as if one were entering a prison. We then went up to the most beautiful dining room. He is a nice man, very agreeable but totally out of touch because he has worked for the Bank all his life and doesn't understand the attacks on him from outside . . . He said the usual stupid things about trade unions and wished the shareholders would play a larger part in companies. He lives in a dream world . . . It occurred to me with a great sort of flash of lightning that this is what is wrong with the City: the people in it don't make any effort to broaden their interests.[66]

A wonderfully Bennite entry, and perhaps unfair to O'Brien, but the larger point holds.

Perhaps above all, the Bank's was a culture that valued an understanding of markets and market psychology far above an academic grasp of economics—indeed, it is arguable that, until the 1960s, the Bank had a positively anti-intellectual bias. 'We were late in building up a body of professionals drawn from outside', Norman privately conceded in 1928, adding that 'we could not draw them from inside because the experience does not exist there'.[67] But this tardiness was more than an oversight. When the Macmillan Committee asked Norman soon afterwards whether he made use of the advisers he now had, Norman allegedly replied (though the answer does not survive in the printed minutes): 'Well, I make up my mind and I ask my experts to explain to me why I've done so'.[68] Did this deep-rooted preference for instinct over reason matter? One moment that it did was in the spring of 1919 in the context of considerable policy confusion over the question of exchange support and maintenance of the gold standard. With the Bank lagging behind badly in the debate, and at odds with the joint-stock banks, Austen Chamberlain observed perceptively that 'when "the City" is acting by instinct and rule of thumb it is amazingly clever and sure, but when it is asked to advise on large new issues, it has no theory or policy to work upon, and is indeed a broken reed.'[69] It was remarkable how little the situation had changed by the post-war period. 'It is hard not to get the impression that the Bank, and the banks generally, do not think at all about credit control as economists do, and indeed that they don't quite understand what it is all about', noted Hall in his diary in 1948.[70] A year later Cobbold was Governor, and in the course of his tenure of office he coined the famous dictum that 'the Bank is not a study group'.[71] A telling insight into the way his mind worked is contained in some private thoughts he jotted down at the end of 1955, a traumatic year for him and the Bank as a whole:

[66] Tony Benn, *Office Without Power: Diaries, 1968–72* (1988), 233–4.
[67] Clay, *Norman*, 311.   [68] Gregory, 'Norman Conquest', 11.
[69] Sir Charles Petrie, *The Life and Letters of the Rt. Hon. Sir Austen Chamberlain* (1940), ii, 141.
[70] Cairncross, *Hall Diaries, 1947–53*, 41.
[71] Jasper Hollom, 'Lord Cobbold', *Independent*, 9 Nov. 1987.

Change of bowling most necessary. Public fed up with hearing about credit squeeze and does not believe it will stop inflation unless forcible attacks made in other directions, notably public expenditure generally and nationalised industries development plans. Further moves in credit field alone unlikely to achieve objectives and likely to discredit policy.

Perhaps worth considering appeal to big industry to go slow in 1956 on development (supported by continued firm credit policy) provided H.M.G. prepared to give firm lead at public and nationalised end, i.e. keep the off-spinner on at one end, but put on a fast bowler at other end with new ball. Must get more directly at the critical points.[72]

Alas, the officer virtues of fortitude and man-management were no longer enough in an England whose cricket team was being captained for the first time by a professional; and when in about 1961 Anthony Sampson spent some time anatomizing the Bank, he was struck by the rarity of graduates, the profusion of 'inarticulate but confident' market operators, and the way in which the institution embodied 'the unquestioning regimental spirit of the public school proletariat'.[73] Over the ensuing two decades, of course, the Bank was to become a far more sophisticated animal, though as late as 1978 there was an echo of Cobbold's dictum when Richardson in his important Mais lecture on the conduct of monetary policy remarked that 'formulating a line of practical policy and trying to stick to it, while yet remaining appropriately flexible amid the uncertainty of day-to-day affairs, feels very different from devising ideal solutions in the seclusion of a study'.[74] Historically, for good as well as ill, the City has always exalted practical man.

Butler, giving evidence to Radcliffe in 1958, tactfully delineated what he saw as the essential differences between the two bodies that sought in their distinctive ways to serve government:

I think that there are things the Bank can do that the Treasury cannot, and things the Treasury can do that the Bank cannot. The Bank is more instinctively intuitive, and the Treasury is more instinctively deliberative—at least, so it seems to me—and so the two partners rather supplement each other. The management of the day-to-day market, which is the fundamental job of the Bank, apart from their agency functions in relation to the debt, the note issue and so forth, is a different sphere from the more deliberative long-term policy aspect of the Treasury.[75]

How, though, did the Treasury view the Bank over the years? There is, in fact, surprisingly little hard evidence. Hamilton in the late-Victorian and Edwardian period was only a selective admirer of individual Governors, but rarely failed to emphasize the need for an attitude of deference on tech-

---

[72] Bank of England Archive, G1/73.
[73] Anthony Sampson, *Anatomy of Britain* (1962), 366.
[74] *Bank of England Quarterly Bulletin*, 18 (Mar. 1978), 33.
[75] Committee on the Working of the Monetary System, *Minutes of Evidence* (1960), q 12,381.

nical matters. This particularly applied to the weekly ceremony of tenders for Treasury bills, indispensable to the short-term funding of government. 'One must practically follow the advice of the Governor & Deputy Governor', he noted on one occasion, 'one of course defers to the judgement of the Governor & Deputy Governor' on another.[76] Over half a century later the tone was very similar when Sir Edward Bridges, Permanent Secretary to the Treasury, informed Radcliffe that, in monetary matters, 'policy springs to a very sharp extent out of the practical experience of the Bank'. And he described the Bank's senior officials as having had 'long and intense training and experience in their particular field', being 'specialists who have risen to the top through their skill and experience in dealing with financial matters'. Such expertise was in marked contrast to their counterparts at the Treasury, whom Bridges described as 'laymen in the sense that most of them do not spend much of their lives in becoming experts in any particular subject'.[77] The direct result of this wide disparity in familiarity with the markets, especially the gilt-edged and foreign exchange, was that, Michael Moran has argued, 'an attitude of deference was induced in the Treasury'.[78] Is this really plausible, granted the legendary intellectual firepower of the Treasury? 'Deference' is perhaps too strong a term. One catches a whiff of a different spirit when in February 1952, with Robot at its planning stage, Otto Clarke at the Treasury waited impatiently 'for the East End mountain to give birth';[79] while through that decade, Sir Robert Hall never lost an opportunity in his diary to castigate the Bank and its Governor for their sadly limited intelligence.[80] Nevertheless, it does seem that the Treasury's traditional view of the Bank's inhabitants was, as in Sampson's helpful phrase, 'a foreign tribe who must not be interfered with'.[81] That view may have been a touch condescending, but it was also watchful—and, ultimately, respectful. Over ensuing decades the Treasury became more comfortable with the markets, but the Bank for its part became more like a government department, and so that respect continued, at least on the monetary side if not necessarily on the fiscal. The Bank's success in the early 1970s in pushing through Competition and Credit Control, almost entirely off its own bat, was graphic testimony to where, as long as an issue was perceived as being sufficiently technical, the monetary whip-hand continued to lie before the 1980s.[82]

It is difficult to make useful generalizations about the attitude to the

---

[76] British Library, Add Mss 48,641, 48,644.

[77] Committee on the Working of the Monetary System, *Principal Memoranda of Evidence* (1960), iii, 47.

[78] Moran, 'Power', 54.   [79] PRO, T 236/3240.

[80] Hall perhaps marked Cobbold too low; Fforde, by contrast, is surely on the generous side.

[81] Sampson, *Anatomy*, 367.

[82] Michael Moran, *The Politics of Banking: The Strange Case of Competition and Credit Control* (1984).

Bank of the Treasury's modern masters. Lord Randolph Churchill may have had a panic attack outside the Bank on his first visit there,[83] but few in the twentieth century held it in such awe. The notable exception was Snowden, who on becoming Chancellor in 1924 was bowled over by Norman. 'I had seen caricatures in the Socialist Press of the typical financier—the hard-faced, close-fisted, high-nosed individual', he recalled. But in fact, he found someone Herculean in his efforts, of an international cast of mind, and with 'one of the kindliest natures and most sympathetic hearts it has been my privilege to know'.[84] More typical, on the positive side of the ledger, was Macmillan's attitude towards Cromer. Although generally grudging in his attitude towards finance, wanting industry to be more proud, he recognized in the Governor a figure of substance. 'Although "sound" ', he noted in his diary in 1962, 'Lord C. has a nose. He is not a Baring for nothing—a long business and financial tradition'.[85] Two years later came the Cromer–Wilson confrontation—Cromer, according to one of Wilson's biographers, 'found Wilson slippery and unsound and made little attempt to hide the low opinion he held', while 'Wilson for his part found Cromer hectoring and bigoted.'[86] But successive Labour Chancellors later in the 1960s had a higher regard for Cromer's less patrician successor. 'Modest, quiet, considerate of the views of others but firm in his own beliefs, he was technically proficient': so Callaghan described O'Brien, and Jenkins seems to have concurred.[87] Similarly in the 1970s, when, although the Bank found itself in the doghouse over its management of sterling in the spring of 1976, both Callaghan as Prime Minister and Healey as Chancellor had generally good, constructive working relationships with Richardson.[88] Granted the rapidly enhanced importance of financial markets from the mid-1970s and their atavistic dislike of any Labour government, perhaps Callaghan and Healey had no alternative, but their attitude was very different from that of Attlee's Chancellors. Dalton was typically condescending towards Catto, describing him in his diary as 'a splendid little asset';[89] Cripps let it be known that he had only appointed Cobbold because he was unable to get anyone else and that Cobbold had turned out far worse than had been expected;[90] while Gaitskell in January 1951, contemptuous of Cobbold's attempt to have Bank rate raised on 'purely psychological' grounds, wrote in his diary: 'I must say that I have a very poor opinion not only of him—he is simply not a very intelligent man—but of

[83] Winston Spencer Churchill, *Lord Randolph Churchill* (1906), ii, 183.
[84] Philip Snowden, *An Autobiography* (1934), i, 613–15.
[85] Harold Macmillan, *At the End of the Day, 1961–1963* (1973), 381.
[86] Philip Ziegler, *Wilson: The Authorised Life of Lord Wilson of Rievaulx* (1993), 194.
[87] James Callaghan, *Time and Chance* (1987), 195; Roy Jenkins, *A Life at the Centre* (1991), 240.
[88] Bernard Donoughue, *Prime Minister: The Conduct of Policy under Harold Wilson and James Callaghan* (1987), 102; Denis Healey, *The Time of my Life* (1989), 375.
[89] Ben Pimlott (ed.), *The Political Diary of Hugh Dalton 1918–40, 1945–60* (1986), 362.
[90] Cairncross, *Hall Diaries, 1947–53*, 66.

also most of the people in the Bank. Whether they are right or not in matters of judgement, they are singularly bad at putting their case, and judging by experience they are usually wrong in their conclusions.'[91] Labour politicians are congenital scribblers, but it is much harder to know what, say, Neville Chamberlain or Butler or Barber really thought about the Bank. Still, we do have the voluminous memoirs of Lawson, Chancellor for longer than anyone since the First World War, as well as Financial Secretary to the Treasury for two important years. It would be hard to describe his attitude as one of wholehearted admiration. He portrays the Medium Term Financial Strategy as having been introduced in 1980 despite Bank attempts to 'neuter' it, an opposition based on the Bank's wish 'to retain complete and unfettered discretion over monetary policy'; he blames the Bank for its 'inability' that same year 'to foresee the scale of the rise in £M3 when the corset was eventually lifted'; he remarks on the Bank's lack of creative input into monetary policy discussion by the time he became chancellor in 1983; and he strongly denies retrospective suggestions that the Bank tried to put the brakes on the credit boom of 1986–8 forever associated with this Chancellor's name.[92] If the mission of Thatcherism was to reverse British economic decline, it seems that Lawson saw the Bank as one of the symptoms—indeed, arguably one of the causes—that needed to be addressed.

There was one Tory Chancellor not just critical of the Bank but wholly disenchanted. In May 1927 Churchill sent Niemeyer at the Treasury a letter in which he poured out all his frustrations:

We have assumed since the war, largely under the guidance of the Bank of England, a policy of deflation, debt repayment, high taxation, large sinking funds and Gold Standard. This has raised our credit, restored our exchange and lowered the cost of living. On the other hand it has produced bad trade, hard times, an immense increase in unemployment involving costly and unwise remedial measures, attempts to reduce wages in conformity with the cost of living and so increase the competitive power, fierce labour disputes arising therefrom, with expense to the State and community measured by hundreds of millions . . . We have to look forward, as a definite part of the Bank of England policy, to an indefinite period of high taxation, of immense repayments and of no progress towards liberation either nominal or real, only a continued enhancement of the bondholders' claim. This debt and taxation lie like a vast wet blanket across the whole process of creating new wealth by new enterprise.

Churchill the politician saw no way beyond this 'strict, rigid, highly particularist line of action' and could only blame the Bank for his intellectual captivity.[93] His personal relations with Norman deteriorated sharply, so

[91] Philip M. Williams (ed.), *The Diary of Hugh Gaitskell, 1945–1956* (1983), 227.
[92] Nigel Lawson, *The View from No. 11: Memoirs of a Tory Radical* (1992), 66–71, 82, 450, 638–9.
[93] PRO, T 175/11.

much so that, according to his private secretary, 'he got into the habit of almost spitting out comments on the presumed enormities of "that man Skinner" ', Skinner being the private secretary in whose name Norman used to reserve his passages across the Atlantic.[94] In later years Churchill continued to brood. 'The biggest blunder in his life', he told Moran and assembled company one evening in September 1945 as he convalesced by Lake Como, 'had been the return to the gold standard. Montagu Norman had spread his blandishments before him till it was done, and had then left him severely alone.'[95] There was a significant coda to his sense of betrayal. When in 1952 the Bank, in alliance with the Overseas Finance section of the Treasury and the Chancellor himself, sought under the Robot Plan to make sterling convertible at a floating rate, Churchill's opposition as Prime Minister was decisive.[96] It was an opposition stiffened at least once by Cherwell, whom Churchill had drafted into the cabinet as Paymaster-General. Cherwell's letter to Churchill of 18 March was a cardinal and in its way brilliant document:

It is at first sight an attractive idea to go back to the good old days before 1914 when the pound was convertible and strong and we never had dollar crises. No doubt the bankers honestly believe that, if only the pound could be left to market forces, with the Bank of England free to intervene when necessary by varying the Bank Rate at their discretion, all would be well. The country's economy, they think, would be taken out of the hands of politicians and planners and handed over to financiers and bankers who alone understand these things . . .

After arguing that the consequences of such a policy were likely to be 'an 8% Bank Rate, 2 million unemployed and a 3/- loaf', Cherwell wound up with a peroration that played on Churchill's most sensitive spot:

Sterling, I repeat, cannot be made strong by financial manipulation. It is the real things that count—more steel mills in Britain, more ship loads of British manufactures crossing the Atlantic, more Australian farmers growing wheat and meat for England, more cotton plantations in the Colonies. That is the way to make sterling strong. It is a hard way and it will take time. But it is the only way. I trust we shall not allow ourselves to be persuaded that there is a painless, magical way—by leaving it all to the Bank of England.[97]

Robot was arguably the great turning-point in post-war British economic history that failed to turn. The outcome might well have been different but for Churchill's personal history.

Finally, what did the Bank itself make of the politicians? Here one has virtually nothing to go on, but it is surely a plausible surmise that they tended to be regarded as an inherently unsatisfactory breed, prone to

[94] P. J. Grigg, *Prejudice and Judgement* (1948), 193.
[95] Lord Moran, *Winston Churchill: The Struggle for Survival, 1940–1965* (1966), 303–4.
[96] For a recent account of the episode, see Stephen J. Procter, 'Floating Convertibility: The Emergence of the Robot Plan, 1951–52', *Contemporary Record*, 7 (1993).
[97] PRO, T 236/3242.

taking decisions more geared towards short-term electoral advantage than the long-term financial health of the country. There is no doubt, for instance, that through much of the spring and summer of 1949 the Bank's view was that those ministers who were pushing for devaluation were doing so as 'an easy way out', a way of avoiding the fundamental issues of excessive public expenditure and lax monetary policy.[98] A similar attitude almost certainly prevailed in July 1966.[99] And when six years later the decision was taken to float sterling, it was seen by the Bank, which had long forgotten its Robotic aberration, as, in the words of Middlemas, 'a surrender to a perennial political temptation to evade a fixed-rate discipline'.[100] One could hardly expect otherwise. In his governorship Norman went through nine Chancellors, Cobbold seven; Cromer managed three, O'Brien four, and Richardson four. The Bank, in a word, could afford to play the long game. 'I hardly like to say "welcome home"', the Deputy Governor Mynors wrote to Cobbold shortly before Christmas 1955, 'because one of the unanswerable questions you left behind has been answered, and one or two new ones have cropped up. We are still in the doldrums, with the Treasury pretty fractious because miracles do not happen.'[101] Clearly there was much frustration on the Bank's part about the dictates of the political process; yet perhaps the miracle-seekers could have done with a little more imaginative sympathy than they tended to receive.

Influencing Policy

It is possible, at the risk of being over-schematic, to identify various stratagems and methods, not always adopted consciously, by which the Bank sought to influence economic policy-making. A favourite was to ally with the Treasury against the politicians and the wider political process. Examples in the first half of this century include the 1914 financial crisis (according to the most recent reading); the rise in Bank rate to 7 per cent in April 1920; the return to gold in 1925 (when Norman and Niemeyer could hardly have acted more closely in their combined assault on Churchill's sensitivities); and the immediate aftermath of the 1931 financial crisis, when briefly it seemed that MacDonald intended to produce direct Cabinet control over monetary policy, before Treasury and Bank came effectively together to manage sterling in the new era.[102] Or from a later period take Radcliffe, when whatever its recent dissatisfaction with the

[98] Alec Cairncross, *Years of Recovery: British Economic Policy, 1945–51* (1985), 189.
[99] Wilson, *Labour Government*, 251–2. [100] Middlemas, *Power*, ii, 334.
[101] Bank of England Archive, G1/73.
[102] John Peters, 'The British Government and the City–Industry Divide: The Case of the 1914 Financial Crisis', *Twentieth Century British History*, 4 (1993); Howson, 'Dear Money'; D. E. Moggridge, *British Monetary Policy, 1924–1931: The Norman Conquest of $4.86* (Cambridge, 1972); Williamson, *National Crisis*, 497–501.

Bank's conduct of monetary policy it does seem that the Treasury tacitly decided to close ranks with the Bank in the face of outside scrutiny and probable criticism.[103] In May 1957, as the Committee met for the first time, it was hardly an adversarial tone that Sir Roger Makins, Permanent Secretary to the Treasury, adopted towards Cobbold. After expressing the hope that 'each of us will keep in touch with the other's thinking while we prepare our positions', he went on:

I certainly want you to know what we are doing. To that end I intend to keep the Bank fully informed, and I hope that you will authorise your people to do the same. As our work proceeds, I am sure that we shall feel the need for your advice, and when such occasions arise I hope we may ask for it. I need not say that we shall be glad to have your comments on our work at any time.

To which Cobbold replied: '*Monetary Enquiry*. We had a word this morning and I now have your letter of today's date. We are, I think, in full agreement and I foresee no difficulty in practice.'[104] Nor was there, as an exasperated Hall noted in his diary later that year:

The thing that I find most irritating about all our proceedings with Radcliffe is that the central fact is not being brought out and I do not suppose it can be brought out, which is that the Bank hardly collaborate with the Treasury at all in internal policy matters—the Chancellor talks to the Governor in private and the Bank neither give us their assessment of the situation, nor of the part they expect monetary policy to play in it. Now I feel that the Governor has hypnotised Roger Makins.[105]

Ultimately the Radcliffe Report did call for a new approach, but Cobbold's monetary skeletons were kept firmly in the cupboard.

Hall was right to be irate, for it was at the heart of the Norman-Cobbold approach that discussion of high policy was only to be undertaken by the men at the top and conducted on an essentially personal basis. It was a revealing moment when Norman mentioned to the Committee of Treasury in 1930 'that the advent of the BIS had altered the time-honoured relations between the Bank and the Treasury', in that it necessitated 'frequent interviews and consultations between officials of the Treasury and the Bank with the result that the Governors are not and cannot be the sole connecting link'. Norman added that he 'viewed this situation with some disquiet'.[106] It is arguable that the almost complete identification of Norman with the deflationary policies of the 1920s ultimately did the Bank more harm than good, but Cobbold in the 1950s was even more 'personal' in his approach. Hall, looking back in 1956 on the phase of Cobbold's governorship between 1951 and 1955 that had ended so disastrously, referred to 'the

[103] E. H. H. Green, 'The Influence of the City over British Economic Policy, *c.* 1880–1960', in Youssef Cassis (ed.), *Finance and Financiers in European History* (Cambridge, 1992), 205–7.
[104] PRO, T 233/1407.
[105] Alec Cairncross (ed.), *The Robert Hall Diaries, 1954–61* (1991), 135.
[106] Diane B. Kunz, *The Battle for Britain's Gold Standard in 1931* (1987), 30.

vicious system under which he saw R.A.B. alone and there was no record of their talks'.[107] Cobbold, like Norman, had a strong personality that cannot have been easy to resist, but there was a significant down side. 'To imagine that access to a chancellor or permanent secretary gives special control over policy betrays an outmoded notion of how modern government works', Moran has written. 'When government is a large and complex organisation intervening in a wide range of social and economic affairs, policy-making becomes a bureaucratic business: decisions are ground out of a network of committees, not independently made by a few highly-placed individuals.'[108] This especially applied on the non-monetary side, where for all Cobbold's repeated exhortations to successive Chancellors to rein back public expenditure he never made much impact. Cobbold's successors, certainly from O'Brien on, relied less on the personal approach. Even so, when Lawson in 1979 'became the Ministerial contact between the Treasury and the Bank', this 'greatly upset Richardson, who felt that, as Governor, his relations should be exclusively with the Chancellor except when he wished to see the Prime Minister' and that 'on no account should he be required to talk to a mere Financial Secretary'.[109] The City's traditional parlours have always placed an inordinate value on personal contact, and Richardson had been a merchant banker before he became Governor—perhaps the last one to do so.

The Bank, even after nationalization, never divulged its secrets readily, epitomized by annual reports that for a long time were a travesty of the genre. 'I'm not against an inquiry because I've discovered that the Bank of England is a closed book to us all', Jenkins remarked to Crossman in 1968, backing the idea that the Select Committee on the Nationalised Industries should seek to penetrate Threadneedle Street. Hardly a conspiracy-minded politician, he added that 'we don't know nearly enough of what's going on because they don't let us into their secrets'.[110] Though the resulting inquiry did secure certain revelations about the Bank's working practices (matters of 'policy' remained strictly off limits), leading to tighter Treasury checks, when he became Chancellor in 1974 Healey was struck by the Bank's essentially non-democratic character, in that 'it still attempted to maintain the cabbalistic secrecy of its most famous Governor, Montague [*sic*] Norman, seeing itself as the guardian of mysteries which no ordinary mortal should be allowed to understand'.[111] A deliberate retention of mystique, an exploitation of the adage that 'knowledge is power', a rarely questioned assumption that it alone understood the markets and what was required to maintain or restore their confidence—all these things could make the Bank a daunting proposition to mortals.[112] Few were made to feel more mortal

---

[107] Cairncross, *Hall Diaries, 1954–61*, 69.   [108] Moran, 'Power', 55.
[109] Lawson, *View*, 84.
[110] Richard Crossman, *The Diaries of a Cabinet Minister, ii* (1976), 667.
[111] Healey, *Time*, 374.   [112] Green, 'Influence of the City', 202 explores this theme.

than MacDonald and Snowden during the whirlwind of August 1931.[113] Intent on saving sterling, not on overthrowing the Labour government, Harvey (standing in for the ill Norman) wrote to Snowden on the 6th. After explaining that the Bank had virtually exhausted its foreign exchange in the previous few weeks, he went on:

What particularly impels me to write to you at this moment is the discussion we had in our Committee this morning and the view of the situation taken by the Bank's most trusted advisers—men in intimate touch with the foreign markets— was, I cannot disguise the fact, extremely grave. However black the Governor may have painted the picture in his discussions with you, his picture cannot have been more black than theirs today.

I feel compelled to write to you to tell you this. We are doing all that we can but our power to act is rapidly diminishing. As I tried to explain to you last week, the reports which reach us all show that the sign which foreigners expect from this country is the readjustment of the budgetary position, and this attitude on their part has again been forcibly expressed today in messages from both Paris and New York. I am most anxious not to step beyond my province but I feel I should be fail- ing in my duty if I did not say that with the prospects as they present themselves today the time available for the Government to reach decisions on this subject (as a means of safeguarding the value of sterling) may be much shorter than recently seemed likely.[114]

Twelve increasingly critical days later he wrote again:

Reports from both the Stock and Exchange markets say that whilst things are some- what quieter today there is a general atmosphere of nervous hesitancy, everybody anxiously awaiting the announcement of the Government's programme. I earnestly hope that it may be possible for such announcement to be made as soon as possi- ble as markets are meanwhile the prey of all sorts of rumours, and so long as the present tension lasts there must always be the danger of a sudden break taking place in some quarter and becoming the signal for a general *sauve qui peut*.[115]

These were powerful, seemingly omniscient communications, which at the least did much to frame the terms of the argument that brought down the government; yet later in the month, after the government's collapse, MacDonald was able to observe in all sincerity that 'the bankers never interfered with political policy'.[116] The Bank's control of all the high cards would never be quite so perfect again, as financial knowledge became more widely disseminated, but successive Governors used successive sterling crises—and even non-crises—to attempt, with varying degrees of success, to bounce governments into 'sound money' policies. 'The feeling of the markets both here and abroad is quite clear', Cobbold wrote to Macmillan

[113] Williamson, *National Crisis*, 255–424, brings this out well in his account of the 1931 financial crisis.

[114] Bank of England Archive, G3/210.   [115] Ibid.

[116] Philip Williamson, 'A "Bankers Ramp"? Financiers and the British Political Crisis of August 1931', *English Historical Review*, 99 (1984), 794.

in December 1956 after the trauma of Suez. 'They have been shocked by the weakness exposed by recent developments and they have their eyes firmly fixed on what they regard as three question marks; our willingness to live within our means, our overseas commitments and our productive capacity (or will to work)'. And, he added, 'unless these questions are answered to their satisfaction, the underlying pressures will remain against us and will become stronger'.[117] As late as July 1976, Callaghan was explicitly asking Richardson to name a figure for what size of public expenditure cuts would be sufficient to hold the currency.[118] Markets by then, in the post-Bretton-Woods world, were in the process of becoming so volatile that soon no central banker could plausibly claim a unique capacity to read the tea-leaves.

This raising of the stakes, often with a sharp twist of emotional pressure, was deliberate. The country would pull through, Norman said privately before he left to convalesce in August 1931, 'if we can get them frightened enough'.[119] 'Them' were MacDonald and Snowden. Over the years it was an enormous help in attempts to put on the frighteners, and generally to get politicians to see things the Bank's way, that the Bank retained what Samuel Brittan in the 1960s memorably called its 'odour of sanctity'.[120] Again and again one is struck by the moralism. Praising dear money, and advocating still dearer, Cokayne in February 1920 commended the recent Bank rate rise to Austen Chamberlain as having 'shown the intention of this country to face facts'.[121] Five years later Norman began his formal case to Churchill for an early return to gold with a series of propositions:

National Credit needs not only a strict financial policy and healthy economic conditions but also good faith and a liquid Reserve.

Gold is the guarantee of good faith.

A liquid Reserve must be internationally valid: there is no internationally valid Reserve except Gold (or its equivalent).

A Gold Reserve and the Gold Standard are steps in the evolution of Finance and Credit: as such they are necessary: so is a Police Force or Tax Collector: it is as dangerous to abandon the former as the latter.[122]

No wonder that the historian of 'the Norman Conquest' has described it as 'ultimately an act of faith ... undertaken for largely moral reasons'.[123] Norman himself did his best as Governor to attempt to create an impression of the Bank as above the sordid fray. 'It is only by refraining rigidly from any intervention in matters of a political character', he wrote to a correspondent in 1931, 'that the Bank can hope to convince politicians and the

[117] Bank of England Archive, G1/74.

[118] Edmund Dell, *A Hard Pounding: Politics and Economic Crisis, 1974–1978* (Oxford, 1991), 225.

[119] Williamson, 'Bankers Ramp', 791.

[120] Samuel Brittan, *The Treasury under the Tories, 1951–1964* (1964), 308.

[121] PRO, T 172/1384.   [122] Moggridge, *Monetary Policy*, 270.

[123] Ibid. 228.

public of their complete impartiality in the discharge of their responsibilities towards successive Governments.'[124] Snowden for one, in his memoirs not long afterwards, bought the essential neutrality of the high priest of high finance: 'I know nothing at all about his politics. I do not know if he has any.'[125] Cobbold's approach was similar, almost obsessively concerned as he was that the newly nationalized Bank should not forfeit a certain inalienable independence of mind. The classic statement of the Bank's core mission occurred in October 1951, when shortly before that month's general election he sent the Treasury a detailed exposition of the Bank's views on the current situation and its generally harsh remedies—cuts in government expenditure, private consumption, and investment, bulwarked by a tighter credit policy—and requested his memorandum to be placed before the new chancellor. Cobbold concluded portentously:

Assessment of the political practicability or expediency of particular lines of policy is no part of the Bank's function. The Bank consider it their duty to set out for submission to His Majesty's Government, on formation of a new Administration, the very serious view which they take of the situation and the general lines of action which, without regard to political considerations, they judge necessary to protect the currency.[126]

Four months later Cobbold was heading a Bank deputation to Churchill in order to advocate the Robot plan. 'He reported', Donald MacDougall noted in his diary of Churchill's reaction before Cherwell got to work on him, 'that they were a fine, patriotic body of men, anxious to do what was right for the country.'[127] Patriotism would soon no longer be enough to confer automatic authority on the Bank's economic and monetary opinions; the economists were on the march and the corporatist state was starting to flex its peacetime muscles. But there never quite disappeared a lingering desire for that sacerdotal odour denied to vote-grubbing politicians and squalid interest groups.

Mediating between City and Government

What the City has traditionally wanted is to be left alone by government. During the nineteenth century, following the passing of major currency and banking legislation during the thirty years after Waterloo, government largely obliged. The Bank, like the rest of the City, seems to have been entirely happy with this state of affairs. Yet whenever there was a financial crisis, as there frequently was, the Bank was to the fore in attempting to persuade government that it should bale out the City. In 1825 it vainly sought the suspension of gold; in 1837 the Governor and his deputy called

[124] Bank of England Archive, G3/198.   [125] Snowden, *Autobiography*, ii, 615.
[126] Fforde, *Bank*, 401.   [127] Donald MacDougall, *Don and Mandarin* (1987), 88.

hopefully on Downing Street, but Melbourne and his Chancellor adroitly passed back the buck; and ten years later the Bank more or less forced the government's hand over suspension of the Bank Charter Act.[128] 'I never did anything so unwillingly in my life', reflected the Chancellor of the day, while according to George Grote, private banker turned historian of Greece, 'the cry of *"must not let merchants fail"* is used just in the same way as that of *"must not let poor people starve"* in regard to Ireland'.[129] It was much the same story in 1857, when, although Governor Neave deemed it prudent not to ask formally for suspension, he did admit to the Chancellor, in the course of their crucial meeting, that 'one Director, a consistent and heretofore staunch supporter of the Bill and well capable of judging the actual condition of affairs', had 'declared to his great regret that he saw no safety to the Bank or to the Mercantile Interest but in a relaxation of the restrictive Clause'. Almost certainly that faintheart was Montagu Norman's grandfather, George Warde Norman.[130] In 1866 pressure to suspend came less from the Bank directly than from what Gladstone in his diary called 'City magnates',[131] but in the Baring crisis of 1890 it was the Bank, and above all its redoubtable Governor, at centre stage.[132] Goschen as Chancellor did his best to resist—'if I act, and disaster never occurs, Parliament would never forgive my having pledged the National credit to a private Firm'[133]—but Lidderdale was adamant that the Bank could act only under a large umbrella provided by government. On 14 November, in conference in Downing Street, he played his highest card:

I told Lord Salisbury I could not possibly go on with the matter at the Bank's sole risk; that the Bank had been taking in Baring's Bills all the week . . . that they were probably coming in fast now that alarm had set in, and that unless Government would relieve us of some of the possible loss, I should return at once and throw out all further acceptance of the Firm.[134]

This threat prevailed. Salisbury, on behalf of the absent Goschen, in effect gave Lidderdale just under twenty-four hours to save Barings, promising that government would bear half the loss resulting from taking in Barings' bills up to early afternoon the next day. Lidderdale returned to the City and successfully set up a fund that in effect guaranteed the Bank against any losses arising out of advances made to Barings to enable that firm to

[128] Kynaston, *City*, 69–70, 109–10, 158–60.

[129] D. P. O'Brien (ed.), *The Correspondence of Lord Overstone* (Cambridge, 1971), i, 397; Mrs Grote, *The Personal Life of George Grote* (1873), 179.

[130] Kynaston, *City*, 194–5.

[131] H. C. G. Mathew (ed.), *The Gladstone Diaries*, vi. *1861–1868* (Oxford, 1978), 436.

[132] The best account of the crisis remains L. S. Pressnell, 'Gold Reserves, Banking Reserves, and the Baring Crisis of 1890', in C. R. Whittlesey and J. S. G. Wilson (eds.), *Essays in Money and Banking, in honour of R. S. Sayers* (Oxford, 1968), 192–207.

[133] Arthur D. Elliot, *The Life of George Joachim Goschen, First Viscount Goschen* (1911), ii, 171–2.

[134] Bank of England Archive, G15/189, G15/192.

discharge its liabilities. 'Goschen has at last found a happy land as protector of City princes', was Beatrice Potter's sour verdict on the crisis,[135] a crisis that in turn did much to reinforce the Bank's status as indispensable mediator between City and government.

The Norman era, which began six years after the Bank in 1914 had again looked successfully to government to help rescue the City, saw the Bank still doing all it could in non-emergency times to keep government out of the City—and, equally, the rest of the City out of government. Far more than any previous Governor, Norman exercised a moral and sometimes even functional authority over the different component parts of the City. During the first half of the 1920s, for example, he did his bit for the government's (not to mention his own) gold standard strategy by putting merchant banks and others under powerful informal pressure not to make foreign issues that were deemed inadvisable. A voluntary, self-regulating system, administered by the Bank, was, he was convinced, far preferable to formal government intervention.[136] Or take the clearing banks. In 1924 Norman hammered out with Snowden a concordant over future amalgamation policy; eight years later, at the time of the massive conversion of the national debt, it was Norman who on the government's behalf squared recalcitrant bankers.[137] In a sense, the most interesting City–government episode of Norman's governorship came right at the end. This was when, by the autumn of 1943, it became clear that—twelve years after the identification of the 'Macmillan gap' and in the context of new initiatives being taken for post-war reconstruction—Whitehall was looking to the creation of an ambitious development corporation to meet the gap in the provision of long-term finance to medium-sized companies. Norman swung into action and managed to get on side at least some of the leading clearers, including Clarence Sadd of the Midland. 'My purpose', Norman wrote to him early in 1944, 'is to satisfy Whitehall: to keep them out of the banking business and free of malevolence towards the bankers'.[138] The outcome, established after Norman's governorship, was the Industrial and Commercial Finance Corporation, forerunner of the modern 3i, whose shareholders comprised the Bank itself as well as the often reluctant clearers. Government was thus kept out of the sensitive finance–industry nexus, in which excluded position it would remain in continuing attempts to meet the long-running gap.

The mediator's role is by definition an invidious one, and City suspicions between the wars that the Bank was becoming the government's tool were, not surprisingly, sharpened by nationalization in 1946. From the Bank's point of view, the privatizing of the steel industry in the 1950s proved

---

[135] Norman and Jeanne Mackenzie (eds.), *The Diary of Beatrice Webb*, i (1982), 349.

[136] John Atkin, 'Official Regulation of British Overseas Investment, 1914–1931', *Economic History Review*, 2nd ser., 23 (1970).

[137] Sayers, *Bank*, i, 242–3; ii, 443–5.   [138] Fforde, *Bank*, 704–23.

especially testing in this respect. During the crucial market preliminaries in the spring of 1953 the Bank played a key role in orchestrating the issuing consortium, a role that David Colville of Rothschilds explicitly repudiated in a memorandum to the other merchant banks involved:

What the Bank of England is in fact doing is to use its influence in the City, acting as the nationalised agent of a Government controlled by a political party, to obtain the support of private enterprise to help implement the election promises of that party. In effect, private enterprise is being suborned by a nationalised institution for political ends and the Bank is, moreover, seeking to throw the whole political onus and possible loss on the City, without taking either risk or responsibility.[139]

Colville's objections, however, fell on unreceptive ears, for the other bankers trusted Cobbold—not only for his judgement but also for his instincts. Put another way, they knew that, if it came to a conflict, Cobbold would bat for the City, if he possibly could. In a sense, that was the price the Bank paid for exclusively representing the City in all matters concerning government. Cobbold, perhaps even more than Norman, was determined to retain that exclusivity. It was, one might argue, the Bank's post-nationalization virility symbol, the visible confirmation that it still had an independent power-base in the City.

The long-running question of credit controls accurately reflected where the Bank's loyalties lay. In January 1951, when Gaitskell rejected Cobbold's 'psychological' argument for a Bank-rate rise, he instead pushed for Bank co-operation over restricting the increase in advances. Cobbold, a little over two years after Catto had vigorously rejected Treasury notions of a compulsory ceiling on bank advances, was blandly reassuring. 'We keep continually before the banks', he informed Gaitskell, 'the need of their co-operation in restricting the increase of advances and we shall take further opportunities of reminding them of the importance which we attach to this policy'.[140] Or, as Cobbold put it some months later in an internal memorandum: 'I believe in the voluntary system by which our banking arrangements are run and I believe that once we get into direct Government interference in the credit system we run into very deep waters.'[141]

Over the next few years Butler let the Bank get on with it, but then came 1955, that *annus horribilis* of the monetary system. In April—on the morning of the budget, with Butler cutting taxes and the economy overheating—Hall was full of woes in his diary:

In addition the Bank of England haven't been as co-operative on monetary policy as they might have been. They have never been too keen on being tough with the Banks. Now the Governor tells the Chancellor that he *is* being tough with them, but Oliver Franks (now Chairman of Lloyds) tells me that this is not so . . .

---

[139] Kathleen Burk, *The First Privatisation: The Politicians, The City, and the Denationalisation of Steel* (1988), 95.

[140] Bank of England Archive, G1/71.
 [141] Ibid.

Altogether we are working up to some sort of *éclaircissement* with the Governor, but whether the Chancellor will support us I don't know—he has always felt that the Governor is in the saddle and that it is a very serious thing to disagree with him.[142]

For some weeks Hall was reasonably sanguine ('I must say that the Bank of England has been tougher and more resolute than I expected them to be', he noted in May),[143] but for him, and Butler, disenchantment soon followed. By the end of June the Treasury belatedly realized that the Bank had been almost completely ineffective in persuading the banks to apply a credit squeeze, and soon afterwards Butler issued a statement calling directly on the banks to reduce their advances. 'It seems to me', Hall told Butler, 'quite clear *either* that the Bank of England did not understand that the policy was meant to be serious *or* that they failed to tell us that it would not work properly unless there was some statement such as that of yesterday . . . In either case, the channels of communication are inadequate and the Government and the country have suffered as a result.'[144] Some hectic exchanges of views ensued, but a Cobbold diary entry for 4 August revealed the Governor at his most adamantine. It recorded a visit to Bridges, who 'wanted much closer contacts with the Bank about credit policy' and 'would also like to know a good deal more about what the Clearing Banks were actually doing'. However:

I said that there were two points—

(*a*) The operative side of credit policy run by the Bank. This remained a Bank responsibility, subject to agreement on the top about policy. I was perfectly content to give the Treasury more information about market operations if they wanted it, though I thought that in fact they were pretty well informed . . .

(*b*) Relations with the Clearing Banks and Clearing Bank operations. I said that the accepted method of dealing with Whitehall relations with the banking community was at the top level through the Governors of the Bank of England. I thought this worked well and I was not prepared to agree to any departure from this arrangement. I was naturally willing to bring the Chairman of the Clearing Banks' Committee to see the Chancellor at any time when any one of us thought it necessary.[145]

During the autumn the banks did notably reduce their advances, but Cobbold was determined that *action directe* should not go to anyone's head. 'The Governor hoped that there would be no new public exhortation of, or request to, the banks', a Treasury memorandum noted at the end of the year. 'While Mr Butler's public request of July was right then, anything we now wished the banks to do could be best put to them privately.'[146]

So the dance went on. When Macmillan in March 1956 floated to Cobbold the idea of announcing in his budget that the Bank would hence-

[142] Cairncross, *Hall Diaries, 1954–61*, 33.   [143] Ibid. 37.
[144] PRO, T 230/384.   [145] Bank of England Archive, G1/73.
[146] PRO, T 230/384.

forth impose a liquidity ratio on the banks, Cobbold successfully insisted that the banks had already been squeezed as severely as was possible, adding typically that it was the expenditure side of things that really needed the Chancellor's attention. The Governor then upped the stakes:

I find people abroad beginning to wonder whether we are losing faith in the capitalist system and in our banking and monetary systems, which they have been brought up to regard as a pattern.

This period is clearly one of experiment and of trial and error in the monetary field as in many others. By all means let us have criticism and let us be on our toes to keep the system up to date. But can we not start from the premise that our system is the best, and not the worst, in the world? And would it not strengthen our credit if the Chancellor were to reaffirm his faith in that system and to make it clear that, in our recent troubles as on other occasions, the authorities have had the entire co-operation of a banking system which is both ready and able to carry on its business with full regard to public policy?[147]

In the event Macmillan offered only muted praise of the banks in his budget speech, but that was more than Thorneycroft would have been inclined to do some eighteen months later. September 1957 is remembered for 7 per cent Bank rate and the infamous 'leak', but earlier that month there was a memorable show-down between Chancellor and Bank over credit policy. The inside account comes from Hall:

The Chancellor wanted to call for a 5% reduction in advances, which would certainly have been logical, but the banks would not accept it and the Governor refused to give them a direction. The Chancellor was advised that the 1946 Act did not give him powers either to direct the Bank to direct the clearing banks, or to dismiss the Governor, both of which courses he was contemplating! and as I thought rightly on the basis of his own policy.

R. Makins was horrified as *he* thought it would complete the débâcle over the £ if the Chancellor now began to direct or dismiss in the banking world—all the rest of us could not see how the £ could be weakened by measures aimed at strengthening the control over money. But in the end the Chancellor would not push it through.

Accordingly, with Mynors (standing in for Cobbold) obdurately resisting any formal quantitative limit on bank advances, there was no alternative to a significant rise in Bank rate. Thorneycroft wanted 6 per cent, the Bank demanded 7, and the Bank won. Thorneycroft, according to Hall, was so cross about this sequence of events that he set up a working party on 'how to control bank credit' and 'how to amend the law to give the Treasury power it thought it had already'. The Bank, naturally in Hall's eyes, 'tried hard to sabotage' the working party and 'had to be more or less instructed to collaborate'.[148]

---

[147] Bank of England Archive, G1/74.
[148] Cairncross, *Hall Diaries, 1954–61*, 126–7; Fforde, *Bank*, 680–4.

But in the end, as the events of September had shown, it was political will that counted—and that political will had not been shown. Macmillan admitted as much the next year, when he wrote to his new Chancellor, Heathcoat Amory, advocating a scheme of special deposits to restrict credit: 'I . . . understand that the Bank of England can force the Bankers to obey but the Treasury cannot force the Bank of England to obey. This is not thought—and I agree—to be of practical importance.'[149] The Treasury, as one would expect, was well aware of where the land lay. Thus in the winter of 1957–8, as Radcliffe considered the question of 'Alternative Techniques' of credit control, there evolved a Bank/Treasury consensus that resisted the compulsory approach.[150] A Treasury memorandum, written by Sir Edmund Compton in December, implicitly spoke volumes: 'The Bank of England evidence points out the risks of rigidity and dislocation of bank practice involved to a greater or lesser extent in any choice of alternative techniques. The Treasury should admit this and therefore agree that if the choice has to be made, the technique should be selected that disturbs as little as possible.'[151] Eventually, in 1960, a system of special deposits was introduced that involved a compulsory element. It was, however, hardly Draconian and seems, in Compton's parlance, to have little disturbed the banking system.[152] Cobbold had fought a long, hard, and successful fight on the City's behalf as well as the Bank's.

Over the next two decades there were some strong continuities. Cromer, as befitted his ancestry, was an especially jealous defender of the City's privileges, epitomized by his effective encouragement of the growing Euromarkets as a government-free zone.[153] Especially telling was his short, sharp squall with Wilson in the autumn of 1965, when shortly before the declaration of UDI the Prime Minister requested details of Rhodesian sterling holdings (official and private) in London. Cromer, arguing on the grounds that his foremost consideration had to be the City's time-honoured reputation for integrity, was thoroughly obstructive; and when, after UDI, Wilson wanted to interview personally the Bank official who until recently had been Deputy Governor of the Reserve Bank of Rhodesia, Cromer (in the words of one of Wilson's biographers) 'put his man on the slowest possible boat for the return passage so as to ensure that his information was out of date by the time he got back'.[154] So too in the 1970s, when the major City episode of that decade, the secondary banking crisis, was largely resolved by the Bank behind closed doors with little government interference—and then the ensuing 1979 Banking Act, moulded more or less according to Bank wishes.[155] A particularly vexed aspect of the triangular

[149] PRO, PREM 11/4199.   [150] Green, 'Influence of the City', 206–7.

[151] PRO, T 233/1410.

[152] M. J. Artis, *Foundations of British Monetary Policy* (Oxford, 1965), 46–7.

[153] John Plender and Paul Wallace, *The Square Mile: A Guide to the New City of London* (1985), 32; *Central Banking*, 4 (Spring 1994), 49.

[154] Ziegler, *Wilson*, 235–6.   [155] Middlemas, *Power*, iii, 30–4, 124–5.

relationship by the mid-1970s, as government debt soared, was the question of gilts. Donoughue recalls the story, from his vantage-point at Number 10:

The Policy Unit conducted long discussions on how to produce a more even flow of gilt sales and I put some suggestions to the Prime Minister in June 1978. These included variable-rate stocks with convertibility, index-linked bonds, and the encouragement by tax change of unit trust participation in the gilt market. We also recommended the introduction of a tender system to replace the traditional poker game between the Government broker and the institutions . . . The Treasury was sympathetic but the Bank of England was at first extremely hostile. However, the Prime Minister followed our suggestion of setting up a working group to look into ways of improving the operation of the gilt market. The working party's interim report in the late summer favoured the early introduction of a new convertible stock. However, this (and the final report in November) rejected most of our long-term suggestions—including index-linked gilts and tender selling—on the basis that the present system worked successfully and that the markets would be upset if these arrangements were disturbed. It was clear that the Bank considered its own mode of working both to be perfect and nobody else's business.[156]

Markets, in short, remained the Bank's inalienable, practitioner-based preserve.

In reality much changed in the post-Cobbold era.[157] The Bank, starting to become more integrated into the wider policy-making machinery, was no longer regarded by the City as the automatic guardian of its interests; while the City itself—increasingly meritocratic and international—was less and less cowed by the Governor's eyebrows. Arguably the key figure is O'Brien. There was little sense in which he was a City grandee; but he was instead, in the words of a recent profile, 'the very model of a public servant' and 'particularly close to the top officials at the Treasury'.[158] His governorship will always be associated with Competition and Credit Control, a policy less than wholly welcome to what was still a semi-cartelized banking system. And, giving evidence in 1970 to the Select Committee on Nationalised Industries, he seemed to distance himself from the square mile when asked to comment on the notion that the Governor of the Bank represented the City point of view in the Treasury:

It is one about which in my opinion there is a great deal of misunderstanding. This partly flows from the fact that the Bank is very old, has grown up in the City and from City institutions by which so far as the Court is concerned it was manned almost exclusively until comparatively recent times and existed in a world where the position of government was quite different from what it is today. There is not any doubt at the present time that the Bank is an arm of Government in the City. The Governor's prime responsibility is as agent of Government to carry out a variety of functions as efficiently as possible in line with Government policy. The Governor's principal job is to advise the Government on what the policy should be in all these

---

[156] Donoughue, *Prime Minister*, 143–4.
[157] The best guide to these broad changes is Moran, 'Power'.
[158] *Central Banking*, 4 (Spring 1994), 51.

areas with which he is concerned. However, in the execution of policy, he has of course to influence the conduct of many institutions. This has traditionally been done by persuasion as much as by instruction and statutory limitation. Also, having been in the City all these years, I think it is fair to claim that the Bank has an understanding of the legitimate interests and needs of City institutions. The knowledge that they have this understanding gives City institutions in general confidence in the Bank so that they know they can go to the Bank with their complaints and troubles and get a fair and understanding hearing. However, that does not mean— and I have said this more than once in print—that the Bank stands ready to push vis-à-vis Government in Whitehall City interests without regard to whether the Bank think it is sensible or not. If City institutions come to me with a complaint which I think has force I will then go and make it known on their behalf. I think I can bring something to the making of the complaint which will add to the possibility of its being heeded. If, however, I think that what they are asking for is contrary to the national interest I will tell them to go away and think again. I am not then the representative of the City but I do represent City interests where I think it is right and proper to do so. I believe I can do that better than many other people could.

O'Brien was also asked about the question of direct City–government relations, unmediated by the Bank. 'I do not invite direct access,' he replied. 'I hope that the City institutions in the main will not think it necessary or desirable. However, if they did, I would not wish to impede them.'[159] This was a new tolerance—and one that O'Brien's successor did not share. Healey long afterwards recalled what happened:

I do not regard the Bank of England as the markets. I did introduce an innovation when I was Chancellor because before I became Chancellor the Bank would not allow Chancellors to talk to people in the City because it regarded itself as God's appointed ambassador on earth from the City to the Treasury. It is one of the few things I had an argument with Gordon Richardson about . . . One of the arguments I had with him was that I said I wanted to hear not from the chairmen of the banks, who are usually time servers, but from the chief executives who are often very, very able indeed like Alec Dibbs who was at NatWest in my time and Tony Tuke. I said I wanted to have them in myself and talk to them about their problems. 'Oh, no; this has never happened before'. In the end they agreed but only on condition that I had a spy from the Bank of England, Charles Goodhart, who I like to hope was perhaps a double agent in the end.[160]

Healey might have added that the clearing banks themselves made many direct representations to government over what became the 1979 Banking Act. As the City started to fragment into a cluster of discrete pressure groups, club-like notions of exclusive representation by the club's patron simply lost credibility.

[159] Select Committee on Nationalised Industries: Bank of England, *First Report* (1969–70, vi), qq 1986, 1994.
[160] Treasury and Civil Service Committee: The Role of the Bank of England, *Minutes of Evidence* (1993–4, HC 98–II), q 275.

Did the 1980s, that decade of strong-minded government riding rough-shod over any last vestiges of gentlemanly conviviality, further tilt the balance? Moran, writing in 1988, had no doubts: 'A generation ago, the Bank was a City institution with a voice in government; now it is a government institution with a voice in the City.'[161] There is much evidence to support this assertion: the Bank's failure to lobby effectively on behalf of the clearers when they were confronted by punitive fiscal measures in the first half of the decade;[162] the question of indexed gifts, introduced in 1981 against Richardson's acute opposition;[163] the Bank's limited input into the 1986 Financial Services Act, a highly legalistic approach to the regulation of the City and deeply unpopular there;[164] and in 1987, the humiliating episode of the BP issue, when, according to Lawson's account, the Bank bowed to City pressure in advising—but in vain—the Chancellor to pull the issue.[165] Against all that, though, the Bank does seem to have played a fundamental role behind the scenes in shaping the Parkinson–Goodison accord that led to Big Bang in 1986, through which the Stock Exchange got itself off the OFT hook;[166] the Bank did persuade government that it should remain the key player in banking supervision;[167] and, in a markets-oriented decade, the Bank's acknowledged expertise inevitably fortified its City standing. By the end of the 1980s the Bank could take a fair degree of pride in the way it had helped to steer government policy towards making the City of London a far more competitive international financial centre than it had been at the start of the decade. That was an achievement that Norman above all would have applauded. But, amidst the swirling mass of new entrants who did not even recognize an eyebrow when they saw one, he probably would not have relished much else.

The Prospect of Independence

In November 1988, in the sixth year of his chancellorship and still preoccupied by the problem of securing permanent low inflation, Lawson sent Thatcher a memorandum proposing 'to give statutory independence to the Bank of England, charging it with the statutory duty to preserve the value of the currency, along the lines already in place and of proven effectiveness for the US Federal Reserve, the National Bank of Switzerland, and the Bundesbank'. He went on:

[161] Michael Moran, 'City Pressure: The City of London as a Pressure Group since 1945', *Contemporary Record*, 2 (Summer 1988), 30.

[162] Margaret Reid, 'Mrs Thatcher's Impact on the City', *Contemporary Record*, 2 (Summer 1989), 22.

[163] Lawson, *View*, 114–17.   [164] Reid, 'Thatcher's Impact', 22.

[165] Lawson, *View*, 769–73.

[166] Margaret Reid, *All-Change in the City: The Revolution in Britain's Financial Sector* (1988), 43–6.

[167] Lawson, *View*, 408.

Such a move would enhance the market credibility of our anti-inflationary stance, both nationally and internationally. It would make it absolutely clear that the fight against inflation remains our top priority; it would do something to help de-politicize interest rate changes—though that can never be completely achieved; above all there would be the longer-term advantage that we would be seen to be locking a permanent anti-inflationary force into the system, as a counter-weight to the strong inflationary pressures which are always lurking.[168]

It was not, Lawson stressed subsequently, that he had any 'illusion that the Bank of England possesses any superior wisdom'. Instead, the benefit lay in 'the logic of the institutional change itself', through which an independent central bank would necessarily enjoy a far greater degree of market credibility than a government ever could; and, 'this extra market credibility is what would make the successful conduct of monetary policy less difficult'.[169] Thatcher was appalled:

My reaction was dismissive ... I did not believe, as Nigel argued, that it would boost the credibility of the fight against inflation ... In fact, as I minuted, 'it would be seen as an abdication by the Chancellor ...' I added that 'it would be an admission of a failure of resolve on our part'. I also doubted whether we had people of the right calibre to run such an institution.[170]

Faced by Thatcher's insistence that the control of inflation was ultimately a political problem, not amenable to institutional solutions, Lawson was compelled to let his proposal rest. However, less than a year later, his resignation speech of October 1989 gave him the opportunity to launch the proposal publicly. The genie was out of the bottle.

Over the next few years, as debate quickened on the subject, there steadily built up a considerable body of support for the Bank's independence. The official attitude of the post-Thatcher government remained agnostic, although certain steps were taken that seemed to presage eventual independence. By the end of 1993 not only was the Bank publishing quarterly an independent Inflation Report to be shown to the Treasury only 'in its final form', but it had also been given discretion over the timing of interest-rate changes, though with the last word on whether to change still resting with the Chancellor. By the spring of 1994, however, the Chancellor of the day, Clarke, seemed to be indicating that because of continuing doubts over the question of accountability, there was no immediate prospect of independence as such. Most commentators were agreed that there could be no more appropriate three-hundredth-birthday present, but government as ever was the party-pooper.[171]

Nagging doubts remain. Can one really place a *cordon sanitaire* around monetary policy and divorce it from the rest of economic policy? Does not

---

[168] Lawson, *View*, 1059–60.   [169] Ibid. 868–9.

[170] Margaret Thatcher, *The Downing Street Years* (1993), 706.

[171] A leading article ('Questions for the Bankers') in the *Financial Times*, 9 June 1994, is a good example of the pro-independence school of thought.

monetary policy itself have political and social dimensions that cannot be simply left to the technicians? Is it not ultimately a negation of democracy, whatever the inbuilt safeguards for accountability, to try do so so? Not long after the end of his ten-year governorship, Leigh-Pemberton (by now Lord Kingsdown) addressed some of these concerns with commendable candour when he spoke on BBC Radio in May 1994:

I think most people in the street are pleased with the concept of price stability—the idea that we don't have to go on living for ever in circumstances in which we assume that prices are going to go up. But of course if the price of that is that economic expansion is somewhat slowed and rates of unemployment either go up or don't fall as quickly as people would like, well, there is a tension there, and it's a very understandable one. And should there be some change in the status of the Bank of England, of course this would be the real challenge for the central bank under this new position—to read the mood of the country, to reconcile that with its commitment to monetary stability, and to make sure that the two can march side by side. And there would undeniably be times I think when the central bank would come under pressure. 'It's been too restrictive'. 'It doesn't know what life is like out there, sitting in that great white building in the middle of the City'.[172]

At the start of the Bank's fourth century, the descendants of Powell, Norman and Cobbold were poised to display political skills that Peel, Gladstone and Harcourt had believed, in their naïvety, to belong to parliamentary statesmen alone.

[172] BBC Radio Four, *Analysis*, 26 May 1994.

3 The Bank of England and the British Economy

ALEC CAIRNCROSS

For most of its existence the Bank of England has been a joint-stock bank differing from other banks mainly in its close relations with government. It came into existence to raise money and lend it to the state and has continued to have the state as its principal customer. In return it was granted privileges as a bank of issue in its Charter and came to occupy a dominant position as a supplier of paper money, acquiring a monopoly of the note issue in the London area at an early stage but not becoming the sole bank of issue in England and Wales until the 1920s. When bank money superseded notes and coin as the main means of payment, however, the Bank could not keep pace with the expansion of the banking system, and by the twentieth century it was a relatively small element in it. On the other hand, its responsibilities expanded as it came to discharge the various duties of a central bank.

The Nineteenth Century

Apart from acting as the financial agent of the government so that it was deeply involved in debt management, the Bank did not assume central banking functions until the nineteenth century and its earlier history is consequently of limited interest. It was in the nineteenth and early twentieth century that the Bank's role as a central banker developed and its functions came to include the establishment of a sound currency, the maintenance of convertibility of that currency into gold, the safeguarding of the financial structure, and the development of instruments and techniques of control over banking operations. At the same time the Bank remained a privately owned commercial bank with obligations to its stockholders to earn what income it could.

A Sound Currency

How did the discharge of these functions impinge on the economy? Taking first the need for a sound currency, the frequency of bank failures in the nineteenth century after a run on the bank left no doubt of the economic damage resulting from a loss of confidence in the notes issued by any of the country banks. After the collapse of many local private banks in 1825–6 the Bank took steps to promote the wider use of its own notes in order 'to give solidity and strength to the whole [note] circulation of the country'.[1] With the concurrence of the government and without any expectation of profit, it set up branches in eleven English towns between 1826 and 1829, specifically for this purpose.

The Bank's branches were welcomed in areas where local banks had collapsed, but in some other towns there was public opposition to an 'uncalled-for interference on the part of the Bank of England' and petitions were made against the establishment of a branch. The Bank was less interested in taking the place of local banks than in attracting banks as customers and developing its own role as a bankers' bank. It entered into agreements with private banks under which they discontinued the issue of their notes and used Bank notes instead, receiving some notes free of interest and others through a credit line with a Bank branch at 3 per cent. As security, bills were deposited which were payable in London and credited, as they fell due, to the account of the private bank with the Bank of England. The private bank was freed from the need to hold gold against its notes and was more secure against a possible crisis since it could obtain additional credit at 3 per cent—an attractive rate. Through the use of 'circulation' accounts of this kind or open accounts with no lower limit, the Bank had considerable success. In the Liverpool area, for example, provincial banknotes were displaced altogether by 1840 and the circulation of trade bills in the area ceased.[2] Nevertheless in 1841 the circulation of Bank of England notes in the provinces was no more than about £4 million compared with £5.8–£6.8 million by private banks, and £3.4–£4 million by joint-stock banks.

The 1844 Act set an upper limit to the issue of bank notes by all issuing banks in England and Wales, while the issue of Bank of England notes was regulated by the gold holdings of the Issue Department. Withdrawals of gold from the Issue Department reduced the cash reserves of the Banking Department and led to a more restrictive credit policy or the sale of investments. Thus the Act aimed to regulate the stock of money more or less automatically by the state of the balance of payments, money at that time being regarded as notes and coin.[3] Needless to say, regulation of money and credit without reference to domestic needs invited a succession of crises which duly occurred in 1847, 1857, and 1866 and forced the suspension of the Act on each occasion.

---

[1] J. Horsley Palmer, Governor of the Bank, in evidence to a government committee in 1832, quoted in D. Ziegler, *Central Bank, Peripheral Industry: The Bank of England in the Provinces, 1826–1913* (Leicester, 1990), 5–6.

[2] Ziegler, *Central Bank*, 13.

[3] Ibid. 31.

After the 1844 Act, the Bank concentrated entirely on its London business, expecting an early disappearance of the provincial banknote and adopting the view that the Banking Department, which was also responsible for the branches, should be conducted as a normal commercial bank. It refused to rediscount bills for provincial banks; and London banks did not do so on principle. The Bank was retreating from being a lender of last resort and requiring banks of all kinds to keep their portfolios so liquid that rediscounting was unnecessary. Circulation accounts dwindled, but in the thirty years after 1844 country bank issues to the value of £2 million lapsed for one reason or another, while the circulation of Bank of England notes continued to grow. By 1900, after the banking amalgamations in the 1890s, the circulation of provincial banknotes was down to about £2 million or 7 per cent of the total note circulation.[4]

Convertibility

The main responsibility of the Bank was to preserve the convertibility of the currency into gold. This carried with it the maintenance of the gold standard and a fixed rate of exchange. Price stability as such was not a Bank objective except in so far as the gold standard contributed to it. It was on external rather than domestic pressures that the Bank was obliged to concentrate. While there were seasonal fluctuations in the domestic stock of money, and corresponding fluctuations in the circulation of gold coins drawn from the Bank's reserve, the larger and more erratic movements were in the balance of international payments. It was these movements, frequently associated with events abroad, that gave the Bank most concern and obliged it to find ways of operating on the economy so as to limit and, if necessary, reverse them. The Bank's field of vision had thus to be international in scope. As Sayers puts it: 'It was the world outside Britain that seemed to matter most. The tides encountered by the Bank operated on it through various parts of the City, but they did in the main come from outside the City and were recognised as such'.[5]

The Bank in turn had to react to these tides. It could do so by raising Bank rate and making it effective. In the nineteenth century the Bank came to rely heavily on this weapon, using a variety of ways of raising market rates nearer to Bank rate. As the commercial banks grew in size, however, and in periods when the market was flush of funds, the Bank was liable to experience difficulty in making its rate effective and had to devise ways of reinforcing upward pressure on market rates. This was first accomplished as far back as 1830 by borrowing from money-market institutions through repurchase agreements. This technique became increasingly common in the second half of the century. On occasion the Bank supplemented this

[4] Ziegler, *Central Bank*, 36–8, 41–3.
[5] R. S. Sayers, *The Bank of England, 1891–1944* (Cambridge, 1976), i, 9.

method of putting pressure on bank reserves by selling Consols, but if the buyer turned to the Bank for the necessary funds, nothing was gained. More commonly the Bank would borrow in the market against government securities, or, after Treasury bills came into existence in 1877, it could adjust the size of the tender or its own bill portfolio to mop up cash and reduce bankers' balances.

A rise in Bank rate helped to reduce an outflow of funds or to draw funds from other financial centres, so reducing the pressure on the exchange rate. In the years before the First World War the Bank hesitated to rely exclusively on Bank rate, conscious that higher rates would depress domestic activity. For the forty years from 1874 to 1913 Bank rate was raised above 5 per cent on only eight occasions, and never for more than a month or so, except in the winter of 1906–7 when a 6 per cent rate was maintained for three months and in 1907–8 when the rate rose to 5½ per cent at the end of October, climbed to 7 per cent a week later, not returning to 5 per cent until mid-January. Such high rates had a powerful effect on the movement of funds and could cause some liquidation of stocks or lead to a postponement of investment, thereby producing an improvement in the balance of trade. But the Bank preferred less disruptive devices except in emergency: small and frequent changes in Bank rate, selling operations to push market rates up to or above Bank rate; offering a higher price for gold or making difficulties hindering international gold movements so as to widen the 'gold points'.[6] It could also collaborate with other central banks, notably the Bank of Japan and the Bank of France, and borrow funds or gold from them, or put pressure on them to provide help by threatening to raise Bank rate.[7]

In preserving convertibility, the Bank could rely only on an exiguous reserve of gold, most of its stock of gold being immobilized as cover for the note issue. Fortunately sterling was in such good repute internationally that it was in extensive use as a medium of international exchange, so that quite small changes in Bank rate were sufficient to attract support from many sources. The good repute of sterling, in turn, rested heavily on the continued existence of a substantial balance of payments surplus throughout the forty years before 1914. The United Kingdom was a more or less consistent creditor and was acquiring an unprecedented accumulation of external assets that added to its financial power. Not that the outflow of capital in those years did not at times cause strains in the balance of payments or that there were no fluctuations in the level of activity, with periodic depressions. But the convertibility of the pound at the fixed rate of exchange was never in serious danger.

The inadequacy of the Bank's gold stock and the consequent need for frequent changes in Bank rate aroused the concern of the commercial banks

[6] R. S. Sayers, *Bank of England Operations, 1890–1914* (1936).
[7] Sayers, *Bank*, i, 40–11, 55, 59; Ziegler, *Central Bank*, 94.

in the years immediately before the First World War. Where the Bank had once been a giant among pygmies it was now the large commercial banks that were the giants and some of them, led by the Midland, were determined to hold their own gold reserve and claim an influence over its use in preserving stability in the exchanges.

Safeguarding the Financial Structure

The Bank came to have an additional responsibility for assisting in the development of a healthy financial system. It aimed from an early date to become a bankers' bank and as such to contribute to the solvency of banks in difficulties by acting as a lender of last resort. But it did not do so consistently. It was in the process of becoming a lender of last resort in the period before the passing of the Bank Charter Act of 1844. That legislation, however, by providing for a separation of the Issue Department from the Banking Department, encouraged the idea that the note issue, with a gold backing against all but the fiduciary issue, would be self-regulating, expanding or contracting as gold flowed in or out with the balance of international payments; and that the Banking Department was free to engage in ordinary commercial banking as well as meeting the financial needs of the government. This caused the Bank to reconsider the assistance it could offer to what it might now regard as competitors, although it continued to avoid entering into direct competition with private or joint-stock banks for commercial business. Rather than act as lender of last resort it preferred to urge on the banks the need to maintain sufficient liquidity in their portfolio to survive difficult times unaided. From the 1870s, when the City of Glasgow Bank collapsed, with a portfolio including highly illiquid investments, there were virtually no bank failures in the English provinces. This might seem to indicate a revival of the Bank's unwillingness to act as lender of last resort and success in the application of the principle. But there was in fact little contact between the Bank and the country banks in the 1880s and 1890s. Rather the country banks had learned the need for 'sound banking' to ensure their survival:

It was precisely the non-availability of a lender of last resort that forced them to keep their portfolios liquid. Instead of investing in *de facto* long-term lending to industrial and other provincial borrowers, a number of provincial banks went over to investing a growing share of their resources on either the London money market or the London Stock Exchange.[8]

An example of a different kind of Bank reaction to a threat to the financial structure was the prompt intervention of the Governor in 1890 to obtain the guarantees that enabled Barings to survive the crisis, which was

---

[8] Ziegler, *Central Bank*, 12, citing M. Collins, 'The Banking Crisis of 1878', *Economic History Review*, 2nd ser., 42 (1989), 512.

associated with issues of investments in the Argentine, although there was at that time no institutional provision for underwriting the issues of such investments. The intervention not only saved Barings but prevented other consequential failures that would have intensified the depression that followed.

During the 1880s and 1890s the Bank found itself faced with a series of problems. One was the growing size of the joint-stock banks, some of which after the amalgamations of the 1890s were already bigger than the Bank. A second was the difficulty of making Bank rate effective when market rates had fallen to unusually low levels. The Bank turned to new devices for this purpose, such as re-purchase agreements, borrowing in the market, and selling Consols or other gilt-edged securities. A third problem was the difficulty of maintaining the Bank's income as interest rates fell.

Maintaining the Bank's Income

In the mid-1890s when Bank rate stood at 2 per cent for two-and-a-half years, the Bank was obliged to cut its dividend and draw on hidden reserves. Here the Bank's provincial branches came to the rescue. In the fourteen years before 1889/90 there had been only one year in which the provincial branches as a group showed a profit. From 1889/90 onwards until the outbreak of war in 1914 they were consistently in profit and for much of the time in very large profit. By 1906/7 profits reached a peak of £214,000, an improvement of £225,000 over 1888/9. This may have been less than 10 per cent of the gross profits of the Banking Department, but it compared with a rise in the profits of the Banking Department over the same period of about £540,000.[9] On this showing, the branches were responsible for about 40 per cent of the improvement over those years—a large contribution at a time when the Bank was desperately in need of additional income.

That the branches were able to make such a contribution derived from a change in their lending practices. The fall in the Bank's income disposed it to connive at methods of extending credit that were previously disallowed. In Birmingham, for example, the Bank's agent expanded lending from under £200,000 in 1885 to an average of nearly £1 million in 1890–7, accepting as collateral local securities and book debts that were anything but liquid. Much of the additional lending was to industrialists and stockbrokers, in direct competition with the commercial banks which it purported to serve as central bank, and made use of London funds that would otherwise have formed part of the central bank's inadequate reserves.[10] Even after the agent was retired, loans of the same kind continued, in spite of a

---

[9] Based on Tables 2.12 to 2.16 in Ziegler, *Central Bank*.

[10] Ziegler, *Central Bank*, 109. About half the loans on collateral in Birmingham in 1892–4 were to the Chamberlain Group.

change in the rules in 1894. The Bank expressed its doubts through the Deputy Governor but rarely rejected requests from the new agent.

Conclusion

The contribution of the Bank to the economy in the nineteenth century was primarily to the economic environment within which business was conducted. Its branches, it is true, began to provide credit to provincial enterprises in a variety of industries; and the Bank was for much of the time a major operator in the bill market. To that extent the Bank provided services similar to those of a large joint-stock bank. But its more important function was as curator of the financial system, ensuring that the currency was sound and stable, that its external value was also stable, and that financial intermediaries followed practices that would permit them to survive. None the less there were damaging fluctuations and periodic crises to which the mistaken ideas of the 1844 Act contributed. The banking system gained strength through mergers and the lessons of experience as the century progressed; and the Bank itself acquired a better understanding of how best to exercise control over currency and credit and deal with upsets in the balance of payments.

In the second half of the century the Bank was operating in a more propitious environment. In spite of the difficulties of maintaining employment and coping with the outflow of capital and labour while international competition grew ever keener, there was a stability in the system that greatly eased the task of the monetary authorities.[11]

The Inter-War Years

Domestic Monetary Policy

In the years after 1918 the Bank remained an independent corporation but one linked increasingly closely with the Treasury. Monetary policy changed in two ways. One was a change in how Bank rate was viewed: more emphasis was put on its impact on the domestic economy. A second was in the greater importance attached to debt management and to the links between debt management and monetary policy.

Up to the First World War the Bank, as we have seen, made limited use of Bank rate and concentrated on its influence in helping to maintain convertibility at a fixed rate of exchange, playing down its influence on

[11] For conflicting views of the later years see W. A. Lewis, *Growth and Fluctuations, 1870–1913* (1978) and my contribution to his Festschrift, 'Economic Growth and Stagnation in the United Kingdom before the First World War', in M. Gersovitz *et al.* (eds.), *The Theory and Experience of Economic Development* (1982).

domestic activity. As Sayers points out, 'in the Treasury view in 1914 there is no trace, as yet, of any notion that a rise in Bank rate is important as prompting a general rise in interest rates in order to depress real investment generally'.[12] In the Cunliffe Report of 1919, however, it was argued that a rise in Bank rate 'necessarily led to a general rise in interest rates and a restriction of credit. New enterprises were then postponed and the demand for constructional materials and other capital goods was lessened ... The result was a decline in general prices' which corrected the adverse balance of trade.[13]

Debt Management

Sayers suggests that this new stress on the repercussions on domestic investment and activity stemmed from the attention given by economists since the beginning of the century to the problem of the trade cycle. But there was another reason. The increasing scale of government borrowing, both on short term and long, meant a corresponding increase in the government's influence on interest rates, short and long. Debt management, which had been almost entirely separate from monetary policy in the nineteenth century, when the national debt was drifting slowly downwards, bore heavily on it in war-time, as private borrowing had to be made to give way before the needs of war-time finance; and one means of securing a reapportionment of national savings in favour of the public sector was by raising long-term rates of interest. After the First World War the greater weight of debt and its increasing financial needs made the government a persistent element in the market at all maturities so that it was impossible to draw a line between debt management, viewed as an endless flow of borrowing operations on the part of government, and monetary policy designed to influence the ease or difficulty of borrowing generally. If Bank rate could be shown to affect the whole range of interest rates, so also could a change in long rates bring pressure on all shorter rates.

Debt management in the inter-war period began to form an important element in monetary policy. It had always been true that in an inelastic bond market heavy government borrowing was likely to add to the stock of money and generate excess liquidity. Now it was also appreciated that, by funding or unfunding, and so varying the average maturity of outstanding government debt, or by conversion operations involving the replacement of debt at one maturity by debt at another maturity, it was possible to influence the structure, and even the level, of interest rates. The most striking example is the conversion of 5 per cent War Loan in 1932, as described below, when the long-term rate of interest on the converted

---

[12] R. S. Sayers, 'Bank Rate in Keynes's Century', *Proceedings of the British Academy*, lxv (1979), 195.
[13] Ibid. 196–7.

bonds was cut from 5 per cent to 3½ per cent and the structure of interest rates changed radically, with dramatic effects on house-building.

Debt management during the Second World War affected interest rates altogether differently. Why? The answer lies in the use by government of powers not available in peace-time. The government could take steps to exclude other borrowers from the market and dictate the terms on which it was prepared to borrow, appealing at the same time to its citizens to show their patriotism by saving more. A firm decision was taken to fight a '3 per cent war' and to announce that no higher rate would be offered for the duration of the war. The government took pains to prevent the additional resources available to the banks (through its failure to raise enough on long term) from being re-lent to the private sector or made the base for an enormous expansion of credit. Thus it raised from the public at long term and from the banks at short term what approximated to forced loans made on terms of its choosing. There were, however, limits to the government's powers over interest rates, as Dalton discovered when he tried to reduce them after the war was over.

The Return to Gold

There was general agreement in the years following the First World War on the need for an eventual return to the gold standard as recommended by the Cunliffe Committee, with little support for the ideas of Keynes and McKenna in favour of a managed currency. The material question was one of timing and on this the Bank took the lead. It was Norman who opened the debate by calling for the appointment of the Chamberlain–Bradbury Committee (and suggesting the membership) in the spring of 1924, and it was he who first named a date (three years away) for the resumption of gold exports. This was followed by a proposal to the Committee in June 1924 from Norman's colleague, Sir Charles Addis, to free gold exports at the end of 1925, when existing legislation restricting gold exports expired.[14] Norman had adopted this view by the time he returned from a visit to the United States and gave further evidence to the Committee in January 1925.[15]

At this stage the Treasury was still elaborating the arguments in favour of an early return to gold for the benefit of the Chancellor who did not finally make up his mind until the middle of March. There was no disagreement between Treasury officials and the Bank, except over Norman's negotiations for a credit of $300 million from the United States to provide a cushion to maintain the exchange rate. There were objections in the Bank, too, but these were overcome by fears of withdrawals of balances in gold

---

[14] D. E. Moggridge, *British Monetary Policy, 1924–1931: The Norman Conquest of $4.86* (Cambridge, 1972), 27–8.
[15] Ibid. 43–4.

once a free market in gold existed. The Treasury queried the need for a loan and the size of the loan, and doubted their power to borrow for the purpose. In the end a credit of $300 million was arranged.

The return to gold was attacked on the ground that it left the pound seriously overvalued in relation to the dollar. More to the point, the pound was overvalued in relation to a balance of payments that inhibited action to bring down unemployment. Between 1924 and 1929, however, there was no deterioration in the current account and very little change in unemployment. The depression that followed had effects in the early 1930s that dwarfed the ill-effects of overvaluation in the late 1920s and were probably not much swollen by reason of any initial overvaluation in 1929. A lower exchange rate in 1925 would have speeded up adjustments and improved employment prospects, but how much would have survived the slump?

As became clear in the 1930s after the gold standard was suspended, the main drawback of the return to gold was the need to maintain higher interest rates than were appropriate in conditions of industrial depression. The Treasury might protest whenever Bank rate was increased, but the increases were the price of returning to gold at a parity that was too high. They were also in keeping with the Treasury's anxiety to fund the national debt. Another consequence was an accumulation of short-term liabilities; and the disclosure of their unexpectedly large amount in the Macmillan Report in June 1931 contributed to the flight from the pound in the months that followed. On that occasion, as in 1925, it was the Treasury that made the final decision while the Bank sought to raise funds abroad.

In the 1930s the Treasury remained the dominant influence, with the Bank acting as its agent in the foreign exchange market as it already did in debt management. The Exchange Equalisation Account was created alongside the gold reserve and was used in the management of a floating pound to keep the rate of exchange down to a competitive level. The Bank carried out the operations but the Treasury took responsibility for the policy. In domestic policy the Bank maintained an unchanged Bank rate of 2 per cent from 1932 to the outbreak of war. The key decision was the conversion in 1932 of a great weight of war debt from 5 per cent to 3½ per cent, and here it was the advice of the Bank that emboldened the government to go to 3½ per cent rather than 4 per cent. The consequence was a long spell of cheap money both at long term and short for the better part of a decade. This started off a housing boom and brought about a rapid industrial expansion, with an increase in industrial production by 45 per cent in five years. Although unemployment was still well over a million at the outbreak of war in 1939, monetary policy had succeeded in transforming the economy in a relatively short time.

Industrial Reconstruction

One of the most interesting developments of the inter-war years was the direct involvement of the Bank, at the insistence of a determined and powerful Governor, in industrial reconstruction. He was equally involved in international financial reconstruction in Europe, but this is of limited relevance to the part played by the Bank in the British economy.

The Bank's involvement in industry began with the problems of Armstrong Whitworth, a customer of the Newcastle branch of the Bank engaged in armaments production. It had diversified its activities after the war with no lasting addition to its profits and was in deep trouble by 1925 over a newsprint-manufacturing venture in Newfoundland. After a financial reconstruction, the Bank found itself in control of the Newfoundland mill and was unable to disengage completely until 1944. The Bank was also involved in repeated financial reconstructions of Armstrong's domestic business. Through a profit guarantee for five years it helped towards the formation of a new company, Vickers-Armstrong, that took over the armaments and naval shipbuilding business of both Vickers and Armstrong. Armstrong's other assets were taken over by a new holding company, Armstrong Whitworth Securities Company Ltd., in which the Bank held a controlling interest. This took it into many branches of heavy industry in the north: coal, steel, locomotive building, shipbuilding, and heavy engineering.

Successive reorganizations were no doubt intended to make for an improvement in efficiency and eventually reduce the Bank's losses. They also reflected the Governor's concern to guide the reconstruction of British industry. In the end, however, as was true later in its interventions in the steel industry, the Bank was largely 'an unwilling accomplice of [the companies'] own development plans, which were not very much to the Bank's taste'.[16]

Next came involvement in the reorganization of the Lancashire cotton-spinning industry. As with Armstrong's, the scheme for a comprehensive merger in the Lancashire Cotton Corporation had government support but no government money. The Governor gave it his backing and participation, 'partly to help the cotton industry, partly to keep the question away from politics, but more especially to relieve certain of the banks from a dangerous position'.[17] The plan was carried through with the Bank of England's financial help in spite of continued opposition from all interests involved, and in spite of the resounding failure of a £2m. debenture issue.

The Bank took a hand in the reconstruction of other basic industries. It made advances to National Shipbuilders Security Ltd. The Governor

[16] Steven Tolliday, *Business, Banking, and Politics: The Case of British Steel, 1918–1939* (Cambridge, Mass., 1987), 197.
[17] Sayers, *Bank*, i, 319.

personally was heavily engaged in complicated negotiations with the North Atlantic liner section of the British shipping industry and, under pressure from the Treasury, the Bank advanced £500,000 towards the completion of a transatlantic liner by Harland and Wolff. Most important of all was the Bank's ultimate involvement in the steel industry, starting with the Lancashire Steel Corporation and Beardmore's at the end of the 1920s. After the flotation of the former company early in 1930 it was suggested to the Governor that the financing pattern adopted of associating City firms with the Bank might take more lasting shape—a suggestion that led to the foundation of the Bankers Industrial Development Company.

Another industry in which the Bank became involved was shipping. Norman took a keen personal interest in negotiations over the financial difficulties of the Royal Mail Group in 1929–30 because of the Group's ownership of Harland and Wolff and so of its subsidiary David Colville and Co., the largest of the Scottish steelmakers. In 1930, after a formal request from the Treasury, the Bank advanced £250,000 and, after a second pressing request, a further £250,000 to tide the Group over its immediate difficulties. Through its success in co-ordinating the response of various creditors and bankers, the Bank facilitated 'an imposed reconstruction which narrowly averted a major public crash in May 1930'.[18] On the other hand, the problems that emerged, according to one study of the crisis in the Group's affairs, 'severely weakened the Bank of England's initiatives in remodelling British industry' by destroying Norman's hopes of 'reconstructing the British staple industries through the formation of large holding companies'.[19] Later, Norman took an active part in the merger in 1933 between the White Star Line, part of the Royal Mail Group, and the Cunard Steam Ship Co.[20]

The growth of the Bank's commitments outside its normal activities reflected Norman's conviction that this work was his most effective contribution to the revival of British industry and the reduction of unemployment. He believed in a case-by-case approach to the rationalization of basic industries—and of basic industries only—to reduce their costs and get them going again in a way 'a mere credit expansion would do nothing to solve and much to delay'.[21] He took steps to bring on to the Court several Directors with industrial experience such as Stamp, Duncan, the accountant Cooper, and the trade unionist Frank Hodges.

Two new bodies were brought into existence to continue the work: the Securities Management Trust, a wholly owned subsidiary of the Bank formed at the end of 1929 with the Governor as Chairman and (from

[18] Tolliday, *Business*, 203.
[19] Edwin Green and Michael Moss, *A Business of National Importance: The Royal Mail Shipping Group, 1902–1937* (1982), 118–19.
[20] Sayers, *Bank*, i, 327–30.
[21] Ibid., i, 323, quoting a Bank paper on 'Bank of England and Unemployment', in Dec. 1929.

March 1930) Sir Charles Bruce Gardner as Managing Director; and the Bankers Industrial Development Company (BIDC), formed in March 1930 with a capital of £6m., subscribed as to three-quarters by the clearing banks and other financial institutions and one-quarter by the Bank. The capital was not substantially called up but formed a kind of guarantee fund. It was 'to receive and consider schemes for the reorganisation and re-equipment of the basic industries of the country when brought forward from within the particular industry, and, if approved, to procure the supply of the necessary financial support'.

The Bank's industrial commitments were put in the name of the SMT and for most of the time it was the experts in the SMT who investigated and discussed schemes of industrial reconstruction. In January 1930 an open invitation was made to business and industry to produce such schemes; but as the depression deepened there was no new era in British industrial finance. The new agencies were not the engines of rationalization in one industry after another but were occupied mainly in supervising the unwinding of the Bank's existing commitments and those into which it was presently driven.

When it came to raising funds for reorganization, the BIDC had no intention of drawing on its capital and aimed to transfer the burden to the issuing houses as soon as possible through the promotion of public issues. Most of the issuing houses participated under the impression that the creation of the BIDC was more or less a gesture and that BIDC funds would be used only for short-term financing. Not that its £6m. would have gone far in a wholesale reorganization of British industry. An obvious source of funds was the government. But it was Norman's explicit object in forming the BIDC, as was well understood in the City, to prevent government intervention in industry. When William Graham, the President of the Board of Trade, supported by Ernest Bevin, proposed the creation of a public utility company to reorganize the steel industry, the Bank successfully blocked the move by threatening to suspend all its own efforts.[22]

In April 1931 the Bank concluded that it could not raise further financial support from the public and would have to support schemes of industrial reconstruction from its own resources. Such schemes were almost all in the steel industry. They included Stewart and Lloyd's new steelworks at Corby, to which the Bank made an advance of £½m. through the BIDC that allowed a start to be made in construction; an electric steel-works at Jarrow in which the Bank invested £200,000; the Richard Thomas plant at Ebbw Vale to which the Bank subscribed one quarter of the £6m. promised; and the strip-mill built by John Summers and Sons in Shotton to which the Bank subscribed £1m. in November 1938 while the United Steel Co. subscribed about £1.3m.

---

[22] Tolliday, *Business*, 208.

One other organization created was the Special Areas Reconstruction Association Ltd. (SARA), which co-operated in making loans towards the establishment of new industries in the Special (or Depressed) Areas. It was a forerunner of the ICFC and raised two-fifths of its ordinary capital from the Bank, which also made advances to cover the early business. Its contribution was, however, an extremely limited one. While its purpose was to supplement existing financial facilities, it was run on principles that were not very different. It provided loan capital only, charging market rates of interest and requiring at least half the capital needed for a project to be provided by its promoter. It much preferred to lend to established businesses rather than new ones, restricted its lending to small firms, and in seven years advanced a total of only £754,000 to 145 concerns (of which 40 per cent had already been repaid at the end of seven years).[23]

The SMT and BIDC were not intended to have a long life; they were allowed to die or vegetate. But even before the war the Bank 'was taking the lead in bringing a wide circle of City institutions into some permanent and public link between finance and industry'.[24] The BIDC and SARA prepared the ground for the establishment of the Finance Corporation for Industry and the Industrial and Commercial Finance Corporation, although neither could come into existence until after the war.

Thus the Bank made a beginning in reshaping banking institutions to the needs of industrial reconstruction and helped to raise capital to meet those needs. But it aspired to a role that it could not fulfil without a more active involvement in the promotion of mergers, with managerial and financial responsibility for their success. Instead of carrying out coherent plans for rationalization, as the Governor intended, the Bank found itself embroiled as a third party in struggles between conflicting interests and on occasion using its influence against mergers that, in principle, it favoured.[25] It relied too much on the prospect that in an industry like steel, constricted by its history, plans for reorganization would somehow emerge, or that plans sketched by experts like Brassert would be readily adopted. It was also opposed in principle to state participation and unwilling to play a part that made it appear to be an agent of government policy, even when the scale and political implications of its proposals brought them automatically within the range of government concern.

The Post-War Years

From 1945 the Bank's relations with the economy were those of a central bank under government control. Its aims were necessarily subordinated to

[23] Carol E. Heim, 'Limits to Intervention: The Bank of England and Industrial Diversification in the Depressed Areas', *Economic History Review*, 2nd ser., 37 (1984), 533–50.

[24] Sayers, *Bank*, ii, 551.   [25] Tolliday, *Business*, 235.

those of the government; and the policies pursued, whatever their origin, were policies conforming to the views of the government. It is not possible, therefore, to attribute to the Bank responsibility for the impact of those policies on the economy. All one can do is to provide some account of the Bank's part in the formulation of government policies, dwelling on the Bank's own ideas and seeking to establish the matters on which it was in disagreement with the government. Such an account has to be based almost entirely on published sources although for the latter part of the post-war period there can be no certainty, in the absence of access to the records, that the full story is discernible.

At the end of the war the economy was in serious difficulty both domestically and externally. Domestically there were all the problems of demobilization and reconstruction: the need for high investment to make up for war-time arrears and improve the competitive power of British industry in face of public eagerness to enjoy the fruits of peace, draw on their savings for that purpose, and save little out of current earnings. There was an acute danger of inflation unless consumer spending was held down in favour of an urgent need to increase investment on the one hand and exports on the other. Externally, exports would have to be increased fivefold or more in order to pay for necessary imports; and since only the Western Hemisphere was in a position to supply most of those imports, there was an even more awkward imbalance in trade with that area, and especially with the United States, to which Britain exported relatively little. There was a further problem in the form of huge debts contracted in war-time, much of them to poor countries such as India and Egypt, and in the simultaneous liquidation of a large portion of British foreign investments. These not only burdened the current account of the balance of payments with interest payments abroad and loss of income from foreign investments; they also, in the absence of adequate reserves, posed an ever greater danger to the capital balance if withdrawals were made by Britain's creditors from their liquid balances of sterling. On top of all this was yet another problem: a sharp rise in import prices in relation to export prices. By 1948 the import bill was about one-sixth larger, in terms of the exports needed to make payment, than it would have been ten years earlier in 1938.

The American Loan

These changes raised major problems for the Bank of England. Its attitude to them diverged markedly from that of the Treasury, then dominated by Keynes. The difference of view went back to Keynes's war-time proposals for an International Clearing Union in preference to the development of the war-time network of payments agreements and arrangements, including the Sterling Area. Keynes had, indeed, outlined as one possibility just such a development, supported by exchange controls and trade restrictions, for a post-war transitional period that might last five years. But he had come down in favour of the much more radical and ambitious proposal, in the expectation that the United States would insist on a multilateral and non-discriminatory system of trade and payments, and he had persuaded Treasury officials, and ultimately the Cabinet, to make his proposals the basis of their approach to the Americans.

The Bank of England was distrustful of Keynes's vision and concerned to find a way of resolving immediate and urgent problems through the use of a machinery that was already in being. They favoured international economic co-operation in the use of exchange stabilization funds on the model of the 1936 Tripartite Agreement and the adoption of what was later called 'the key currency approach'. They were conscious also of an underlying hostility in the American administration to the pooling of dollar earnings in London by members of the Sterling Area and to the continued existence of Imperial Preference. So far from sharing American views, the Bank regarded existing arrangements with satisfaction in the light of war-time experience and looked forward to the contribution they could make in peace-time to exchange stability. Above all, they felt that it was a mistake to concentrate attention on long-term aims when it was more important to convince the Americans that exchange controls, trade controls, and bilateral agreements must be the framework of policy for years to come.[26]

While the Bank's view of the future proved to be realistic, it was not a view that the Americans could be persuaded to adopt in 1945–6. The United Kingdom was in no position to insist on acceptance by the Americans of its ideas. On the contrary, if it wished for American co-operation and assistance—particularly financial assistance—it would have to subscribe to the eventual adoption of the multilateral, non-discriminatory system of trade and payments on which the Americans had set their hearts. They could seek for concessions as supporters of such a system that would be denied them if they started from other premises. The length of the transition period, a scarce currency clause, freedom to preserve the Sterling Area, and financial assistance in the early years of reconstruction were matters for negotiation within the American scheme of things. But if America were unsympathetic and denied British co-operation on terms acceptable to America, the future would indeed be black.

From 1941 onwards the Bank was nearly always at odds with Keynes and the Treasury. They distrusted large, visionary plans for what they saw as a distant future and preferred to think in terms of the adaptation of existing arrangements to the widely different circumstances of a variety of trading partners. It would be better to build on the use of the dollar and sterling in international payments arrangements than set about limiting their use by attacking the system of payments within the Sterling Area.

[26] John Fforde, *The Bank of England and Public Policy, 1941–1958* (Cambridge, 1992), 37–48.

They wanted to deal with the sterling balances by informal arrangements, concentrating on India and Egypt, not by some formula applicable to all. They were also against seeking a large long-term loan from the United States and favoured some form of continued US aid or interest-free credit, or even a loan on commercial terms without strings. The Bank was particularly concerned to find that in July 1945 Keynes was reconciled to abandoning the idea of a transitional period and expected to have to concede to the Americans acceptance of the full Bretton Woods obligations from a fixed date, likely to be one year after VJ day.

By the time Keynes left to lead the Loan Negotiations in Washington he had been warned by Will Clayton and others that there was little chance of an outright grant from the USA or of a loan in excess of $5bn. Others had joined the Bank in expressing doubts about accepting the Bretton Woods obligations at an early date, and Lord Brand had questioned Keynes's view that the Americans would insist on such an undertaking. Keynes, however, was now proposing external convertibility world-wide, not just for Sterling Area countries. He intended to ask for a grant of $5 billion, not a loan, in spite of Clayton's advice and although the assistance required to permit early convertibility was recognized to be well over $5bn. He was gambling on his ability to persuade the Americans that a grant of $5bn. was what justice to their ally required and had no fall-back position. The Bank had expressed reasonable doubts at a meeting with Keynes on 23 July 1945, but in the month that elapsed before Keynes's departure it had no further exchanges with him.

Keynes's gamble did not come off. The Loan Agreement committed the United Kingdom to convertibility from a date that many in Britain realized it would be impossible to honour. It did, however, provide just enough dollars to tide over Britain's urgent requirements until the Marshall Plan came into effect. Ironically, within two years the Americans committed themselves to a far more ambitious plan of European reconstruction that was in keeping with Keynes's vision rather than with the Loan Agreement, while the Bank of England busied itself with the conclusion of payments agreements along the lines for which it had argued unsuccessfully. The dollar shortage lasted much longer than anyone had foreseen in 1945; and the eventual shape of international payments embraced neither full convertibility nor a resurrection of sterling. The hopes of the Bank for the greater use of sterling in European payments arrangements—even in some versions for an extension of the Sterling Area to cover Western Europe—came to nothing. A convertibility crisis in 1947 and a devaluation of sterling in 1949 did nothing to persuade Europeans to put their faith in sterling.

Nevertheless, given the evolution of Congressional attitudes, the strength of the movement towards closer integration in Europe, and the weakness of the British economy with its war-time debts, it is doubtful whether Britain could have hoped for a more satisfactory outcome by 1950; and it is hard to see how sterling could have played a larger part in world recovery.

Monetary Policy

The influence of the Bank on monetary policy (so far as there was such a thing) was distinctly limited. In the early years after the Second World War it was symptomatic that it was not represented on the National Debt Enquiry in the spring of 1945 and received no copy of the Report until 20 October, months after it was submitted. In Dalton's drive to reduce longer-term interest rates, the Bank's advice was sought on tactics only, not on the policy. It specifically warned against an attempt to float a long-term or irredeemable 2½ per cent stock, arguing that 'it was not safe for the moment to go beyond extending the date for a new issue of 3 per cent stock'.[27] The Bank was consulted over the cut in short-term rates to ½ per cent and the Governor, after discussion with the clearing banks, gave his agreement, provided the reduction was not accompanied by a cut in Bank rate. The Bank was more alive than the Treasury to the danger of a retreat from 2½ per cent that might result in rates higher than at the start; the difficulty of disposing of vast amounts of gilt-edged in exchange for equity holdings in the industries to be nationalized; and the problems likely to attend a premature effort to achieve convertibility.

Even more limited was the Bank's subsequent influence on interest rates in the years of Labour government. The Bank made repeated attempts to secure government agreement to an increase in Bank rate. The need for some revival of monetary policy in post-war conditions had been recognized in war-time, but at the end of the war a rise in Bank rate was judged to be out of the question politically, and it was the possibility of a reduction that was first discussed by the Bank—and rejected. There would appear to have been no proposal for an increase during the convertibility crisis, but some increase to accompany devaluation was envisaged by officials in the Treasury. The Bank then sought to make a reduction in public expenditure a pre-condition for a rise in Bank rate, but the government would have none of it. In 1948–9 there had also been a reversal of Dalton's policy of boosting the price of gilt-edged, even at the cost of adding to the stock of money. The Treasury called on the Bank to check the growth of deposits and, more particularly, the growth of bank advances. To this the overall Budget surplus under Cripps was expected to contribute, but the Bank was also expected to put itself in a position to prevent the stock of money from increasing and if necessary to impose a ceiling on bank advances. This latter suggestion was rejected with some indignation by the Governor and instead the banks were asked informally to keep the rise in

---

[27] Fforde, *Bank*, 334.

advances to a minimum. Monetary deflation without a rise in interest rates proved too difficult. As Mynors put it in January 1950: 'The present trouble is in fact only the application in the monetary field of the familiar principle elsewhere, that you can control price or quantity but not both. . . . We are accused of an inadequate system of rationing or allocation'.[28]

The debate soon concentrated on the case for higher rates, but the Government continued to refuse the slightest increase. A rise in Bank rate would have been quite costly to the Government—a 4 per cent Bank rate meant an addition of £120m., net of additional tax revenue, to floating debt charges, and might have added up to £70m. to the balance of payments cost. But this was not the main ground of opposition. What accounted for the Government's resistance to higher interest rates until they lost office in October 1951 was a rooted objection in principle: an objection (unsupported by officials) even to slightly higher market rates at an unchanged 2 per cent Bank rate. Long-term interest rates on government bonds were, however, allowed to rise gradually to 4 per cent.

In 1945–51 the Bank had tempered its proposals to the known views of the Treasury and the Chancellor. It had hesitated, for example, to suggest any larger increase in short-term rates than ½ per cent. The arrival of a Conservative government, less willing to rely on controls and given to talking of 'freeing the pound', seemed likely to make for a more congenial relationship. It was already clear that yet another exchange crisis was in prospect at no very distant date.

The Bank put it to the new Chancellor (Butler) that it was necessary to make a start at once with the reactivation of Bank rate, but that monetary measures by themselves were not enough and must be accompanied by 'heavy cuts in expenditure and investment programmes'. This was part of the Bank's post-war prescription and was urged on Chancellors on many different occasions from 1949 onwards. Just as there had to be accompanying measures to make devaluation effective, so changes in Bank rate needed reinforcement by cuts in public expenditure and other means. At the same time the Bank did not hesitate to claim decisive results from a substantial rise in Bank rate on its own. As Cobbold told the new Chancellor in 1951: 'Monetary policy . . . would begin really to bite and bite hard with Bank Rate at 4 per cent and upwards with the shake-outs and upsets that this would cause'.[29]

Cobbold saw no incompatibility between the two views. He regarded excess demand as a continuing problem and budgetary deflation as a continuing need. 'Overspending, over-consumption and over-investment in the United Kingdom are the prime cause', he told Bridges, 'of the threat to both internal and external value of the currency'. In a crisis, or at a turning-point, however, what was needed for early results was a package of

[28] Fforde, *Bank*, 379.   [29] Ibid. 403.

which a rise in Bank rate should form part, but other measures should be included too.

Convertibility

The Chancellor adopted all the Bank's proposals in early November 1951. Cuts were made in imports and hire-purchase restrictions were introduced for the first time. But as the crisis deepened and it began to look as if the reserves would fall below the danger level, much more radical ideas were advanced. Plans emerged for (non-resident) convertibility of sterling combined with a blocking of sterling balances and a floating rate of exchange.[30] These plans originated in extensive discussions in the Bank but were far from agreed Bank proposals when Otto Clarke in the Treasury provided a remarkable exposition into which they all fitted. This was followed by a paper outlining the desperate situation if the expected fall in reserves of over $2,000m. in the year to the end of March were to continue and leave no effective defence against massive depreciation. The plan (Robot) was one that united most of the Bank with most of the Treasury and had strong Ministerial support. But it was defeated. After it did not feature in the Budget in March while deflationary measures did, including a rise in Bank rate to 4 per cent, there was little or no further drain from the reserves and the crisis passed without the adoption of any part of the plan. When it was revived in June at the suggestion of the Governor, it was not even submitted to Cabinet.

The Bank still felt the need to drive on to full convertibility. Fresh proposals for a 'collective approach', involving collaboration with a nucleus of other countries aiming at convertibility, were elaborated. These plans, which had the strong support of the Bank, rested on the assumed provision by the United States of a large support fund for use by members of the group in need of assistance. But when the United States was approached by a British mission in 1953 it rejected the plan as 'premature' and offered no assistance.

The Bank was still finding it difficult to operate a system of effective exchange control. It kept drawing attention to leaks in the system that allowed foreign traders to acquire large amounts of 'cheap sterling' at cut rates for the purchase of Sterling Area commodities. This made it continue to hanker after early convertibility, fearing that the leaks in the system would make it progressively inoperable.

In 1954 it united the various brands of sterling used in monetary agreements into a single brand of 'transferable sterling', to be traded in overseas markets alongside official sterling; and in February 1955 sought

[30] For a full discussion see ibid. 426–73; Alec Cairncross, *Years of Recovery: British Economic Policy, 1945–51* (1985), ch. 9; Donald MacDougall, *Don and Mandarin* (1987), ch. 5.

the agreement of the Chancellor to action that would make sterling *de facto* convertible at a slight discount. The Bank had in fact proposed intervention in the market for transferable sterling as early as 1953 (before the market actually existed) so as to bring the rates for transferable and official sterling closer together. It had coupled the proposal with the idea of a wider spread in official dealing rates and hoped for a stand-by from the IMF to provide support. When the proposal was revived in 1955, the idea of wider spreads was ultimately dropped after it had caused the exchange rate to weaken and aroused opposition in OEEC. It was to be nearly four years later that full *de jure* convertibility of sterling was established in conjunction with other European currencies.

Progress towards convertibility in the 1950s was a painful and laborious process and the source of constant friction between the Bank and the Treasury, within the Treasury, and between Britain and other members of the European Payments Union. Things were not made easier by the frequent changes of front in British policy, the periodic exchange crises in sterling, and the inability to accumulate adequate foreign-exchange reserves. The Bank of England, acutely conscious of the difficulties of inconvertibility, agitated throughout for a speedier approach to convertibility, in disregard of any pre-conditions that had been agreed, and without the effective collaboration of other members of the European Payments Union (which convertibility would have destroyed). The Bank had sought throughout to maintain the international acceptability of sterling, and had shown no enthusiasm for other arrangements for intra-European payments, such as the EPU. It was hoping for greater use of sterling in Europe and to safeguard the Sterling Area. But the Bank's sense of urgency in pushing for convertibility was shared neither by Western European countries nor by the United States. Western Europe regarded the elimination of discrimination in trade with the USA as a prerequisite of convertibility, whereas the United Kingdom wanted convertibility first and was in no hurry to give up discrimination.

The 1950s

The Bank's use of monetary policy developed gradually through the 1950s. It approached the use of higher interest rates with some caution in a climate of opinion that associated higher interest rates with deflation and unemployment and dwelt on their cost to the Exchequer and their deterrent effect on industrial investment and housing. The revival of Bank rate in 1951–2 did not carry it beyond 4 per cent—in real terms probably a negative rate—and had an eye mainly on foreign opinion. Until 1956 Bank rate was never raised above 4½ per cent and was changed only once, or at most twice, a year from 1951 to 1958. The Bank regarded small increases as highly effective and attributed the short depression in 1952 largely to the 4 per cent Bank rate announced in March, although some observers were rightly sceptical. In 1955, when Butler cut taxation and put his faith in 'the resources of a flexible monetary policy', the Bank made no move to raise Bank rate further than the 4½ per cent it had reached in February, and contented itself with pressure on bank liquidity that was met by sales of investments without any tightening of bank credit. In the absence of any much more drastic use of Bank rate, the buoyancy of investment in the mid-1950s remained largely out of control. Monetary policy alone provided little check and even the reinforcement of an autumn budget had little immediate effect on the boom.

What was seen in the Treasury as a failure by the Bank to tighten monetary policy in the spring of 1955 led to renewed pressure for a direct limitation of bank advances. In July the Chancellor called for 'a positive and significant reduction in total advances over the next few months' and the banks subsequently agreed to aim for a 10 per cent reduction. Controls over bank lending, once introduced as the government's main anti-inflationary weapon, were continued into 1956 and a Bank–Treasury committee was appointed to discuss how the volume of credit might be controlled more effectively. The Bank, as before, saw the downside of control over bank advances. The Governor warned that a stage might be reached when a credit squeeze would do more harm than good and argued that there had been too much 'fiscal and other encouragement to expansion and investment' in 1954. Debate continued and in April 1957 the Chancellor appointed a committee on the working of the monetary system under Lord Radcliffe.

Later in the year the Chancellor (now Thorneycroft), advised by Lionel Robbins, decided to make a stand against inflation. Although his ideas were expressed in terms of the stock of money, it was the growth of money GNP that he tried to stabilize. He wanted a standstill on current government expenditure, a ceiling on public investment, and a 5 per cent cut in bank advances. Protecting sterling by raising Bank rate to 7 per cent was almost an afterthought. For the first time the government was prepared to see unemployment increased to 2–3 per cent by deflationary measures. From the point of view of the Bank of England the main interest of this episode, which led to Thorneycroft's resignation, lay in its ability to resist the 5 per cent cut in bank advances by refusing to issue a directive requiring such a cut. The Chancellor discovered that under the 1946 Act he could neither oblige the Bank to issue a directive nor dismiss the Governor and Court as he contemplated.

Yet another committee of officials on the control of bank credit was appointed in 1958. It reported, against strong opposition from the Deputy Governor, in favour of a variable liquidity ratio combined with what took shape eventually as Special Deposits. In 1959 the Radcliffe Committee also recommended Special Deposits and they were introduced for the first time in 1960. They proved, however, a rather feeble instrument and were aban-doned in favour of the corset in 1973.

Relations with the Treasury

Up to the time of the Radcliffe Committee, contact between the Bank and the Treasury on monetary policy was almost exclusively through the Governor. His normal practice

was to call for policy advice from individual members of the small home-finance team and for the most part adamantly to disallow prior discussion by his officials with Treasury officials, except at 'technical level'. Having held a meeting, made up his own mind and more often than not written his own brief, he would then argue the Bank's case personally with the Chancellor or the Permanent Secretary . . . All of this was a procedure for resolutely retaining some worthwhile degree of inde-pendence and authority for the Bank and resisting encroachment from Whitehall.[31]

This was bound, however, to be 'a task of increasing difficulty and ten-sion', given the legal subordination of the Bank through the 1946 Act and the growing political importance attached to monetary policy. The Bank's statistical and economic services were also relatively undeveloped and the information available for devising monetary policy was equally incomplete. The Bank had two very able economists in Mynors (Deputy Governor from 1954) and Allen (Economic Adviser from 1950), but this was far from pro-portionate to the need.

Since the Radcliffe Committee, major changes have occurred, bringing the staffs of the Bank and Treasury closer together and expanding the Bank's economic and statistical staff to around 200. The Bank has been represented on the Treasury's Budget Committee and its senior staff are in direct contact with their opposite numbers in the Treasury. The Bank also publishes its own *Quarterly Bulletin* with articles and comments on mone-tary and economic developments, reports of speeches by the Governor and others, and a comprehensive digest of current monetary statistics.

The 1960s

The 1960s began with attempts to limit inflation through incomes policy ('the pause') without any simultaneous use of monetary policy for the same purpose. The emphasis throughout the decade was on economic growth, and on resolving the balance of payments difficulties that kept recurring, rather than on combating inflation. Reliance was placed on con-trols—exchange control and measures to limit outgoings across the exchanges on the one hand, and control over the level of bank advances on the other. The Bank of England played a subsidiary and complemen-

---

[31] Fforde, *Bank*, 612.

tary part alongside the Treasury, taking part, for example, in the construction of an international system of currency swaps, helping to raise funds from the IMF and other central banks in times of crisis, as in November 1964, and urging stronger deflationary measures, notably after the 1967 devaluation. Monetary policy was rarely in the limelight and consisted largely of a combination of credit rationing and small adjustments in interest rates.

As inflation accelerated at the end of the 1960s and monetarist ideas spread, the Bank was increasingly conscious of the disadvantages and limitations of the various controls over the banks. They required the suppression of competition, distorted the financial structure, and became of more limited and more doubtful value as instruments of demand management. In 1969 credit ceilings had given rise to much friction with the clearing banks. In 1971, under the banner of 'competition and credit control', credit ceilings were removed and the banks were encouraged to compete with one another, bidding for the necessary funds in the wholesale market. Interest rates rose, with distortions in the structure of rates that gave rise to 'round-tripping' and inflated the monetary aggregates. The result of the new policy, which was originated by the Bank and not the Treasury, was to produce an extraordinary expansion in bank credit and bank deposits just when the pace of inflation had already accelerated markedly and was about to accelerate again in the commodity boom of 1972–3 and the oil shock that followed. It would seem that credit ceilings had been more effective in restraining monetary growth than the alternative methods of control to which the Bank now turned.

A second change at the end of the 1960s was increased attention to the monetary aggregates as a more reliable indicator of inflationary pressure than changes in nominal interest rates that might be overtaken by larger changes in prices, and be robbed of their intended disinflationary effect. It was not only the Bank that began to pay more attention to the money stock: financial markets everywhere did so too, to the point at which week-to-week fluctuations in the monetary aggregates came to dominate financial opinion to an extraordinary extent. The Bank, although far from monetarist in outlook—its philosophy usually leant more in the direction of the nineteenth-century Banking School—was swept along by monetarist currents and found it useful to publish monetary targets from 1976 in order to regain the confidence of the markets. The preparation of monetary targets began earlier, in 1973, partly because of the Bank's anxiety to anchor its policy to a suitable financial magnitude when it could no longer use a fixed exchange rate after the pound was allowed to float in June 1972. Publication of the target began only in the autumn of 1976, by which time confidence in sterling had sunk very low. It had little immediate effect on confidence in sterling, which went on falling; it took the arrival of the IMF to make sterling rise in late 1976.

What effect the targets had on the tightness of the policy pursued is not easy to say. The targets were probably nearer to estimates by the Bank of the likely change in money under existing conditions than warnings that the Bank would vary its policy to make the actual increase conform to the target increase. The targets were never hit. But they did oblige the Bank to trim its operations in the direction they indicated and strengthened the growing tendency to regard failure to hit the target as linked to failure to control inflation.

A third change that was always at work was financial innovation, and the development of new institutions, new practices, and new markets. One such change was the growth of the Eurodollar market during the 1960s to about £40bn. at the end of the decade, and vastly more in later decades. Another was the trebling of the sterling deposits with the accepting houses, overseas banks, and other banks in the 1960s, and a rapid increase in their number. The development of liability management, changes in bank reserve requirements, the removal of exchange control, and many other changes were in progress, complicating the task of interpreting familiar indicators and the selection of appropriate responses.

The 1970s: Monetary Targets

The Bank had begun the 1970s by removing credit controls. By the end of 1973 it had re-introduced control in the form of the 'corset' (the Supplementary Special Deposits scheme) but that, too, had disappeared from the scene by the end of the decade. Monetary targets came into operation, starting with M3, then £M3, then a variety of monetary aggregates that kept changing, with a reliance also on supplementary indicators including the exchange rate, interest rates, and inflationary expectations. For a time, importance was attached to DCE (Domestic Credit Expansion), but once the country was out of debt to the IMF, this soon disappeared as an indicator. Later targets were related to the Government's Medium Term Financial Strategy, which planned for a decline in inflation over a period of years.

The use of monetary targets in no way implied a conversion to the tenets of monetarism. The Governor, for example, was still commending the use of incomes policy in 1975 (though he was not inclined to put great faith in it at that time). The adoption of M3 rather than M1 was also more in keeping with the ideas of the Radcliffe Report than the quantity theory. It seemed more appropriate to the Bank because it could see ways of operating directly on M3 that had no counterpart in the case of M1. It was not convinced that M3 provided reliable evidence of the rate of inflation, and recognized that M1 was a better indicator. But it did not imagine that control of M1 or M3 would automatically conquer inflation. As it stated in 1984:

The Bank has never felt that the containment of inflation should, or could, be left to the sole responsibility of monetary policy. Throughout the years the Bank has argued that monetary policy needs to be coherently supported by other policies, notably fiscal policy. It has never . . . felt that economic relations were sufficiently predictable, or the financial system so static, that the conduct of policy could be safely placed on a quasi-automatic basis with the adoption of constant rules.[32]

It was one thing to announce a monetary target but quite another to decide by what means the target could be hit. The pre-war method of operating on the money stock had been through open market operations and changes in Bank rate. These instruments had been sufficient to alter bank reserves and force or induce the banks to curtail or expand credit with a corresponding effect on bank deposits. But the system no longer worked that way. The banks had found other ways of replenishing their reserves either by cashing government securities or borrowing appropriate liquid assets. The public treated bank deposits as they had once treated currency. Just as they had drawn on or run down their bank accounts to adjust their holdings of cash, they could now adjust the size of their bank account to what they required by drawing on or adding to alternative assets of high liquidity or by reducing or adding to their bank overdrafts. Raising Bank rate, which had once made for greater economy in the use of money, was now apt to cause an increase in time deposits as they came to earn a higher return. The surest way of reducing the money stock was to reduce the level of economic activity. This would reduce the demand for money whether prices fell or not, and would make it easier to hit the target, if it called for less money to be in use. But it could hardly be the object of a lower target to lead to a depression; there was presumed to be a financial *modus operandi* that allowed the Bank to achieve a financial aim through financial changes within its control.

Other countries appeared to be able to control the growth of the money stock in just such a way, by operating on the monetary base. In 1979–80 it was contended that the Bank should follow their example and a controversy ensued in which the Bank expounded the difficulties involved in the proposal. It pointed out that since 1945 the monetary authorities had always provided the banks with the necessary reserves and 'to the extent that there has been any causal relationship . . . it has run *from* money to the base rather than the other way round'.[33] Strict control of the base and enforcement of specified reserve ratios would put an end to all lender-of-last-resort facilities and

would continually threaten frequent and potentially massive movements in interest rates, if not complete instability . . . The greater the emphasis on control of the base

[32] Bank of England, *The Development and Operation of Monetary Policy, 1960–83* (1984), 4.

[33] M. D. K. W. Foot, C. A. E. Goodhart, and A. C. Hotson, 'Monetary Base Control', *Bank of England Quarterly Bulletin*, 19 (June 1979), 152.

the less the possibility that the central bank could intervene to ameliorate any interest-rate fluctuations.[34]

These objections, the Bank admitted, did not hold to anything like the same extent in circumstances in which banks were given sufficient time to make adjustments. In practice, monetary base control would be unlikely to work well unless it gave rise to a change in the structure of financial markets making it easier for the authorities to control the volume of sales of government debt to the non-bank public; but such changes ought to be considered quite separately and on their own merits.

In the end, after the issue of a Green Paper by the government in 1980, and clear indications of government support for some form of monetary base control, the difficulties urged by the Bank were judged to be decisive and the proposal was dropped.

Later Developments

Although inflation was brought under control in the 1980s and fell to a fairly low level in the middle of the decade, it would be difficult to attribute this to a slowing down in the growth of the money stock, which was just as fast as in the 1970s, with a fourfold increase in the decade. Controversy moved to other issues. Of these, the first was over entry into the Exchange Rate Mechanism (ERM) and then over entry into European Monetary Union (EMU) and all that this implied, including a common European currency, the independence of central banks, and the establishment of a European central bank.

These are not matters to be dealt with in a paragraph or two, but they go to the root of the job central banks are expected to do. So long as there are separate governments, answerable to separate electorates, pursuing separate economic policies in economies with separate labour markets, can these governments completely forgo separate monetary policies so long as they have separate budgets? Can one really divide economic policy in two, leaving one half to government and surrendering the other half to an international central bank independent of governments? These and many other questions arising out of them are not easy to answer. The Bank of England has shown itself to be in favour of independence for central banks, national and international, of agreed rules limiting governmental discretion in the framing of budgets, of a common European currency, and much else contained in the Maastricht Treaty. In a way, it has gone to the opposite extreme, in its vision of its place in Europe, from its vision of 1945 with the restoration of sterling as an international currency to which Europe might be increasingly attracted. Has it again misjudged the trend that events will take as Europe moves into yet another century?

---

[34] Foot *et al.*, 'Monetary Base Control', 153.

4 The Bank of England in its International Setting, 1918–1972

P. L. COTTRELL

UNLIKE many of its peers, the Bank of England is an international central bank, an aspect of its corporate character which has deep historical roots. Developments arising from Britain being the first industrial nation made the pound sterling an international currency from at least the decades following Waterloo, with the consequence that, for much of its history, the Bank has operated within a world environment.

The Bank of England was the guardian of sterling and that custodianship took a variety of forms. During the eighteenth century the relationship to sterling was tenuous and developed organically as both sterling itself changed and the Bank became established. War-time inflation and subsequent threats to convertibility thereafter in 1825 and 1839 sparked debates both inside and outside the Bank over its responsibility to the currency, which ultimately led to legislative rules in 1844. Those rules, and with them the gold standard, then became almost sacrosanct and were not to be successfully challenged until 1931. Rules, however, were not sufficient by themselves and discretion—the essence of central banking—remained.

The development of central banking, although the term was not really used until the early 1920s, involved the evolutionary deployment from the early 1870s of a variety of techniques to establish control. This was called for, on the one hand by the nature of the world economy after the early 1870s and, on the other, by the general ineffectiveness of Bank rate as a tool of management until 1907. Crisis, both before and after 1844, led to what would now be called central bank co-operation. Until the 1870s it largely arose out of the cosmopolitan community of European commerce and finance; thereafter until 1914 it was frequently a product of the Bank of France offering assistance in order that the problems of London, the world's financial centre, would not spill over disastrously to affect Paris.

Due to limitations of space, this chapter focuses on the era from the Armistice of 1918 to the end of the Bretton Woods system in 1972. These years saw a formalization and institutionalization of international central banking, a development reflected in the Bank's own organization by the establishment in 1926 of a Central Banking Section within the Chief

Cashier's Office, which became a fully fledged department in 1932. Inevitably this review relies heavily upon the Bank's own historians— Sayers and Fforde—but wherever possible the opportunity has been taken to incorporate the fruits of other scholarship, especially that of economists and historians who have studied the Bank's development and cast fresh light upon it.

Post-War Perspectives

At the time of the Armistice the Bank completely misread the situation. The Governor looked to a rise in interest rates to take sterling rapidly back to its pre-war parity. These misconceptions continued until early in the spring of 1919, as there was an expectation within the Bank that war debts would be settled at Versailles, so removing a major barrier in the way of international monetary reconstruction. The new realities only became clear by April 1919. On the one hand, the government, which had complained of a '5 per cent war' during its final year, now resisted any further rise in interest rates, while on the other, City bankers forced an embargo on the export of gold as the only conceivable mechanism to prevent such outward flows. A Bank plan for immediate restoration of gold, but involving no internal metallic circulation, was consequently lost. Since neither the Bank nor the Treasury had the necessary resources, the pound floated and, inevitably, sterling moved further and further away from its pre-war parity. However, the Bank never lost sight of the objective of restoration and regarded Bank rate as the weapon to control the exchanges, rather than credit rationing as suggested by the Chancellor and some commercial bankers.

The dangers of a world of floating currencies were there to be seen in the inflationary post-war stockpiling boom. The Governor only started to gain ground from autumn 1919, but both greater control over London's liquid financial markets and a rise of Bank rate to 6 per cent on 6 November had no effect on sterling's exchange rate against the dollar, which continued to sink. The spiralling internal price level finally convinced the Chancellor that deflationary action—but gradual rather than sudden—was required. Bank rate went to 7 per cent on 15 April 1920, just as the inflationary bubble was about to burst.[1] The slump that followed was deep and severe and, for the authorities of countries like Germany, provided an example of the consequences of the medicine of Anglo-Saxon monetary orthodoxy. It was now clear that there could be no rapid return of sterling to its pre-war position; equally there seemed to be a continuing disorder within Europe rather than a quick return to normalcy.

---

[1] R. S. Sayers, *The Bank of England, 1891–1944* (Cambridge, 1976), i, 115–20; Susan Howson, 'The Origins of Dear Money, 1919–20', *Economic History Review*, 2nd ser., 27 (1974).

The restoration of sterling's pre-war position was in practice given a timetable set by the Gold and Silver (Export Control) Act of 1920 (following the Order in Council of March 1919) which, like all legislation of its type, had a life of five years.[2] Britain's difficult position during the early 1920s was blamed on the world depression in trade and finance. Consequently, Governor Norman[3] gave first priority to defeating inflation on the continent of Europe, reconstructing the European economy, and loosening some of the entanglements of the Versailles peace settlement. For this he sought American aid and involvement, and the participation of wartime neutrals to depoliticize the economic war of reparations that was gathering pace.

In October 1919 Vissering, the Governor of the Netherlands Bank, brought together a group of bankers and experts known to one another from the Versailles conference. They discussed Europe's finances and considered the feasibility of a major international reconstruction loan to be raised in the United States and 'neutral centres'. There was a further meeting in November, and Keynes drew up the resulting report and suggested that it should be put to the Economic Section of the first Assembly of the League of Nations. The ground was prepared by various national airings during December 1919 and January 1920 to canvass for further signatures, followed by an appeal to governments on 16 January 1920.[4] Humanitarians joined bankers to present the Keynes–Vissering memorial to the Chancellor of the Exchequer.[5]

The merchant bankers and clearing bankers in the delegation accepted the priorities of establishing fiscal rectitude and reducing international indebtedness. But they saw a role in the provision, with government assistance, of £20m. credits for exports to central Europe, even if this meant tied trade. The necessary machinery might be constructed by an international conference, despite the negative attitude that had already been shown by the United States government. Kindersley argued that there was a direct British interest, since a post-war entrepôt trade through London was straining the exchanges. There was no direct outcome from this initiative, but it may have played a part in shaping the Supreme Economic Council's final report which recommended convening a general economic council.[6] This was taken up by the League of Nations as a conference, to be twice postponed before it finally met in Brussels during September 1920. In the mean

[2] Sayers, *Bank*, i, 135.

[3] For biographies, see: Sir Henry Clay, *Lord Norman* (1957)—a product of a close relationship; and, although less reliable, Andrew Boyle, *Montagu Norman: A Biography* (1967).

[4] Elizabeth Johnson (ed.), *The Collected Writings of John Maynard Keynes*, xvii, *Activities, 1920–1922* (1977), 128–30, 136, 147, 149–50.

[5] PRO, T 172/1175.

[6] Carl H. Pegg, *Evolution of the European Idea, 1914–1932* (1983), 17.

time some of central Europe's still pressing requirements were relieved by the International Committee for Relief Credits.[7]

Cullen represented the Bank at Brussels[8] and, through trenchantly expressing Bank opinion, had a very direct impact on that part of the Conference's report dealing with 'Currency and Exchanges'. This had first been drafted by Vissering, who had stressed credit rationing as the most appropriate mechanism and had seen no value whatsoever in high interest rates. The final outcome was very different, with Cullen commenting to Norman that 'We managed to get a more or less "dear money" Report out of a more than less "cheap money" Committee'. The process of that reversal also had a personal effect upon Vissering, who subsequently became one of Norman's closest allies in the development of connections between Europe's central banks. At the time of the Brussels conference these intra-European contacts had barely started.

The European collapse from the summer of 1920 further emphasized that the Old World would not be able to put itself right; it required the assistance of the New World. However, Washington remained insistent that government-to-government aid had ended with Versailles and that the proper channel for a trans-Atlantic flow of dollars had to be constructed by private capitalism, which would ensure their investment for productive purposes. Bankers in Europe largely agreed with this perspective. Norman's early training in an Anglo-American merchant bank meant that he was very familiar with American ways, whilst since September 1916 contacts between the Bank of England and the Federal Reserve Bank of New York had been increasing.[9] Norman had met Strong[10] when the American central banker had come to London after the war and, by the time of the Brussels conference, a close personal friendship had been established between the two men. They recognized that fate appeared to have given them a major task, since the world's politicians seemed to have been exhausted by the experience of Versailles. Reparations were proving to be a running sore, whilst there were early indications that inflation would take a terrible toll in central Europe. Norman, in particular, was prepared to grasp the nettle, having a taste for international diplomacy which he cloaked in a preference for anonymity.

Within six months of the Brussels conference, Norman was approached by the League of Nations to aid a Geneva-sponsored scheme for Austrian economic and financial reconstruction.[11] Despite the Governor's best

---

[7] Nicole Pietri, *La Société des Nations et la reconstruction financière de l'Autriche 1921–1926* (Geneva, 1970), 26.

[8] On the conference generally see Anne Orde, *British Policy and European Reconstruction after the First World War* (Cambridge, 1990), 105–7.

[9] Sayers, *Bank*, i, 120–1.

[10] See Lester V. Chandler, *Benjamin Strong, Central Banker* (Washington, DC., 1958).

[11] See generally, Orde, *British Policy*, 123–9; the Bank's account is given in Bank of England Archive, OV28/62, F. W. R. Laverack, 'Outline of the General Scheme for the

efforts, it was unsuccessful, tainted by the political objectives of the members of the Entente against which Norman had stood firm. The Bank had also had a particular interest in Austria since 1914, when it had taken up the 'moratorium bills' of the London offices of the Anglo-Austrian Bank and the Länderbank. During the early 1920s, in conjunction with the London bank Glyn, Mills, the Bank played a large part in the anglicization of the Anglo-Austrian Bank.

Norman, and the London merchant bankers to whom he had turned, were now committed to assisting Eastern Europe, and when the Governor went to America during the summer of 1921, he attempted to raise American interest in proposed schemes. This went along with furthering the Bank's relationship with the Federal Reserve Board and, above all, Strong's Federal Reserve Bank of New York. A major international loan for Austria remained out of even the Governor's reach, but the Bank, together with its progeny—the Anglo-Austrian Bank[12]—was the intermediary in the transmission of assistance to Vienna from the British government during the winter of 1921/2, partly undertaken in concert with Czechoslovakia, France, and Italy.

Co-operation and Autonomy

Austria's problems were considered in the corridors of the Genoa conference of Easter 1922.[13] This was an inter-governmental affair, but Norman played a considerable role in the preparations for, and the outcome of, some of its debates. Within the Bank a review was undertaken of its relations with sixteen central banks, including the Fed, which occupied a category of its own. This crystallized the basic tenets of Norman's approach to international central banking, which had been coming to the fore as a result of his now lengthy discussions and correspondence with Strong and, equally important, an almost continuous dialogue with Strakosch. They were: co-operation, exclusiveness, balances, and autonomy.

For Norman the most important were co-operation and autonomy. Co-operation was shorthand for consultation, which might generate co-ordination, or at least establish sufficient room for individual institutional manœuvre. Co-operation, in these senses, was also related to exclusiveness

Rehabilitation of Austria with Special Reference to the Part Played by the Bank of England' (April 1927).

[12] Alice Teichova, 'Versailles and the Expansion of the Bank of England into Central Europe', in Norbert Horn and Jürgen Kocka (eds.), *Law and the Formation of the Big Enterprises in the 19th and early 20th Centuries* (Göttingen, 1979); P. L. Cottrell, 'Aspects of Western Equity Investment in the Banking Systems of East Central Europe', in Alice Teichova and P. L. Cottrell (eds.), *International Business and Central Europe, 1918–1939* (Leicester, 1983).

[13] See generally, Carole Fink, *The Genoa Conference: European Diplomacy, 1921–1922* (Chapel Hill, NC, 1984).

and balances, and thereby especially the Bank's problems in the London market, still of considerable significance despite the post-war rise of New York. Although floating, sterling remained a hard currency and so was a reserve asset, while other central banks used it as an intervention currency. These operations took place mainly in London, and Norman desired that they should occur only through an account with the Bank of England, so providing re-insurance for co-operation. As a general principle this would restrict central banks to only holding accounts with one another. This went against the tradition and practice which had developed since the last decades of the nineteenth century and had led central banks, as they were now increasingly styled, to have accounts with a range of London institutions. To encourage the restriction on central banks to hold accounts only with one another, the Bank offered to employ on a remunerative basis central bank balances placed exclusively with it. In fact, there was more in this than simply offering a carrot of interest-earning balances in return for exclusiveness.

Norman did not intend European monetary reconstruction to re-establish the pre-1914 standard in which gold had been the major reserve asset. Many English commentators anticipated a gold shortage in the post-war world, so that foreign exchange reserves would have to come into play to make up the shortfall in international liquidity. Two of the key pre-war currencies—the franc and the mark—were out of play due to domestic economic difficulties and political problems. French controls on capital exports, and German inflation and the reparations issue, ruled them out, at least for the time being. A way forward was for the establishment of a gold-exchange standard based on London and New York as the gold centres, with other central banks using mainly dollar and sterling denominated assets. Central bank balances placed exclusively with the Bank of England would be critical in this development.

Of equal importance with co-operation in Norman's mind was autonomy. The need for central bankers to be masters in their own houses had been forcibly impressed upon Norman when he had been Deputy-Governor during the Bank's struggle for control in 1919/20. Then the Chancellor had needed much persuasion and, even after he had largely been brought round, had once, in July 1920, stood his ground against a rise in Bank rate. Like many politicians, the Chancellor had some of the characteristics of Janus—putting to the Cabinet the Bank's view, and to the Bank the financial consequences of his ministerial colleagues' policies. Furthermore, as a hangover from wartime practice, it was customary to consult the clearers before a final decision was taken. All this experience convinced Norman of the Bank's need for full autonomy in order to discharge properly what he considered to be its public duty[14] to the currency. Whatever lessons had

---

[14] Sayers, *Bank*, i, 119, 123.

been learnt by Norman in July 1920, they were reinforced by the subsequent monetary paths taken in Central Europe, resulting from politicians cranking the printing presses to produce notes of increasingly lower purchasing power. Autonomy had been accepted at the Brussels conference. Autonomy became sacrosanct in Norman's mind, and he subsequently refused either to entertain Ministers of Finance at Threadneedle Street or to visit countries which lacked a central bank. This attitude had its drawbacks, but was meant to ensure that central bankers could co-operate freely, knowing that their conversations and confidences would stay within a professional caste which had a common purpose.

The loosely framed and generalized Resolutions that concluded the Genoa Conference were given an edge by some specific recommendations from the French delegation. These called for the Bank of England— Norman—to organize a review meeting to digest the deliberations at Genoa, but possibly going so far as to frame an International Monetary Convention. Norman took up what proved to be a gauntlet, or rather a double-edged sword. Seized with the success of the Genoa Conference, Norman attempted to convene the meeting in September 1922, giving it the aim of establishing his gold-exchange standard. Many of the replies to Norman's invitations were hesitant, and the grand opening meeting of the central bankers' club never took place. Norman's dashed hopes were camouflaged by the deterioration of the German reparations problem and the closely related issue of German inflation, which from the summer of 1922 was clearly out of control. Reparations had been considered by all to be the obstacle that had to be surmounted before European monetary reconstruction could realistically commence. Another was inter-Allied debts, for which the US Congress had established a timetable.[15] However some ground had been made merely in the preparations for the abortive meeting. Sayers has suggested that the necessary correspondence and personal meetings to plan the event ultimately proved more important than either the Brussels or Genoa conferences in bringing central bankers into contact.

The path followed later by French policy during the 1920s would suggest that the Gallic galvanizing of central bank co-operation at Genoa was a device to ambush Norman so as to ensure that his vision for monetary reconstruction failed to gain credibility. French policy-makers regarded the gold-exchange standard as at best a temporary expedient—a transitory stage in a return to pre-1914 conditions. As far as Europe was concerned, they argued that the gold-exchange standard was really a sterling standard under which there was only a theoretical right of gold convertibility and, furthermore, that this was a right that few countries would have the temerity to exercise. Consequently the gold-exchange standard was regarded in Paris as a means to sustain British financial power—a force which had

---

[15] Ibid. i, 155–62.

greatly declined following the payment of the costs of the First World War. The French also had economic objections as well as those arising from international relations. They considered the gold-exchange standard to be inherently inflationary and that it would not permit effective monetary management by central banks in secondary, non-gold, financial centres.[16]

Although Genoa only provided the new cadre of central bankers with personal contacts, important though this was to be, the Financial Committee of the League of Nations did become an umbrella organization for central banking action against hyperinflation. Kindleberger has seen the consequent institutional relationships as a forerunner of the IMF. Since the Brussels conference this League committee had become a think-tank for reconstruction schemes; as its first attempt to tackle Austria's problems had shown, it could draft plans but lacked the financial resources to give them substance. The committee was dominated by British experts—Strakosch, but above all Niemeyer—and had close connections with some of Norman's confidants such as ter Meulen, all of which increased French anxieties, although it had been Jean Monnet who had first identified Norman as the *geldmenger*.

Despite there being no central bankers' conference in September 1922, it was then that a second League plan for Austria at last gained the necessary diplomatic momentum. Norman was instrumental in arranging the international flotation, involving substantial American participation, of the 1923 Austrian stabilization loan. This enabled the creation of a Genoa-style independent Austrian central bank, which, although it did not receive Norman's desired foreign central banker at its head—causing a *frisson*— accepted a foreign adviser. The long-delayed League initiative for Austria provided a model in 1923–4 for comparable action for Hungary.[17] Over the same period Norman, and Norman rather than the Bank, was involved in quelling the German maelstrom, but the arising friendship with Schacht provided further fuel for growing French concerns.[18] During the course of 1923–4 the Bank, and in particular Norman himself, had become the central node, although this was not generally apparent, for League action, and this relationship was to continue through the second half of the 1920s until the formation of BIS.[19]

[16] Judith L. Kooker, 'French Financial Diplomacy: The Interwar Years', in Benjamin M. Rowland (ed.), *Balance of Power or Hegemony: The Interwar Monetary System* (New York, 1976).

[17] György Péteri, 'Central Bank Diplomacy: Montagu Norman and Central Europe's Monetary Reconstruction after World War I', *Contemporary European History*, 1 (1992).

[18] Sayers, *Bank*, i, 167–83; [Hans Kernbauer], *Das Österreichische Noteninstitut*, iii.1. *1923 bis 1938, Währungspolitik in der Zwischenkriegszeit* (Vienna, 1988), 53–85; *A Magyar Nemzeti Bank Története*, i. *Az Osztrák Nemzeti Banktól a Magyar Nemzeti Bankig 1816–1924* (Budapest, 1994), 501–65.

[19] See generally, Stephen V. O. Clarke, *Central Bank Co-operation, 1924–1931* (New York, 1967), and Kenneth Mouré, 'The Limits to Central Bank Co-operation, 1916–36', *Contemporary European History*, 1 (1992).

The British Return to the Gold Standard

The economic and political stabilization of Central Europe from autumn 1922 clipped back two of the thorny hedges—inflationary discord and reparations—in the way of a British return to gold. The third, requiring a compact over war debts to America and its execution, was achieved in 1923. During the second half of 1922 there had been a growing general expectation that sterling would soon return to gold, clearly displayed in the foreign exchange market, but the gains so made from sentiment were lost over the third quarter of 1923. This forced a rise in Bank rate on 3 July 1923 by one percentage point to 4 per cent, and put into abeyance Bank plans for shipping gold to the US to force up American prices. Norman and the Bank also became aware that the continuing British slump was causing disaffection from the goals set by the Cunliffe Committee, with a growing preference emerging for simple price stability. However, the international arena for a return was very promising during early 1924, with a final settlement of the German question apparently in sight. But, with the British economy remaining in the doldrums, pointed up by no amelioration of the unemployment figures, and the dollar exchange rate 11 per cent below pre-war parity, the technical task was now much greater than it had been six months earlier. Assistance was given by the trans-Atlantic repayment of war debts, which had generated more, wider-ranging, technical discussions, whilst the new Labour Chancellor, Snowden, proved to be as staunch a supporter of the Cunliffe goals as any of his predecessors.

The first necessary step was to amalgamate the war-time Treasury notes into the Bank of England note issue, so as to get back fully to the 1844 Bank Act settlement. Norman proposed the necessary investigatory committee and suggested its membership to the Treasury on 16 April 1924. The composition of the body which emerged (which has become known as the Chamberlain–Bradbury Committee) largely replicated that of the preceding Cunliffe Committee and it began its work in the summer of 1924. However, there was also a recognition that the real purpose of this committee was wider—to plan for full restoration—which was stressed by Norman, its first witness. When the committee began its deliberations sterling was 9 per cent below its pre-war parity to the dollar. The Bank held Bank rate at 4 per cent to gain every advantage from declines in New York short rates, achieved by keeping a tight rein on the money market, whilst dampening overseas capital issues activity in London. In New York Strong had embarked upon a policy of easy money, conducted through open market operations, as a mechanism to transfer short- and long-term funds to Europe to aid the continent's monetary reconstruction. When a Conservative government replaced the minority Labour administration in November 1924, sterling stood at $4.62, 5 per cent below the pre-war par, a gap which in early 1923 had seemed relatively easy to close. However the outside world could clearly read that, by November 1924, there was little statutory life left in the 1920 Embargo Act that forbade the export of gold and had acted accordingly. There was a growing speculative pressure on sterling, buoying it up during the autumn of 1924 and given further fuel by the installation of a Conservative British Chancellor in November.

The Chamberlain–Bradbury Committee had not been prepared in early drafts of its report to fix a definite timetable for return because of the continuing disparity between American and British price levels. This would have left the Bank with the task of maintaining a tight monetary policy until a return to $4.86 was achieved, and the autumn of 1923 had indicated how rapidly political opposition could arise, jeopardizing both the policy goal and the route to achieve it. The advent of the Conservative administration went hand-in-hand with an improvement of sterling against the dollar. With these somewhat contrary signals of the past year before him, Norman sought a stand-by American credit for the British government to assist the restoration of the pre-war parity, facilities which he personally negotiated with J. P. Morgan & Co. in New York. American optimism encouraged the Governor, so much so that on his return to London he changed tack to favour an early return to the gold standard. Moreover, American conditions for these credits required that Norman should remain Governor.

Senior directors on the Committee of Treasury—the Governor's sounding-board—did not share Norman's recast view that an early return was feasible. They thought that sterling was being held up by speculative movements, masking the rate justified by the underlying balance of payments, and opposed the device of an American cushion of credits. The Court, too, had reservations, to the extent that Norman was accompanied by Sir Charles Addis when the Bank gave a second round of evidence before the Chamberlain–Bradbury Committee. In the hearing the two were divided over the timing of return and whether American credits should be deployed, but Norman won to the extent that the committee's final report largely followed his approach. Some of the costs of this victory were indicated in the need for Bank rate to rise at the end of February to offset a heralded increase in New York. Although Norman supported return, and now early return, he recognized that the ultimate decision had to be taken by politicians, who he was most concerned should accept the responsibility for their actions. By 20 March the Chancellor, Churchill, had taken that necessary step, after continuing interchanges between himself, the Treasury, and the Bank. But the timing of the return was both pushed by a determined Norman and affected by conditions in the United States, since the American credits required publicity if they were effectively to deter speculators. Preparations at home included suppressing the internal circulation of gold through the clearing banks, whose reluctant co-operation only continued until 1928, and attempting to control foreign flotations on the London market by the use of informal channels that had been developed during war-time.[20]

The return to gold by Britain appeared to have completed Norman's work since the moment he had put his wholehearted efforts towards achieving European monetary reconstruction. However, the ensuing years were to prove to be bitter ones for both Norman and Churchill. In March 1930 the Governor publicly stated that 'the main consideration in connection with movements of the Bank Rate is the international consideration, and that especially over the last few years so far as the international position is concerned—certainly until the last few weeks—we have been continuously under the harrow'.

The Long Island 'Club' and the 'Reparations Bank'

Underlying developments during the mid-1920s brought the problem of a world gold shortage to the fore. It had been offset by maintaining monetary restriction, but this gave a deflationary bias to the direction of the world economy. The consequent difficulties were at the forefront of the meeting of central bankers that took place at Long Island in July 1927 hosted by Strong. Serious problems arising from economic trends were joined by those caused by a growing clash between Britain and France over the effects of further financial stabilization plans upon European diplomacy and inter-state power relationships. Since mid-1926 the Bank of France had been acquiring reserves at a premium, in part to regulate the movement of the franc upon the foreign exchange market during the run up to *de facto* stabilization at the end of the year. As a consequence, over the six months from November 1926 the Bank of France increased its sterling holdings by £145m. For a variety of reasons, domestic and international, Moreau, the Governor of the Bank of France, decided in May 1927 to convert dollars and sterling into gold. Norman regarded Moreau's actions as 'capricious' and considered that they would wreak 'havoc' with the gold standard. French opponents of the gold-exchange standard could have received no greater confirmation of their opposition. Moreau subsequently got his gold through the Bank of England buying in the open market, borrowing from the Federal Reserve, and selling dollar reserves. Consequently, France's sterling balances were on the agenda of the Long Island meeting.[21]

Moreau was more determined after 25 June 1928, when the French franc returned *de jure* to gold. In preparation for this formal stabilization, the Bank of France had accumulated £237m. of gold and £203m. in

[20] D. E. Moggridge, *British Monetary Policy, 1924–1931: The Norman Conquest of $4.86* (Cambridge, 1972), 37–97; Sayers, *Bank*, i, 133–52.

[21] Sayers, *Bank*, i, 336–46; Moggridge, *British Monetary Policy*, 133–6.

foreign exchange balances. From mid-1928 the French central bank pursued a policy of accumulating further gold, remaining concerned about inflation rather than deflation. The Bank of France allowed its array of contracts for buying foreign exchange forward to expire, which reduced its holdings of such balances by net £87m. (involving a decline of £97m. but a rise of $50m.), and in their place would only accept gold. France and the United States became the world's gold sinks during the late 1920s, which had substantial effects upon the Bank of England's reserve, which had reached a record level of £173.9m. in September 1928.[22] Norman responded with an even greater reliance upon co-operation with other central banks, although Strong's untimely death in October 1928 removed one major pillar of support. To this weakened structure were added efforts to ensure that the London money market did not deviate from the course set by Bank rate, backed up by continuing personal control over capital exports, although outwardly this segment of the City had been unfettered since November 1925.

Intra-central-bank co-operation was cemented by an interchange of staff, with members of the new independent banks formed in Europe in the wake of League stabilization loans regularly arriving in Threadneedle Street. Similarly Bank staff members went on tours of visits to central banks in major and minor centres. Another marker of co-operation was the £75m. of central bank balances held by the Bank, as well as the transactions conducted in the London gold market by the Bank on behalf of a limited number of its peers. The only major meeting was the Long Island 'conference' of July 1927, which was attended by Strong, Norman, Schacht of the *Reichsbank*, and Rist of the Bank of France deputizing for Moreau. In practice it proved to be a series of interrelated bilateral conversations, of which the most important and continuous were between the old allies, Norman and Strong, who had designed the meeting. The major outcome was reduction in American discount rates between early August and mid-September 1927, assisting American conditions which indicated a recession, but more importantly preventing European centres from having to raise their rates further and so having a marginal impact upon the growing skewed world distribution of official gold stocks. Gold problems were also ameliorated by technical market adjustments which eased conditions somewhat for 18 months. At the end of that period Norman thought that Long Island and subsequent co-operation with the Fed had assisted the distribution of £80–100m. of what he deemed to be surplus gold.

Strong's ill-health and subsequent death prevented a further meeting of the Long Island 'club'. A new forum for greater contact arose from the pro-

[22] R. W. D. Boyce, *British Capitalism at the Crossroads, 1919–1932* (Cambridge, 1987), 158–72; Moggridge, *British Monetary Policy*, 258–9; Kenneth Mouré, *Managing the Franc Poincaré: Economic Understanding and Political Constraint in French Monetary Policy, 1928–1936* (Cambridge, 1991).

posal for a 'Reparations Bank' aired before the Young Committee which was reviewing the technical operation of the Dawes Plan. This gained substance with the formation of the Bank for International Settlements (BIS), which was given the additional function of promoting central bank co-operation. During the formation of the BIS the intermeshing of politics and international finance that Norman had confronted since his first involvement with Austrian stabilization in mid-1921 occurred once more. Furthermore, by the late 1920s, the objectives of central bankers were no longer shared by politicians and public commentators, especially in Britain. None the less the Organisation Committee and subsequent discussions between the heads of the major central banks produced an agreement by which the BIS would be independent of governments, to the extent of neither accepting government accounts nor making advances to governments. However, the BIS's origins in the reparations issue, which had flared up again during its creation, meant that American representation consisted of three commercial banks rather than the Fed. The new international institution was not all that Norman had desired and the clashing of national aspirations during its gestation meant that he refused to allow the secondment of Harry Siepman, who had been the foreign adviser to the National Bank of Hungary during the 1920s and was therefore well qualified to establish the BIS's Central Banking Department. In the end Norman was prevailed upon to allow Francis Rodd, one of his advisers, to join the new staff at Basle, where he was to play a major role in attempting to deal with the 1931 crisis.

BIS took deposits from central banks, although its initial deployment of them was not always to Norman's liking in terms of prudence. More importantly, its monthly meetings provided exactly the context for private meetings of central bank governors that Norman had always sought. He clearly indicated the value that he attached to the Basle weekends by his regular attendance, and stressed the gains made from informal mealtime discussions and quiet talks outside the dining room.[23] Those conversations were to have even greater importance as a financial crisis engulfed Europe from May 1931, beginning with the collapse of the Austrian Credit-Anstalt.

The Crises of 1931

The Austrian Crisis

There had been growing fears regarding stability in Central and Eastern Europe as the depression gathered momentum from 1929. Plans were drawn up by both British and French draughtsmen during 1930 and 1931

---

[23] Sayers, *Bank*, i, 352–9.

for an injection of further capital into the agrarian states of Eastern
Europe. Kindersley and the Bank of England had been involved in these
proposals[24] but British central bankers were none the less taken by surprise
that the 1931 liquidity panic began in Austria. In January 1931 concerns
over 'future dangers' arising from 'serious trouble with private credit institutions . . . which might easily induce the bulk of foreign lenders to with-
draw short term credits if distrust was spreading from one bank to another'
had been expressed within the Bank of England. It was an exceedingly
accurate prediction of what was soon to happen, and it was recognized at
Threadneedle Street that, under these conditions, a central bank might well
be forced to intervene. However, a private estimate of Austrian short-term
indebtedness appeared reassuring. It led to the conclusion that 'even the
largest withdrawal of foreign funds [from Vienna] could apparently be easily dealt with by the central bank'. A more pessimistic annotator of this
memorandum wondered how the Austrian National Bank deployed its foreign exchange holdings and, consequently, heavily underlined 'apparently'.[25] This staff member may have remembered that the Bank of
England had been informed in 1929 that part of the Austrian central bank's
reserves had been indirectly placed with the Credit-Anstalt to assist its
acquisition of a collapsed major bank—the Boden-Credit-Anstalt.

On 11 May 1931 it was publicly announced that the Credit-Anstalt, the
greatest of Vienna's great banks, had foundered and, with its interests
throughout the successor states, it was clear that this would have grave
effects upon the whole of Eastern Europe.[26] The Austrian government had
been informed on 8 May, while the bank's continuing delay in publishing
a balance-sheet for 1930 was a message that had already been read by some.
The Austrian government planned to meet the situation by a fresh injection
of capital. The state was to supply the majority, along with the Austrian
National Bank and existing shareholders, which included the Bank of
England as a result of the Credit-Anstalt's acquisition of the Austrian
branches of the Anglo-Austrian Bank in 1926. The initial basic difficulty
arose from the Austrian government not having the required funds to hand.
The state budget was already in deficit due to a depression-induced conjunction of mounting unemployment relief and falling customs revenues.
The Austrian government looked to raising an external loan, but this
required the permission of the states which had guaranteed the 1923 stabilization loan. As a result of Austria's putative customs union with

[24] Clarke, *Co-operation*, 179.

[25] Bank of England Archive, OV28/3, 'Note', 23 Jan. 1931.

[26] The following section is drawn from P. L. Cottrell, 'Austria between Diplomats and
Bankers 1919–1931', in Gustav Schmidt (ed.), *Konstellationen Internationaler Politik,
1924–1932: Politische und wirtschaftliche Faktoren in den Beziehungen zwischen Westeuropa
und den Vereinigten Staaten* (Bochum, 1983); see also Dieter Stiefel, *Finanzdiplomatie und
Weltwirtschaftskrise: Die Krise der Credit-Anstalt für Handel und Gewerbe 1931* (Frankfurt-a.-
M., 1989).

Germany, there was opposition on the Committee of Control established by the 1922 Geneva protocols, especially from France and Czechoslovakia. The Austro-German Customs Union was already on the agenda of the League of Nations, but the discussions there were overtaken by the announcement of the Credit-Anstalt's difficulties. Politics were to complicate greatly international bankers' handling of the Austrian financial crisis from its inception and, ultimately, to its cost.

A day before the news release, the Bank of England, with other central banks, was informed opaquely by the Austrian government of the growing financial disaster that was engulfing Vienna. Norman's approach came immediately into play, in that Siepmann maintained that he could not directly advise the Austrian government, whilst any arising central banking problems would be considered by the central banks acting through the BIS. Reisch, the President of the Austrian National Bank, understood this response immediately, and was in any case already in touch with Basle. In all this, the Bank of England's view was that its relationship with the Austrian National Bank (to which it had granted a credit facility in 1926) stood, and so still held good in substance, but had changed in form following the creation of the BIS. This was re-emphasized personally by Norman to Reisch at Basle, Norman insisting that the establishment of the BIS 'had necessarily brought about a radical change in the direct relations between central banks individually, by making concerted action not only possible but obligatory'.

At Basle over the weekend of 17–18 May central bankers were briefed regarding the position of the Austrian National Bank, especially its losses of foreign exchange. The public result of their deliberations was that the central banks through the BIS would provide a credit of 100m. schillinge, of which the Bank of England took a lead share of 10m. schillinge. The Austrian National Bank planned to take up this facility in two ways: 40m. was to be 'employed' in Vienna, whilst the balance was to be used through the BIS rediscounting Austrian bills, thereby supplying foreign exchange to bolster, if necessary, the Austrian central bank's reserve. At Basle Norman learnt from Reisch of the Austrian central banker's two major private concerns. The first was the effect of re-discounting for the Credit-Anstalt: Reisch was going to put into play the 40m. schillinge from the BIS, as this 'employment of money' would not have to be declared in his bank's public returns. Second, he was anxious regarding the consequences arising from possible withdrawals of the Credit-Anstalt's foreign deposits.

There had been talk of a Credit-Anstalt foreign creditors' committee at Basle and, when Norman returned to London, he busied himself trying to discover the exact position of the Austrian bank and establishing ways of preventing it from deteriorating further. However, the creation of an international body of creditors, since it involved banks from every Western financial centre, took time. While Norman's associates tried to give the lead, Austrians were encashing Credit-Anstalt *Kassenscheine*—transactions which reached panic proportions by 23 May—and the bank's foreign liabilities were falling due. The Credit-Anstalt's staff now thought that a credit of £10m. was required to meet the increasingly adverse situation that they faced and, furthermore, an Austrian banking moratorium was looming. The BIS felt that these matters were beyond its competence and consequently looked to Norman. Norman saw a solution in the form of an Austrian state guarantee of the foundered bank's liabilities, with its reconstruction taking place under the supervision of the state in conjunction with the bank's foreign creditors. A foreign creditors' committee was publicly announced in London on 26 May, but it did not encompass all the Western banks involved for some days after. The necessary guarantee law for the Credit-Anstalt was passed by the Austrian parliament on 29 May. This provided the context for the dispatch of a range of Western experts to Vienna: Van Hengel (who had reorganized the Rotterdamsche Bankvereeniging) for the Credit-Anstalt, Rist (of the Bank of France) for the Austrian budget, and Bruins (who had been involved in the Dawes scheme) for the National Bank, all joining Rodd of the BIS.

With all the delays, some understandable and some arising from political friction provoked by past memories and the current Austro-German Customs Union proposal, a banking crisis in Vienna was transformed into a currency crisis. Between 17 May and 5 June the Credit-Anstalt's rediscounts with the Austrian National Bank rose from 116m. to 628m. schillinge (and Reisch had initially thought that an increase of only 50m. would be publicly acceptable), whereas the central bank lost 350m. in foreign exchange. Withdrawals of foreign exchange from the Austrian National Bank took cover for the Austrian currency down to 57 per cent and, although above the legal floor of 40 per cent, since the hyperinflation of 1921–2 the Austrian public had looked to a high proportionate cover; it had averaged 78 per cent during the year up to May 1931. The foreign advisers thought that the National Bank required a further credit of 100m. schillinge from the BIS, which was agreed at Basle on the condition that it would only be available once the Austrian government had raised the external loan it required to inject new capital into the Credit-Anstalt. The proviso arose from conflicting political interests amongst those present, so much so that the Bank of England got a waiver allowing individual central banks to act alone, if they judged this to be required by the developing situation. Concerted action by central bankers through the BIS was to be outwardly maintained, and any individual action was to be disguised. However, discussions over the second BIS credit for the Austrian National Bank clearly indicated that central bankers were fettered by the diplomatic intentions of their respective states.

Matters came to a head in mid-June, when Gannon of the Chase National and Kindersley, a partner in Lazards and a Bank director, went to Vienna to conclude an agreement on behalf of the Credit-Anstalt's foreign creditors. They found 'a situation which could not continue' and which the Austrian National Bank felt could only be met by a moratorium. Norman offered to try to cut through the Gordian knot of European politics in which an Austrian external issue of Treasury bonds had become enmeshed. As Kindersley and Gannon concluded an agreement freezing the Credit-Anstalt's foreign liabilities, the French government issued an ultimatum, consisting of politico-economic conditions for floating the Austrian Treasury bonds on the Paris market, which the Austrian government had only four hours to accept. While the Austrian government reached a decision to resign, the Bank of England supplied a 150m. schillinge credit to the Austrian National Bank. Threadneedle Street was well aware through Rodd of the increasingly precarious state of the Austrian currency, and Norman had received a note from the francophobic Chancellor of the Exchequer, Snowden, expressing deep concern and emphasizing 'the great importance in the public interest of providing financial assistance for Austria without delay'.[27] The Governor also knew that the next return of the Austrian National Bank—for 15 June to be published on 18 June— would show a foreign exchange loss of 100m. schillinge, which was a central banking problem involving dangers for the gold-exchange standard. The French Ambassador in London commented: 'Je n'ai pas de sympathie personnelle pour M. Norman, dont les dispositions ne sont pas francophiles. Mais je dois constituer qu'il vient d'accomplir un acte très audacieux et dont le retentissement dans le monde sera très grand'.[28]

By 17 June 1931 'the note circulation and prices [were] at normal levels' in Vienna in the view of Bruins, while Kindersley now thought that the situation there was under control. Their fears now had their origins in Berlin and they hoped that the improving Austrian situation would quickly be reflected in the German capital. However, a week later the Reichsbank received an international credit of $100m. and the monetary order that central bankers had played a large part in constructing during the early 1920s was about to collapse. Not only was much of Norman's effort of the past decade being undone, but the financial and monetary collapse east of the Rhine had grave implications for the stability of many of the City of London's financial institutions.[29]

---

[27] PRO, FO 371 15151 C 4543.

[28] Archive of the former Ministry of Finance, France, F^{30} 628, Fleuriau (London) to Ministry of Foreign Affairs, 18 June 1931.

[29] See Edward W. Bennett, *Germany and the Diplomacy of the Financial Crisis, 1931* (Cambridge, Mass., 1962); Karl Erich Born, *Die deutsche Bankenkrise 1931: Finanzen und Politik* (Munich, 1967); Harold James, *The German Slump: Politics and Economics, 1924–1936* (Oxford, 1986); and Theo Balderston, 'The Banks and the Gold Standard in the German Financial Crisis of 1931', *Financial History Review*, 1 (1994).

The British Crisis

Initially the European banking and currency crisis of spring and early summer 1931 strengthened sterling, as short-term capital retreated, albeit temporarily, to the apparent safety of London.[30] International confidence
appeared to be rebuilt following the Hoover moratorium of 20 June. On 9
July Norman went so far as to put down a boom before further international aid to the Reichsbank. This stemmed from the Governor expecting
that his action would lead to a cancellation of reparations, while, with
regard to German monetary conditions, Norman thought they were largely
of domestic origin, and best dealt with by controls and deflation. Technical
debates were ended by the collapse of the Darmstadter Bank on 13 July,
which froze another tranche of London's claims on Central European
banks. Sterling now came under severe strain, close to panic proportions
on 15 July, due to sales by continental European holders. The sudden and
radically changed situation deeply troubled Norman, who advised the
Cabinet either to prepare for exchange controls and a moratorium or to
accelerate the convening of the London conference which was to address
the German situation. Once more political action appeared to hold the
dam, as sterling revived to the extent of postponing a rise in Bank rate.

However, the London conference revealed once more the European divisions that had been clearly evident with regard to Austria's problem during the immediate past months, and clefts in the British minority Labour
government. The conference only resulted in limited measures to solve the
crisis in German finance that had been developing since the late 1920s.
Foreign short claims became the subject of a standstill agreement, whereas
Germany's future financial needs were to be investigated by the BIS. This
did not quell the European liquidity panic, which now focused upon sterling because of the imbalance in London's international short-term liabilities and long-term assets made plain by the Macmillan Report published
on 13 July. Bank rate was increased to 3½ per cent on 23 July, and the Bank
of England obtained accommodation from the Bank of France and the
Federal Reserve Bank of New York, measures forced by gold losses which
had risen from £2m. a day to £5m. a day during the previous week.
Kindersley went to Paris to negotiate credits, a journey which marked both
the fading of the Bank's previous objections and a more responsive mood
in the French capital arising from fears that its own financial institutions
would be next in the firing-line.

By 23 July the prospect of sterling being forced off the gold standard was

[30] The following section is largely drawn from Philip Williamson, *National Crisis and
National Government: British Politics, the Economy and Empire, 1926–1932* (Cambridge, 1992),
which supersedes his 'A "Bankers Ramp"? Financiers and the British Political Crisis of August
1931', *English Historical Review*, 99 (1984). See also: Sayers, *Bank*, ii, 387–415; Alec Cairncross
and Barry Eichengreen, *Sterling in Decline* (Oxford, 1983), 27–110; Diane B. Kunz, *The Battle
for Britain's Gold Standard in 1931* (1987).

being faced in both the Bank of England and the Treasury. Norman thought that foreign confidence in sterling might be rebuilt by the application of measures that he had discussed with the Chancellor at the beginning of the year. An increase in the fiduciary issue would make more gold available for export, while deflation, induced by a high Bank rate, could, through reducing domestic costs, right the British balance of payments and have a remedial effect upon the fiscal deficit. British budget difficulties were emphasized in the May Report, available to senior ministers and Norman on 23 July, which estimated a deficit of £120m. for 1932–3, an astronomical figure for the time. This prediction meant that American bankers, such as J. P. Morgan & Co., were not prepared to lend to the British government unless state expenditure was reduced.

By the end of July, efforts to stabilize sterling in the face of the gale that had struck the British currency over the past fortnight had succeeded. Gold losses to Paris had been reduced to nothing and the Bank was now turning its attention to stem the flows to minor European financial centres. None the less, sterling remained weak, which led the Bank, encouraged by Chancellor Snowden, to prepare for a temporary increase in the fiduciary issue of £15m., of which the first step was to raise Bank rate to 4½ per cent on 30 July. However, Norman was now unwell, a recurrence of the nervous illness that had plagued him before, and which had no doubt been triggered by the alarming course of events since the middle of the month. The forced departure of the Governor may have been responsible for others in the Bank deciding to activate the American and French support credits, totalling £50m. and equivalent to the gold and foreign exchange which had recently been lost in the July crisis. Their receipt was publicly announced on 1 August, to show as clearly as possible the international institutional backing that sterling had received. All involved in London now believed that any crisis, political or financial, had at least been staved off until the autumn.

The Bank put misplaced confidence in the ability of the publicity given to the credits to change market sentiments towards sterling. As a result of this mistaken view, official support for sterling on the Paris market was removed and the Bank tolerated an outward leak of gold. This all appeared as drift to international holders of sterling, which led to a flight from 5 August—not to be stayed by deploying the American and French credits from 7 August. Harvey and Peacock, now in charge at the Bank, supplied the Prime Minister and the Chancellor with full details of the losses that the Bank had experienced, for which they thought that the only remedy was to indicate to remaining foreign holders of sterling that the budget would be balanced. Conservative and Liberal leaders were also informed of the Bank's anxieties for sterling. The Bank still regarded devaluation as a 'major disaster', which could be avoided by savings in government expenditure broadly following the May Report (which had been an all-party affair), and an emergency tariff. A return to fiscal balance remained the concern of American bankers, who were approached again over a loan to the British government sought by the Prime Minister to hold the situation until Parliament reassembled after the summer recess.

By 21 August the Bank of England considered that it had sufficient resources to defend sterling for only four further days. The Bank had been preparing contingency plans since 18 August for sterling's suspension from gold and it now looked likely that they would have to be put into effect. The decisions of that day's Cabinet meeting were regarded by the Prime Minister, the Chancellor, and Bank directors as more likely to undermine further, rather than improve, market sentiment towards sterling. This dire emergency, after three days of intense political discussions, produced a National Government, initially intended to have a limited life linked to putting robust budget proposals into legislation. On the day that it was established, a wayward *Times* editorial caused the Bank to lose £12m. across the exchanges, which was only covered by a transfer of dollar securities from the Treasury and assistance from the Fed. New credits to the British government totalling £80m. from French and American banks were obtained in a week of intense negotiations. Indications that the new Cabinet was prepared to take whatever measures were necessary steadied the markets until 26 August, but then the underlying lack of confidence once more surfaced.

The National Government's emergency budget failed to halt the outflow from London, so that by 17 September half of the foreign credits had been consumed. The Bank attributed this to a number of causes: one was Britain's balance of payments deficit, which it estimated to be £60–100m., another was that the situation in Central Europe was continuing to deteriorate, and these factors were now joined by banking problems on both sides of the Atlantic. The situation called for the difficult mobilization of British overseas investment, but it was being primarily unsettled by anxieties over what a British parliamentary election might produce. In these circumstances renewed foreign trust in sterling could only result from political continuity at Westminster and in Downing Street. The Bank certainly thought that it lacked sufficient resources for sterling to see a general election out, especially one where the three parties campaigned independently, a prospect which appeared to be increasingly likely. A banking crisis in Amsterdam, aggravating the effects of the so-called Invergordon Mutiny, caused the Bank to experience exchange losses in excess of £10m. on 17 September, and an even greater outflow on the following day. As a result the Bank decided that the fight for sterling had come to an end, not being swayed by either an offer of a further French credit, or trans-Atlantic advice to keep on in the hope that something might turn up. To show that the towel had been thrown in, the Bank allowed sterling to fall and further losses to take place, amounting to £18m. The Prime Minister was informed late on 18 September of the Bank's decisions, which involved support for sterling on Saturday 19 September to give time for legislation and announcements on Monday 21 September. Through consultations with the Treasury, Cabinet, Privy Council, the clearers and the Stock Exchange, the Bank made the necessary preparations. Bank rate was to go to 6 per cent, the Stock Exchange to be closed, a bank holiday made ready as a contingency, while all banks in the United Kingdom were to restrict foreign-exchange dealings. Sterling's departure from gold was publicly attributed to external developments beyond the Bank of England's control. At the end the Bank's prime concerns were to ensure the maintenance of British creditworthiness, partly undertaken by indicating that the summer's international facilities would be repaid in gold, and to prevent other currencies following in sterling's wake as far as was possible.

A new policy for sterling was developed during the autumn of 1931. Within the Bank it was shaped by the Special Committee on Foreign Exchange, which had been established just prior to the sterling crisis. Its members, led by Kindersley, were initially concerned about the inflation that the floating of sterling might produce and, equally, the turbulence caused by continued capital movements between the world's monetary centres. By 24 September 1931 it had been concluded that a return to $4.86 was out of the question so that the direction of policy was to allow sterling to fall further, whilst maintaining an orderly market. As these decisions were reached, it was agreed between the Bank, the Treasury, and J. P. Morgan & Co. of New York to sell sterling at $3.90 and to operate in the forward market. All this enabled a policy to be shaped that looked to the gradual stabilization of sterling in the long term, but under which neither the target stable rate nor the timetable for its achievement were specified. The need for the utmost caution soon became apparent as winter set in. Very rapidly the acquisition of exchange reserves turned to the support of sterling and advice from the specialist departments of the clearers now assisted the Bank. However, the Bank's resources were 'too meagre' to allow anything but initially checking the speed of sterling's fall, and then forced a total withdrawal of intervention. Sterling's problems of differing kinds during December 1931, and then March 1932, resulted in the creation of the Exchange Equalisation Account (EEA).[31]

Norman's policy was to hold Bank rate at its crisis level of 6 per cent until the Bank had accumulated sufficient foreign exchange with which to liquidate the credits that had been received during the summer of 1931. His approach came under fire within the Court during February 1932, as sterling gained strength and then remained strong within a band of $3.40–46. Consequently, by 25 February the Bank had command of half of what was required to meet the liabilities of the summer of 1931, whereas sterling was

---

[31] Sayers, *Bank*, ii, 416–22.

now rising speculatively to the extent that the situation was threatening to go out of control. Bank rate was reduced to 4 and then 3½ per cent, although this did not check the inflow into the London market which allowed the Bank to accumulate £20m. during March 1932. The Exchange Equalisation Account was announced in the spring budget of 1932 and began operating from 1 July 1932. This ensured that the Bank did not suffer from losses arising from foreign exchange dealings and provided a mechanism to undertake operations beyond the scope that the Bank could easily manage. These were not to be made public. The establishment of the EEA made the Treasury the principal, and this facilitated the balancing of international flows in and out of sterling, ideally by countervailing movements in holdings of Treasury Bills. Furthermore, unlike operations conducted directly by the Bank, the Account's dealings would have no effect upon domestic credit conditions.[32]

The Sterling Area and the Wider World

Sterling's departure from the gold-exchange standard in September 1931 came to be seen as the end of an epoch that stretched back to 1821, or even to the last quarter of the eighteenth century. It proved not to be a temporary expedient—a limited peace-time 'escape'—as in 1847, 1857, and 1866, which some French officials thought, or hoped, would be the case.[33] It also led to the creation of the Sterling Area, as many countries tied politically, or economically, or both, to Britain decided to retain a fixed exchange rate with sterling so that their own currencies floated up and down with sterling on the foreign-exchange markets. There were no formalized monetary ties within the Sterling Area before 1939;[34] indeed, although it was one of the currency blocs of the 1930s, its borders were not demarcated by exchange controls. The Sterling Area was primarily a product of the international monetary disarray of the early 1930s, but its earliest origins can be tracked back to the late nineteenth century and the then greater growth of holding

---

[32] Sayers, *Bank*, ii, 425–30. More generally, see 'The Exchange Equalisation Account: Its Origins and Development', *Bank of England Quarterly Bulletin*, 8 (1968); Susan Howson, *Sterling's Managed Float: The Operations of the Exchange Equalisation Account, 1932–39* (Princeton, NJ., 1980).

[33] Ian M. Drummond, *The Floating Pound and the Sterling Area, 1931–1939* (Cambridge, 1981), 122–3.

[34] The term 'Sterling Area' only came into use with the introduction of exchange controls as a result of the Second World War. During the 1930s the proto-Sterling Area consisted of the British Commonwealth (with the exception of Canada), and Egypt, Iceland, Iraq, Ireland, Portugal, and the Sudan. Estonia and Siam became members in 1933, as did Scandinavia, in effect, following the dollar's float in 1933. Other countries—Argentina, Bolivia, Greece, Japan, and Yugoslavia—pegged their currencies to sterling for lengthy periods, but applied various types of exchange controls.

sterling within official reserves not only within the British Empire but also by some Latin American and European states.[35]

An opportunity to consolidate at least part of the Sterling Area arose with the Imperial Economic Conference, held at Ottawa in 1932. The British Treasury and the Prime Minister's advisers favoured an 'Empire Sterling standard'. Numerous advantages were seen in terms of sustaining trade, maintaining the use of sterling for financing world trade, and giving sterling greater international stability. But all recognized that the crux of the matter lay in confidence in sterling, which, in turn, meant confidence in the Bank of England's management of the currency in the turbulent floating world of the 1930s. Norman wanted Imperial monetary co-operation, although in 1931–2 he still had his eye on sterling's return to gold. The Governor was prepared to encourage this co-ordination through the Bank's provision of limited credits to Sterling Area members experiencing temporary exchange-rate difficulties, but not for those of their own making, such as those produced by adventurous domestic fiscal, or monetary, policies. The Bank was represented at Ottawa by R. N. Kershaw, its expert on Imperial monetary concerns. However, despite all the excitement and campaigning that had occurred during the run-up to the Conference, its monetary proceedings did not produce a report with proposals for institutionalizing the Sterling Area. Rather there was an exchange of views in which Britain showed that it would try to keep sterling steady, while such an international regime would be assisted by the Empire maintaining stable exchange rates based on sterling.[36]

Some co-ordination was given to the Sterling Area through the Bank of England's encouragement of the development of central banking in the Dominions and colonies.[37] This pre-dated the emergence of the Sterling Area during the early 1930s and had run in parallel with Norman's work in Central and Eastern Europe. In fact, many of Norman's ideas were honed in discussions with Strakosch, who between 1919 and 1920 had been largely responsible for the creation of the South African Reserve Bank.[38] The link between the two banks was further developed by Norman's releasing Clegg, the Bank's Chief Accountant, to be its first Governor. To further these developments during the early 1920s, Peacock, a director of Baring Brothers of Canadian birth, was deliberately made a Bank Director

[35] David Williams, 'The Evolution of the Sterling System', in C. R. Whittlesey and J. S. G. Wilson (eds.), *Essays in Money and Banking in honour of R. S. Sayers* (Oxford, 1968). For one example of how the Empire was affected by the events of 1931, see B. R. Tomlinson, 'Britain and the Indian Currency Crisis, 1930–2', *Economic History Review*, 2nd ser., 32 (1979).

[36] Drummond, *Floating Pound*, 1–27.

[37] See A. F. W. Plumptre, *Central Banking in the British Dominions* (Toronto, 1940), esp. ch. 7.

[38] See Gerhard de Kock, *A History of the South African Reserve Bank, 1920–52* (Pretoria, 1954).

with the intention that he would preach the central banking gospel throughout the Dominions and India.

With the post-war creation of the Imperial Bank of India, Norman saw this as the institutional foundation for a central bank. He encouraged its Managing Governors to use the Bank's London office to subsume the Government of India's transactions within the City. The Commonwealth Bank of Australia was another embryonic Imperial central bank, which took a further step in this direction with legislation in 1924. Requests came from this bank during the ensuing years to enable it to become a fully fledged central bank and Harvey, the Bank's Comptroller, visited the southern continent in 1927, followed by Niemeyer in 1930. Personal contact was important, but much of the Bank's connections with its Imperial peers consisted of correspondence. This was coupled with managing these banks' London sterling balances as 'money employed', alongside holdings of British Treasury bills and the national debt. From November 1928 a regular fortnightly letter was sent from Threadneedle Street to the new central banks of the Empire; it was compiled by new cadres within the Bank staff consisting of a nascent intelligence section and the Bank's advisers.[39]

The difficulties arising from the initial phase of the Great Depression led to Niemeyer advising New Zealand in 1930 regarding the establishment of a central bank. However the gestation of the subsequent proposals was long and drawn out, which led inevitably to changes in their direction and content. The New Zealand Reserve Bank was finally created in 1933[40] and the Bank of England gave advice on the necessary legislation and nominated Lefeaux, its Deputy Chief Cashier, as the first Governor, an appointment which proved to be less than successful.[41]

Despite a rather passive attitude to the Ottawa conference, Norman placed great stress on the Empire and its central banks, and had considered in 1933 the creation of an institutionalized forum. In 1935 the Governor thought of holding a London conference of governors, who would be attending George V's jubilee. Ultimately this notion was put to one side, but it was taken out again for George VI's coronation in 1937. The Bank prepared a series of technical and background papers, but the latter were largely concerned with Europe, whereas at the meetings each central bank presented a paper. During the year before this meeting the Bank had conducted some 3,000 operations involving £670m. on behalf of all other central banks in which 2,230 international cables to the five Imperial central banks had played a part.[42] Those cables also indicated the continuing physical remoteness of the Imperial central banks as opposed to the proximity of the Bank of England's counterparts in Amsterdam and Paris.

---

[39] Sayers, *Bank*, i, 201–10.

[40] G. R. Hawke, *Between Governments and Banks: A History of the Reserve Bank of New Zealand* (Wellington, NZ, 1973).

[41] Sayers, *Bank*, ii, 516–18.   [42] Ibid. ii, 525–7.

As in the 1920s, the Bank's further encouragement of central banking during the 1930s consisted of specific action, arising from particularly opportune circumstances. Addis, a Bank Director, was a member of the 1933 Canadian Royal Commission, which investigated central banking for the Dominion, assisted first by Fisher and then by Kershaw as the adviser from the Bank of England.[43] This led to the creation of the Bank of Canada in 1935 and J. A. C. Osborne, who had served as the Secretary of the Bank of England, was its first Deputy-Governor. These North American developments ran in parallel with the Bank's role, through advice given by Harvey and Clegg, assisting the creation of the Reserve Bank of India. Norman was again asked to nominate the first Governor and named Osborne Smith of the old Imperial Bank which, however, as with New Zealand, proved to be an unhappy choice.[44]

Efforts to Stabilize International Currencies

Europe's and the world's post-war problems had been considered at both the Brussels and Genoa conferences; the effects of the Great Depression led finally to the convening of a World Economic Conference in London in 1933. That the conference was ill-fated was clearly indicated by the disarray of the preparations. During autumn 1932 Britain came under pressure from France and the United States to peg sterling, so giving it a gold value. The Bank of England felt that the continuing uncertainty in the exchange markets and, above all, in the world economy meant that it was impossible to determine sterling's correct international parity. Beyond sterling, the Bank saw a world full of structural impediments whose persistence would mean that sterling would face the sort of crisis that occurred in 1931 all over again. A repeat of such a crisis could be avoided by Britain's having higher gold reserves, but these could only be built up by domestic deflation—absolutely contrary to the policy that had been pursued since 1932. Consequently, the Bank would only go as far as restricting sterling's movements within a narrow band, the dimensions of which were not to be declared, so this policy could hardly form a conference brief.[45] However, during subsequent preparatory discussions there was some acceptance of British desiderata for reforming the gold standard, but this did not go as far as agreeing to British officials' plans for redistributing world gold stocks. Finally, the grounds for the conference were changed when Roosevelt took the United States off the gold standard in March 1933, thus

---

[43] George S. Watts, 'The Origins and Background of Central Banking in Canada', *Bank of Canada Review* (May 1972).

[44] Sayers, *Bank*, ii, 512–15, 518–19; [Reserve Bank], *History of the Reserve Bank of India (1935–1951)* (Bombay, 1970).

[45] Drummond, *Floating Pound*, 135–6.

halting gold exports; both measures were taken without any advance warning to Britain and France.[46]

During the conference, representatives of the central banks and finance ministries of Britain, France, and the United States discussed exchange-rate stabilization, but to apply only for the duration while the world discussed its problems.[47] Their proposals involved a central rate of $4 with a 3 per cent spread for Britain (thought intolerable by the Treasury two months earlier), but to be sustained only as long as an expenditure of 30m. ounces of gold allowed. This plan ran foul of Roosevelt, who was irked by British and French defaults on war debt payments to the United States. The lack of a clear American policy, together with leaks and rumours, led to chaos on the European exchanges. However, Britain was not prepared to countenance the long run stabilization of sterling, let alone a link with what was to be the future European gold bloc of the mid-1930s.[48]

Currency stabilization efforts continued after the World Economic Conference;[49] however, Roosevelt's decisions meant that the Exchange Equalisation Account had to operate mainly in francs, which led to a drawing together of the Bank of England and the Bank of France. Roosevelt's gold-buying initiative of autumn 1933 caused Norman to sound out Harrison of the New York Fed over the target exchange rate that the American President was aiming at. This led to informal approaches from Harrison to the Governor of the Bank of England, seeking to discover whether central bankers could generate proposals for their respective governments, although foremost in the American's mind was a trans-Atlantic return to gold, with sterling perhaps at $4.86. Roosevelt's autumnal experiment came to an end in early 1934, which fixed the dollar against gold at $35 per ounce, while the $2,000m. profits from the exercise were to be used to manage the American currency against sterling. However, despite the impression that Morgenthau, the Secretary of the Treasury, gave publicly, British institutions were not approached to stabilize the sterling : dollar rate until March 1935.[50]

American intimations regarding stabilized currencies were not taken up in London during mid-1935, either by the Treasury or the Bank, whose officials pointed to the United States still absorbing the world's gold. Equally they felt that the prospects for an indicated French devaluation were poor, since it would not be politically acceptable. Similarly, British officials and their political masters were not prepared to take up French invitations to

[46] Drummond, *Floating Pound*, 137–9, 143.

[47] Patricia Clavin, ' "The Fetishes of So-Called International Bankers": Central Bank Co-operation for the World Economic Conference, 1932–3', *Contemporary European History*, 1 (1992).

[48] Drummond, *Floating Pound*, 162–73.

[49] Stephen V. O. Clarke, *Exchange Rate Stabilization in the Mid-1930s: Negotiating the Tripartite Agreement* (Princeton, NJ., 1977).

[50] Drummond, *Floating Pound*, 181–4.

discuss stabilization within the context of tariff reductions.[51] The British view was that currencies had not yet reached equilibrium exchange rates, whereas, and more importantly, there was no wish to see domestic recovery, based upon liberal credit, endangered in any way. Morgenthau made approaches to London again in the spring of 1936, which he widened from June to include Paris. These were once more rebuffed in both European capitals, but Washington felt that it was London that was the centre of opposition, so preventing both a franc devaluation and a subsequent three-way stabilization of exchange rates.[52] Finally, Morgenthau was forced to bring London and Paris together, especially after French politicians began to indicate publicly that they were prepared to consider a devaluation of the franc within an international agreement.

London received the details of France's envisaged devaluation on 22 July 1936. The package involved a substantial international depreciation of the franc, which was in practice to join the Sterling Area, if sterling was maintained between $4.75 and $4.97. Officials in London found the consequences for Britain that this would generate totally unacceptable. None the less, the French initiative, for which French officials had prepared the ground in Washington, needed some reply, and Chamberlain explained the British position to the French Premier. The French put forward the same proposals in September, but the British government was not prepared to go further than again promising not to retaliate if the new rate was 100 francs : £1 as had been previously indicated. A formal agreement was not sought in London, as there was no intention to peg sterling beyond damping daily movements in the market. What emerged from a further round of monetary diplomacy between France, America, and Britain through discussions in Paris, was a willingness for the public declaration of three independent, but none the less related, statements.

The British statement was released on 26 September 1936 and confirmed that British external monetary policy would both continue in the same vein as the recent past and not respond aggressively to the French devaluation. It also pointed to co-operation between the central banks of Britain, France, and the United States. This built upon the growing relationship between London and Paris that had developed since the World Economic Conference, now to be augmented by an inter-play with a French equalization fund. Such collaboration would be extended across the Atlantic, but did not involve any commitment to a particular conjunction of exchange rates.[53] More importantly, as trans-Atlantic co-ordination developed with respect to the foreign exchange markets, Morgenthau agreed to sell gold to the Fed's partner banks, or rather the stabilization funds. This personal initiative helped to cement what has been called the 'tripartite monetary agreement' of September 1936, and provided an incentive for others to join

---

[51] Ibid. 190–3.   [52] Ibid. 194–9.   [53] Ibid. 201–14.

it.[54] The Tripartite Agreement of 1936 largely anticipated the essential structure of the gold-dollar standard of the Bretton Woods system during its 'convertible phase', which lasted from 1959 until March 1968.[55]

Paying the Price

Bretton Woods grew out of the bitter international experience of the 1930s and particularly from war-time Anglo-American finance and the plans that it involved for post-war reconstruction.[56] Article VII of the Mutual Aid Agreement of February 1942, which envisaged trade liberalization and built upon the economic hopes of the Atlantic Charter in terms of eliminating 'all forms of discriminatory treatment in international commerce', was critical. Here, Americans were particularly concerned to remove Imperial Preference, which Cordell Hull considered 'the greatest injury, in a commercial way, that has been inflicted on this country since I have been in public life'.[57] Subsequent conversations showed that Washington might oppose import and exchange control. Moreover, distaste there of Imperial Preference also embraced objections to the Sterling Area's common dollar pool, the product of war-time external finance.[58]

The development of the British response to these American intentions, regarding both the post-war transition and the international economic foundation for the peace, led to the Bank disagreeing with the Treasury over appropriate policies for the United Kingdom. However, in war-time debates the Bank was both overshadowed by Keynes and his Atlanticist aspirations, and suffered from a reputation dented by the particular experience of sterling on gold between 1925 and 1931 and, more generally, the gold-exchange standard and its collapse.[59] Indeed, American officials and politicians were concerned that central bankers should play the smallest role in the new post-war world, with Morgenthau stating in 1946 that his primary objective had been to 'move the financial centre of the world from London and Wall Street to the United States Treasury' and to create a new concept between nations of international finance under the control of 'sovereign governments and not of private financial interests'.[60]

[54] Drummond, *Floating Pound*, 220–4.

[55] Michael D. Bordo and Barry Eichengreen (eds.), *A Retrospective on the Bretton Woods System: Lessons for International Monetary Reform* (Chicago, 1993).

[56] See L. S. Pressnell, *External Economic Policy since the War*, i. *The Post-War Financial Settlement* (1986).

[57] Quoted in Robert M. Hathaway, *Ambiguous Partnership: Britain and America, 1944–1947* (New York, 1981), 21.

[58] See, generally, R. S. Sayers, *Financial Policy, 1939–45* (1956).

[59] John Fforde, *The Bank of England and Public Policy, 1941–1958* (Cambridge, 1992), 34–5.

[60] Quoted in: David Reynolds, *The Creation of the Anglo-American Alliance, 1937–41: A Study in Competitive Co-operation* (1981), 270.

Those involved in Threadneedle Street foresaw the need during the post-war transition for trade regulation, discrimination, and quantitative restrictions to buttress monetary control—a very different perspective to that of Washington. In this the Bank wished to build pragmatically upon the foundation consisting of the 1936 Tripartite Monetary Agreement and subsequent compacts with regard to international monetary movements and payments that had been forced by war conditions.[61] The Bank also became more concerned than the Treasury, and somewhat earlier, with regard to the problem of sterling balances, which mounted rapidly with British wartime expenditure in the Middle East and India. Where the Bank gained ground with its views during these early war-time deliberations was with regard to the Sterling Area. Bank staff, and especially George Bolton, were able to persuade Keynes in particular and the Treasury more generally that the continuance of the Sterling Area, now hedged by war-induced controls, would provide the context for a stable exchange rate, sterling having being fixed at \$4.03 with the outbreak of hostilities.[62] Yet by the spring of 1942 it was evident that a substantial gulf existed between the Bank and the Treasury, a divide which was underscored by the central bank having only 24 hours to comment upon the developed version of Keynes's Clearing Union proposal.[63]

During mid-1942 the Bank concentrated upon the problem of the sterling balances, especially those held by states outside the Sterling Area. The arising proposal that such threats to Britain's reserves might require controls in a world divided into currency areas was not accepted by the Treasury. Similarly the Bank discovered that its ideas for the post-war monetary order would not strike a chord with American officials,[64] while it was becoming apparent that the prospective size of Britain's post-war balance of trade deficit would inevitably lead to American aid being sought. In February 1943 the Bank received a copy of the White Plan, which, *inter alia*, contained proposals for funding the sterling balances through a proposed international monetary fund. Overall, however, Threadneedle Street found the American proposals for the post-war international monetary order not to its liking, indeed puzzling in their details and intent.[65]

The Bank of England consolidated its approach to post-war planning with the production in April 1943 of a paper, 'Sterling after the War'—a developed version of Siepmann's work since the Cabinet had approved Keynes's Clearing Union. In this it was argued that sterling should continue to be a key currency in terms of current-account convertibility, yet

[61] Pressnell, *Financial Settlement*, 68–74: Fforde, *Bank*, 38–9.

[62] Pressnell, *Financial Settlement*, 94–6; Fforde, *Bank*, 39–41.

[63] Fforde, *Bank*, 44–8.

[64] See, generally, Sir Richard Clarke (ed. Alec Cairncross), *Anglo-American Collaboration in War and Peace, 1942–1949* (Oxford, 1982).

[65] Fforde, *Bank*, 50–2.

would only be backed by at best a weak reserve position, given the war's disastrous effects upon the British balance of payments. The square could be circled, would have to be circled, by only allowing the free international use of sterling to develop slowly through a framework of controls. In this approach there would be discrimination between the Sterling Area and the rest of the world. The Sterling Area was regarded as a source of assistance for Britain's extremely difficult post-war balance of payments position, to be augmented through the free use of sterling, but it was the rest of the world where controls would have to be applied most vigorously.[66] Links between the Sterling Area and the rest of the world, especially non-sterling members who held sterling balances, could be developed through monetary agreements, either new or old—as in the case of the Argentine or Brazil. All this was couched in terms of fulfilling the world's need for practical working relationships while White-style or Keynesian global institutions came to fulfilment. It also implied a world payments system where central bankers played a major role.

During mid-1943 it was realized that American proposals would have to be generally accepted and all that British officials and negotiators could achieve was their modification. The Bank and Keynes agreed about the items requiring further consideration and reformulation, namely: elasticity regarding exchange-rate changes; the Fund not being empowered to intervene on the markets; the gold content of national subscriptions to the Fund; and a scarce currency clause, reflecting the dollar shortage since 1918.[67] None the less the Bank, especially Norman, still maintained that an alternative to a world institution should be considered. Once more Bank staff were concerned about the need for practical working arrangements— 'certain general basic principles'—rather than 'a mass of complicated technical and mechanical detail' as Cobbold termed it. However, this was not accepted in either Whitehall or Downing Street, whereas Keynes, accompanied by Thompson-McCausland of the Bank, was able to obtain in Washington during autumn 1943 the modifications of the White scheme that the British authorities sought.[68]

Opposition within the Bank to the way that the Anglo-American discussions were gelling came in late 1943 from Clay. He argued that Britain's problem during the inter-war period had been structural, arising from the decline of the staple export-orientated industries, and, moreover, he considered that his diagnosis was equally applicable to the prospective severe strains of the post-war transition. Consequently, he opposed the re-creation of the pre-1914 world of trade liberalism and fixed exchange rates that he considered American policy and the White Plan implied. As a result,

[66] Pressnell, *Financial Settlement*, 97; Fforde, *Bank*, 52–4.
[67] See M. E. Falkus, 'United States Policy and the "Dollar Gap" of the 1920s', *Economic History Review*, 2nd ser., 24 (1971).
[68] Fforde, *Bank*, 54–6.

the Bank and some Treasury members, led by Catto, concentrated on developing outline policies for Britain's post-war transition.

The Bank's continuing opposition to Keynes and the American proposals came to a head during January 1944 and focused on what was considered to be the damage that a Fund would inflict on sterling as a reserve currency and on the unity of the Sterling Area. The Bank was concerned that the Fund would not assist in attaining the goals of exchange-rate stability and the provision of liquidity. This was based on the conclusion that the Fund required an unsustainable commitment by Britain to sterling being convertible, which in effect meant a return to the gold standard. Furthermore, it was argued that the proposed starting-base was curious, to say the least, in terms of policies for the transition and for the Sterling Area. With regard to the latter, it would inevitably be broken up by the role that the Fund was likely to play, whereas the transition would commence with the irony of blocking war-time accumulated sterling balances. Essentially, the Bank considered that Keynes, and other international draughtsmen, had not comprehended either the nature of the Sterling Area or its development, which, for instance, had led to an exaggeration of its likely post-war dollar deficit. The Bank's concern also encompassed an anxiety towards Keynes's proposals for meeting Britain's post-war transition balance of payments deficit by obtaining a loan from the United States. Bank staff thought that a better way forward consisted of maintaining controls and developing an export policy, which, in turn, could be based upon sustaining sterling's fixed war-time rate in conjunction with bilateral monetary agreements with European and Latin American countries. These proposals would be evolutionary, rather than testing an untried international system, and, moreover, saw the IMF progressing rather as a consultative body.[69] The Cabinet noted the Bank's dissenting views, but Keynes characterized them as 'old arrangements and old-fashioned ideas'.[70]

In June 1944 Catto, now Governor of the Bank, was concerned about the convertibility obligations of the IMF as matters were debated at Bretton Woods. He wanted to restrict the commitment to external current-account convertibility after the transition, as he thought that three years for reserve sterling balances was too short an arrangement and would therefore generate instability. This made some impact upon Whitehall[71] and eventually the United States accepted that a nation always had sovereignty over its currency and therefore could vary its exchange rate, which led to article XIV of the IMF as a qualification to article VIII.[72] However, even after Bretton Woods, which had been attended by Bolton on behalf of the Bank, there was confusion over what precisely was meant by convertibility, especially with regard to reserve balances.[73]

[69] Pressnell, *Financial Settlement*, 141–3.   [70] Fforde, *Bank*, 57–61.

[71] Pressnell, *Financial Settlement*, 148–9; Fforde, *Bank*, 33, 61.

[72] Pressnell, *Financial Settlement*, 160–1.   [73] Ibid. 170.

The US Post-War Loan to Britain

Whatever doubts there might have been regarding Bretton Woods, Washington's terms for a post-war dollar loan to Britain were contingent upon adherence by the United Kingdom to the Bretton Woods agreement, together with its associated trade-policy regime—the ultimately abortive International Trade Organisation. Britain and Keynes were warned in good time of these tight terms by Will Clayton, who had used the excuse of attending an UNRRA meeting in order to let his counterparts across the Atlantic know the mood in Washington. Actually, the Anglo-American Financial Agreement required the introduction of current-account convertibility for non-resident sterling within a year of its ratification, whereas Bretton Woods had held out the prospect of a transition period of five years. In practice the transition was meaningless in any case, as Western hemisphere countries, such as Argentina, would have inevitably required British post-war deficits to be settled in either convertible sterling or dollars, and Eastern hemisphere countries, such as Belgium, which were in surplus with Britain, would have been in a position to restrict their acceptance of sterling. This was recognized in the Treasury by the autumn of 1947, if not earlier.[74] Furthermore, Dalton, the Chancellor, realized as soon as the Anglo-American Agreement was initialled that its 'conditions will have to be revised long before AD 2001, and that, even in the next year or two, circumstances may require a large revision, which might even be "unilateral" '.[75]

The Bank had made counter suggestions to Keynes's 'Justice' proposal. Deputy Governor Cobbold linked the question of the sterling balances with the need for an American loan. He opposed any uniform treatment of the sterling balances run up during the war, preferring bilateral settlements concluded as each balance peaked. Cobbold thought that what should be sought from America was a grant to cover essentials and for Britain alone, not the entire Sterling Area. Here, he was harking back to the Bank's wartime proposals, as the grant would be employed to enable Britain to develop her existing payment agreements, with consequently only a gradual movement towards convertibility. Catto was even more trenchant, having argued that the brief for the approach to Washington should consist of a claim for retrospective Lend-Lease and the negotiation of a secured credit, with the acceptance from the beginning that, if the credit could not be repaid within a decade, the collateral would have to be surrendered. A year later Cobbold grumbled that the Agreement had had the result of Britain losing its independence with respect to the conduct of monetary policy.[76] As the loan's

[74] PRO, CAB 134/47, 'Overseas Payment Problems', note by the Treasury, 20 Sept. 1947.
[75] Hugh Dalton, *High Tide and After: Memoirs, 1945–1960* (1962), 257.
[76] Bank of England, G1/101, memorandum 'Convertibility', Cobbold to Eady (Treasury), 20 June 1947.

dollars ran out over the subsequent months, the Bank considered devaluation, with guidance provided by previous lows—$3.26 in February 1920 and $3.17 in November 1932—although 'something lower' was considered to be required in the aftermath of the Second World War.[77]

During the first year of peace, the pattern of British international trade, with soft surpluses and hard deficits,[78] was leading to a situation in which the American loan would be exhausted prematurely. Dalton was aware of this and so was Cripps, who commented in November 1946: 'We must try to get nearer to balance not only of our total trade but hard currency trade as well and unless we succeed in doing that in the next year or two we shall find ourselves in the position of having to take some drastic action to carry on'.[79] The rate of outward flow of Britain's dollar drain was increased as a consequence of the gradual development of current-account convertibility for sterling. The first bilateral agreement was signed with Argentina in October 1946 and others followed, so that sterling's convertibility developed like the opening of a fan from autumn 1946 to meet the due date of 15 July 1947.[80] Under these arrangements, the responsibility for both supervising the transferable accounts and ensuring that withdrawals were only made for current transactions was placed with the monetary authorities of each foreign state. Gardner has subsequently maintained that the implications of such arrangements were never made clear to those concerned in the United States.[81] In the case of a number of European countries, sterling convertibility procedures were supplementary to monetary agreements concluded during 1944 and 1945. Cobbold wanted to ensure that, with current account convertibility, transfer facilities would only apply to the net sterling holdings of European central banks, whilst these institutions would accept sterling from any quarter. The expectation that Belgium would use any accumulation of sterling to discharge inter-government debts was dashed, with the Belgian Ministry of Finance denying that it was in any way bound by understandings reached between central bankers. By March 1947, within a week of the formal inception of current-account convertibility of sterling throughout Europe, Belgium had changed £4m. into dollars.

During May 1947 the outflow of dollars from Britain was running at such a rate as to have grave implications.[82] This drain was due to the impact of the Eastern hemisphere's demand for dollars (including the Sterling Area) upon Britain's currency reserves and the unbalanced—soft–hard—nature of Britain's international accounts. Eastern hemisphere countries arranged their international payments so as to obtain the dollars they required through convertible sterling. Dollars were short and the dollar area was to

[77] Bank of England, G1/101, 'Devaluation of Sterling', 28 June 1947.
[78] Clarke, *Anglo-American Collaboration*, 73–5.
[79] *The Times*, 29 Oct. 1946.   [80] PRO, T 236/1667.
[81] Richard N. Gardner, *Sterling–Dollar Diplomacy* (1969 edn.), 313.
[82] See also Alec Cairncross, *Years of Recovery: British Economic Policy, 1945–51* (1985), 121–66.

run a surplus of $3,266m. in its trade with the rest of the world during 1947. The post-war hardness of the dollar was further increased by the rise in dollar prices of some 10 per cent after 1945, which, together with the delay in the recovery of the Eastern hemisphere's economy, augmented Britain's dollar deficit. This amounted to $1,733m. for the United Kingdom alone and $2,700m. for the Sterling Area. International payments problems were further increased by institutional flows of $969m., of which $234m. consisted of subscriptions to the IMF and IBRD.[83]

Dalton, the Chancellor, had attempted to take countervailing action from January 1947. His problems were made worse by the fuel crisis,[84] caused by extreme winter conditions, to the extent of £100–200m. of exports being lost through energy shortages. The extent of these difficulties was indicated by the Bank of England's request to the Treasury to raise the level of monthly drawings on the American loan from $100m. to $200m., the necessity for which was accepted in March 1947. The Bank also warned that 'Full transferability is going to cost a good deal more but no one can say how much more'.[85]

As one of a range of dollar-saving measures, Dalton now insisted that the settlement of each sterling balance would have to involve an element of cancellation. Some of his advisers went further and reopened the question of freezing balances. Eventually, in late April 1947, it was decided that, while generally British negotiators should attempt to obtain some contribution from Sterling Area members with excessive balances, equally they were to be allowed to fall back on securing the maintenance of minimum balances when reaching an agreement. Each of these objectives was found difficult to achieve, as was discovered when Cobbold, together with Eady of the Treasury, tried to negotiate a gentleman's agreement with India, involving a scaling-down of the sub-continent's sterling balance. This provoked a strong reaction in Delhi. By the end of May Cobbold had come round to a partial freezing plan which also involved American assistance. His scheme was for gold, not dollar, loans for Egypt, India, Iraq, and Palestine so as to take advantage of the difference between the official and local prices of gold.[86]

By late May 1947 it was becoming apparent that the monthly level of drawing on the American loan needed to be raised again, which brought even closer the point at which the loan would be exhausted. At the begin-

---

[83] Economic Cooperation Administration, Special Mission to the United Kingdom, *The Sterling Area: An American Analysis* (1951), 66.

[84] Cairncross, *Recovery*, 354–84; Alex J. Robertson, *The Bleak Midwinter: 1947* (Manchester, 1987).

[85] PRO, T 273/3, [Sir Hugh Ellis-Rees], 'The Convertibility Crisis of 1947', Treasury Historical Memoranda no. 4, 19.

[86] On the further development of aspects of this problem, see B. R. Tomlinson, 'Indo-British Relations in the Post-Colonial Era: The Sterling Balances Negotiations, 1947–49', *Journal of Imperial and Commonwealth History*, 13 (1985).

ning of 1947 it had been expected that the loan would last until September 1949; it now looked as if Britain and the Sterling Area would be dependent solely on pooled reserves by the spring of 1948. Cuts in the Import Programme requested by the Treasury ran into ministerial opposition and procrastination, despite fresh reviews which pointed to the loan being all gone by October 1947. By mid-June the Treasury and the Bank had begun contingency planning, although officials were clear about the effects of suspending convertibility. European trade would be gravely affected and sterling would be finished as a world trading currency, which would mean that Britain would have to face dollar invoicing for its imports.

Cobbold saw an 'economic Dunkirk' looming. He argued that this would mean that the British government would have to reject ruthlessly all international entanglements, irrespective of political loyalties. It was thought that Britain's most important Western hemisphere suppliers—Argentina, Brazil, Canada, and Uruguay—would introduce dollar invoicing as an insurance against any depreciation of the pound. Similarly, it was expected that Europe would be forced back onto the monetary agreements, which would involve ganging up at the likely time for the implementation of the Marshall proposals. Finally, it was clear that the Sterling Area would be weakened through outsiders demanding either dollars or pounds backed by a gold guarantee. On the home front it was considered that any decision to end convertibility, before further American aid was within reach, would cause capital flight through lags on trade transactions and shifts from gilts to shares on the Stock Exchange. The conclusion drawn by the Deputy Governor was to persevere. Although Cobbold had opposed the introduction of convertibility, he now felt that 'having accepted the principle of convertibility and having agreed to put it into force so shortly after the end of the war, it is probable [,] however difficult the future may prove to be [,] we cannot in any circumstance cancel convertibility without destroying sterling as an international currency'.[87] Given the increasingly desperate situation, it is surprising that the visit of Clayton and Douglas to London, between 24 and 26 June, was not used to brief these American representatives fully.

Convertibility was achieved by 15 July 1947, but had been accompanied by the dollar drain turning into a flood—increasing from $112m. net over the week before 15 July to $155m. over the subsequent seven days. It was against this background that Dalton was briefed by Bridges regarding Alternative Action, a programme which had been drawn up by the Bank and the Treasury. Dalton's own notes began their ministerial rounds in preparation for a series of committee and Cabinet meetings from 28 July. However, on the eve of the parliamentary debates of early August, it seemed that the tide of the dollar drain had turned. The early July flood

---

[87] Bank of England, G101/1 'Convertibility', 20 June 1947.

had been in part due to British commitments in Germany and the pattern of Canadian wheat shipments. The latest figures led Dalton to reduce the amount to be drawn on the American loan on 11 August from $300m. to $150m., although a further call on the facility was pencilled in for 25 August.[88]

The dollar drain was not subsiding. There may have been a pause in late July, but thereafter Britain's dollars flowed out at an increasing rate as a speculative bear run on sterling began. During early August it became clear that both Argentina and Brazil were selling more pounds than they had readily available in view of their likely future requirements. Similarly, Belgium was continuing to run its sterling balance down. On the other side of the account, no gold had been received from South Africa for three weeks, while it now seemed that the gold loan from the Union, for which negotiations had begun on 2 August, would amount to only £60–80m., rather than £100m. as had originally been expected. Remaining international confidence in sterling was shattered by Dalton's speech in the House on 6 August, in which he declared that the American loan would be all gone within two months, after which Britain would be left with reserves of only £600m., the remaining balance of £125m. on the parallel Canadian loan and £320m. of IMF drawing rights against liabilities of £3,660m. composed of the sterling balances. Following this speech and the debate, Siepmann at the Bank thought that there was a general attempt by holders of transferable sterling 'to take cover without delay'. Between 11 and 15 August $41.5m. was for American accounts, $27.7m. for Argentina, $20m. for Canada, and $16.2m. for the Sterling Area, as far as it was then possible to identify elements in the outward flow.[89] The Treasury, like the Bank, had suspected speculation against sterling, but Whitehall was not to receive anything like a full measure of the extent until the evening of Wednesday 13 August, when news of it burst like a bombshell. The Treasury was reliant upon the Bank, normally through Cobbold, for all balance of payments statistics.[90] The magnitude of the dollar flood on 13 August was conveyed by Siepmann with the comment 'the avalanche [was] upon us'.[91] It now appeared that Britain would be temporarily out of dollars by 18 or 19 August, so that plans had to be developed for approaching the Fed for a bridging credit.

The Bank may have been stung by Treasury criticism of the lateness of its warning of the resurgence of the dollar drain, but Threadneedle Street staff were also concerned that nothing precipitate was undertaken in the first flush of a crisis. They regarded 'the politics of exhaustion of a credit

[88] PRO, T 267/3, Ellis-Rees, 30.
[89] Bank of England, G1/102, [Note by] HAS, 14 Aug. 1947; 'United States Dollar Figures', 15 Aug. 1947.
[90] Clarke, *Anglo-American Collaboration*, 59.
[91] Bank of England, G1/102 letter [?Eady to Cobbold], 16 Aug. 1947.

at an unexpectedly early date by apparent capital movements' as 'particularly touchy'.[92] What was in their minds was 1931 and the adverse criticism that had been made then, to the extent that Bank officials maintained that Britain could not now repudiate when there was still a reserve of £600m. This was particularly felt to be the case as the formal completion of the convertibility arrangements on 15 July had been announced 'in a blaze of publicity'. Therefore, Threadneedle Street urged partial use of the exchange reserve and reiterated the proposal for withdrawing support of sterling on the American market, a tactic which it was thought would have a psychological effect upon Washington. Catto continued with the line that fences should not be rushed, if only to allow the British team going to Washington a chance to sense the American mood.[93]

Current account convertibility for non-resident sterling was suspended on 20 August 1947. Britain's international monetary arrangements now consisted of the Sterling Area, with its dollar pool from which individual members' drawings were to be kept 'as low as possible',[94] and the European monetary agreements dating from 1944. Sterling Area arrangements were discussed at the first Sterling Area Conference held in mid-September. Beyond the Sterling Area, it was a question of trade and monetary controls involving discrimination concluded by bilateral arrangements.[95] The result was a variety of types of sterling. 'American' sterling referred to balances held by the United States and a group of Central American countries for current account purposes, and was freely transferable into dollars. From 1947 there existed 'transferable account' sterling, with regard to a heterogeneous group of states which agreed to accept sterling for trade payment purposes, to hold it as a monetary reserve, and to block war balances.

Before 20 August 1947 ministerial discussions had placed great emphasis upon the Commonwealth as both a source of British imports and an earner of dollars, the roles that it had played before the war. Dalton considered the Sterling Area Conference, the first, to have yielded some useful results. The British government took the opportunity to stress the gravity of the situation and the importance of the measures that had been taken before and after 20 August. It was also emphasized that Sterling Area members should ensure as far as possible that dollar purchases were kept to a minimum, particularly until mid-1948. Lastly, the discussions ranged over what, and how, additional resources could be added to the

[92] Bank of England, G1/102, 'Figures Meeting', L. P. T.-McC, 13 Aug. 1947.

[93] Bank of England, G1/102, 'Diary of Events Leading to Suspension of Transferable Sterling Exclusive of Sterling Area', Catto.

[94] Ronan Fanning, *The Irish Department of Finance, 1922–58* (Dublin, 1978), 397.

[95] PRO, CAB 134/47, 'Current or Pending Trade Discussions', Note by the Board of Trade, 20 Sept. 1947; 'Treasury Negotiations with Countries Outside the Sterling Area', 21 Sept. 1947.

Area's pooled reserves.[96] The clearest success of the conference was the gold loan agreement with South Africa, for which negotiations had begun in early August. Not only would this provide £80m., but South Africa also undertook to replace in gold 'any net deficit in third currencies, which [Britain was] called upon to meet on her account.' Furthermore, arrangements had been concluded covering both 'undesirable capital movements' and British foodstuff purchases for the ensuing three years.

There were no bilateral discussions with either India or Pakistan during the conference. This meant that the British Treasury had to continue to work on the basis of an estimate of an Indian component of the continuing dollar drain of $60m. for the second half of 1947 with regard to an all-India sterling balances agreement. For its part, the Treasury gained the impression that, while the Indian authorities claimed to be doing all that could be done to economize on hard currencies, they were nevertheless purchasing immediately any food grains that came on the market. Treasury officials thought that it would be possible to reach a settlement with Delhi, whereby during the first half of 1948 India drew on the IMF, while repaying to the Sterling Area's reserves any amount above $60m. that had been drawn from the pool during the second half of 1947. All that could be deduced regarding Pakistan was that the Karachi government intended a complete separation from India, including 'such pre-existing services as are on the India side of the India-Pakistan border'.

One objective gained from the conference and its associated talks and informal discussions was the 'desirability of a constant exchange of information'. As a result the British Treasury followed up the suggestion that Australia and New Zealand should be more effectively represented in London, which would overcome the need to telegraph to Canberra and Wellington for additional information as and when required. More generally, it looked likely that an effective machinery involving all major members of the Sterling Area could be established, although Ceylon, Palestine, and India were special cases.[97] The creation of a Sterling Area Statistical Organisation in London commenced in late November 1947, following discussions over the British non-dollar balance of payments programme.

American intentions to accelerate the post-war liberalization of the world economy through the negotiation of the Anglo-American Financial Agreement had been precipitate. The suspension of sterling's convertibility and the collapse of the ITO talks in Geneva during mid-summer 1947 clearly revealed that the post-war transition was fragile and could not be accelerated. One major underlying problem was the 'dollar gap', a feature

[96] PRO, CAB 134/215, EPC (47) 1st meeting, Economic Policy Committee, 9 Sept. 1947; David Lee, 'Protecting the Sterling Area: The Chiefley Government's Response to Multilateralism, 1945–1949', *Australian Journal of Political Science*, 25 (1990).

[97] PRO, CAB 134/215, EPC (47) 19, 'Sterling Area Conference', note by the Chancellor, 19 Nov. 1947.

of the period running from the 1920s until the 1960s. However, Cobbold, for one, rightly recognized that the IMF would not declare the dollar a scarce currency—unless arrangements could be made for a more rapid use of quotas at the Fund meeting of September 1947.[98] Although the Board of the IMF agreed in August 1947 that there was a case for the dollar being declared scarce, since there was 'an unusual need and demand for dollars', it was maintained that this had arisen from a shortage of productive facilities in Europe with which to earn dollars, rather than the United States curtailing imports as a reaction to a slump.[99]

The world's dollar imbalance was recognized in Washington from February 1947. The American Treasury suggested that the United States would have an aggregate balance of payments surplus of $20–$25bn. over the ensuing five years and one recipient of this estimate in the State Department commented that 'there was the probability of a bankrupt world thus we had to give priority to an aid program'. In late May 1947 Clayton proposed to Marshall that the United States should grant Europe $6–7bn. of goods every year for at least three years.[100] However, Marshall's speech of 5 June 1947 created—at least in London—misplaced hopes that the American cavalry would arrive before sterling collapsed, and it came as a shock that Congress might not hold the necessary special session during autumn 1947.[101] The early stages of planning for the European Recovery Programme acted to complicate the sterling crisis of the summer of 1947.

Devaluation

After August 1947 the convertibility of sterling was low down on the list of objectives of the British monetary authorities, though it remained there. Managing inconvertible sterling became particularly difficult as the controls over its international use frequently sprang leaks. International markets developed on which sterling of various categories was traded at a discount to the official rate (especially New York and Zürich), which necessitated further plumbing in the form of tighter and more complex controls. This all inevitably weakened the role that sterling could and might play as a key currency.[102]

---

[98] Bank of England, G1/102, 'Scarce Currency Clause', n.d. [? 5 Aug. 1947, from position within file].

[99] J. Keith Horsefield, *The International Monetary Fund, 1945–1965: Twenty Years of International Monetary Co-operation*, i. *Chronicle* (Washington, DC, 1969), 193.

[100] Imanuel Wexler, *The Marshall Plan Revisited: The European Recovery Program in Economic Perspective* (Westport, Conn., 1983), 14.

[101] PRO, CAB 124/1045, telegram 7531, Foreign Office to Washington, 25 July 1947.

[102] Fforde, *Bank*, 219–49. More generally, see Graham L. Rees, *Britain and the Postwar European Payment Systems* (Cardiff, 1963); Brian Tew, *The Evolution of the International Monetary System, 1945–88* (1988).

Sterling's status was also affected by the devaluation of 1949.[103] It was clearly recognized that the maintenance of the fixed war-time rate of $4.03 was an artificiality and the Bank had been considering devaluation since at least the strains and stresses of mid-1947. The circumstances of the transition ensured that the question of devaluation had to be addressed and this was acknowledged by both the Bank and the Chancellor from the beginning of 1948. However, in many respects the 1949 devaluation was forced by the United States in two distinct ways. One was the downturn of this crucial, if protected, dollar-earning market for British exports; the other was that the American authorities sought sterling's devaluation as part of a round of parity readjustments between the Old World and the New to prepare the ground for a greater movement to economic liberalism during the penultimate year of the Marshall Plan.

E. M. Bernstein, Director of Research at the IMF, foresaw the need for European devaluations when America experienced its first post-war depression. This proposal met opposition within his staff, including from Maurice Allen, an Assistant Director and later an Executive Director of the Bank of England. In order to persuade his colleagues Bernstein wrote a paper on 'The marginal incremental rate of exchange', presented to the Washington Chapter of the Statistics Association which used as an example a devaluation of sterling from $4.00 to $2.80. Bernstein considered the wave of devaluations that were to take place in 1949 'as the readjustment of the international economic position of the reset of the world to the United States, as it had been affected by the Great Depression and the war'. With the onset of an American recession, the US Executive Director of the IMF sought negotiations in early 1949 to consider European devaluations. Bernstein opposed talks between Executive Directors on the grounds that it would lead to speculation in the foreign-exchange markets, while the Bank of England, for similar reasons, was against a European tour by Bernstein and the Managing Director of the IMF. Eventually Bernstein, with Allen, saw Cobbold and learnt that the Bank of England was contemplating devaluation; however, Cobbold declared that the extent was still being considered and also pointed out that ultimately it was a political decision. Bernstein's diagnosis of the British problem stressed leaks from blocked sterling balances into dollars, which he thought could be minimized at a sterling : dollar rate of $3.[104]

Some alternatives were considered in London but rejected as first-line options, since they would not only challenge the precepts of Bretton Woods, but also required both an abandonment of 'cheaper money' and an early re-establishment of London's foreign markets. Consequently a return to the world of floating currencies was only regarded as a contingency

---

[103] See also Cairncross and Eichengreen, *Sterling*, 111–55; Cairncross, *Recovery*, 165–211.

[104] Stanley W. Black, *A Levite Among the Priests: Edward M. Bernstein and the Origins of the Bretton Woods System* (Boulder, Colo., 1991), 62–3, 66–8.

plan—to be taken out of the drawer if the dollar shortage became even more adverse. However, the timetable for any decision was shortened by growing American pressure, including opaque but none the less very public pronouncements, from February 1949. This pressure also involved the use of the IMF to bring about European devaluations, which caused resentment in London, particularly with the press commentary that it attracted.

Losses from the reserves from the summer of 1949 were a further factor preventing the British authorities from devaluing sterling in their own time. However, devaluation also raised questions over domestic policy—yet further austerity to be coupled with that which had had to be introduced from the summer of 1947—and the manner in which London institutions could regain their global role within the context of the sterling balances—an objective of the Bank which also considered American assistance to be fundamental to securing it. A Bank report on devaluation, drawn up in June 1949, anticipated consequent advantages if domestic policies were changed, but no gains with respect to external issues such as convertibility, the sterling balances, and the post-war dollar debt. The Governor considered the critical problem to be the establishment of an associated understanding with North America that would reduce Britain's dollar drain by which the rest of the world was trying to meet the dollar gap. As in the summer of 1947, the Cabinet was not prepared to introduce the further retrenchment which the Chancellor, with the benefit of Bank advice, had seen as the only alternative to devaluation.

Continuing reserve losses, which it was estimated would take holdings down to £300–325m. by mid-September, finally led junior ministers to the conclusion that devaluation had to be accepted, which was agreed by the Cabinet on 28 July. As in 1931 and 1947, the political problem arose from associated increases in domestic austerity and retrenchment. The Governor indicated two further, contextual problems—that of sterling leading a world round of devaluations and, second, the need for a greater devaluation of sterling if it was forced rather than being conceived as a central feature of a general reshaping of policy. The Bank had looked to and was still considering an external route, but this had now been overtaken by events. It had consisted of a further round of American assistance to the United Kingdom and sterling, which would aid the liberalization of world trade and payments. However, American officials in Washington had come to focus solely upon a sterling devaluation.

By late August the Governor recommended the devaluation of sterling, if only because it was now so widely expected, and suggested $2.75, which involved a margin of undervaluation. The new rate of $2.80 was determined at a meeting in the British Embassy in Washington on 12 September attended by Cripps and Bevin, who had reluctantly accepted the need for a rate below $3.00. The decision was taken amidst tripartite talks between

Britain, Canada, and the United States. The public announcement took place on 19 September after the Bank had made the necessary international and domestic preparations. The Governor saw it as a once and for all change.

Sterling's devaluation was followed by a global realignment. The Sterling Area, with the exception of only one or two members, kept a fixed rate with sterling, as did Scandinavia and the Netherlands. No other European currency was devalued to the same extent, with the result that the trade-weighted effective devaluation of sterling was somewhat less than 10 per cent, as opposed to the 30 per cent nominal change against the dollar. These devaluations came to change the eventual nature of the Bretton Woods international monetary regime. It had originally been conceived as an adjustable peg system, but the experience of the global exchange adjustments of 1948/9, it has been argued, led to no major devaluations taking place between 1958 and 1971—during the full convertibility phase of Bretton Woods.[105] In the case of Britain, with the domestic measures that were also taken, the 1949 devaluation proved more successful than either the Treasury or the Bank had hoped. British dollar earning exports increased and the reserves rose to total more than $2bn. by mid-1950.[106]

Towards Convertibility

Monetary policy in peace-time changed for the first time in nearly two decades with the announcement on 8 November 1951 that Bank rate was to be increased to 2½ per cent. This was rapidly followed by the re-opening of London's exchange markets with respect to spot and forward rates in sterling. The latter was designed to reduce the risk exposure of the Exchange Equalisation Account and to deal with the problems of speculative 'leads and lags' that had been apparent since 1947. These two changes started to have an effective impact just as sterling faced what can be regarded as its third and final post-war crisis—caused by the global economic effects of the Korean War. Britain's reserves declined rapidly and suddenly from the autumn of 1951. This sudden outflow re-emphasized the problems that sterling had faced since 1947, in terms of the impracticality of controlling non-resident holdings, the now perennial difficulty of the sterling balances, and the ever-continuing dollar gap. At the Bank Thompson-McCausland and Bolton thought that a solution lay in moving to convertibility—even at a floating rate, but this was only foreseeable with American assistance coupled with further domestic policy changes.[107] Some

---

[105] Michael D. Bordo, 'The Bretton Woods International Monetary System: A Historical Overview', in Bordo and Eichengreen, *Retrospective*, 3, 49.
[106] Fforde, *Bank*, 276–304.   [107] Ibid. 417–21.

of this thinking went to the Commonwealth Finance Ministers' Conference of January 1952.[108]

A clear crisis developed during the first quarter of 1952, to the extent that there were predictions from the Treasury that the reserves could rapidly fall to $1,400m. These very gloomy estimates prompted the conception of drastic ideas, or the crystallization of lines of argument that had been developing amongst some Bank staff since the beginning of the decade. It seemed that the post-1939 controlled sterling system now had little future, but any new start involved putting the 'house in order', a phrase that had been increasingly used since 1949. If domestic measures taken by Britain and the Sterling Area were successful, there still remained the problems of low reserves and free markets in sterling,[109] both of which were sources of scepticism regarding sterling remaining at $2.80. These difficulties might be resolved by freezing a high proportion of sterling balances, making remaining 'free' sterling convertible within a wider parity band against the dollar, and bolstering the reserves by commercial borrowing in New York and drawing on the IMF. The need for action was pointed up by the coming publication of the reserve figures in April 1952, which would show the first quarter's losses. These proposals, as they were developed within the Bank and the Overseas Finance section of the Treasury, became known as the Robot Plan.[110] However, it was undone by political insistence that the arising radical, strategic measures would have to be included in the 1952 budget—producing an almost impossible timetable—and by the lack of full prior consideration within all the relevant sections of Whitehall, which sparked a ferocious opposition. Instead the budget, which included raising Bank rate to 4 per cent and other measures which would later be regarded as of the 'stop' variety, stemmed the reserve losses.[111]

Over the 1950s Britain enjoyed a surplus on current balance of the order of £118m. per annum on average, which was equivalent to 0.7 per cent of GNP. This was largely due to a favourable shift in the terms of trade, while the extent of the improvement in the international position was in no way sufficient to liquidate the financial heritage of the Second World War. Sterling crises persisted, as in 1954, and in 1957 the underlying situation was characterized by Cobbold as sterling being on a see-saw, with adequate confidence in the currency being retained by only a slender margin.

The recovery of reserves immediately after the crisis of the spring of 1952 did not diminish officials' concern over the precarious state of the post-war sterling system. As a result the Bank and Treasury persisted with developing Robot by considering its wider ramifications, but this too was rejected

[108] See also B. W. Muirhead, 'Britain, Canada and the Collective Approach to Freer Trade and Payments, 1952–57', *Journal of Imperial and Commonwealth History*, 20 (1992).

[109] Catherine R. Schenk, 'Closing the Hong Kong Gap: Hong Kong and the Free Dollar Market in the 1950s', *Economic History Review*, 47 (1994).

[110] Cairncross, *Recovery*, 234–71.   [111] Fforde, *Bank*, 426–51.

by the Cabinet's Economic Policy Committee in mid-1952, despite growing indications of an autumnal sterling crisis. Fortunately, sterling got through the autumn of 1952 untroubled, while the rejection of Robot resulted in a growing acceptance within Whitehall of the need for Britain to participate in, indeed lead, a return to convertibility, to be undertaken by all the major Western European economies in terms of key currencies.

The new British plan—'Collective Approach to Multilateral Trade and Payments'—was reasonably well received by Commonwealth officials in early autumn 1952, but European countries still opposed an early resumption of convertibility, however defined. The European Payments Union,[112] which had operated in practice since mid-1947, and its associated regime governing trade appeared to be working well. Across the Channel there was significant consensus that saw the introduction of convertibility resulting in either heightened barriers to trade or a further appreciation of the dollar. The only gain that the Bank was able to make was to ensure, through the forum provided by the BIS, that an EPU report was to be largely technical in its review of current-account convertibility. However, any advantage was lost by the Governor's misunderstanding when he made a visit to North America immediately prior to the Commonwealth Prime Ministers' conference. Cobbold gained the impression, as did other Bank staff, that Washington favoured an informal approach by Britain regarding its plans for convertibility. Whatever anxieties this might have caused in European capitals, a behind-the-scenes approach would be difficult because of the communiqué that would automatically follow from the gathering of the Commonwealth. That announcement, when made, looked forward to the convertibility of sterling through the co-operation of the United States, Europe, and the international organs of Bretton Woods.

Members of the EPU remained hostile to convertibility, given the low reserves of its members and the continuing dollar shortage. They saw greater advantages arising from the further development of the EPU and the IMF, which had recently agreed in principle to stand-by facilities. Furthermore, they expected prior consultation by the British government before the British made any approach to Washington. European central bankers, almost like the Bank of England during the mid-1940s, placed their trust in existing institutions—such as the EPU—rather than the totally untried British initiative—now conceived in Whitehall as a new joint IMF–GATT committee of twelve. Washington also heard of continental European concerns and anxieties caused by the developing British proposal.

The Treasury stuck to its plan for approaching Washington first, but turned to the Bank for advice about proposals concerned with superseding the EPU. Thompson-McCausland suggested maintaining the EPU as a

---

[112] Jacob J. Kaplan and Günther Schleiminger, *The European Payments Union: Financial Diplomacy in the 1950s* (Oxford, 1989).

policy discussion forum, but replacing its trade-support credits through automatic and unconditional IMF stand-by facilities. The British government made no headway with the Americans in talks held in March 1953. Basically Washington doubted whether the British economy had the necessary resilience, while for its part the Eisenhower administration was not prepared to tackle Congress on either further trans-Atlantic financial assistance or the liberalization of United States commercial policy.[113]

From 1947 until mid-1953 British designs for sterling had evolved, understandably and naturally, because of the general problems of the Sterling Area, both real and monetary. By the autumn of 1953 the international position began to be considered more in the light of the increasing de-control of the British economy and the gradual re-emergence of the City as a global financial centre. Cobbold explored with the Chancellor the possibility of introducing technical changes in the control of sterling which could sustain the movement towards convertibility. What he had in mind was to simplify the regulation of non-resident transferable sterling (other than that held on the American account) in order to allow a market in it to develop, parallel to the official market. There was talk within the Bank of re-opening London's free gold market. However, whilst the Chancellor was anxious for a positive agenda for the next round of Commonwealth discussions, the Treasury was hesitant and, indeed, puzzled by oblique references to the 1936 tripartite monetary agreement. Finally, following international soundings, the Chancellor agreed to the initial stage of the Bank's 'technical progress' plan, namely the simplification of controls on non-resident sterling and the re-opening of the London gold market, measures which became operative on 22 March 1954.[114]

Further technical progress came up against political barriers caused by the question of the succession at 10 Downing Street and the electoral cycle. However, sterling's underlying problems were pointed up by reserve losses from the autumn of 1954, which had initially been thought to be seasonal. Sterling's weakness was re-emphasized by trading at a discount in offshore markets. Resolving these difficulties was addressed by the Bank and the Treasury during the opening months of 1955. It also had the effect of reopening the cracks between advisers that had been apparent during the early Robot discussions, with one root cause now being the appropriateness of official intervention in the market for transferable sterling. In the end the Bank got its way and the rise in Bank rate to 4½ per cent on 24 February 1955 was combined with intervention, which the Bank had maintained the markets would expect and, in any case, for a long time had sought as part of technical progress.[115] Although it received very little publicity, intervention in transferable sterling made it to all intents convertible, at a discount of 1 per cent to the official rate from the end of March 1955.

---

[113] Fforde, *Bank*, 477–92.   [114] Ibid. 492–505.   [115] Ibid. 512–27.

In late 1955, British reserves amounted to £750m. ($2.12bn.), only £150m. more than they had been in either mid-1947 or early 1952, whereas the sterling balances were broadly at the same level as in 1945—£3,750m.— but of which one-fifth were now held outside the Sterling Area. During the opening months of 1956 talk of devaluation was once more in the air and distrust of sterling was shown within the Sterling Area through the increasing diversification of members' individual reserve holdings. The problem of the sterling balances was also acquiring a new twist with decolonization. Then, from late July, came the Suez affair.

The fall, actual and extrapolated, in the reserves over the last quarter of 1956 looked as if their crisis floor of $2bn. would not only be reached but severely breached. However, pressure on sterling in the exchange markets abated at the time of the cease-fire on 6 November. In this situation Bolton at the Bank recommended a drawing on the IMF of $1bn., reiterating a joint Bank–Treasury contingency review of September. However, an open exchange crisis was feared when the Suez-induced reserve losses were to be published in early December. Inevitably the situation meant a British approach to Washington and, while that was being prepared from 19 November, the Bank argued, and the Chancellor agreed, that reserves should be used to hold sterling firm. The Governor was also suggesting a combination of major international borrowing and domestic measures to clear up the situation which had pertained since 1947. If this proved feasible, some Bank staff members saw the occasion as opportune for establishing a single rate for sterling, so closing cheap markets such as Hong Kong and Kuwait.

American financial assistance only came after some of the political divisions arising from the Suez adventure had been publicly mended. The British announcement of withdrawal on 3 December 1956 was rapidly followed by the publication of the reserve losses, but reduced to $279m. by some portfolio shuffling. The American key to the IMF was immediately turned, which released four tranches of Britain's quota, with the third and fourth being in the form of a stand-by. These were coupled with an Export–Import Bank line of $700m. for oil imports, to make $2bn. in all. The Bank felt that this assistance would hold the situation but not revive confidence in sterling, which it was thought in Threadneedle Street would only come about as a result of major fiscal changes.[116]

The underlying weakness of sterling was once again revealed during the summer of 1957 as a result of European currency speculation following on from a devaluation of the French franc. Movements in the market, which cost the British reserves $203m. directly, centred on an anticipated revaluation of the Deutschmark, but were further complicated by the German elections. The Bank looked to international action to resolve the situation,

---

[116] Fforde, *Bank*, 543–65.

although the Treasury opposed using the situation to develop exchange-rate adjustment through altering the top limits on European currency bands. The loss of British reserves forced a movement of Bank rate to 7 per cent on 19 September (a level not reached for 37 years), and a drawing from the Export-Import Bank facility.[117] Little noticed at the time, a further measure was introduced which restricted the international use of sterling, in terms of financing world trade, to credits within the Sterling Area. The attrition of the twelve years since the war had resulted in the beginning of the public acknowledgement of sterling's decline as a major international currency.

Britain's international accounts improved markedly during 1958. It was against the background of a substantial current-account balance, falling sterling balances, and rising reserves that convertibility was introduced within the framework of the European Monetary Agreement of 1955. The question of marrying official and transferable sterling was considered at the beginning of the year in a discussion between the Governor and the Treasury. The Bank seized the opportunity and maintained pressure until the spring, which led to the preparation of briefing papers for Downing Street ranging over all possible options. Generally, Whitehall and Threadneedle Street agreed on maintaining a fixed rate but differed over whether it would be advisable to lift sterling's top, the Treasury being concerned over both the necessary approach to the IMF and the practicalities, whereby a working top of $2.88, if achieved, would damage exports. The Bank official responsible for foreign exchange continued to maintain that sterling required a wider spread since it would reduce pressure on the reserves by checking speculation. However, there were senior Treasury dissidents who felt that Britain's underlying position was insufficiently strong and therefore feared another 1947 débâcle as a consequence. Floating, which was seen as a political option, was cast by Bolton at the Bank as 'inevitable . . . but make no attempt to force the pace until it becomes more acceptable to the Western world as a whole'. After receiving all this advice Downing Street decided to postpone any decision until the autumn, which disappointed the Governor and other Bank officials.[118]

The continuing improvement of Britain's international economic position finally convinced all the responsible senior Treasury officials that it was the time for full current account convertibility. A necessary cushion could be provided by renewing sterling's Suez IMF facilities. The 1958 autumnal round of international meetings would provide a forum for informal and more direct discussions of Britain's putative policy line for sterling. All that arose negatively was Jacobsson's opposition to the manner in which Britain envisaged the involvement of the IMF, with the consequence that the

---

[117] Ibid. 566–72.   [118] Ibid. 585–91.

British monetary authorities had to rely upon the recently augmented United Kingdom Fund quota.

The experience of the disastrous international presentation of the 'Collective Approach' may have led the Bank to counsel that the unification of sterling rates needed preparation involving substantial European discussions. The Bank recommended that these should begin with the central banks of France and Germany and then be progressively widened to all other members of the EPU.[119] Political and economic conditions in France were emphasized by the EPU, which reinforced the Bank's cautious approach to what had been dubbed 'Operation Unicorn'. Other members of the nascent EEC welcomed the inception of formal convertibility under the European Monetary Agreement of 1955, but indicated that they would follow any lead that Paris might give. Consequently Cobbold took two rounds of central bank soundings to prepare the ground.

European economic politics led to the Bank playing a critical part, through discussions with the Bank of France which revealed that the franc would probably be devalued following presidential elections in late December 1958, although the final decision would be taken by de Gaulle, the expected victor. This intelligence changed the attitude of British ministers, who had previously been cautious, since they now feared that Unicorn, rather than having to be postponed, would be trumped by a devalued, yet convertible, franc. The Bank continued to be the channel of communication between London and Paris and established that there would be no French opposition if sterling and the franc moved together. European political collaboration arose from informal talks at the OEEC Ministerial meeting in Paris in mid-December, during which a German offer of financial assistance to France was made.

The final difficulty that had to be resolved during the days before Christmas arose from the termination of the EPU and the creation of the European Fund under the now dated European Monetary Agreement. With this out of the way, it was agreed between Bonn, Paris, and London that European convertibility would be introduced on 29 December 1958, which effectively gave three days to finalize the pan-continental operation. That time was largely absorbed by dealing with fresh difficulties raised by the German authorities and outright opposition from the Norwegian central bank and government.[120] Convertibility for sterling came at what was to be the post-war apogee of the ratio of official reserves to net external sterling liabilities. This had risen from 18 per cent in 1952 to 28 per cent in 1958 and thereafter was to fall, reaching 19 per cent in 1964 and 21 per cent in 1967.

---

[119] Fforde, *Bank*, 592–5.   [120] Ibid. 595–605.

Shoring up Sterling

Convertibility did not solve sterling's problems. During the 1960s they became more difficult as Britain's international accounts deteriorated—but that trend was frequently overestimated in the first publication of official figures (and it has become far less marked in subsequent revisions of that data). It would now appear that over the decade (1960–9) the deficit on the current account averaged £49m., equivalent to just under 1 per cent of GNP.

Sterling's *de facto* convertibility from 27 December 1958 was joined in May 1961 by *de jure* convertibility under Article VIII of the Bretton Woods Agreement, but sterling encountered a series of crises—1961, 1964, 1966, and 1967—which led to 'stops' being introduced as the opposite phase to the British government's economic policy of 'go'. These 'stops' between 1958 and 1966 involved the British authorities applying 'every technique and tool' that the OECD Working Party 3 was to recommend for establishing an external equilibrium.[121] Britain's problems over the 1960s, in comparison with other major industrial countries, consisted of a combination of slower economic growth and a higher underlying rate of inflation.

During the 1960s there was one new global monetary factor. The world dollar shortage, which had been evident since 1918 and extreme since 1945, suddenly came to an end in 1958. However, the United States continued to have a visible trade surplus until 1972, and the main causes of the fall in the American gold reserve from 1958 were, in declining order of importance, American corporate overseas investment, other private transfers, and United States government expenditure abroad. Consequently the world economy of the 1960s had the problem that both the major key currencies—the dollar and sterling (which was still used to finance approximately 27 per cent of world trade in the early 1960s)—were becoming progressively weaker and, in their decline until the early 1970s, sterling may well have been the 'fall guy' for the dollar. As a result, in these terms, the experience of sterling was closely intertwined with that of the dollar. Certainly Washington took this view so that, unlike the experience of most of the 1950s, the British authorities could generally rely on American support during the sterling crises of the 1960s.

The relationship between the Bank of England and sterling during the 1960s has necessarily to be viewed from a different perspective. Current histories of the Bank finish their consideration in 1958, whereas the '30 year

---

[121] Bordo, 'Bretton Woods', 52–4. The General Agreement to Borrow led to regular meetings of finance ministers and central-bank governors from the 'group of 10' countries. The personnel involved almost exactly coincided with the composition of W[orking] P[arty] 3 of the Economic Policy Committee of the OECD on balance of payments disequilibria, the report of which was published in 1966.

rule' means that public papers and the Bank's own archive are generally not available for much of this period. Consequently, a view from the windows of Threadneedle Street towards either the City or Whitehall is necessarily barred, and all that is available is the odd snatched glimpse from pavement into the Bank. Therefore, the treatment in this last section of the review of the Bank's international dimension is necessarily very different from those that have preceded it.

The first challenge to the Bretton Woods system came in the autumn of 1960, when the international monetary system planned in 1944 had only been fully operational for barely 21 months. A currency confidence crisis, induced by devaluation fears that largely centred on the dollar against gold, led to the so-called 'gold rush' of October 1960, which pushed up the price of gold from \$35.20 per ounce to \$40 on the London free market. This increased the pressure on the dollar, which had already arisen from European central banks switching their reserve holdings from dollars to gold. On 20 October the United States Treasury publicly denied any intention to devalue the dollar, and this statement was coupled with an agreement between the New York Fed and European central banks for 'effective monetary control, with particular reference to the price of gold'. In the short term, speculative gold purchases were offset by the United States Treasury supplying the Bank of England with sufficient gold to maintain its price close to the official rate of \$35. This measure was augmented by the monetary authorities of six European countries joining Anglo-American collaborative action through deciding that they would not buy gold if the price was above \$35.20 per ounce. These understandings led to the formation of the London gold-pool, which was announced officially in November 1961 as a measure to peg the price of gold at \$35. This institution stabilized the dollar against gold at its 1935 price until the aftermath of the devaluation of sterling in 1967. However, during the 1960s the American monetary gold stock continued to decline because central banks replenished their own gold holdings through exchanging dollars for gold with the United States Treasury. The relationship between the dollar and gold also came under pressure because of the policies pursued by France from 1965 under the direction of de Gaulle and Rueff and which, for instance, led to France leaving the gold-pool in June 1967. Consequently, the Bank of England, through the London gold-pool arrangements, was a net seller of gold from 1966. The growing weakness of the dollar was similarly not reversed by restrictions imposed in 1964 on American investment abroad.[122]

The London gold market had barely been stabilized before sterling came under pressure in the spring of 1961, arising from market-induced German

---

[122] Tew, *Monetary System*, 102–5; W. M. Scammell, *International Monetary Policy: Bretton Woods and after* (1975), 179–80; Bordo, 'Bretton Woods', 69.

and Dutch revaluations on 4 and 6 March. To some degree it was a repeat for sterling of the experience of 1957, though then it was a franc devaluation and an anticipated revaluation of the Deutschmark that were responsible. London, in its determination to maintain sterling's parity, and backed by comparable American resolve, met the situation through European central bank co-operation providing swap facilities of a similar kind to those which had been discussed during the spring of 1955 in the preparations for the European Monetary Agreement.[123] To deal with the speculative movements on the foreign-exchange markets of spring 1961, three-month swaps, or credits, were agreed through the forum of the BIS at Basle. As a result sterling was supported by a £325m. facility which ran between March and July. Publicity was given to these arrangements from the start through central bank governors collectively stating that rumours of further parity changes were unfounded and that there would be collaboration between eight central banks to that effect.[124] However, the sterling crisis was only overcome by the British government's introduction of severe deflationary measures on 25 July 1961, coupled with a drawing of £536m. (in Belgian francs, French francs, Deutschmarks, guilders, lire, Swedish kronor, and yen, as well as Canadian and United States dollars), and a stand-by credit of £179m. from the IMF. The Fund's support for sterling replaced the Basle credit and was, in turn, repaid by August 1962, although the stand-by was retained by the British authorities. Britain, through the Bank of England, once more had recourse to facilities arranged through Basle in February and March 1963, and they were to feature again during subsequent sterling crises of the decade.[125] In parallel, IMF one-year stand-by facilities were agreed, and these were renewed in July 1964. Swap arrangements were also further developed, with a reciprocal facility of $50m. between the Bank and the Federal Reserve Bank of New York being established in May 1962; this was then developed to the extent that it totalled $2bn. by late 1968.[126]

The British current balance deteriorated substantially and, even more importantly, erratically during the mid-1960s. To the problems that this gave rise to for sustaining sterling at $2.80 was added the expectation that the first act of the Labour government, elected in October 1964, would be devaluation. This seemed a very likely reaction to the mounting monthly trade deficits recorded from the beginning of the year. Actually the new Labour government, especially the Prime Minister, Harold Wilson, with his personal memories of 1947 and 1949, was staunchly opposed to even contemplating devaluation. This was a political decision shaped by history and

[123] Fforde, *Bank*, 531–2.
[124] 'The Overseas Work of the Bank of England', *Bank of England Quarterly Bulletin*, 7 (1967).
[125] Tew, *Monetary System*, 121–3; Scammell, *International Monetary Policy*, 173–5.
[126] 'The Exchange Equalisation Account', *Bank of England Quarterly Bulletin*, 8 (1968).

experience of it since 1931, and the new Cabinet paid little heed to briefs, of whatever stance, from the Bank and the Treasury regarding sterling.

Initial political intents were challenged within a month by a mishandled increase in Bank rate to 7 per cent, but the need for a political considera- tion of devaluation was removed from the table of 10 Downing Street by the Bank obtaining $3bn. of international support for sterling, initially from the Federal Reserve and the Bundesbank, to add to its current Basle swap network facilities of $1bn. The reserves were subsequently bolstered by the use of these swaps dating from 1963 and 1964, and by the Bank's new arrangements of November. Furthermore, the IMF agreed on 2 December to a request from Britain to draw on the whole of the stand-by of $1bn. Market speculation against sterling, which had led to a fall of nearly £350m. in overseas holdings, was stopped, and the deployed autumn credits were funded through the United Kingdom making a large drawing on the General Agreement to Borrow. This facility had been developed in September 1961 through the Group of Ten, supplementing the IMF's now meagre resources by supplying, initially, $6bn. It became operative in October 1962 when it was anticipated that it would be largely used by either Britain or the United States.[127]

Despite the complex support operations that the Bank deployed during the winter of 1964, market pressure on sterling continued until the spring of 1965. Devaluation being anathema, the government imposed trade con- trols in the form of import surcharges and export bounties, measures which provoked a storm of international protest. The concurrent tightening of exchange-control measures appears to have had little general effect upon the reserves. Sterling was to be continually buffeted until its devaluation in November 1967, but the Bank of England attempted to hold the market through relieving 'the pressure on the spot [rate] by forward dealings'. These were to be on a very substantial scale and consequently far greater than had been resorted to during the 1950s.[128]

As in 1949, but reigning over a longer period, there was a growing con- sensus that sterling would be devalued, in part formed by international scepticism over the effectiveness of the British government's economic pol- icy. Consequently, sterling remained weak and its market position was frag- ile. Sterling sales reached crisis proportions by mid-July 1965, with important consequences for the reserves. A summer mini-budget failed to change sentiment and there was a further major run on the pound during August. International support for sterling, organized by Washington, was announced on 21 September; it was supplied by Europe (although not France) and North America, with the IMF contributing 1,400m. SDR. This proved sufficient to hold the situation until February 1966.[129]

---

[127] Cairncross and Eichengreen, *Sterling*, 156–70; Tew, *Monetary System*, 116–18; Scammell, *International Monetary Policy*, 175.
[128] Cairncross and Eichengreen, *Sterling*, 184–5.   [129] Ibid. 176–8.

By the time of a yet further sterling crisis during the summer of 1966, opinion within the Cabinet was changing. Brown was now openly in favour of devaluation, while a group of ministers was attracted by the option of floating sterling. The need for radical views was underscored by the rapid deterioration of the monthly trade figures within an international context of rising interest rates. A seamen's strike acted as the catalyst, but once more sterling received international institutional support. Basle group arrangements were made in June 1966, which were to be twice renewed— in March 1967 and March 1968—and ran until 1971. They provided swap facilities to contain reductions in Britain's reserves arising from fluctuations in overseas sterling balances, as measured against a spring 1966 base.[130] However, this central banking co-operation was insufficient to underpin confidence in sterling, which was affected not only by the publication of British economic data but also by political turbulence.

Political responses to the crisis of summer 1966 were slow and drawn out and Bank rate was not raised to 7 per cent until 14 July. However, resignations from the Cabinet and leaks of different ministers' views acted to destabilize the markets further. The Cabinet was divided over further deflation, especially cuts in public expenditure, and the extent of the disagreements included the Chancellor joining the ministerial group favouring devaluation. It was the force of the Prime Minister which convinced the Cabinet to keep to its existing course regarding sterling, while Wilson for his part took the responsibility of announcing the cuts to the House.[131] During the winter 1966/7 the balance of payments improved, but unemployment mounted and it was this factor which shaped the budget of 1967.

Sterling weakened again during the summer of 1967, due to a range of factors. Bank rate was reduced, cutting the return on international holdings of sterling. The expectation of a devaluation was reinforced by the announcement in May of Britain's intention to join the EEC. It was thought that this would have very adverse effects upon Britain's balance of payments so that entry into Europe would be accompanied by devaluation. Further pressure on sterling arose from the Six Day War, the associated closure of the Suez canal, and the consequent implications for the price of oil and oil imports. The British government, however, was more concerned with combating a domestic recession and consequently introduced reflationary measures from 7 June. Furthermore, the export drive ran into the barrier of a three-month dock strike which commenced in September.

The reserves fell from May onwards, but on this occasion it seemed unlikely that sterling would receive further international institutional support. This did indeed prove to be the case, as another major Basle operation was abortive. All that came in its place was some limited assistance from the major Swiss commercial banks and from the BIS itself, the latter

[130] Tew, *Monetary System*, 123–4.
[131] Cairncross and Eichengreen, *Sterling*, 179–81.

refinancing an IMF repayment due in December. This proved ineffectual, as did two increases of Bank rate on 19 October and 9 November 1967. By 4 November, with public European statements referring directly or indirectly to a sterling devaluation, the Prime Minister and the Chancellor began to accept what they had previously stood steadfastly against in public. The Chancellor preferred the option of floating, whereas Wilson was concerned that a devaluation of sterling would trigger comparable action along the western edge of the Pacific rim and in Europe. General political agreement to devalue to $2.40 was only reached by 15 November, and even then with considerable reluctance. The Prime Minister's anxiety over the international ramifications proved to be justified, as within Europe Denmark, Ireland, and Spain devalued, as did Ceylon and New Zealand and a number of former British possessions.

Devaluation was nearly avoided by last-minute American attempts to amass a further major international facility to back sterling, but this received little European support. The grudging acceptance by the British Cabinet of devaluation had the result that officially prepared contingency plans could not go smoothly into action. The IMF only received one hour's notice of Britain's intention, and devaluation took place without the support of a stand-by. Subsequent negotiations provided a stand-by of $1.4bn., while central bank co-operation generated another $1.6bn.[132]

Sterling's problems on the exchange markets remained unresolved by the November 1967 devaluation, so much so that the decline in the reserves forced a further round of international borrowing. Sterling also proved to be the fall guy for the dollar. Pressure on sterling during the autumn 1967 had been accompanied by a wave of speculative transactions on the London gold market—in reality against the dollar, now the key currency, and regarded as being overvalued against gold—which peaked in March 1968. This experience led to the closure of the London gold market during the latter part of March 1968 after losses of $2.75bn., while the central banks involved in the gold-pool decided to halt open gold sales. From spring 1968 central banks only sold gold to one another as a reserve asset and $35 per ounce became the price of gold as a monetary asset.[133]

Britain's balance of trade, and with it sterling, only began to improve from late 1968, which followed on from government cuts announced in January and a deflationary spring budget. These measures were reinforced by further deflation in November following an exchange crisis that focused on the franc.[134] Before the improvement of the British trade accounts, further measures were taken to deal with remaining sterling balances. Following six months of discussions initiated by the Bank of England, in September 1968 a second Basle agreement was announced which, through

[132] Cairncross and Eichengreen, *Sterling*, 186–91.
[133] Tew, *Monetary System*, 109–11; Scammell, *International Monetary Policy*, 180.
[134] Cairncross and Eichengreen, *Sterling*, 194–5.

renewal, ran until September 1973. It involved the provision of $2bn. through the BIS, most of which had been repaid by mid-1969. The aim of this support for sterling was to deal with fluctuations in overseas officially and privately held sterling balances below an agreed base of £3,080m. A dollar value guarantee was given by the United Kingdom for the larger part of these balances, while official holders of sterling for their part were to continue to hold sterling as part of their reserves. Furthermore, sterling balance holders were encouraged to place a proportion of their non-sterling holdings with the BIS as representative of the Basle 'club'. The United Kingdom drew $600m. to finance earlier reductions.[135] Although the Basle Agreement of 1968 was intended by the British authorities to sustain sterling as a reserve asset, in practice its nature marked the end of the Sterling Area. None the less, the Basle agreement provided a control rod for confidence to the extent that overseas official holdings of sterling rose from £1.5bn. in mid-1968 to £2.7bn. by the close of 1971.

International monetary turbulence continued on into 1969 and remained centred on European currencies. The closure of the gold-pool was followed by market expectations that the franc would be devalued and the Deutschmark revalued. The extent of this pressure forced the closure of the European exchange markets for a week after 20 November. Again, during spring 1969 there were comparable speculative transactions which affected sterling. Even after the devaluation of the franc in August 1969, pressure on sterling persisted, until in the autumn the Deutschmark was allowed to appreciate before finally being officially revalued in October.

The two-tier gold market that followed the closure of the London gold-pool, if not sterling's second devaluation, marked the beginning of the end of the Bretton Woods system. In the midst of the March 1968 gold rush the United States removed the 25 per cent gold requirement against Federal Reserve notes, whilst, with the closure of the gold-pool, the world was now on a *de facto* dollar standard.[136] But the world flood of dollars, the rising tide since 1958, meant that there was now little confidence in the dollar, a stance which was given a political edge by substantial opposition to American policy in South-East Asia. A retreat of the dollar flood, with the United States recording international surpluses on a reserve transaction basis during 1968 and 1969, proved to be temporary; it arose from a technicality connected with the recycling of Eurodollars. The dollar flood resumed with a marked deterioration in the American balance of trade so that the balance of payments deficit in 1970 was a staggering $9.8bn. The result was mounting speculation against the dollar, largely consisting of switches into the Deutschmark (but also from the franc to the Deutschmark), to the extent that on 5 May 1971 the German authorities allowed the Deutschmark to float.

[135] 'Overseas Sterling Balances 1963–1973', *Bank of England Quarterly Bulletin*, 14 (1974).
[136] Bordo, 'Bretton Woods', 70, 72.

The fixed presidential electoral cycle of the United States forced Nixon to take radical action in August 1971. The Bretton Woods era was finally ended by the closure of the 'gold window' at the United States Treasury, so drawing the curtain across the full convertibility phase which had reigned since the beginning of 1959. This was coupled with a devaluation of the dollar against gold by 8 per cent, which the market had twice previously attempted to force during the turbulent 1960s. However, the Nixon measures to improve the American balance of payments through a 10 per cent import surcharge, backing up threats of a world trade war, forced a responsiveness to a request for a world currency realignment against the dollar. This produced the Smithsonian Agreement of 1971, which encompassed a devaluation of the dollar (including a further change against gold of 8.5 per cent) and a compact for a return to fixed exchange rates. However, the Smithsonian Agreement was only to last 15 months and fresh sterling problems played a part in limiting its lifespan.

During the late 1960s the British balance of payments problem seemed to have been cured by the 1967 devaluation of sterling to $2.40, and current account surpluses were recorded in mid-1970 and mid-1971. Thereafter the pattern was disturbed by industrial unrest, especially the miners' strike, resulting power-cuts, and a dock strike in July 1972. These all led to growing pessimism regarding the future development of the British balance of payments, notwithstanding that published data indicated an overall surplus of £300m. for 1972 on an annual basis. The first intimation of the dock strike on 15 June 1972 reawakened fears of a further sterling devaluation, which led to an outward flow of funds. All the signs of preparation for a sterling devaluation were apparent, with overseas borrowing of sterling from British banks and leads and lags in the payments for imports and exports. Sterling had entered the European 'snake' in May, and received intervention support, which by 22 June totalled £1,001m., undertaken by the Bank of England with five other central banks. This ceased on 23 June and the London exchange market was closed until 27 June.[137] The size of flows across the exchanges during mid-June and their rapidity heralded the exchange turmoil which has come to be characteristic of recent decades.

Initially, sterling's float was officially regarded as a temporary measure, but by the end of July 1972 sterling had already moved by 6¾ per cent from its agreed Smithsonian parity and the extent of subsequent fluctuations reactivated use of the Exchange Equalisation Account from mid-1973. The inception of the float was accompanied by an extension of exchange controls to the Sterling Area. Only twelve countries decided to peg their currencies so as to allow them to float with sterling, and in the case of South Africa this decision lasted for only four months. The floating of sterling from mid-1972 accelerated the trend, begun with the 1967 devaluation,

---

[137] 'Commentary', *Bank of England Quarterly Bulletin*, 12 (1972), 303–26.

towards independently managed currencies and diversification away from sterling in reserve holdings. The share of sterling in world reserves fell over the post-war period from 20 per cent in the mid-1940s to 10 per cent by the early 1960s, and then to about 5 per cent by 1973. This decline in sterling's share was particularly marked during 1967 and 1968, although during this period it was also affected by the burgeoning United States balance of payments deficit. By 1972 there were indications that the Deutschmark may well have replaced sterling as the second most important reserve currency.[138]

The Norman Bequest

International central banking, as that term is now understood, was largely a creation of Governor Norman, who personally linked the late nineteenth-century world of Anglo-American merchant banking with the European, and then world, financial diplomacy of the mid-twentieth century. His lifetime's experience witnessed the decline of sterling from its global apogee and a significant change in the Bank's custody of sterling. Two world wars, and especially the second, greatly and gravely changed Britain's international financial position. War finance and then policies for resolving sterling's continuing international role brought Westminster and Whitehall to the fore. From 1933 the Bank increasingly became the day-to-day manager of sterling and an alternative source of official advice regarding sterling. Equally, from 1932 government domestic policies meant that there was a very different context to discussions, either domestic or international, over sterling's international role. From 1944 the international institutional environment was also greatly changed.

Opportunities for international central banking only really became available again from 1958 with European convertibility. Until 1958 the Bank had attempted to nurture sterling's international role, but frequently decisions were forced by crisis. Only in 1958 was the Bank able to catch the tide of opportunity. Thereafter central bank co-operation through Basle, a forum that Norman had valued highly, was repeatedly used to assist the British government in its designs for sterling. An epoch had ended in 1931, whereas an era closed in 1972. However, the fortunes of the City, in which the Bank stands at the centre, and of sterling had drifted apart during the mid-twentieth century. In 1972 the City was as international as it had been in 1694, although now populated by a growing multitude of banks from all over the world rather than merchants and financiers attracted from Europe.

[138] 'Overseas Sterling Balances'.

5 The Bank of England and Central Bank Co-operation 1970–1994

ROBERT PRINGLE

THE modern era of central bank co-operation began in 1961, with the first in a series of bilateral arrangements that were to lead to a large 'swap' network of mutual credit lines among major central banks. The purpose of the arrangements, initiated by the US Treasury and taken over the following year by the Federal Reserve Bank of New York, was to defend the dollar, which had come under attack in the foreign exchange markets for the first time since World War II. The swaps made foreign currencies available to the United States to finance intervention in the foreign exchange market. The first was between the New York Fed and the Bank of France; the Fed agreed to pay $50m. into the account of the Bank of France in New York against payment of an equivalent sum (245m. frs.) by the Bank of France to the account of the Fed in Paris. This resulted in an increase in the foreign reserves at the disposal of both countries at the stroke of a pen. Swap credits were later used extensively by other countries, notably Britain. They were very flexible and short term; unless renewed, the swaps were unwound at the end of three months at the same exchange rate, eliminating exchange risk. They survived the move to floating rates. By 1994 the New York Fed had swap facilities totalling $30bn. with fourteen central banks and the Bank for International Settlements.

These credits were a continuation, in modern guise, of the practice under the gold standard whereby central banks occasionally (if somewhat reluctantly) borrowed gold from each other at times of strain. The Bank of England arranged a credit with the Bank of France in 1836–9, and in the Baring crisis in 1890 Lidderdale arranged gold loans of £3m. from the Bank of France and £1.5m. from the State Bank of Russia.

Central Banks' Defences Overwhelmed

In the Bretton Woods system, as in the gold standard days, the purpose of central banking co-operation was to hold the international monetary sys-

A version of this article first appeared in *Central Banking*, 5/3, winter 1994–5.

tem together. According to central bankers like Gerald Corrigan, President of the New York Fed from 1985 to 1993, central bank co-operation was the key to the preservation of the Bretton Woods system in the 1960s. But swaps were only one of the means used to paper over the cracks; another was the gold-pool. Meeting in Basle in 1961, central banks agreed to try to stabilize the gold price in the market around its official $35 parity by making $270m. worth of gold available for open-market operations by the Bank of England. There were no written rules, and officials denied there was even a gentlemen's agreement (asked about it, the French Minister of Finance, Wilfrid Baumgartner, said 'Il n'y a jamais eu de gentlemen's agreement de Bâle, mais il n'y a à Bâle que des gentlemen'.[1]) The pool worked well for a period, but France itself withdrew in 1967 and the sterling devaluation of that year triggered a large demand for gold. After March 1968, gold was left to find its own price.

Certainly, the period illustrated the limits to central bank collaboration: neither mutual credit lines nor attempts to fix the gold price could prevent the system from falling apart. As persistent inflation in the United States eroded America's competitive position and confidence in the dollar in the late 1960s, so European central banks and governments grew increasingly reluctant to absorb surplus dollars. Some, such as France, regarded the system as giving unfair privileges to the United States by allowing it to sustain a large capital outflow—using surplus dollars to buy up French and other European companies. President de Gaulle indeed sounded the death-knell of Bretton Woods as early as 1965: 'Nous tenons donc pour nécessaire que les échanges internationaux s'établissent, comme c'était le cas avant les grands malheurs du monde, sur une base monétaire indiscutable et qui ne porte la marque d'aucun pays en particulier'. 'Pour toutes ces raisons, la France préconise que le système soit changé'. And France was in a position to enforce change: it had large dollar balances which it could present to America for conversion into gold. Such conversions, allowed under the rules of the system, threatened to bring the system down since nobody expected that America would allow its gold stock to be depleted: as the alternative of devaluing the dollar against gold and all other currencies had been ruled out, it would have to suspend convertibility of dollars into gold, as President Nixon eventually did in August 1971. Central bank co-operation can do little against such strong economic or political forces.

But central bankers have a remarkable facility for snatching victory from the jaws of defeat—and for adjusting their convictions to the needs of the time. Having to a man defended the fixed exchange-rate system until it collapsed, they soon learnt to live with the regime of floating rates. It certainly served their institutional interests. For the advent of flexible rates paved the

---

[1] Quoted in Fred Hirsch, *Money International* (London, 1967).

way for the new era of central banking, by making independent national monetary policy feasible. True, they made a mess of the transition. Under pressure from the oil crisis and governments' demands for economic growth, central banks followed inflationary policies during the 1970s. The Bank of England, under the governorships of Leslie O'Brien (Lord O'Brien) and Gordon Richardson (Lord Richardson), was no exception—indeed, UK monetary policies were even more inflationary than those of most other countries. But central bankers could blame the resulting inflation on governments—at the time only the Bundesbank and the Fed had any degree of policy autonomy. So by the time that the public was ready for a return to monetary stability, in the 1980s, governments had become discredited; it was only natural that central bankers should step into the breach.

One clear success of central bank co-operation during this period was in the arrangements made to wind down sterling's role as an official reserve currency. This role had undoubtedly been at the centre of the concerns of the Bank of England since the war—as any reader of John Fforde's recent history will be aware. Yet the role had come to be criticized at home for leaving the economy too vulnerable to sudden speculative attacks on the currency (the argument being that private holders were made nervous about sterling by fear that official holders might demand conversion into dollars at times of strain).

Sterling also proved a stumbling-block to Britain's entry into the European Community. French presidents, including de Gaulle and Pompidou, took a quite remarkable interest in this somewhat arcane subject. They said that sterling's world role could cause tensions when (or if) Britain entered the Common Market. At Basle, central bankers had put together various credit packages to support sterling during the 1960s. But the Bank of England was forced to offer dollar guarantees on a high proportion of the holdings, and France refused to join in co-operative efforts to shore up sterling. It is not clear when the Bank became reconciled to the end of sterling's role, but the sterling devaluation of 1967 persuaded many Sterling Area countries of the need to diversify their reserves, and several wanted to hold the bulk of their reserves in dollars. Thus political and financial imperatives pointed in the same direction; in 1977 a final Basle credit arrangement was concluded to assist the UK in winding down the sterling balances (this role later staged a limited comeback but that is another story).

The Hazards of Prudential Supervision

In the mean time, the financial instability that accompanied the breakdown of the fixed-rate system provided fertile ground for the extension of central bank co-operation in another field—banking supervision. The 1973–8 period saw the Herstatt failure in Germany, an event which had far-reaching implications for supervisors; the real estate investment trust débâcle in America; the failure of the Franklin National Bank; the secondary banking crisis in Britain; and severe problems at the Japanese securities houses. The financial markets were developing rapidly and central bankers had to be concerned with the broad stability of the system. This led in the mid-1970s to the setting up under the Bank of England's man, George Blunden, of a committee at the Bank for International Settlements to co-ordinate prudential supervision. From this small beginning there developed over the next 20 years a massive structure of international banking supervision. Throughout, the Bank of England played a leading role—especially, for instance, in forcing through an agreement on capital adequacy in 1986. (In this case agreement was reached first on a bilateral basis between the Bank of England and the Federal Reserve, and then sold to other central banks, beginning with the Bank of Japan; following that, the others joined in the process which became known as 'the Basle Accord').

But supervision proved even more hazardous ground than monetary policy. Inevitably, if misguidedly, the public and some politicians expected central bankers to prevent bank failures. In the event, the rate of bank failures and near-failures increased in many countries and bank supervisors were all too often forced onto the defensive. Try as they might to remind the public that their job was not to prevent individual banks from failing but only to preserve systemic stability, it was inevitable that they should get blamed whenever a big bank failed, as seemed to happen with distressing frequency, especially in the United States.

The Bank of England, having enjoyed an enviable reputation as the world's best banking regulator (the informal methods traditionally used seeming to be just as effective as the more legalistic systems in Continental Europe and America), then came unstuck with BCCI, the world's biggest and most scandalous financial collapse ever. The facts that the Bank was not responsible for supervising BCCI world-wide (that should have been done by the Luxemburg authorities), and that in 1991 it moved quickly to close the bank once there was clear evidence of fraud, failed to impress. Critics pointed out that BCCI had been effectively run out of London, it had perpetrated fraud on a large scale over a prolonged period (possibly ever since it was founded), and that the Bank, which had harboured suspicions about BCCI almost from the time it set up in London in the 1970s, should have made it its business to find out what was going on. The Bank of England suffered a large dent to its reputation—and so did central banking co-operation, which had so obviously failed in this instance.

Recycling and the Debt Crisis

Some informed critics also charge central banks with having fallen down over the recycling of surplus funds owned by oil-producing countries in the 1970s. Conrad Oort claims that central banks made fatal mistakes, not in their monetary policy role but as supervisors and guardians of the monetary system. Oort is no mere armchair critic: he has been the top civil servant at the Netherlands Finance Ministry, chairman of the Monetary Committee of the EC, half of whose members are central banks, and a long-serving director of a leading Dutch bank. Oort argues that unrestrained bank lending of surplus oil money to non-oil developing countries was a major cause of the crisis, since it prevented the Third World countries from adjusting to the reality of a much higher oil price. Oort recognises that central banks did not have the authority to restrict lending through the Euromarkets (though they did agree to restrict the redepositing of official reserves in the Euromarkets). However, he argues that, as supervisors, 'they could and should have prevented' the build-up of doubtful loans on the books of the banks. 'Central banks must have been fully aware of the impending disaster long before the private markets collapsed after the Mexican default in 1982'.[2]

This is like accusing a train driver of deliberately crashing into the back of another train. In reality, central banks and everybody else were working in a fog. They did not know what the effects of the 1973–4 oil-price hike would be, how large the cumulative OPEC surplus would be, how much the commercial banks would lend or how much oil-importing countries could or should borrow.

The whole tenor of public debate was that the OPEC surplus had to be recycled at all costs, since it was manifestly unfair—and could be politically dangerous—to expect oil-importing countries to adjust immediately. The only way of doing this would have been by synchronized and savage global deflation—at least, that was the view accepted at the time by many governments, including the Labour Chancellor Denis Healey.

Central banks did try to peer through the fog: they started to collate the statistics needed, to analyse the capacity of the banking system to shoulder the burden, and the capacity of the oil-importing countries to service the debt. The Bank of England's efforts in this field were led by Kit McMahon, Executive Director and later Deputy Governor. There was a big argument about whether official institutions such as the IMF should do more, but governments would not agree to more than some quite small expansion in their lending role—after all, the IMF is not supposed to function as a financial intermediary but merely as a revolving fund.

---

[2] See Conrad Oort, 'A Post-Mortem on the Debt Crisis', in A. F. P. Bakker *et al.* (eds.), *Monetary Stability through International Cooperation. Essays in Honour of André Szasz* (Dordrecht, 1994), 353–73.

So the job was left to the markets, which thereby filled a policy vacuum as well as a financing gap. Of course, the allocation of resources by the markets was in no sense economically optimal—far too much went on current consumption rather than investment. However, this was a time when economists were growing increasingly sceptical of the claims of governments to be able to plan or allocate resources—and there was a willingness to try out the markets, almost as an experiment. When the second oil price shock came in 1979, again there was no option but to leave the recycling to the markets, despite the fact that major debtor countries had much higher levels of indebtedness and debt-service ratios (e.g. debt service as a percentage of export earnings) than in the mid-1970s, and despite the fact that banking creditors had much higher concentrations of lending (the bulk being to Brazil, Mexico, South Korea, and the Philippines).

Still, the question discussed at international financial conferences was not, how do we stop banks from lending? It was, how can we assist them to lend even more? Driven by normal competitive pressures, and official encouragement, commercial bankers complied. To reduce risk they relied partly on portfolio diversification, and partly on the expectation that the United States would assist large debtor countries (and thus their bankers) in a crisis and that Germany would protect the interests of its bankers in Eastern Europe (this was known as the 'umbrella theory'), although no OECD government actually gave such assurances. And rescheduling was already an established practice—bankers viewed it as quite normal that a growing economy should have rising levels of indebtedness, and that the credits would from time to time have to be refinanced. Even on the eve of the crisis, in June 1982, the central bankers' club was in two minds: in its annual report, the BIS on the one hand urged stricter prudential guidelines on banks; on the other, it warned that banks' 'growing caution' over Third World lending might extend 'too widely and too indiscriminately to whole groups of countries'.

Indeed, it might all have worked out if it had not been for two further shocks: the sudden change in the entire approach to monetary policy adopted by the Federal Reserve under Paul Volcker's leadership at the end of 1979 (involving the targeting of the money supply and much wider fluctuations in interest rates); and the deflation in the OECD countries in 1980-2. The rapid rise in dollar interest rates in 1980-1 hit economies already burdened with huge dollar-denominated debts, while the slump in the OECD countries tore a large hole in their export earnings. With lower export earnings and higher interest payments, imports had to be cut savagely. But this could not be done quickly enough; so countries suspended interest payments. But central banking co-operation, led by Paul Volcker at the Federal Reserve and Gordon Richardson at the Bank of England, did prevent what could have been a severe threat to the international banking system when the crisis broke. Against oil as collateral and under the aegis of the BIS, the Group of Ten central banks and the Bank of Spain put together a bridging loan for Mexico of $1.85bn. including a contribution from the US Treasury, and the American government promised another $2bn. in advance payments for oil. Bankers' expectations that the big powers would act to prevent a banking crisis were in that sense proved right; the burden of adjustment was forced instead onto developing countries (though most of the banks eventually took large write-offs). At the official level, leadership in managing the debt work-out, involving tortuous negotiations between banks, creditor countries, and debtor countries, was then taken over by Jacques de Larosière, Managing Director of the International Monetary Fund, though central banks continued to be deeply involved.

It all took a long time. Not until 1994 was the World Bank ready to state that for the major debtors the debt crisis was more or less over. But long before then many of these very debtors were already experiencing the opposite problem, a tidal wave of incoming investment (a tide in which some observers were quick to discern seeds of another debt crisis). And these developing countries had found a new label—'emerging markets'—to go with their new credit-worthy status. But as in the 1970s, central banks of developed countries did not see it as their duty to warn or restrain the markets; and in the 1990s they had a new reason for inaction, for the flows consisted largely of portfolio and direct investment rather than bank loans. The default risk was carried by equity and bondholders, as in the nineteenth century. Whether history will judge this hands-off attitude to be wise is another matter.

Still Trying to Fix Currencies

The repercussions of Paul Volcker's 1979 decision to let interest rates rise to whatever levels were needed to bring inflation under control, and restore domestic and international confidence in the dollar, reverberated through the 1980s. In conjunction with the tax cuts and loose fiscal policies of the first Reagan administration of 1981–5, high US interest rates attracted a massive flow of funds and a dramatic appreciation of the dollar. By 1985 there was mounting concern about this 'overshooting' and in the spring, market sentiment began to turn against the dollar; nevertheless, finance ministers and central bank governors chose to give the dollar a downward push later that year. In September 1985, meeting at the Plaza Hotel, New York, they issued a press communiqué calling for 'some further orderly appreciation of the main non-dollar currencies against the dollar', and they followed up their words with $10bn. of market intervention.

It is doubtful whether this was helpful to the cause of exchange-rate stability. By the following year there was already anxiety about the dollar's rapid decline in the markets and by February 1987 the finance ministers and governors declared that their currencies were roughly at the right levels. At this Louvre meeting governments and central banks pledged themselves 'to cooperate closely to foster stability of exchange rates around current levels'. Subsequently many champions of the target-zone approach to exchange-rate management have proclaimed that the world then entered a new era, and that such target zones have existed ever since. This seems far-fetched. Certainly, none were made public, and although it may have been true that in 1987 there was a broad intention to keep exchange rates within a 5 per cent band of the then going rates of 153 yen and Dm 1.80 to the dollar, the margins were 'soft', as Volcker put it. An understatement: by 1994 the dollar had slumped to 96 yen and Dm 1.50.

Central bankers remain sceptical of the benefits of policy co-ordination. True, as a species, they instinctively favour stability—external as well as internal. For instance, the Bank of France is pledged to pursue both kinds of stability, and the French have always preferred the orderliness of stable rates (at the Louvre meeting they suggested setting reference exchange rates, but this was rejected by the others). However, central banks of surplus countries, notably Japan and Germany, fear that their ability to control monetary conditions domestically would be undermined by a commitment to hold the exchange rate at any predetermined level. Many fear that such a political process would be dominated by America and serve US interests (given the absence of agreement on an objective means of establishing equilibrium exchange rates). Thus when in 1994 the Bretton Woods Commission, an independent commission set up to consider the future of the IMF and World Bank, again floated the idea of a reform of the system based on target exchange-rate zones among the three leading currencies—dollar, yen, and Dm—the idea was flatly rejected by both Germany and Japan.

Proposals for a European central banking system were also worked out by central bankers—who saw the opportunity to win a larger measure of independence from politicians. For the proposals would be modelled on the independent Bundesbank. The Bank of England's Governor at the time, Robin Leigh-Pemberton (now Lord Kingsdown), had been a member of the Delors Committee, and went along with its proposals for European economic and monetary union, unpalatable though he knew this would be to the Prime Minister, Margaret Thatcher (now Lady Thatcher). But the ERM, supposed precursor to full EMU, proved to be yet another doomed attempt to fix currencies—an attempt that failed at considerable financial cost with the departure of sterling and the lira in September 1992 and the further collapse of August 1993. For the moment, central bankers had had enough. Those who wanted stable rates, like Denmark, Austria, France, Benelux, and Ireland, pegged to the Deutschmark. Those who wanted domestic monetary autonomy, like Britain, let their currency float. Rates among the three currency blocs were flexible.

The Crash of 1987

If the record of exchange-rate management and Third World debt is patchy, what will history make of Alan Greenspan's 'baptism of fire' in the stock-market crash of October 1987? Under his leadership, central bankers relaxed monetary policies and pumped liquidity into the system—showing, as they thought, that they had learnt the lessons of the 1929 stock market crash (after which they mistakenly tightened monetary policy).

Central bankers believe this response was fully justified. However, it carried two distinct dangers. First, moral hazard. It was prompted at least in part by a need to protect banks from the risks they were exposed to as a result of commitments to firms in the securities markets, and thus arguably signalled an unwarranted extension of the central banks' safety-net to another area of the financial system. Would central banks henceforth feel obliged to support stock markets whenever a fall in prices seemed to threaten financial stability? Secondly, there were risks for monetary policy and inflation. When should a central bank that has relaxed policy to counter a short-term threat tighten policy again? In 1987–8 it is widely agreed that Britain and Japan were among those who failed to regain their grip quickly enough, with resultant overheating in Britain and the 'bubble economy' in Japan. Certainly, the costs of that single episode of central bank co-operation were not negligible, though it is hard to argue with the view that Alan Greenspan's initial response was necessary to avert panic.

Co-operation with the New York Fed

Clearly the Bank of England saw where its duties lay. It followed its instincts—to keep close behind the Fed, the world's lender of last resort in a crisis. Indeed, there has long been a special relationship between the central banks that have offices in the world's two major financial centres. According to Gerald Corrigan, 'this historical relationship between the Fed and the Bank of England is unique'. That special relationship started with Montagu Norman and Benjamin Strong, who became Governor of the New York Fed in 1914, only a year after the Federal Reserve System was set up. It was new, just finding its way, whereas the Old Lady had run the gold standard for generations. But both central bankers were visionaries committed to the idea of central bank co-operation. Strong travelled the world to meet other central bankers, while Norman was the principal moving spirit behind the foundation of the Bank for International Settlements in 1930. Co-operation between the two banks revived in the 1950s and reached a high point during the 1980s, with the LDC debt crisis, the capital adequacy agreement of 1986, and the stock-market crash of 1987.[3]

[3] See 'Interview with E. Gerald Corrigan', *Central Banking*, 4/4 (Spring 1994), 25–30.

Forces Behind Central Bank Co-operation

So much for the story. What about the underlying causes of these attempts at closer co-operation? What can we learn from them about future prospects?

The intensification of central bank co-operation is a natural corollary of the continuing growth in the influence of external factors in shaping national monetary policies. Asked what the biggest single change had been in his job over the past 30 years, Erik Hoffmeyer, the veteran governor of the central bank of Denmark from 1965 to 1994, replied in one word: 'internationalization'. When he started as governor, economies were still largely closed—enabling even a small economy such as Denmark's to enjoy a degree of independence in monetary policy. But all that changed with the abolition of exchange controls over trade and capital movements and the deregulation during the 1970s and 1980s. In the early 1980s, after attempting to follow an independent policy for some years and experiencing rapid inflation and growing external and internal debt, Denmark decided to embark on a hard currency policy—in effect tying the kroner to the Deutschmark.

The success of that policy in stabilizing the economy, despite high initial costs, earned it full public support in Denmark. Exporters, knowing they have to remain competitive at the given exchange rate, have in fact maintained relative competitiveness with German companies. Economists at the central bank freely acknowledge that it is difficult to keep up with the Deutschmark (unlike the British tendency to fasten on weak points in the German performance), but point out that Danish exporters have controlled costs sufficiently to hold their share of markets and allow a strong recovery of the economy in 1992–4.

Another motive for increased central bank co-operation stems more directly from their role as guardians of the financial system: this is the increased risk of bank failure and the increased costs associated with such a failure. Many, perhaps most, central bankers agree that the risk of a failure has grown, as a result of increased competition following deregulation, the rapid growth of derivatives business, and the diminished role of banks in the financial system. This is what Andrew Crockett, General Manager of the BIS, had to say in a paper prepared when he was Executive Director of the Bank of England:

Banks have become highly competitive institutions. They have lost their earlier role as privileged intermediaries between depositors who were relatively insensitive to interest rate considerations and borrowers who were, in the main, of high creditworthiness. They have to compete in the market place for both assets and liabilities. A feature of competition in any industry is that less efficient producers make losses and are forced out of business.[4]

[4] Andrew Crockett, 'National Financial Liberalisation and International Economic Cooperation', in Bakker, *Monetary Stability*.

Yet, as Crockett goes on to say, bank failures are not the same as failures in other sectors of the economy. 'There is a much greater risk of contagion which, because of the central role of banks in the payments system, could have serious consequences for the economy as a whole'. An official response has therefore been needed to deal with the increased potential damage from bank failures in an innovative and deregulated environment. Given the international nature of financial activity, regulatory policies 'need to be effectively coordinated if they are to produce competitive equality along with systemic stability'.

Central banks are thus paying much attention to reducing risk in the payments system and to increasing the resilience of the banking system generally. On the payment system, most central banks agree that the world should move gradually towards a system where each payment is executed the moment the underlying transaction is made, and not at the end of the business day, as is generally the case at present. The main risk with end-of-day settlement is that a bank could fail during the day, freezing all its payments due to others during the day, risking knock-on effects on other banks and financial institutions. Under the preferred 'real-time gross-settlement' system, institutions making payments should be able to do so only when they have adequate funds at the settlement agent (usually the central bank) or they have adequate collateral to finance an overdraft. Gerald Corrigan has also cited the need to strengthen the payments system and risk-management systems in large internationally active financial institutions as a key area for further central bank collaboration. 'There is little doubt in my mind that a major problem or failure in one such institution can all too easily become the instrumentality through which a particular problem can take on a more generalized character'. Corrigan recognized that efforts needed in these areas are costly and unglamorous: 'Three yards and a cloud of dust about captures it'. But 'payments and settlements risk can be the killer'.

Central bank co-operation on these highly intricate and technical issues is essential because of the integration of the financial system. With different time-zones and the need to settle cross-border payments, rules governing payments procedures have to be agreed internationally. As central banks in most countries are responsible for the health of the payments system, and would be in the eye of the storm, they have every incentive to reach agreement on such rules and to ensure their financial institutions practise them. As the central bank of the country with one of the world's leading financial centres, the Bank of England will remain at the forefront of these discussions.

The Balance-Sheet

Central bank co-operation has a mixed record. It propped up the fixed exchange rate system but was powerless to prevent its eventual collapse. It failed to prevent the break-up of Bretton Woods. It did not prevent the spread of banking crises, which, at least until the 1990s, were steadily increasing in scale and the potential for loss. It failed to stop a fraudulent bank from operating with impunity in one of the world's major centres for 20 years. It failed to deliver exchange-rate stability. A cynic might say—as many academic critics have said—that it has even increased the danger of instability, by raising hopes on the part of financial market participants that they would be bailed out, and thus encouraging risk-taking behaviour.

And yet, the forces that produce efforts at co-operation are growing rather than diminishing. Thus, whatever the record, central bankers will go on trying. Perhaps a more favourable verdict is in order; co-operation has not stymied central banks' increasingly successful efforts to deliver price stability. Central bankers have been learning that co-operation is possible and desirable in some fields but not in others. They have learnt that they should not co-operate to fix currencies when that threatens price stability. Thus it is no accident that, by the mid-1990s, the world was nearer to achieving the goals of non-inflationary growth than at any previous time. Central banks may certainly take some of the credit for this.

6 The Bank of England and the City

RICHARD ROBERTS

'THE CITY' is a term with two meanings. Traditionally, it was an abbreviation for the City of London, the physical area of roughly one square mile that is the oldest inhabited part of the metropolis. Today the term is usually used as a shorthand collective term for the banking and other financial services which are the principal activities conducted in the square mile. It is in this latter functional sense that the relationship between the Bank and the City is discussed below. But a brief point about the physical dimension is a pertinent prologue.

Human settlement on the site of the City of London dates back at least as far as Roman times. In the sixteenth and seventeenth centuries the City of London was a thriving port, a commercial and mercantile centre, the site of some of London's principal produce markets, and the location of certain manufacturing activities. It was also a teeming residential neighbourhood. A mile or so to the west was the City of Westminster, a very different place that had grown up entirely separately from the City of London, although building in Holborn and the Strand in the sixteenth century made the two contiguous.[1] Westminster was the home of the royal court, the parliament, and national administration. The physical proximity of government had important consequences for the development of the financial functions of the City. After the Restoration the requirements of courtiers and parliamentarians for cash while in the capital had stimulated the development of private banking. The outcome of the desperate financial needs of the state in the 1690s, and the ability of the City to accommodate its demands, was the Bank of England.

Funding activities on behalf of the state were a vital stimulus to the development of the City's long-term and short-term financial markets. Once established, the capital market and the discount market developed other activities, further enhancing the City's role as a financial centre. In the twentieth century the Bank became involved with the foreign exchange, commodities, and equity markets too. It also provided banking services for its principal client, the government, and for the banking system as a whole. These markets and institutions, plus shipping services and insurance with

---

[1] Alfred James Henderson, *London and the National Government, 1721–1742: A Study of City Politics and the Walpole Administration* (Durham, NC., 1945), 12–13.

which the Bank had relatively little contact, comprised the core of the City's activities. Their complementary operations made the City the world's leading international financial centre, a status that the Bank helped to sustain. This essay explores in turn the relationship between the Bank and each of these dimensions of the City.

The Bank and the Gilt-edged and Discount Markets to 1914

The sale of monopolies was a familiar device for fund-raising by the state in sixteenth- and seventeenth-century England, especially when it was as financially hard-pressed as it was in the 1690s due to England's participation in the wars against Louis XIV. The promoters of the scheme promised a loan to the government of £1.2m.—perhaps £5bn. in today's money or, roughly speaking, the equivalent of the proceeds of the privatization of British Gas in 1986.[2] In return they received the privilege of forming the first and for well over a century the only joint-stock bank in England and Wales, which meant it had a much larger capital than any other bank. The new institution acted as banker to the government, making short-term advances to the Exchequer and other departments and holding deposits on their behalf and on behalf of officials such as collectors of customs and taxes. A few months after its formation it was given responsibility for handling remittances to the armed forces overseas. In 1707 it was appointed 'principal agent' for the issue and circulation of Exchequer bills, short-dated securities that were an important component of the nascent London money market.[3] In the two decades of war prior to the Treaty of Utrecht of 1714 the Bank made a vital contribution to English war finance, whose solvency was a key element in English victories in the field. The following quarter-century was an era of peace and relatively little pressure on the public purse, but from 1739 until 1815 Britain was repeatedly at war with only brief respites of peace. Naturally this put massive strain on the public finances and the Bank played an important role in ensuring that British government finances did not get into the lamentable state of those of its principal antagonist, France.

These years saw a significant shift in the pattern of public financing away from short-term borrowing to long-term indebtedness.[4] In the Nine Years War, 1688–97, over 70 per cent of the state's borrowings were short-term but in the War of the Austrian Succession, 1739–48, the proportion was 14 per cent; and in the Seven Years War, 1756–63, and the American War of

---

[2] Estimate based on calculations by Morgan and Thomas adjusted for inflation: E. Victor Morgan and W. A. Thomas, *The Stock Exchange: Its History and Functions* (1962), 16.

[3] Sir John Clapham, *The Bank of England: A History* (Cambridge, 1944), i, 59; P. G. M. Dickson, *The Financial Revolution in England* (1967), 373.

[4] John Brewer, *The Sinews of Power: War, Money and the English State, 1688–1783* (New York, 1988), 119.

Independence, 1776–83, it was less than 10 per cent. Each renewal of the Bank's charter was bought with an increase in the level of its loan to the government, which by the mid-1780s had increased tenfold. But in the same period the government's long-term indebtedness had grown 380-fold, increasing from £600,000 to £685m. between the first government bond issue of 1693 to the end of the French wars in 1815. These funds were raised by the sale of government bonds, tapping a broader and broader investor base. The issues were conducted by City financiers, known as loan contractors, who bid competitively for the contracts. The Bank played a role in the issuing process, but a minor one, participating in the distribution of the securities, assisting purchasers with advances, and advising the government on terms. However, it provided paying agency and debt management services for a larger and larger proportion of these securities, handling 70 per cent of this work by the 1760s and subsequently all of it.[5] The gilt-edged market was the corner-stone of the burgeoning London capital market and thereby the Bank was intimately involved in its development, though its part was less significant than in relation to the discount market or the banking system.

The century from the Battle of Waterloo to the outbreak of the First World War was generally speaking an era of *laissez-faire* government and balanced budgets, the national debt being smaller at the end of the period than at the beginning. This was despite substantial additions to borrowing to finance the Crimean War, the Boer War, and for other purposes such as the purchase of the Suez Canal Company and the compensation of West Indian slave-owners. By 1914 British government bonds, which in 1860 had constituted more than 50 per cent of the value of all securities quoted on the London Stock Exchange, amounted to only 5 per cent.[6] None the less, gilt-edged, notably Consols, were the largest homogeneous block of securities in the London market and played a vital role in the financial system as a whole, being uniquely liquid and low-risk assets that were a crucial component of bank balance-sheets and investors' portfolios. The Bank continued to act in a routine capacity as paying agent and manager of sinking fund and other operations. An important administrative reform that enhanced the liquidity of the gilt-edged market was the Bank's abolition in 1861 of the traditional quarterly 'shuttings' of the transfer book that periodically disrupted dealings. It also conducted, on behalf of the Treasury, various conversion operations, notably those of 1844 and 1888, though its contribution was described by Clapham as 'purely administrative'.[7] The loan contracting system was revived for the issue of new gilts during the Crimean War, 1853–6, but drawing upon the Bank's expertise as a safeguard against the exploitation of the government's desperate need for funds. The Governor was asked to indicate the minimum terms that he con-

[5] Clapham, *Bank*, i, 102–3.   [6] Morgan and Thomas, *Stock Exchange*, 113.
[7] Clapham, *Bank*, ii, 318.

sidered acceptable and the document was placed in a sealed envelope until tenders had been received. For one of the loans there was only one bidder, Rothschilds, and the terms offered failed to meet the governor's criteria. The Chancellor of the Exchequer refused to depart from the Bank's conditions, which were eventually accepted by Rothschilds.[8] The Bank itself conducted new issues on behalf of colonial governments and other public authorities. It took a leading if much criticized role in the organization of the issues to finance the Boer War, working with the merchant banks Morgan Grenfell, Barings, and Rothschilds in London, while J. P. Morgan & Co. acted as agent for the New York tranches.[9]

The Bank's relationship with the discount market in the nineteenth century and early twentieth century was multi-faceted, and it played a more direct and significant role in its development than it did in relation to the capital market. There were three dimensions to the relationship: the Bank's role as agent for the issue and management of short-term debt; its private discount business; and its provision of rediscount facilities to the discount houses. For short-term needs the government financed its requirements either by borrowing from the Bank or by issues of Exchequer bills that were handled by the Bank. From the 1830s Exchequer bills fell out of favour with banks and other investors, who were presented with a vastly increased range of securities superior to these 'peculiarly cumbersome' instruments.[10] The volume of Exchequer bill issues declined more or less continuously from a peak in 1818, petering out completely in the 1860s. In 1877 a new short-term instrument was introduced, the Treasury bill, devised on the advice of Walter Bagehot, editor of *The Economist*, to closely resemble a commercial bill of exchange. The initiative for this development was the Treasury's, but it was the Bank that sold them to the market. This re-established the Bank's contact with the money market through short-term government securities, but prior to the First World War the volume of Treasury bills in circulation was picayune relative to commercial bills and the Bank had more effective ways of exercising influence over the market.

A significant source of income for the Bank in the second half of the eighteenth century was the discounting of various sorts of paper: orders payable on behalf of officials of the army and navy; private individuals' promissory notes; and inland or foreign bills of exchange.[11] The Bank's conduct of this activity was part and parcel of its right of note issue, discounting being the principal way by which it put its notes into circulation. In order to secure the privilege of being able to discount at the Bank, firms had to have a Director's recommendation, to be located in London, and to

[8] Morgan and Thomas, *Stock Exchange*, 114.

[9] Kathleen Burk, *Morgan Grenfell 1838–1988: The Biography of a Merchant Bank* (Oxford, 1989), 111–23; Vincent P. Carosso, *Investment Banking in America: A History* (Cambridge, Mass., 1970), 510–13.

[10] Clapham, *Bank*, ii, 136.   [11] Ibid. i, 122.

be engaged in trade.[12] An analysis of the pattern of the Bank's discounts on 1 January 1800 undertaken by Clapham shows £3,246,000 outstanding on behalf of merchants in domestic trade, led by the linen and cotton merchants, tea dealers, grocers, and sugar refiners, and £2,961,000 for those engaged in foreign trade, first and foremost the West India interest and then merchants in the Irish, American, Russian, and Peninsular trades. Together they numbered 1,340 firms and Clapham comments that the analysis reveals 'the Bank's close contact with the whole commercial and industrial life of late eighteenth century London'.[13]

The 1790s and 1800s saw a dramatic upsurge in the volume of discounts, the Bank thus assuming an enhanced role in the financing of commerce in these decades. The reasons seem to have been three-fold: increased domestic demand for accommodation due to burgeoning industrial output; the foreign trade boom and the end of the foreign trade facilities traditionally provided by Amsterdam; and, following the suspension of convertibility in 1797, the liberal discounting policy adopted by the Bank, which was intended to induce public confidence. The volume of the Bank's discounts peaked in 1809–10 and declined markedly, if fitfully, over the following two decades. This reversal was due partly to less favourable business conditions but mostly to the rise of competition from commercial rivals. In 1821 the Bank struck back by relaxing its discounting rules to restore its competitiveness. The outcome was an unwitting creation of credit that fuelled the speculative boom which culminated in the financial crisis of 1825. Becoming concerned about the speculative fever the Bank ceased to discount, which precipitated a panic that was only relieved when it performed a volte-face and began to discount freely. In the wake of the crisis of 1825 it was determined that it was no longer appropriate for the Bank's discounting activities to be driven by considerations of private profit, and henceforth discounting became a matter of support for the money market. In order to make up for the resulting shortfall in the Bank's regular revenues it was authorized to open branches in the provinces, which it did with alacrity and highly profitably.

A new phase in the Bank's relationship with the money market opened in 1830, when for the first time bill brokers, the forerunners of the discount houses, were permitted to open 'discount accounts' with the Bank. This allowed these specialist dealers in bills of exchange to take bills of specified standards to the Bank and exchange them for Bank notes, thereby providing them with last resort facilities. This was one of a number of fundamental changes that were transforming the money market in the 1820s and 1830s: the establishment of the Bank of England provincial branches; the rise of joint-stock banking; the establishment of the 'call loan' system, whereby the commercial banks lent to the bill brokers; and the end of the

---

[12] Clapham, *Bank*, i, 205.   [13] Ibid. i, 208.

practice of rediscounting by the London private banks. The Bank's initiative of 1830 was a response to these developments, and was intended to provide an automatic device for the alleviation of the credit shortages that caused commercial crises. Providing bill brokers with the right to come to the Bank in times of credit stringency ensured not only that they could repay outstanding call loans, relieving pressure on the banks, but also pushed money into the economy at large through the discounting of bills for ordinary commercial purposes. 'The significance of the Bank's action in 1830 in allowing bill dealers' accounts to be opened', comments Scammell, the market's historian,

and thereby admitting its own role as lender of last resort, was immense in the general development of British banking and in particular for the discount market . . . By making credit available through one channel, the discount market, the Bank of England could, and of course now [1968] does, control both the quantity and price of credit . . . The realisation by the Bank of England . . . of its own position as the ultimate source of cash; of the need for a means of channelling cash to the economy in times of need; and the conscious choice of the discount market as that means, marks a definite step in the direction not only of the modern discount market but of the modern banking system as a whole.[14]

The 1830s, 1840s, and 1850s witnessed a steady expansion of the discount market. But these years also saw repeated instability stemming partly from abuses of the product in which it dealt—bills of exchange—and partly from malpractices on the part of market participants. The former problems arose largely from the lax behaviour of the joint-stock banks that applied little discrimination to either the quantity or the quality of the bills they rediscounted. Their casual credit practices fuelled the speculative booms that culminated in the crises of 1837, 1847, and, above all, 1857. The right to rediscount at the Bank encouraged the bill brokers to indulge in 'overtrading'.[15] This inflicted a massive strain on the Bank's resources, requiring heavy calls on reserves; for instance, in the crisis of 1857 the Bank's reserves dropped as low as £950,000, a highly alarming state of affairs.[16] The Bank's response was a bombshell. In March 1858 it abolished the right of the discount houses to take bills to the Bank for discount, thereby ending their automatic last resort privilege. Critics accused the Bank of panic or pique and the discount houses felt sorely aggrieved and made representations seeking a reversal of the ruling. A bill broker informed the Governor that he had decided to retire 'on a/c of ill health brought on from overanxiety greatly increased since the Bill Brokers have been excluded from the discount office. He believes that the Profits in Bill Broking will be so much

---

[14] W. M. Scammell, *The London Discount Market* (1968), 142, 147.

[15] Bank of England Archive, C47/30, memorandum on 'Rates Charged on Market Advances', Discount Office, 9 July 1936.

[16] Walter Bagehot, *Lombard Street: A Description of the London Money Market* (1873), 179.

reduced as to render the Business an unprofitable one'.[17] But the Bank was unmoved. Frustrated, the headstrong pair of partners who had recently inherited control of the City's foremost discount house, Overend Gurney & Co., tried to strong-arm the Bank into a reversal of policy by spoiling its management of the currency. Over three days in mid-April 1860 the firm and some sympathizers withdrew £1.6m. in Bank notes and an anonymous letter to the Governor informed him that 'Overends can pull out every note you have, from actual knowledge the writer can inform you that with their own family assistance they can nurse *seven* millions'.[18] This bizarre threat had a certain logic, since at the time the Bank's reserve of notes was no more than £7.7m.[19] But the Bank refused to modify its stance and, realizing that they had overplayed their hand, the Overend partners sued for peace. The withdrawn notes were returned, though in a mutilated state (they were cut in half, apparently for reasons of security), and a message was sent that 'they are sorry for what they have done'.[20] Although the Bank had won the scrap, the cavalier conduct of 'these tricksters', as a Bank Director referred to the Overend partners, was not such as to endear them to the Old Lady should they ever find themselves in need of her favours.

The Overend partners' response to the Bank's curb on bill broking was to develop business in a variety of unrelated and unfamiliar activities, with predictably unhappy results. In the highly speculative climate prevalent in the City in the early 1860s they perceived profitable opportunities in all sorts of directions, becoming railway financiers, grain-traders, ship-owners, and even iron-masters and shipbuilders. Such activities tied up capital in illiquid assets which were thoroughly unsuitable for a firm whose basic business remained bill broking; and besides, many of the investments were made incompetently and became valueless, so that by the summer of 1865 the firm was technically insolvent, though this was known only to the partners. They attempted to resolve their predicament by availing themselves of the recent legislation facilitating incorporation with limited liability, hoping that with this refinancing they could turn the business round. The spring of 1866 saw unsettled conditions in the money market stemming from the trade boom that followed the end of the American Civil War and the threat of the outbreak of war on the continent. A succession of increases in interest rates to protect the reserves inflicted impossible costs on Overend Gurney, which failed in May owing over £5m. The Bank was already aware that Overend Gurney had problems about which it had received a secret report drawn up by a three-man committee.[21] This established that the business was beyond redemption and it was thus decided to

---

[17] Quoted in David Kynaston, *The City of London, i. A World of Its Own 1815–1890* (1994), 199–200.

[18] Clapham, *Bank*, ii, 243.

[19] B. R. Mitchell, *Abstract of British Historical Statistics* (Cambridge, 1962), 444.

[20] Kynaston, *City*, 201.   [21] Ibid. 239.

allow the firm to fail. But other City firms which found themselves temporarily embarrassed at the same time were generously accommodated, the Governor, Lancelot Holland, reporting to shareholders that 'this house exerted itself to the utmost—and exerted itself most successfully—to meet the crisis. We did not flinch from our post . . . before the Chancellor of the Exchequer was perhaps out of his bed we had advanced one half of our reserves'.[22] The contrast between the treatment of Overends and other firms was stark and the lesson was not lost on the City.

The 1860s, 1870s, and 1880s saw the internationalization of the discount market. It was focused more and more on overseas trade finance, becoming the world's most important source of credit for international commerce. One of the factors underlying this development was sterling's adherence to the gold standard, which was managed by the Bank of England. This involved the manipulation of short-term interest rates to replenish the reserves. But the ending of the discount houses' right of discount in 1858 diminished the Bank's contact with the money market and lessened its influence over market rates, and therefore over bullion and capital flows. The Bank found itself in the pathetic position of 'chasing rather than governing' the market rates of interest, which had become critical in the working of the gold standard, an increasingly unsatisfactory state of affairs.[23]

In contrast to the previous three decades, relations between the Bank and the discount market in the quarter-century prior to the outbreak of the First World War were characterized by closeness and co-operation. The turning-point was the Bank's decision in July 1890 to restore the right of discount to the discount houses in pursuit of the objective of making Bank rate the determinant of short-term interest rates. Just how ineffectual the Bank's impact in the market had become was demonstrated only a few months later when, during the Baring crisis, it raised Bank rate to 6 per cent but the commercial banks left their rate at 4.5 per cent. This prompted the Governor, Lidderdale, to observe that since the Bank and the commercial banks were all in the same boat 'it would be for the common advantage of bankers and the country if the rowers would take their time a little better from the stroke oar'.[24] The Baring crisis provoked criticism of the Bank's inability to maintain the gold reserve and to make its interest rate effective. In response the Bank adopted the practice of keeping Bank rate close to the market rate, but at a slight premium, and the usage of open market operations when it wanted to force the discount houses to borrow from it and thus oblige them to follow the interest rate it was setting. The interconnections between the discount houses and the commercial banks put pressure on the latter to bring their rates into line with Bank rate. Moreover, the Governors and Discount Office officials now deliberately

[22] Quoted in Philip Geddes, *Inside the Bank of England* (1987), 93.
[23] R. S. Sayers, *The Bank of England 1891–1944* (Cambridge, 1976), i, 11.
[24] Geddes, *Inside the Bank*, 29.

developed personal ties with the directors and leading executives of the discount houses and commercial banks, enabling the Bank to exert moral suasion over the money market's decision-makers. By the beginning of the twentieth century the Bank had successfully imposed its leadership on the short-term money market.

The Bank and the Gilt-Edged and Discount Markets since 1914

A new era of public finance began with the outbreak of the First World War, which imposed unprecedented strains. In 1914 the national debt was £650m.; five years later the domestic debt was £6,142m. and more was owed abroad. Much the largest part of this amount, £4,500m., comprised long- and medium-term securities, gilts now comprising one-third of the total nominal value of securities quoted on the Stock Exchange, a proportion unknown since the 1870s.[25] In July 1914 the total of outstanding Treasury bills was £15.5m., but in January 1919 it was £1,100m. and the Treasury bill completely dominated the discount market. The rest of the debt comprised £300m. Ways and Means Advances and £200m. in War Savings Certificates. The Bank of England, as the government's agent in both the short-term and long-term money markets, was closely involved in these developments, and in the post-war endeavours to deal with the massively swollen indebtedness of the state.

The bulk of the long-term debt comprised three enormous issues of War Loan of November 1914, June 1915, and January 1917, that were conducted for the government by the Bank. In order to assist the success of the first of these issues, whose terms had been set by the Treasury and were regarded as niggardly, Governor Cunliffe, entirely on his own responsibility, announced that the Bank would make advances to purchasers at 1 per cent below Bank rate against their holdings until March 1918. This 'extraordinary offer' subsequently became an attractive way of borrowing and the Bank ultimately incurred bad debts of £400,000 as a result.[26] Despite such measures to stimulate subscriptions, the first issue of War Loan was not a success with investors, who applied for only £91m. of the £350m. on offer. The Bank was obliged to act in the capacity of an underwriter, its first big underwriting venture according to Sayers, and ended up with 44 per cent of the bonds on its books.[27] The mammoth £2,000m. War Loan issue of 1917, by contrast, was a great success, the market having been adroitly prepared by the Bank. Thereafter there were no more large long-term loans, since for the remainder of the war fund-raising focused on the issue of medium-term National War Bonds and short-term Exchequer Bonds offered on tap and, of course, Treasury bills.

[25] Morgan and Thomas, *Stock Exchange*, 282, Table V.
[26] Sayers, *Bank*, i, 79.   [27] Ibid. i, 81.

At the beginning of the war the business of the discount market was the financing of international trade, with domestic commercial bills and Treasury bills being but minor side-shows. During the period of hostilities, however, trade finance business largely ceased and Treasury bills became the staple. Bank rate was superseded as the regulator of short-term interest rates by the rate on Treasury bills issued through the tap, which was organized by the Bank. The principal purchasers of Treasury bills were the discount houses, financed by call loans from the commercial banks. A notable innovation in 1916 in government borrowing from the banking system was the introduction of Special Deposits that were made by the commercial banks to the Bank of England and then re-lent to the Treasury as Ways and Means Advances.

The post-war years saw the Bank undertaking a series of conversions, redemptions, and new issues as the authorities struggled to manage the avaricious national debt. Montagu Norman took a closer interest in gilt-edged market operations than any previous Governor, and in the 1920s Bank officials became active and adept in preparing the market for new issues. When undertaking a conversion they would buy up maturing stock and convert it; for cash offers they would, in effect, underwrite the issue by taking up any unsubscribed securities. In either case, the new securities would be gradually sold to the public through the Stock Exchange by the Government Broker acting on the Bank's instructions.[28] All the Bank's technical skills were put to the test by the massive War Loan conversion of 1932, the most spectacular financial operation of the inter-war years. The bonds in question were the 5 per cent War Loan of 1917, that alone constituted 40 per cent of all quoted government securities. The level of coupon was proving burdensome for the Exchequer and was an obstacle to the general fall in interest rates that was now public policy. The Governor played a leading part in the planning and negotiations whereby the bonds were successfully converted from a 5 per cent basis to 3.5 per cent. Besides its financial significance, the episode illuminates the 'ways of the Bank' under Norman's leadership:

its determined exercise of all power derived from its position in financial markets, the extent and the limits of its persuasion in informal contacts in the City, its quick adaptability in the face of unforeseen technical problems, and—perhaps for the last time in its history—the fewness of the men who participated in the discussions and took the crucial decisions.[29]

Restrictions on new issues on the London Stock Exchange had been imposed by the Treasury in December 1914 in order to reserve the market for government funding needs and with a view to protecting the value of sterling.[30] The war-time measures were rescinded in November 1919 as part

---

[28] Morgan and Thomas, *Stock Exchange*, 193.　　[29] Sayers, *Bank*, ii, 431.
[30] John Atkin, *British Overseas Investment 1918–1931* (New York, 1977), 28.

of the general process of the dismantling of war-time controls. But both the Bank and the Treasury considered that it was premature to allow open access to the London capital market to overseas borrowers, partly on account of the requirements of domestic borrowers and partly because of foreign exchange considerations, since the outflow of sterling would make it yet more difficult to raise its value relative to the dollar, which was the prerequisite for the restoration of the gold standard at the pre-war parity. For these reasons the Governor operated an informal embargo on foreign loans from January 1920 to November 1925. It was reimposed from mid-1929 to May 1930, and after September 1930. According to Sir Henry Clay, Norman's colleague and biographer:

Without any power of forbidding them, he imposed some regulation on new issues for foreign account. Only his personal influence, based on intimate contacts with all the houses making such issues and backed by the value of his knowledge and advice and . . . in the last resort . . . his power of tightening credit generally, kept within bounds the natural tendency of an organisation like the London new issue market . . . to meet the urgent and apparently limitless demands from their traditional clients.[31]

The 1920s saw the development of closer relationships between the Bank and the discount houses. Under Norman, who kept himself well informed about the affairs of the Discount Office, the Bank accepted responsibility for the orderly functioning of the discount market. This meant that it assumed responsibility for the solvency of its participants, the discount houses, who served as the Bank's intermediaries with the commercial banking system. The commercial banks' call loans to the discount houses exposed them to the risk of losses should a discount house become insolvent for whatever reason. Such a development would have caused intolerable disruption to the money market, the banking system, and the Bank's financial operations on behalf of government, and could not be allowed to happen. It followed that the Bank stood behind the discount houses, being prepared to furnish unsecured loans in support if necessary. The counterpart to the Bank's recognition of its financial responsibility for the discount houses was a more stringent supervisory role.

Since the 1890s Governors and Principals of the Discount Office had cultivated close relations with the discount market and had kept a close eye on the discount houses, requiring them to provide confidential viewings of their balance-sheets. The greatly enhanced scale of government operations in the discount market in the First World War led to the formation of the Discount Market Committee (DMC), on which all the discount houses were represented, that acted as a channel of communication between the Bank and the market during the war and after. In 1920 Norman instigated weekly meetings with the Chairman of the DMC on Thursday afternoons,

---

[31] Sir Henry Clay, *Lord Norman* (1957), 281.

between the Thursday morning meeting of the Court, when Bank rate was published, and Friday's Treasury bill tender, a convenient point for the Bank to convey its views to the market. The others present at these gatherings were the Deputy Governor and the Principal of the Discount Office, and from 1929, as problems mounted, the Deputy Chairman of the DMC also attended.

The Bank's power over the discount market in the 1920s was enhanced by its emergence as a dealer in Treasury bills on a large scale, both on its own account and as the agent of other central banks holding sterling balances. From 1922 Norman used the firm of Seccombe, Marshall & Campion as the Bank's agent for the conduct of its bill business, a relationship that continued until the 1980s. Seccombe, Marshall & Campion also acted as the Bank's eyes and ears in the market, a role akin to that of the Government Broker, Mullens & Co., in the gilt-edged market. Another source of information about the state of the money market was provided by the commencement of the practice of making daily purchases of small parcels of commercial bills from the discount houses, which it was understood would be representative of their bill portfolios, in order to monitor their quality.[32] Thereby the Bank was able to curb what it considered to be undesirable developments, notably the growth of 'finance bills' that were not based on underlying self-liquidating transactions. Pressure on the discount houses to take such bills arose partly from competition from other international financial centres and partly because of the shortage of genuine commercial bills.

At the end of the war, Treasury bills comprised virtually the whole of the discount market. Although the volume fell considerably in the early 1920s, they were a major component of the market throughout the decade, £456m. outstanding in 1924–5 and £512m. in 1929–30. The greatly expanded volume of Treasury bills in the discount market presented the Bank with a plentiful supply of short-term paper convenient for large-scale open-market operations. Thereby from 1922, with the disappearance of the highly liquid conditions of the early 1920s which had made effective credit control impossible, it was able to make Bank rate highly effective. The immediate post-war years saw a rapid revival of the volume of commercial bills as international trade recovered, increasing from £306m. in 1918–19 to £583m. in 1924–5.[33] But in the second half of the decade the volume slipped back and by 1929–30 it was £520m. At the time it was believed that the conditions were temporary and would soon improve, but in fact they were to get much worse for the discount houses before they got better.

The intimate relationship between the Bank and the discount houses that developed in the 1920s proved to be much to the latters' advantage in the very adverse conditions of the 1930s. Indeed, had it not been for the Bank

---

[32] Sayers, *Bank*, i, 279.
[33] T. Balogh, *Studies in Financial Organisation* (London, 1947), 167.

it is unlikely that the firms would have survived. One problem that the Bank could do nothing about was the fall in the quantity of commercial bills that followed the onset of the international sump, the volume declining by half in the years 1929–33 and making little recovery for the rest of the decade. Indeed, the quantity was artificially sustained by the terms of the Standstill Agreement that was negotiated with Bank encouragement between international short-term creditors and German commercial debtors following the moratorium on external payments by Germany in July 1931.[34] Under this agreement German bills remained in the market and were repeatedly renewed upon expiry, the sort of practice which had hitherto caused apoplexy in the Discount Office. The merchant banks which had guaranteed the bills were assisted in the discharge of their responsibilities by special loans from the Bank.

Sterling's departure from the gold standard in September 1931 was followed by the adoption of new monetary tactics—a fluctuating exchange rate, under Bank of England influence, and low interest rates. By June 1932 Bank rate had fallen to 2 per cent, at which level it remained (apart from a few weeks in 1939) until 1951. Other interest rates moved lower as a result; the rate on Treasury bills, which in the 1930s constituted some two-thirds of the discount market, fell to 0.5 per cent and less at times of abundant funds. However, the minimum rate at which the commercial banks would lend to the discount houses was 1 per cent, which meant that they incurred a loss on every transaction. At the instigation of the Bank, which wished to preserve the independent discount houses as a feature of the City, a live-and-let-live gentlemen's agreement was reached between the discount houses and the banks in September 1933: this allowed the former to conduct bill-dealing business without making a loss. Unfortunately they could not make much in the way of profits either, and revisions, also brokered by the Bank, were agreed in November 1934 and February 1935. By the terms of the latter agreement the commercial banks agreed not to compete in the Treasury bill auction, leaving the business to be transacted between the discount houses and the Bank, an arrangement that suited them both very well and lasted until the 1980s. In response to the dismal conditions in their traditional business the discount houses developed dealing activities in short-dated government bonds, though this brought them into competition with Stock Exchange jobbers. Rationalization was Norman's solution to strengthening the discount houses, and in September 1937 he set a target of £300,000 as the minimum capital, which earmarked half a dozen firms as candidates for amalgamation. This directive and the difficulties experienced by the firms in the 1930s resulted in a contraction of their number from twenty-four at the beginning of the decade to eighteen at the end.

There was no crisis in the City upon the outbreak of war in 1939 such as

---

[34] See Richard Roberts, *Schroders: Merchants & Bankers* (1992), 252–62.

had occurred in 1914. The hostilities had long been anticipated and were thoroughly prepared for, a process in which the Bank was closely involved.[35] Plainly war would necessitate greatly increased government revenues, which were to be raised both through taxation, at much higher levels than in the First World War, and by borrowing. Borrowing conditions were very different to those a quarter of a century earlier, because of the comprehensive system of government-imposed controls: capital-issues control reserved the financial markets for the state; price control, rationing, and taxation were an anti-inflationary armoury; while exchange controls prevented the flight of funds abroad. The monetary effect of the controls was to detach the rate of interest from economic conditions, allowing it to be set at a low rate that was cheap for borrowers, that is the state. The outcome was a 'Three per cent War', a strategy strongly supported by Norman and the Bank.[36]

The government's war-time issues were of two types: long-term Savings Bonds with maturities of 24–30 years and 3 per cent coupons; and medium-term 2.5 per cent National War Bonds with maturities of 6–10 years. Overall the three series of Savings Bonds raised £2,800m. and the six series of National War Bonds £3,400m. The war saw innovations and refinements in the Bank's issuing techniques, many of which endured long into the post-war era. All the issues were declared to be fully subscribed, though this was only true in the sense that the bonds for which the public had not applied, sometimes a large proportion, were purchased by the Issue Department of the Bank of England, the Unemployed Insurance Funds, or some other holding-place controlled by the government. Thereafter the bonds were gradually disposed of in the market by the Government Broker, by tradition a partner in the stockbrokers Mullens & Co., who acted on the Bank's instructions. After the débâcle of the first 3 per cent Savings Bonds issued in March 1940, which received a dismal level of public support, issues were made on a 'tap' basis, by which modest amounts were offered continuously by the Government Broker.

At the end of the war the internal national debt stood at £23,373m., of which 52 per cent comprised long-term securities quoted on the Stock Exchange and 48 per cent were short-term borrowings, a much higher proportion than before the war. Treasury bills were the largest part of the short-term indebtedness, the annual turnover rising from £1,820m. in 1938–9 to over £7,000m. by the end of the war. Ostensibly this was a big boost for the discount market, whose commercial bill business had dwindled to almost nothing with the outbreak of war. But the margins on the business were so slim that there was little profit in it despite the increased volume; one firm, whose bill business had grown sixfold, disclosed that this side of its activities generated a third of total expenses while contributing

[35] Sayers, *Bank*, ii, ch. 21.
[36] The phrase was coined by a leading article in *The Economist*, 20 Jan. 1940.

nothing to profits.[37] In mid-1941 the Bank informed the market of the need for further amalgamations to form stronger firms with greater capitalizations. This would enable them to expand their dealings in short-dated bonds. The issue of these securities soared during the war, outstripping the market-making capacity that Stock Exchange jobbers were able to provide. Moreover, the discount houses brought skills developed in dealing with large blocks of Treasury bills that were beyond the expertise of the gilt-edged jobbers. The Bank of England actively promoted the development of the discount houses' business in short-dated bonds, allowing them special borrowing privileges to do so. The expansion of the discount houses' bill and bond portfolios necessitated additional capital. With Bank support, capital issue consent was forthcoming, and seven of the eleven amalgamated firms that now constituted the discount market issued new capital in 1942–3, while others capitalized reserves. By early 1944, all the firms had at least £1m. capital, the figure now stipulated by the Bank as a minimum, and their aggregate resources were £22m.

The development of short-dated bond dealing by the discount houses was their salvation. Unlike bill business it was a profitable activity, running yields on bonds being as high as 2.5 per cent against call loan money at 1.125 per cent. The participation of the discount houses in the short-bond market was very useful for the authorities, since for technical reasons a high proportion of maturing bonds came to be held in their bond portfolios. This enabled the authorities to retire large blocks of bonds before their maturity dates, facilitating refinancing operations. In fact, in the latter war years these operations to smooth the workings of the bond market came to be regarded by the Bank and the Treasury as the primary function of the discount houses.

The election of a Labour government in 1945 was unwelcome to most City men, but for the Treasury bill and gilt-edged markets the new administration's commitment to public expenditure was something of a mitigating factor. Moreover, the maturity schedule of short-term and medium-term war-time bond issues stretched out ahead for at least a decade, ensuring a continuing need for the bond-gathering services of the discount houses. But their ability to fulfil this function effectively was questionable, since the ratio of their portfolios of bills and bonds to their capitals was now twice as large as before the war. The solution, championed by the Bank, was to issue more capital, and the new socialist administration, which was highly suspicious of the City, was surprised to learn that in order to execute its chosen financial policy it was necessary to give priority in the allocation of scarce capital to the discount houses. These operations added £10.6m. to the capital resources of the market in the years 1945–7, marking the high point of the discount market both absolutely and

---

[37] W. T. C. King, 'The Changing Discount Market', *The Banker* (Mar. 1947), 178.

in relation to the banking system. For the duration of the Labour government the discount houses continued to conduct the Treasury bill and short-bond dealing business they had built up during the war, making adequate profits.

The resumption of the usage of interest rates as a lever of economic management in November 1951 had important implications for the discount houses and for their relationship with the Bank. First of all, higher and flexible short-term rates meant that bill business became more profitable but also more risky. The Bank continued to exercise a close supervisory role, the Thursday afternoon meetings providing an opportunity for giving the houses discreet guidance about the direction in which the authorities wanted rates to move. Moreover, when trading conditions were difficult the Bank might allow especially favourable resale margins on its direct purchases of bills from the discount market. The quid pro quo for such privileges and for the Bank's protection was the understanding that the discount houses would not diversify into other activities, but would stick to their last as specialist dealers in bills and short bonds.

The return to flexible rates made bond dealing much more hazardous because of the threat of capital losses if firms' bond portfolios were wrongly positioned for market developments. Naturally, forthcoming changes in interest rates was not something about which the Bank was able to warn, but it could and did keep a close eye on the scale of the discount houses' portfolios in relation to their capital and was quick to admonish houses that assumed excessive risks. Nevertheless some houses did sustain substantial losses when rates rose. In 1955 the Bank was obliged to give emergency support to one house and introduced a range of measures to ease the pressures on the market as a whole.[38] Unnerved by this experience, the discount houses rapidly reduced their participation in the bond market when dangerous conditions returned in 1957, obliging the Government Broker, acting on behalf of the Bank, to assume the role they had relinquished. The following year, however, they resumed a major role in the market and the 1960s saw a more or less continuous growth of their bond holdings. This expansion was underpinned by the Bank's support operations to sustain the marketability of gilt-edged in periods of downward pressure on prices, which incidentally underwrote the discount houses' exposures.

Despite repeated suggestions that the discount houses were an unnecessary anachronism and that their functions could be perfectly well performed by the clearing banks and gilt-edged jobbers, the discount houses survived, sustained by the Bank. In 1980 the Wilson Committee Report observed that they 'play a prominent role in the money markets . . . [being] distinguished from other participants in these markets in that by convention they underwrite the weekly Treasury bill tender and in return have

---

[38] John Fforde, *The Bank of England and Public Policy 1941–1958* (Cambridge, 1992), 757.

privileged access to the Bank of England as lender of last resort'.[39] Deregulation of the securities markets in the 1980s led to amalgamations amongst the discount houses and to the acquisition of some firms by foreign banks, both processes leading to increased capitalizations.[40] By the early 1990s the membership of the London Discount Market Association had fallen to nine. But these firms continued to play a pivotal role as intermediaries between the Bank and the banking system.[41] Some of the larger firms became primary gilt dealers in the reformed gilt-edged market established in 1986. Initially they enjoyed something of an advantage over other participants on account of their established privilege of being able to borrow from the Bank against the security of eligible bills whereas other firms could only borrow against longer-dated securities, though the advantage proved only transitional.[42]

The post-war decades saw a closer involvement of the Bank in the gilt-edged market than ever before in peace-time. Unlike previous periods of peace, which had witnessed reductions in the national debt, these years saw continuous borrowing, though for different reasons at different moments: to meet the costs of nationalization and the capital needs of the nationalized industries; for the conversion or redemption of maturing bonds; to reduce the volume of Treasury bills and other highly liquid assets to curb inflation; to bridge the gap in the budget between revenues and expenditure to finance consumption. The outcome was an increase in the nominal value of the national debt from £12.3bn. in 1946 to £125bn. in the early 1990s.

The usual method of new issues of gilts continued to be by tender, the Bank offering a substantial amount of newly created bonds at or above a specified minimum price. An innovation on pre-war practice was that for most issues a part, often a substantial part, of any unsold bonds were taken by the Bank's Issue Department and were sold subsequently as 'tap' stocks by the Government Broker. Since the war, tap stocks of varying maturities were on offer continuously, the terms of sale varying according to market conditions. When the supply of a particular tap stock ran out it was replaced by a new issue of a similar sort that was taken onto the books of the Bank of England. A significant new departure was the commencement of issue by auction in May 1987. Initially there were considerable differences between the highest and lowest accepted bids, but by the early 1990s the gap had narrowed and the new system was working well.[43] The terms on which bonds were offered varied continuously according to market

---

[39] *Report of the Committee to Review the Functioning of Financial Institutions*, 1980, Cmnd. 7937, cap. 196, 53.

[40] Maximillian Hall, *The City Revolution: Causes and Consequences* (1987), 59–60.

[41] Paul Temperton, 'The London Money Market', in David Cobham (ed.), *Markets and Dealers: The Economics of the London Financial Markets* (1992), 139.

[42] Hall, *City Revolution*, 61.

[43] Richard Harrington, 'The Sterling Bond Market', in Cobham (ed.), *Markets and Dealers*, 71.

conditions, but a noteworthy innovation was the commencement of the issue of index-linked gilts in 1981 (albeit against the Bank's wishes). Another landmark was the ECU 2.75bn. gilts issue in February 1991, the first ECU gilts issue and the largest fixed-rate issue ever on the international bond market.[44]

The Wilson Committee's Report identified four main policy objectives underlying the Bank's operations in the gilt-edged market:

to implement monetary policy by funding the government's borrowing in non-monetary form, so controlling the money supply and influencing interest rates; to encourage the breadth and liquidity of the market so as to maximise the long-term demand for government debt; to maintain an appropriate maturity structure of government debt; and to minimise the cost of debt servicing.[45]

It was noted that unfortunately these objectives were sometimes in conflict. In the immediate post-war decades the Bank gave priority to managing the market, buying and selling gilts to smooth out violent price fluctuations and thus facilitate new issues and redemptions. But towards the end of the 1960s the Bank's price-support activities began to be criticized for fuelling inflation. 'We have found recently and I think will continue to find in the future', Governor Leslie O'Brien told the Select Committee on Nationalised Industries in 1969, 'that it is often difficult to reconcile the pedestrian day-to-day desire for an orderly gilt-edged market and the overall policy desire to let us restrain the money supply'.[46] Indeed, in 1971 it was announced that the Bank's support for the gilt-edged market would be more selective.

The gilt-edged market was drastically reformed in October 1986 as part of the deregulation of securities trading known as Big Bang. The traditional structure of brokers and jobbers dealing on the floor of the Stock Exchange was replaced by dual-capacity gilt-edged market makers, and trading almost immediately became screen-based. A new settlement system, the Central Gilts Office, was introduced under the joint supervision of the Bank and the Stock Exchange. Trading in gilts was largely confined to a set of firms that were officially designated as recognized gilt-edged market makers by the Bank of England, a status conferring both privileges and obligations. Gilt-edged market makers were required by the Bank to be always prepared to make effective two-way prices, thereby ensuring at all times the liquidity of the gilt-edged market. Initially there were twenty-seven gilt-edged market makers with an aggregate capital of £595m., a situation of considerable over-capacity. The position of the gilt-edged market makers was aggravated by the stock market crash of October 1987, in the wake of which there were reduced levels of activity in all financial markets,

---

[44] Ralph J. Mehnert, *Users Guide to the ECU* (1992), 102–3. The issue of British government ECU-denominated securities began in 1988 with the issue of two series of Treasury bills.

[45] *Report of . . . Financial Institutions*, cap. 199, 54.

[46] Quoted in Frances Cairncross and Hamish McRae, *Capital City* (1985), 227–8.

and by the three-year period 1988–90, unprecedented in the post-war era, in which budget surpluses reduced the national debt and there were no new gilt issues. As a result the number of recognized gilt-edged market makers fell to eighteen and their aggregate capital fell to £432m.[47] But the early 1990s saw profitable trading conditions, attracting new entrants and additional capital. In these years, as the public-sector borrowing requirement splurged out of control, it seemed as if the Bank in its original function had come full circle, but the new market arrangements proved effective in coping with the government's bloated borrowing requirements.

The Bank and the Foreign Exchange, Commodities, and Equity Markets

The Bank's relationships with the foreign exchange, commodities, and equity markets were twentieth-century developments. In the First World War the Bank became actively involved in the management of Britain's foreign exchange resources for the first time. At the beginning of the war the government decided not to suspend the convertibility of sterling, despite the pressures that the reserves were likely to experience. This was done with a view to safeguarding the standing of London as an international financial centre; Keynes, a staunch supporter at the Treasury of continued convertibility, argued that 'the *future* position of the City of London as a free gold market will be seriously injured if at the *first* sign of emergency specie payment is suspended'.[48] The policy of a fixed exchange rate and freedom for ordinary trading transactions was sustained throughout the war. The achievement of these goals required raising large sums abroad (mostly in the US), the attraction to London of foreign funds, and the mobilization of Britain's large overseas investments for the war effort. From the outset, the Governor, Cunliffe, was energetically involved in every aspect. In November 1915 he was made chairman of the London Exchange Committee, a body comprising Bank officials and senior clearing bankers, established by the Chancellor, and charged with responsibility for 'the regulation of the foreign exchanges'. It was given wide-ranging powers and had at its disposal all the authorities' gold and foreign currency and the proceeds of sales of securities on foreign markets. It met frequently, sometimes daily, and proved highly effective in sustaining sterling at the wartime pegged value of $4.76 to the pound. This was achieved through a combination of issues of British government bonds and Treasury bills in the US, the sale of dollar securities surrendered by UK owners, gold shipments, and borrowings from US banks, especially J. P. Morgan & Co., the

---

[47] 'The Gilt-Edged Market: Developments in 1991', *Bank of England Quarterly Bulletin*, 32 (1992), 56–9.
[48] Sayers, *Bank*, i, 83.

British government's US agent. For the first two years of the war these borrowings were made in the name of the Bank, not the Treasury. The entry of the US into the war in 1917 considerably eased the task of managing the currency because of the provision of government-to-government credits.

Before the war the foreign exchange market in London was a minor affair, since the bulk of international transactions were conducted in sterling.[49] In the post-war era dealing in foreign currency became a large and very active City market, London being the 'great market for international moneys'.[50] This arose from the enormous increase in the use of US dollars for international financial transactions and the growth in paper currency in international circulation, a sevenfold expansion over the years 1914–19 being the estimate of the National City Bank of New York's economist.[51] The immediate post-war years saw wild fluctuations in the values of the floating currencies, that from March 1919 included sterling. Manipulation of Bank rate was the instrument used by the Bank to achieve a desired exchange rate in the 1920s, both in the years before the restoration of the gold standard in 1925 and subsequently.[52] The summer of 1929 saw pressure on the pound and the Bank decided that an increase in Bank rate was necessary. But the recently elected Labour administration was unwilling to allow this because of other considerations. Instead, the Bank went into the market selling dollars, while the Federal Reserve Bank of New York, acting in conjunction, bought pounds.[53] These operations marked the beginning of modern-style intervention in the foreign exchange market.[54]

The financial crisis of autumn 1931 prompted an important initiative on the part of the Bank, called by Sayers 'one of its most significant domestic innovations', to increase its power in the foreign exchange market.[55] On 9 September 1931, following a decision of the Court a week earlier, a Foreign Exchange Committee was jointly established by the Bank and the commercial banks. This took over the day-to-day defence of sterling, drawing on the skills of the banks' foreign exchange dealing rooms. Thereafter there rapidly developed a much closer relationship between Bank officials and the City's foreign exchange experts, which was essential following the suspension of convertibility that cast the Bank in the role of managing sterling. In the 1920s this had been done by the adjustment of interest rates, but with the adoption of a cheap money policy in the early 1930s this was not an option. A Treasury Order was issued restricting the foreign exchange transactions of British subjects and residents; and the Bank started to build a reserve of US dollars and French francs, buying in the market when

[49] Paul Einzig, *The History of Foreign Exchange* (1970), 182–3.

[50] B. M. Anderson, 'Three and a Half Billion Dollar Floating Debt of Europe to Private Creditors in America', *The Chase Economic Bulletin*, 1 (Oct. 1920), 9–10.

[51] O. P. Austin, 'World's Paper Currency Now Seven Times the Amount in 1914', *The Americas*, 6 (Jan. 1920), 25–7.

[52] Sayers, *Bank*, i, 117.   [53] Ibid. i, 228.

[54] Geddes, *Inside the Bank*, 76.   [55] Sayers, *Bank*, i, 281.

conditions were favourable, to provide itself with the means of intervening in the market.

An unwelcome upturn in the value of sterling in the spring of 1932, threatening the competitive position of British exports, revealed the inadequacy of the Bank's market firepower.[56] The outcome was the establishment in July 1932 of the Exchange Equalisation Account (EEA), a special Treasury account with the Bank holding the nation's gold and foreign exchange reserves. The function of the EEA, which was managed by the Bank, was to implement official exchange rate policy by means of buying and selling in the foreign exchange and bullion markets. With the resources of the EEA at its disposal, the Bank was able to smooth fluctuations so as to reduce uncertainty, thereby encouraging exports and providing protection for the economy from the destabilizing effects of short-term capital flows. The Bank recruited a handful of experienced foreign exchange professionals from the City to run the EEA, amongst them Cameron Cobbold, a future Governor, and George Bolton.[57] It also took steps to organize and discipline the foreign exchange market, which had never had a formal structure and was 'a fragmented trade with many small brokers and some unsavoury practices'.[58] To this end the Bank prompted the formation of the Foreign Exchange Brokers Association, which adopted a code of conduct drawn up with the Bank's blessing. London banks were expected to conduct their foreign exchange business through a member of the Association and members were required to adhere to its rules. By the end of the 1930s the London foreign exchange market comprised some 140 banks and other financial firms with thirty brokers acting as intermediaries.[59] The coming of war and the imposition of exchange control put a stop to the activities of London's foreign exchange market. For the subsequent dozen years, banks obtained such foreign exchange as they were permitted through the Bank of England. The administration of the controls on gold and foreign currency transactions and capital flows overseas necessitated a massive expansion of the Bank's Foreign Exchange Department, whose staff grew from a few dozen before the hostilities to more than a thousand by the summer of 1940.

The commodity markets were an important part of the City's activities, though not one with which the Bank was directly involved before the Second World War. An exception occurred in 1935, when speculation in white pepper led to large losses and to the failure of several firms in the Mincing Lane market.[60] The Bank played a very active role in co-ordinating action to minimize disruption to the market and losses to the banks that had lent

---

[56] 'The Exchange Equalisation Account: Its Origins and Development', *Bank of England Quarterly Bulletin* (Dec. 1968), 377–90.

[57] Richard Fry (ed.), *A Banker's World: The Revival of the City 1957–1970* (1970), 19.

[58] Joe Irving, *The City at Work* (1981), 127.

[59] William M. Clarke, *Inside the City* (1979), 175.   [60] Sayers, *Bank*, ii, 544–6.

to the commodity brokers. Accumulated stocks were gradually liquidated in an orderly manner through a London Pepper Sales Control Committee, and Norman personally chose a number of new company chairmen and directors to fill the places of those discredited by the episode.

Upon the outbreak of war in 1939 the UK commodity exchanges closed, supplies of essential raw materials being secured by government contracts and allocated by new administrative arrangements. Early in 1944 the Bank began to make plans for the post-war re-opening of the commodity markets.[61] It very much favoured the resumption of their operations, which would not only be an effective means of securing supplies, but would also provide a means of reviving the City's international activities and perhaps, through entrepôt activities, ease the country's foreign exchange shortage. The Bank assumed the role of championing the markets in the face of Treasury and ministerial preference for controls, devising regimes that reconciled their operational requirements with exchange control and rigorous economy in foreign exchange. The first fruit of these exertions was the re-opening of entrepôt trade in Latin American coffee in May 1946, a development that represented something of a coup for London, since in the inter-war years the trade had been dominated by Hamburg and Amsterdam. The Bank kept a watchful eye on its protégé, monthly meetings being held with representatives of the Coffee Trade Federation. It was also closely involved with the re-opening of the rubber market in November 1946, the metals markets between autumn 1949 and summer 1953, and the softs markets in the second half of 1953. The Bank's commodities schemes proved successful in its aims of promoting the use of sterling as an international currency and reviving City business. They extended its authority and expertise to another area of City activity and added a further dimension to its role as an intermediary between Whitehall and the square mile.

The foreign exchange market resumed operations in December 1951, though still much constrained by exchange control and other measures. During the war access to foreign exchange had been restricted to 'authorized dealers', that is banks which were prepared to undertake the pettifogging bureaucracy of exchange control.[62] This arrangement was perpetuated by the Exchange Control Act 1947, and until 1979 only banks authorized under this measure could act as principals in the London foreign exchange market, though others dealt through brokers. The Foreign Exchange Brokers Association was revived after the war and London banks were again required to conduct most of their foreign exchange transactions through its members.[63] Membership was restricted to firms 'recognized' by the Bank, a process that involved submitting an application to the Bank supported by at least six sponsoring banks and an undertaking to abide by

[61] J. F. A. Pullinger, 'The Bank and the Commodity Markets', in Fforde, *Bank*, 785–94.

[62] Sayers, *Bank*, ii, 570.

[63] *Report of . . . Financial Institutions*, cap. 3.377, 514–15.

the code of practice required by the Bank. The Bank's grasp on the market was reinforced by the establishment of a Joint Standing Committee, chaired by a Bank official and comprising representatives of the banks and brokers, that kept the market under review. The privileged position of the brokers disappeared in January 1980 when in the wake of the end of exchange control a new set of rules designed to stimulate competition was introduced. The abolition of exchange control by the newly elected Conservative government in 1979 came as a mighty shock to the Bank, especially to the 675 staff of the Exchange Control Department who suddenly had no work to do. Furthermore, since exchange control had provided the Bank with an almost universally applicable means to 'persuade' banks and other institutions to conduct their activities in ways that served its objectives, its abolition weakened its coercive power over the City and led it to rely more heavily on its moral authority.[64]

The Bank's post-war dealings in the foreign exchange market continued to be conducted through the EEA. From 1945 to 1972 its operations were designed to maintain sterling's pegged relationship with the US dollar as required under the Bretton Woods system. In the era of floating exchange rates—between the collapse of Bretton Woods and sterling's entry into the Exchange Rate Mechanism of the European Monetary System in October 1990—intervention was discretionary and more modest. The scale of foreign exchange dealing in London grew apace from the 1960s, stimulated by the burgeoning Euromarkets, and the City re-emerged as the world's foremost foreign exchange centre. In the mid-1970s 220 banks were active participants in the market.[65] By the end of the decade their number had grown to 270 and the daily turnover of the London market was estimated to be $50bn., compared with $40bn. in New York, $10bn. in Frankfurt, and $2bn. in Tokyo.[66] The volume of foreign exchange transactions soared in the 1980s: in 1986 daily turnover in London was $90bn.; in 1989 it was $187bn.[67] Corresponding figures for the leading international financial centres in the latter year were $129bn. in New York and $115bn. in Tokyo, giving London a commanding lead. The massive overall increase in international foreign exchange dealing greatly outstripped the growth of the resources available to central banks to intervene in the markets. The power of the markets was sensationally demonstrated in September 1992, when, despite the Bank's skills and the co-operation of other central banks, it proved impossible to withstand speculative pressure and sterling was forced out of the ERM.

The equity market was not a concern of the Bank before Montagu

[64] Stephen Fay, *Portrait of an Old Lady: Turmoil at the Bank of England* (1987), 105–6.

[65] Nicholas Ritchie, *What Goes on in the City?* (Cambridge, 1975), 70.

[66] *Euromoney* (Apr. 1979).

[67] 'The Market in Foreign Exchange in London', *Bank of England Quarterly Bulletin*, 29 (1989), 531–5.

Norman's governorship. More mindful of the needs of British industry than any previous governor, one of the objectives of his informal embargo on foreign loans of 1920–5 was to facilitate borrowing by British firms for post-war reconstruction. When the Bank began to publish annual estimates of UK capital issues in 1928, the series contained considerable detail of corporate capital raising, suggesting at least an interest in monitoring the market.[68] The sponsorship of the formation of the Bankers Industrial Development Company (BIDC) in April 1930 established a direct Bank involvement in the equity market. Norman himself assumed the chairmanship of the new body, whose purpose, he told the Court, was 'to examine, assist and finance the amalgamation, reconstruction and reorganisation on an economic and rationalised basis of groups of British companies engaged in important industries'.[69] The BIDC played a useful role sponsoring a number of issues on behalf of British manufacturers in the 1930s, though not entirely fulfilling initial expectations. After the war two new institutions—the Finance Corporation for Industry and the Industrial and Commercial Finance Corporation—were launched at the behest of the Bank, the latter becoming one of the largest providers of venture capital in the world.

War-time regulations forbade new issues without Treasury consent. Applications to raise capital were vetted by the Bank, which had authority to permit access to the market to UK borrowers undertaking work in the national interest. Other cases were referred to an advisory body, the Capital Issues Committee, but problematic ones tended to involve the Bank.[70] These controls continued in the immediate post-war years, though they were relaxed in the 1950s and the Capital Issues Committee was abolished in 1959. An enduring Bank constraint on the market was the queuing system for new issues organized by the Government Broker on the Bank's behalf to give priority to its funding operations for the state.[71]

The early 1950s saw a new development in the equity market that aroused much concern at the Bank and in Whitehall—the hostile take-over bid.[72] Sensationally reported bids for J. Sears & Co. and the Savoy Hotel Co. in 1953 led to a search for a means to prevent take-overs, viewed by the authorities as economically and politically harmful. Legislation was ruled out for practical and ideological reasons but the Bank was able to curb take-over activity by issuing requests to banks, both British and foreign, and to other City firms, not to finance 'speculation'. The effect of the Bank's actions in December 1953 was to ensure that take-overs did not

[68] See annual *Bank of England Statistical Summaries*.

[69] Speech to Court, 6 Mar. 1930, quoted in Clay, *Norman*, 329.

[70] Sayers, *Bank*, ii, 581–2.

[71] A J. Merrett, M. Howe, and G. D. Newbould, *Equity Issues and the London Capital Market* (1967), 16; *Report of . . . Financial Institutions*, cap. 188, 51.

[72] See Richard Roberts, 'Regulatory Responses to the Rise of the Market for Corporate Control in Britain in the 1950s', *Business History*, 34 (Jan. 1992), 183–200.

become 'normal commercial exercises' in the mid-1950s, but remained 'financial curiosities'.[73]

Take-overs resumed in the merger wave of the years 1958–61, and have been a feature of City activity ever since. This was due to two developments. One was the relaxation of controls on bank lending in July 1958, which included the rescinding of the Bank's requests against financing speculation. The other was a change of attitude to take-overs on the part of the Bank and the government. Increasing concern about the uncompetitiveness of British industry led them to take a favourable view of take-over bids as a spur to managerial efficiency. The new thinking was expressed by Leslie O'Brien, then Chief Cashier, in a memorandum to the Governor: 'Developments since 1953 have tended to support the view that take-over bidders generally perform a useful function . . . Directors have only themselves to blame if they are dispossessed by more enterprising rivals'.[74] This view was decidedly more advanced than that of City opinion in general, as was demonstrated during the battle for control of British Aluminium in 1958–9, when many of the leading firms formed a consortium to frustrate the ambitions of the hostile bidder. Despite their representations, the authorities declined to act and the City establishment suffered a humiliating defeat. Henceforth take-overs were an everyday part of the City landscape.

The new market for corporate control was politically too controversial to be allowed to operate by the law of the jungle. On the initiative of Governor Cobbold, a secret conference was held at the Bank in July 1959, which was attended by representatives of the Stock Exchange, the banks, merchant banks and the insurance industry to formulate principles for the conduct of take-over bids. The outcome was the issue of a set of guidelines for City practitioners. It soon proved ineffectual and was eventually supplanted in 1967 by the Take-over Code, the Bank again being closely involved. To enforce compliance the Panel on Take-overs and Mergers was established in 1968. The full-time director and his staff were experienced practitioners and were paid to be policemen by the industry. It was the epitome of the sort of poacher-turned-gamekeeper self-regulatory arrangement that the Bank believed to work most effectively in the City and to be in the City's best interests. Despite occasional blunders, the Code and Panel were generally seen as effective and proved an enduring institution with which the Bank worked closely.

---

[73] George Bull and Anthony Vice, *Bid for Power* (1958), 237.
[74] Bank of England Archive, C40/971, f.10, memorandum from Leslie O'Brien to the Governor, 8 July 1959.

The Bank and the Banking System

The relationship between the Bank and other banks has struck a variety of chords, sometimes by no means harmonious ones. The establishment of the privileged tyro in 1694 was much resented by the goldsmith-bankers and its early years saw some skirmishing. Yet there proved to be business enough for all, and the number of private London bankers increased in subsequent years. Relations between the Bank and the country banks that proliferated from the 1750s were often acrimonious, due to rivalry in note issuing. The country banks competed aggressively with the Bank of England in the circulation of their notes, which was their principal source of profit. Many were woefully deficient in providing proper backing for their note issue and their conduct was a source of cost and frustration for the Bank and of instability in the economy. The friction over the note issue was finally resolved by the legislation of 1833 and 1844.

By the mid-nineteenth century the country banks were already on the wane and the rise of the joint-stock banks had begun. The first to open in London was the London and Westminster Bank in 1834, an intrusion that was much resented and resisted by the Bank of England because of the competition that would ensue to its private banking business of deposit-taking and the granting of loans.[75] But more and more the Bank came to recognize that it was not like other banks. As repository of the cash reserve of the banking system and banker to the government, it alone had the resources to meet the demand for cash in times of panic. The effective performance of the function of lender of last resort to the banking system required closer co-operation with the commercial banks, the Bank's joining of the Bankers Clearing House in 1864 being a move in this direction. Personal contacts were developed, yet the Bank took no formal supervisory role and assumed no formal responsibility for individual institutions. Thus the appeal for financial assistance by the City of Glasgow Bank—which suspended payments in 1878, causing great hardship to thousands of small savers—was turned down on the grounds that there was no danger to the banking system as a whole. The collapse in 1890 of Baring Brothers, one of the City's largest merchant banks, presented a hazard of an entirely different magnitude. The firm's failure would cause havoc in the discount market and threatened to undermine the banking system because of its outstanding call loans. This could not be allowed to happen. On the other hand there was no reason why the Bank's shareholders should assume all the risk and all the potential losses. Hence the Governor initiated and organized a rescue fund subscribed to by the commercial banks, the merchant banks, and other City firms, all of whom recognized that it was in their own

---

[75] Michael Collins, *Money and Banking in the UK: A History* (1988), 190.

interest and in the interest of the City as a whole to assist. The Bank's leadership under William Lidderdale ensured that the Baring Crisis was a crisis that never became a drama and won great admiration for its decisiveness and competence.

The 1890s and 1900s saw a spate of amalgamations between the commercial banks, whose outcome was a set of banks with nationwide branch networks and very large resources. Hitherto, the Bank had been not only the foremost banking institution but also the biggest by yardsticks such as capital or deposits. Now it became dwarfed by institutions such as the London City and Midland Bank and the London County and Westminster Bank, whose deposits overtook the Bank's in 1908 and 1909 respectively.[76] Regular dialogue between the Bank and the commercial banks was established on a formal basis in 1911 with the commencement of what became the quarterly meetings of the Committee of the Bankers Clearing House at the Bank. Somewhat disconcertingly for the Bank, such occasions provided the commercial bankers with opportunities to criticize its conduct, and the years preceding the First World War saw regular bickering over the issue of the level of the gold reserves maintained by the Bank, which the bankers argued was inadequate. The closing years of the war saw further bank amalgamations, resulting in the emergence of the Big Five. Alarmed at the increasingly monopolistic nature of the commercial banking industry, the Chancellor appointed a committee of inquiry in 1918. The outcome was a set of rules on further bank amalgamations, their interpretation being entrusted to the Governor of the Bank of England.

The interruption to international remittances which followed the outbreak of hostilities in 1914 posed dire problems for the City's merchant banks, the very important group of firms that specialized in the endorsement of bills of exchange arising from international trade.[77] Many of the merchant banks were faced with failure due to non-remittance from enemy countries and others, notably Russia, since their obligations to pay up on 90-day bills of exchange when they fell due exceeded their capital. This prospect created grave problems for the holders of bills—the discount houses and the commercial banks—and threatened a wholesale collapse of the banking system. It was in order to determine what to do that the partners of twenty-one merchant banks met in the office of Frederick Huth Jackson, senior partner of Frederick Huth & Co., a Director of the Bank of England, on 5 August 1914, the first full day of the war. This proved to be the inaugural meeting of the Accepting Houses Committee. Disaster was averted by the government's declaration of a moratorium on the settlement of outstanding bills and the Bank's undertaking, supported by a Treasury

---

[76] A. R. Holmes and Edwin Green, *Midland: 150 years of Banking Business* (1986), 324; T. E. Gregory, *The Westminster Bank Through a Century* (1936), ii, 316; Mitchell, *British Historical Statistics*, 445.

[77] Roberts, *Schroders*, 152–5.

indemnity, to purchase any approved bill accepted prior to the moratorium. These measures relieved the discount houses and the banks of doubtful assets. The Bank sustained the merchant banks by making available special loans that were not repayable until after the end of the hostilities, enabling them to discharge their outstanding liabilities, though paying 2 per cent above Bank rate for the privilege. These measures successfully resolved the crisis, being hailed at the time by the leading financial journalist Hartley Withers as 'the greatest evidence of London's strength as a financial centre that it could have desired or dreamt of'.[78]

A few of the merchant banks to which the Bank made war-time advances were unable to repay, including Huths. They were kept going by the Bank after the war until a suitable partner could be found, the beginning of the Bank's role as a marriage-broker to City firms. By the 1920s it had become inconceivable that a British commercial bank could be allowed to fail. When in 1928 Williams Deacon's Bank got into trouble, the Bank effected a rescue by persuading the Royal Bank of Scotland to take it over, the deal including as a sweetener the transfer to the Royal Bank of the Bank's West End branch in Burlington Gardens. In July 1931 it provided emergency assistance to the merchant bank Lazard Brothers and two months later to the Anglo-South American Bank, subsequently arranging for it to be absorbed by the Bank of London and South America. The 1980s saw a revival of the Bank's role as a marriage-broker, but this time in the context of the restructuring arising from Big Bang. It has also on occasion played a reverse role and thwarted what it considered to be unsuitable liaisons, for instance the proposed acquisition of the Royal Bank of Scotland by the Hongkong and Shanghai Bank in 1981, not to mention the truly eyebrow-raising suggestion half a dozen years later that the Midland Bank was a suitable sideline for the advertising agency Saatchi & Saatchi.

The members of the Accepting Houses Committee constituted something of an aristocracy amongst City firms, and by the later 1920s it was equally inconceivable that one of them could be allowed to fail because of the contingent damage that would be done to the financial fabric and to London's reputation as an international financial centre. In return for the Bank's tacit guarantee the firms accepted a closer degree of supervision. This was effected by the instigation of regular meetings between the Accepting Houses Committee and Bank officials, and from 1929 the Governor asked to see the balance-sheets of each firm, prepared in 'Bank of England form'.[79] As already discussed, the German suspension of international payments in July 1931 created problems for the merchant banks similar to those of August 1914. Again the Bank was closely involved in resolving them and provided special assistance to some houses.

The Bank of England Act 1946 that brought the Bank into public

---

[78] Hartley Withers, *War and Lombard Street* (1915), 99.
[79] Geddes, *Inside the Bank*, 97.

ownership conferred a range of powers upon it *vis-à-vis* the domestic banking system. It was empowered to issue directives—the Bank preferred the term 'requests'—to the banking system or to individual banks thought in need of corrective action. In fact, the Bank generally preferred to continue to use informal guidance to achieve its aims. This continued to be effective in the 1950s when, as the Governor put it in 1957, 'if I want to talk to the representatives of the British banks, or indeed of the whole community, we can usually get together in one room in about half an hour'.[80] But in the 1960s the internationalization of the City's activities, the influx of foreign banks, and the multiplication of the number of bank-like institutions under the prevailing 'ramshackle system of authorization' began to erode the effectiveness of the Bank's powers of 'moral suasion'.[81] For instance, in the late 1940s it was necessary to issue only a handful of requests to key City bodies to get its views across, but by the end of the 1960s they were going out to more than 260 institutions and monitoring compliance had become very difficult.

The Bank's techniques of credit control were undermined by the report of the National Board for Prices and Incomes published in May 1967, which condemned existing arrangements as uncompetitive. Its line of criticism was endorsed by a Monopolies Commission report that condemned the 'soporific effect' of the prevailing cartelized structure of British domestic banking. In response, the new policy of Competition and Credit Control was introduced in 1971. Its purpose, explained Governor O'Brien, was 'to permit the price mechanism to function efficiently in the allocation of credit, and to free the banks from the rigidities and restraints which have for too long inhibited them'.[82] Although a government measure, the Bank was the architect of the policy and its adoption represented a triumph for its market-oriented inclinations. But the sudden removal of controls led to the property boom of 1971–3 that culminated in the secondary banking crisis which began in November 1973. It soon became clear that a substantial number of 'secondary banks', institutions supervised not by the Bank but by the Board of Trade, were in trouble and that their problems might well infect the major commercial banks. To avert damage to the banking system as a whole, the new Governor, Gordon Richardson, convened a meeting at the Bank and secured the City's support for a rescue fund that became known as 'the lifeboat'.[83] Richardson won much praise for his adroit handling of the crisis, echoing the plaudits bestowed after the Baring crisis.

The 1979 Banking Act, passed to remedy the regulatory deficiencies

---

[80] Quoted in Geddes, *Inside the Bank*, 98.

[81] John Grady and Martin Weale, *British Banking, 1960–85* (1986), 37.

[82] Quoted in Geddes, *Inside the Bank*, 99.

[83] A colourful account of the meeting at the Bank and its background is provided by Charles Gordon, *The Cedar Story: The Night the City was Saved* (1993).

exposed by the secondary banking crisis, imposed a comprehensive system of statutory bank supervision for the first time. The measure greatly strengthened the Bank's role in bank supervision, the Board of Trade's part being eliminated. In July 1974, well before the legislation, the Bank had created a new Bank Supervision Department which adopted a much more active and intrusive approach to bank supervision than hitherto. Nevertheless, the Bank failed to spot the serious problems that were engulfing Johnson Matthey Bankers in 1984 until it was almost too late. The lapse led to much criticism and to the Banking Act of 1987, that gave the Bank and the authorities swingeing new powers of control. Although the need for rigorous supervision to safeguard depositors and the banking system was universally recognized in the City, some regretted the greater and greater intrusion of the statutory form of regulation. 'If we go on chipping away at the flexibility and the old customs of the City', observed Lord Seebohm, a director of Barclays Bank, 'we shall sooner or later find that the City loses its prominent position as the financial centre of the world'.[84]

The Bank and London as an International Financial Centre

At the time of the formation of the Bank of England, Amsterdam was the world's leading international mercantile and financial centre. Its supplanting in these roles by London in the eighteenth century was partly due to the expansion of the scale and scope of British trade, a process in which British feats of arms played a considerable part. By bolstering British war finances the Bank contributed very materially to these developments. The other factor was the decline of Dutch mercantile activity. Three episodes warrant special mention. The crisis of 1763 that followed the end of the Seven Years War, during which Dutch merchants as neutrals had enjoyed a massive boom, had a devastating impact in Amsterdam and there was a heavy crop of bankruptcies.[85] But London's merchants were largely unscathed thanks to the Bank's cool-headed extension of discounting facilities so that there was no credit crisis in London and no loss of confidence. Indeed, it also provided extensive credit to foreign merchants, thereby enhancing its standing abroad. The next milestone was the Anglo-Dutch war of 1780–3, which saw the decimation of Dutch maritime commerce, the annihilation of its navy, the seizure of its colonies, and the collapse of the Bank of Amsterdam, the institution formed in 1609 that had provided something of a model for the Bank of England.[86] Finally, the French invasion of Holland in 1795 put paid to Amsterdam's role as an international

---

[84] Quoted in Geddes, *Inside the Bank*, 110.

[85] C. H. Wilson, 'The Economic Decline of the Netherlands', *Economic History Review*, 9 (1939), 123.

[86] Ibid. 125–6.

capital and acceptance market, functions which migrated to London along with a fair number of Dutch financiers. This may have been an important reason for the Bank's soaring discounts in the late 1790s and early 1800s discussed earlier; Clapham's breakdown of foreign and domestic bills showed a much larger proportion of the former than might be expected.[87]

From 1795 to 1914, London was the world's leading international financial centre, though the meaning of the title is different in the first and second halves of the era. In the years from the 1790s to the 1860s London functioned as an international capital market, diverting British savings into relatively high-yielding foreign bonds, predominantly sovereign loans but increasingly those financing infrastructure developments, especially railways in North America. The rapidly expanding discount market was overwhelmingly concerned with the finance of domestic trade, though the proportion of foreign bills was growing, rising from perhaps 14 per cent of the total in the mid-1840s to around 45 per cent by the mid-1860s.[88] The Bank of England's contribution to these developments was indirect, its focus being thoroughly domestic, though its role in respect of the evolution of the banking system and the discount market, and the convertibility of sterling into gold, were helpful in the sense that they engendered favourable conditions.

The decades from the 1860s to 1914 saw the development of an international network of financial centres—Paris, Amsterdam, Frankfurt, Hamburg, and latterly Berlin being the other principals—with London at the apex of the structure. This was the age of the international gold standard *par excellence*, with the Bank of England playing a key role as manager of the system. In these years, it gradually perfected the technique of Bank rate control by which it orchestrated the international gold standard. Sterling became the key currency for the denomination of international bonds, the finance of international trade, and the international reserve currency. Foreign banks established branches in London to participate in the international money and capital markets. The first arrived in 1865 and by 1910 there were 28 of them.[89] By then there were also sixty or so British colonial banks.[90] This institutional framework, underpinned by sterling which was regarded as guaranteed by the prestige and practice of the Bank of England, made London the world's leading international financial centre.

All this was shattered by the First World War, which undermined sterling and brought an end to international bond issues and to the role of the discount market in the finance of international trade. Furthermore, it

[87] Clapham, *Bank*, i, 205–8.

[88] Scammell, *Discount Market*, 162; Shizuga Nishimura, *The Decline of the Inland Bill of Exchange in the London Money Market, 1855–1913* (Cambridge, 1971), 93.

[89] W. F. Spalding, 'The Establishment and Growth of Foreign Branch Banks in London', *Journal of the Institute of Bankers* (Nov. 1911), 438.

[90] 'Colonial and Foreign Banks: Their Position in this Country', *Bankers' Magazine*, 77 (1904), 352–63.

boosted the prestige of the US dollar and turned New York into a centre for international capital raising, the British government showing the way, and for international trade finance. The return to the gold standard was seen by the Bank and by the City as the key to the restoration of London's leading role as an international financial centre. They were right, and the City enjoyed a revival of international activity from 1925, although it was short-lived.

The 1930s, 1940s, and 1950s were decades in which the City relinquished its role as a leading international financial centre, save in relation to the Sterling Area. But the Bank, especially its flamboyant Executive Director, George Bolton, retained international aspirations for London.[91] The growth of dollar deposits with London banks from the late 1950s was welcomed and encouraged by the Bank. It fostered the growth of the Euromarkets through a combination of a light regulatory touch with an open-door policy for foreign banks. The latter mounted a veritable invasion, their number soaring from 114 in 1967 to 447 to 1986.[92] The Bank's informal and sympathetic regulatory approach was greatly appreciated by foreign bankers, most of whom were used to much more legalistic frameworks. The attraction of the Bank's method was summed up in 1986 by the chairman of Chase Manhattan when he remarked that it made the City 'a very warm place for doing business'.[93] The outcome of the dynamic development of the Euromarkets from the 1960s was London's re-emergence as a leading international financial centre, one of the top trio with New York and Tokyo.

The Big Bang restructuring of the 1980s enhanced London's competitiveness as an international financial centre. Though not originally set in motion by the Bank, the reforms were adroitly managed by it once the process was underway. More recently, the Bank has played a key role, in conjunction with Whitehall, in securing the location of the European Bank for Reconstruction and Development in the City; has lobbied hard, though unsuccessfully, for the placement of the European Monetary Institute in the square mile; and has taken initiatives such as the issue of ECU-dominated gilts to promote London's role as the leading European international financial centre. Although the International Division disappeared in the internal reorganization of the Bank announced in April 1994, the promotion of London as an international financial centre continued to be a key objective.

Patterns and Perspectives

The last 300 years have seen many changes in both the Bank and the City. In the eighteenth century the Bank loomed large and powerful both

---

[91] Fry, *Banker's World*, 29–38.   [92] *Banker* (Nov. 1986), 69.
[93] John Plender and Paul Wallace, *The Square Mile: A Guide to the New City of London* (1985), 32.

in relation to other City institutions and to the government. The nineteenth century saw a waning of its power as other City institutions, notably the joint-stock banks, increased in size, and the government's financing requirements became routine. However, it enjoyed a waxing of its prestige and mystique and its role in the City's Edwardian heyday has been likened to that of the conductor of an orchestra.

For the twentieth century, generalizations about its role are problematic. One reason is the multiplicity of parts it has played: a player, a policeman, a fireman, a marriage-broker, an immigration officer, an impresario, and others. For many years it became more and more an agent of government, but the shift towards greater independence from the early 1990s may reverse this process. Recent decades have witnessed an unprecedented increase in its statutory powers—but, because of growing globalization, a decrease in its authority over markets and their participants.

Finally, there is the uncertainty over its future in relation to the advent of a European Central Banking system that will probably assume a form something like the Federal Reserve System of the United States. If the Bank of England emerged from this process with a status and operational role like that of the Federal Reserve Bank of New York, the City would receive a shot in the arm. But a standing akin to, say, the Federal Reserve Bank of Minneapolis would, of course, be a very different matter.

7 The Governors, Directors and Management of the Bank of England

ELIZABETH HENNESSY

THIS chapter examines the people chosen by the Bank to be its Governors, Directors and senior managers, traces the methods of selection from the establishment of the Bank until 1994, its tercentenary year, and makes some assessment of the effectiveness with which the internal management of the Bank has been carried out.

Governors and Court

The first Governors of the Bank of England in 1694 swore, on election, that to the utmost of their powers they would by legal ways and means endeavour to support and maintain 'the Body Politique or fellowship of the Governor and Company of the Bank of England and the liberties and privileges thereof'. The twenty-four Directors swore, in their turn, to be 'indifferent and equall to all manner of persons' and to give their best advice and assistance for the support and good government of the corporation.[1] The diarist John Evelyn asserted that the new corporation had been put 'under the government of the most able & wealthy Cittizens of Lond';[2] and the composition of this earliest Court of Directors set a pattern which was to be followed faithfully for well over 200 years and which is still clearly discernible today.

The draft Charter of the Bank had laid down that the qualification for the office of Governor should be a holding of £4,000 stock of the corporation, £3,000 for Deputy Governor, and £2,000 for a Director. Governors and Directors were to be chosen each year between 25 March and 25 April by the proprietors of not less than £500 of Bank stock. Most of the first Directors were wealthy City merchants, many of them with close

---

[1] W. Marston Acres, *The Bank of England from Within, 1694–1900* (Oxford, 1931), i, 13–14.
[2] E. S. De Beer (ed.), *The Diary of John Evelyn*, v. *Kalendarium, 1690–1706* (Oxford, 1955), 185.

connections with the Court and the Court of Aldermen of the City of London. Sir John Houblon, the first Governor, was a future Lord Mayor (1695–6), Master of the Grocers' Company in 1696, and a Lord of the Admiralty (where he earned the friendship and respect of Samuel Pepys) from 1694 to 1699. After his years as Governor from 1694 to 1697, he remained a Director of the Bank until his death in 1712. Two of his brothers, James and Abraham Houblon (the latter was Governor from 1703 to 1705), were among the first Directors of the Bank, and a brother-in-law of the three Houblons, John Lordell, was also one of the first Directors. Of these original 26 members of Court, six were or became knights, one was a baronet, ten were Aldermen, and six served as Lord Mayor. One of these, Gilbert Heathcote, a merchant dealing in Spanish wine, was twice Governor of the Bank at separate periods (1709–11 and 1723–5) and achieved this position without serving as Deputy Governor; he was the last Lord Mayor to ride on horseback in his own Lord Mayor's Show. It came to be normal practice for a man to serve two years in the office of Deputy Governor followed immediately by two years as Governor, and this, as Clapham remarks, 'led to a great continuity, and ultimately to a great conservatism, in the direction of Bank policy'.[3]

Seven of the first Directors were descended from Protestant refugees from the continent: the Houblons, John Lordell, James Bateman, Theodore Janssen and Samuel Lethieullier, a descendant of a Cologne family and a member of the Grocers' Company. Several more such descendants were chosen for the Court at the next election in 1697. At this period many of the most prominent City merchants were of foreign extraction, particularly the descendants of the French Protestants who had taken refuge in England when persecution was at its height on the continent. They naturally supported the Glorious Revolution of 1688, which had put the Protestant William of Orange on the throne, and had made substantial contributions to the capital raised to establish the Bank of England in order to prosecute the war with the French: it was all too clear to them what position they would be in if James II should regain the English throne with the help of Louis XIV. Their names and those of relatives and connections by marriage were to become familiar in the lists of Directors, for from the earliest days family as well as business relationships were strong predisposals to selection for the Court.[4]

In August 1694, a month after the establishment of the Bank, a meeting of the General Court of Proprietors agreed that a committee should be set up to prepare the By-Laws. Seventeen were duly prepared, most of them based on the provisions of the Charter or on clauses of the 1694 Bank of

---

[3] Bank of England Archive, ADM 30/1; A. A. Houblon, *The Houblon Family, its Story and Times* (1907), i, 260–83; Sir John Clapham, *The Bank of England: A History* (Cambridge, 1944), i, 37–41, 108.

[4] Acres, *Bank*, i, 21–8.

England Act. One, which was evidently framed to prevent the Bank falling into the hands of a small and powerful clique, would have prohibited more than two-thirds of the retiring Directors from being re-elected for the ensuing year, and limited the tenure of office by the Governor and Deputy Governor to two years only. This draft By-Law was strongly opposed and was thrown out on this occasion, but an Act of 1697 (Act 8 & 9 Wm III, cap. 20, sec. 52) did include a clause which embodied the first of the two provisions.[5]

This state of affairs was not always convenient, but no change appears to have been seriously considered until 1848, when it was suggested that at least twenty of the Directors should be eligible for re-election; however, any alteration had to be agreed by parliament and the matter was allowed to drop. In 1857 the Court of Directors asked the Governor to allow five-sixths (i.e. twenty) of the Directors to be re-elected instead of two-thirds (sixteen), but again no action was taken, possibly, as Acres suggests, because the financial crisis of that year was preoccupying the Governors. Fifteen years later, in 1872, a Special Committee of Directors recommended that application should be made to parliament for power to remove the restriction, so that in forthcoming elections seven-eighths instead of two-thirds of those who were Directors in the previous year could be chosen again. This was agreed, and the Bank's solicitors drafted a Bill which was approved by the General Court of Proprietors and which received the Royal Assent on 18 July 1872 as the Bank of England, Election of Directors Act. It remained in force until 1897, when the Proprietors passed a resolution repealing the By-Law which prevented the re-election of more than twenty-one of the retiring Directors.[6]

In the two hundred years in which these varying restrictions were in force, they led to the formation of a group, varying in number, who during their intervals out of office were referred to as 'ex-Directors'. It was usually only the comparatively junior Directors who were required to stand down, and once a Director had 'passed the chairs' by serving as Deputy Governor and/or Governor, he was no longer required to do so. He also became eligible for membership of the Bank's senior and most influential committee, the Committee of Treasury.

The Act of 1697 added two regulations concerning the yearly 'recompense' to be paid to the Governors and Directors—a General Court, or meeting of the proprietors of Bank stock, on 26 April 1695, having agreed that the Governor and Deputy Governor would be allowed £200 per year and Directors £150 per year each. These rates were not reviewed until 1804, when they were doubled; 80 years later there was a further readjustment, when the Governor and Deputy Governor were allowed £1,000 per year each, and Directors £500. In 1892, by which time it was recognized that

---

[5] Clapham, *Bank*, i, 40.   [6] Acres, *Bank*, ii, 542.

their terms of office in the Bank were requiring most of their time—which had not been the case much before this period—the Governor's remuneration was raised to £2,000 a year and his Deputy received £1,500.[7]

The Directors soon faced their first serious problems, when war expenditure caused rocketing inflation: their efforts to combat this were successful, but it almost certainly led to the death of one of their number, the first Deputy Governor, Michael Godfrey. Godfrey, only 37 at the time of his death, was one of the most prominent promoters of the Bank and its interests. He was killed by a cannon-ball in the trenches at Namur in July 1695; why he had gone there has never been exactly determined but it seems likely that he was in Flanders to draw the personal attention of the King to what was being done in London to counteract the fall in the value of the guinea. Further economic troubles ensued in 1696, including the first serious run on the Bank, and were also successfully withstood by the Directors.

The original By-Laws of 1694 authorized the Court to appoint any sub-committees they found to be necessary. The Court itself, after an initial period of daily meetings, met weekly, as it has continued to do with barely a week missed since, and each year, after the elections, it appointed the various standing or permanent committees. These were the House Committee, which looked after the interests of the staff and premises; the Committee in Waiting, composed of a rota of Directors who superintended day-to-day business, including advances and in later years discounts; and one originally described as the 'Committee for ye Trea'ry', later known as 'The Committee to Attend the Lord Treasurer' or, more commonly, the Committee of Treasury.[8] This was the most influential of all the Bank's committees and its chief directive body; it was finally abolished with effect from March 1994. In the immediately preceding years it had fallen into disuse—a distaste for an inner group within the Court prevailed, and after its abolition its functions were split between the Audit and Remuneration Committees.

From its inception the Committee of Treasury consisted of the Governor, Deputy Governor, and the most senior of the Directors, most of whom had served as Governor. It soon took over the work of another standing committee, the original Committee for Accounts, and thus had the books of the Bank under continuous review, as well as being in direct, official contact with government. There are no minute-books of this committee before 1779. Clapham considers it unlikely that earlier books have been lost, as the first record consists only of a rough note made by the then Deputy Governor: if this had been one of a series, he suggests, 'it is a fair inference from the known history of records that something tidier and more formal would have evolved'. Its increasing power and influence were symptomatic of the fact that the direction of the higher affairs of the Bank was increasingly held in fewer hands.[9]

---

[7] John Giuseppi, *The Bank of England: A History from its Foundation in 1694* (1966), 148.
[8] Clapham, *Bank*, i, 108–12.   [9] Ibid. i, 110.

Stability in the Eighteenth Century

Once the alarms and agitations of the early years (including the South Sea Bubble) were safely behind it, and the move to Threadneedle Street had been accomplished in 1734, the Bank settled into a steady, unruffled routine which was to last for some 50 years. The General Court had ceased to be very influential. In the first years of the Bank it had frequently been required to give rulings on constitutional matters or to back up Directors in their efforts to prevent any infringement of the Bank's position or privileges by government or anybody else. But the need for its support gradually diminished, and by the middle of the eighteenth century it only forgathered for its statutory meetings, which according to the terms of the Charter had to be held quarterly. It met twice a year, usually in January and July, to declare the dividend; and once in March or April to elect Governors and Directors. The fourth meeting was presumably held merely to fulfil the requirements of the Charter; additional meetings were called when renewal of the Charter was being considered or if a vacancy occurred among the Directors.[10]

During the second half of the eighteenth century, however, vacancies were infrequent. Many of the Directors were long-lived, and served for periods of thirty years or even more. The government and policies of the Bank remained firmly in the hands of these long-term Directors, and the predominant inner council remained the Committee of Treasury, which by 1769 had absorbed another of the standing committees, the Exchanges Committee. It also, as Clapham notes, conducted much business which might have been considered the prerogative of the House Committee, including matters concerning 'keys and porters and watchmen, the pensioning of servants, Christmas boxes for the out-tellers [the clerks who went out to collect money due on bills and notes], the giving of a gratuity to the widow of a glazier who fell while at his work and was killed, and how a woman spent the night with the Officer of the Bank Guard'—the last case having three pages of minutes devoted to it.[11]

The powers of the Committee of Treasury came in for criticism from outside the Bank. A Lord Mayor of London, Alderman William Pickett, who was never a Director, stated fiercely in 1788 that 'by whom, when and by what contrivance, the dark and concealed system of management by a *Treasury Committee, without the deliberation of the whole Court, has been established,* is a consideration of the first magnitude for the Proprietors .. . it was certainly not provided for in the Charter'.[12]

Agitation over the amount of the dividend payable on Bank stock led to

[10] Ibid. i, 111–12.   [11] Ibid. i, 200.
[12] William Pickett, *An Apologie to the Public for a continued Intrusion on their Notice . . .* (1788), 36, quoted in Clapham, *Bank*, i, 200.

a stirring of movement from the General Court in the same year, and for a while the numbers of proprietors attending its spring-time election meetings rose quite considerably, from the 100 or so which had long been the average, to 524 in 1789. It was further stirred when Pitt the Younger, in 1790, threatened to remove unclaimed dividends from the Exchequer and Audit Roll (a record of government money which passed through the Bank to be paid out in dividends). The Directors, supported by the General Court, which was affronted by this threat to private property, successfully thwarted Pitt's intentions.[13]

The Committee of Treasury was responsible among other things for drawing up the lists of proposals for Governors' and Directors' elections, thus further ensuring that the *status quo* remained largely undisturbed. This concentration of policy and administration into 'so few hands, some of them old and perhaps feeble', had unhappy results. Few of the Directors took much interest in the administration of the staff, which by now numbered over 400: frauds and forged notes, both perpetrated by clerks, began to come to light, and special internal committees were set up in 1783 and again in 1790 to enquire into the 'mode and execution of the business . . . in the different parts of the Bank.' Their reports suggested reforms which were duly carried out and eliminated some of the worst lapses in security, such as keys to the Bank lying forgotten overnight on a table at the entrance and the unquestioning admittance of strangers who claimed to have business in the Bank. Stockbroking business carried out on the premises by clerks from the Stock Transfer Offices, despite rules to the contrary, was forbidden once more (although they continued to use the Rotunda in the Bank until finally expelled in 1838), but the nature of the Bank's central government remained unmodified, and the Committee of Treasury continued to rule by 'precedent and routine'.[14]

Significant reforms concerning the 'rotation of the chairs' were introduced in 1848, after the failure in the previous year of Robinson & Co., a firm of merchants whose head, W. R. Robinson, was Governor at the time. It had gone bankrupt following 'imprudent operations in Corn'; and several Directors and Governors had become insolvent in the previous decade. It was decided that in future the Court of Directors would, in principle, recommend to the Proprietors the man they considered the most fitted for the job; and this would have the added advantage that initial election to the Court could be at a more mature age, whereas up until then it had been considered that newcomers should be below middle age so that when their turn as Deputy and Governor came round, they were not too old to fill the posts satisfactorily. The formal rotation of the chairs was also repudiated (although in practice it continued until the First World War), and new Directors were no longer required to undertake to serve as Deputy and

---

[13] Clapham, *Bank*, i, 201–2; ii, 480–1.   [14] Ibid. i, 202–3.

Governor when their time came round, or to retire. Private bankers continued to be ineligible for a place on the Court, in order to preserve confidentiality—one banker should not be privy to the secrets of a competitor, and the Bank of England was still at this period transacting considerable amounts of private banking business.[15] But after 1848 there was a new emphasis on experience and capability, and the Court as a whole became a better qualified group; and similarly from this date the Bank began the process of disengaging itself from active participation in the discount market, preferring to attempt to regulate the market by varying Bank rate. As Kynaston points out, 'the implication was clear enough that considerations of profit were now becoming secondary to those of central banking'.[16]

There had never been any formal decision, taken by vote at a General Court, that a Director should be drawn from the merchants of London, or the merchant bankers who were evolving from them. Nor had it ever been formally decided that a Deputy Governor from their number should serve for two years and then immediately serve as Governor for two more, but this practice had become virtually fossilized by tradition. One Governor served two years twice in the reigns of Queen Anne and King George I, and three Governors in the eighteenth century and five in the nineteenth served an extra year; the vast majority followed the general rule, however, and only two Deputy Governors served for three years.

A Call for Reform

Towards the end of the nineteenth century, and after a series of financial crises, a scathing attack was made on the practices, by then almost two centuries old, by which the Governors and Directors of the Bank were chosen. Walter Bagehot's *Lombard Street*, published in 1873, devoted a chapter to 'The Government of the Bank of England', which was certainly the most cogent and intelligent criticism levelled on this subject to date. He begins by acknowledging the fairness and lack of 'favour' shown in the selection process: 'Very few selections in the world are made with equal purity', and there is a sincere wish on the part of the Directors to 'provide, to the best of their ability, for the future good government of the Bank'. Age is a primary consideration. The oldest and most senior Director who has not been in office almost inevitably, with only a few exceptions made on grounds of ill-health or 'special temporary occupation', becomes Deputy Governor and then immediately Governor. It is usually about twenty years from the time of his first election that he arrives 'at the chair'. 'And as the offices ... are very important, a man who fills them should be still in the vigour

[15] R. S. Sayers, *The Bank of England, 1891–1944* (Cambridge, 1976), ii, 595, apps., pp. 1–2.
[16] David Kynaston, *The City of London*, i. *A World of Its Own, 1815–1890* (1994), 165.

of life. Accordingly, Bank directors, when first chosen by the board, are always young men.'

Bagehot continues by assessing the influence of the Committee of Treasury, composed of 'the older members of the board', over the Bank and the government. He views this as changing with the character of the changing Governor: even so, 'the influence of the Committee of Treasury is always considerable, though not always the same. They form a cabinet of mature, declining and old men, just close to the executive; and for good or evil such a cabinet must have power.'

He has no real quarrel with these facts, but is deeply troubled by the lack of continuity of the government of the Bank which is implicit in the change, every two years, of Governor and Deputy—other old-fashioned institutions, such as the East India or Hudson's Bay Companies, did have long-serving Governors. He allows that a permanent Governor is not a realistic possibility. Such a post would attract the wrong type of man—'we should not be sure of choosing a good Governor, and should indeed run a great risk, for the most part, of choosing a bad one'. What Bagehot proposes is a 'humbler scheme': a permanent Deputy Governor, on the lines of the Permanent Under Secretary of State in parliamentary offices, who remains in place despite changes in administration. Such a man would avoid the problems inherent in a permanent Governor: he would not be a 'king' in the City, and there would be no danger of attracting the vain and the idle well-to-do candidate who might otherwise be drawn to the position. This new office should go to a trained banker, who should give his whole time to the post, rather than, as now, being engaged in his own business, and would thus be able to give full attention to the affairs of the Bank just when those affairs require that attention the most, i.e. at times of anxiety or panic in the City. He should be a Director and a man of good position; he must not have to say 'Sir' to the Governor—'such a person would give to the decisions of the Bank that foresight, that quickness and that consistency in which those decisions are understandably now deficient.'

This was the most pressing and necessary reform identified by Bagehot, but another should be the end of the exclusion of London bankers from the Court. They are now, he noted, as they had not been at the time of the Bank's foundation, the principal depositors at the Bank, and are therefore especially interested in its stability. If the house of Rothschild is represented on the Court, then English bankers should be so too, for 'according to continental ideas Messrs Rothschild are bankers, if anyone is a banker'. The Committee of Treasury should be chosen on principles of competence rather than seniority. Bagehot suggests that the Court is perhaps too numerous, at twenty-six, to carry out any real discussion of difficult business in a short weekly meeting—and if it sits longer than an hour or so, the Stock Exchange and the money market become excited. Perhaps 'the knowledge of impatience without must cause haste, if not impatience, within'.[17] The call for what would, in effect, have been a General Manager, or Managing Director, of the Bank, produced no discernible effect in Threadneedle Street at the time, but as described below such a post was indeed created for a short while in the following century.

Between 1890 and 1946 the formalities relevant to the election of the Court, and to meetings of the General Court, were altered only once, under the Supplemental Charter of 1896. This recognized that only two meetings of the General Court were necessary each year instead of the previous four, and empowered it to fix the number of Directors who should not be immediately re-elected.[18] From 1900 onwards all the Directors were re-elected each year; after the report of the Revelstoke Committee in 1918 an age-limit of 70 came into force. In the latter years of the nineteenth century and the early years of the twentieth there were still some very aged men on the Court: Sayers notes that four who died between 1900 and 1918 each served for 50 or more years, and in the early years of Norman's Governorship 'the senior Director [Sir E. A. Hambro] had been on the Court since 1879, when the United States went on the gold standard; he died (a Director to the end) in the last weeks before Britain's return to gold in 1925'.[19]

The First World War and After

The First World War finally broke the pattern of rotation which had lasted with few exceptions for over 200 years. Governor Lidderdale was one such exception: he had been elected for a third year in office because of his successful handling of the Baring crisis of 1890, and in order to negotiate the renewal of the Bank's Charter two years later. The swift and effective actions to calm panic in the City and sort out the troubles of the money markets taken by Governor Cunliffe on the outbreak of war in 1914 led to his re-election after his two-year term as Governor, which would normally have ended in the spring of 1915. He was re-elected in that year and the two following years; no previous Governor had ever served so long, and his colleagues were happy at first for him to continue to run the Bank, advise the Treasury, and maintain relationships with the City. But his overbearing, bullying manner, which was manifest outside the Bank as well as within it, led him, fatally, to act without consultation with the Committee of Treasury. In 1917 a head-on clash with the Chancellor of the Exchequer, Andrew Bonar Law, had far-reaching results as far as the Governorship was concerned.

Cunliffe's actions, which amounted to a complete flouting of the Treasury's wishes without any reference to the Chancellor, led the Prime

---

[17] Walter Bagehot, *Lombard Street: A Description of the Money Market* (1873), ch. 8 *passim*.

[18] Acres, *Bank*, ii, 542. [19] Sayers, *Bank*, ii, 595.

Minister, Lloyd George, to ask the Governor to sign a memorandum agreeing that while the war continued the Bank must act in all matters on the direction of the Chancellor whenever the latter felt that the national interest was involved. When Cunliffe refused to sign without consulting his colleagues, Lloyd George spoke of the possibility of the government 'taking over the Bank'. Under this threat the Committee of Treasury prepared a memorandum requesting Cunliffe to express his regret over the way certain telegrams had been dispatched about the transfer of gold in Ottawa without consulting the Chancellor, but also pointing out that the course of action taken was the only one that had seemed possible at the time. Eventually the Governor did apologize and undertook to consult the Chancellor 'before taking any action during the war involving the general conditions of national credit or substantially affecting the gold holdings of the Bank'. He expressed the opinion within the Bank that this climb-down would ultimately lead to nationalization.[20]

In any case his Governorship was now certain to come to an end. His colleagues were glad to take the opportunity of getting rid of him—several openly said that they thought he was insane—and in 1918 Brien Cokayne (later Lord Cullen) was recommended by the Committee of Treasury to become Governor, with Montagu Norman, who had been a Director since 1907 and had spent increasing amounts of time in the Bank, as his Deputy.

By this time the outside world had begun to question the whole topic of the Bank's duties and functions: *The Economist* in September 1917 had said that it was too secretive, suggested that it should make more use of industrialists and bankers, and questioned the advisability of concentrating too much power in the hands of one man. Although the Bank usually maintained a lofty disregard of external opinions, these happened to chime with many expressed inside. In October 1917 a committee chaired by Lord Revelstoke, who had been a Director since 1898, was appointed to examine the position. Its report, approved by the Court in February 1918, allowed that much of the external criticism had been justified. The Committee agreed that the Governor should be prevented from exercising autocratic control, primarily by keeping the Committee of Treasury informed of the Bank's affairs and his own actions. The Committee of Treasury itself should be reconstituted from its traditional composition of the Governors *ex officio*, plus nine or ten Directors, to consist of not more than nine members in all, including the Governors. The Committee should have at least three members who had not passed either chair and should be elected each year by free and secret ballot. It also recommended the continuation of the relatively recent practice of having the Secretary or his Deputy to attend its meetings, in order to relieve the Deputy Governor of his task, undertaken certainly since 1779, of taking the minutes.

[20] Sayers, *Bank*, i, 99–109.

A further concern addressed by the Revelstoke Committee was the composition of the Court. It saw no reason to depart from the principle that members of the clearing banks and of the discount houses should not become Directors, but in view of the fact that fewer candidates of the 'time hallowed mercantile type' were now appearing, it recommended that members of British banks with branches in India, the Colonies, and South America should be considered eligible. Directors should in future be expected to retire at the age of 70.[21]

In April 1918, after the election of Cokayne and Norman as Governor and Deputy, Revelstoke's main recommendations were accepted and implemented swiftly. A new post, that of Comptroller—answering quite closely to Bagehot's recommendations for a permanent Deputy Governor—was created, and filled by Sir Gordon Nairne, previously the Chief Cashier. It was a unique position: he attended meetings of Court without being a Director, and also meetings of the Committee of Treasury and all Standing Committees, and was given special responsibility for coordination of the work of the 'two sides [i.e. stock and cash] of the Bank' and its internal affairs in general. This was an important innovation, which created the first stepping-stone between Governors and Court and the rest of the officials and staff. Nairne was the first of only three people to fill the post of Comptroller, which he relinquished after seven years when he was elected to Court as a Director—the first member of the Bank's staff ever to be so, in a step that was another major turning-point for the Directorate.[22]

Governor Norman and Modernization

In 1920 Montagu Norman become Governor. He had been a Director since 1907, and during the First World War had devoted virtually all his time to the affairs of the Bank, acting as an unofficial assistant to Cokayne, then Deputy to Cunliffe. Norman had always been convinced of the desirability of, as he wrote to the US banker Benjamin Strong in 1927, a group of full-time professionals on the Court. Although the Revelstoke Committee recommendations in this respect had had little immediate effect—Sir Charles Addis, London manager of the Hongkong and Shanghai Bank, was the only 'overseas' banker to join the Court in the wake of the Committee's report—once Norman became Governor its whole composition began to change swiftly. Sayers has analysed the proportion of the 'new breed' and of the 'conventional recruits' in the period between the Revelstoke Report and the outbreak of the Second World War, noting the gradual swing from the traditional City figures such as Goschen, Wallace, Whigham,

---

[21] Ibid. ii, 596–7.   [22] Ibid. ii, 619; Giuseppi, *Bank*, 143–4.

Whitworth, Hambro and Spencer-Smith to industrialists like Sir Josiah Stamp, Sir Andrew Duncan and Lord Hyndley.[23]

The annual election of Governors and Directors in 1929 included one appointment of especial interest. The fact that Norman had undertaken an increasingly onerous and time-consuming burden of work since he became Governor had thrown a corresponding increase of work-load on the Deputy Governors, who had continued to be elected on the old system of rotation. But it was clear by the end of the 1920s that what was needed was a full-time Deputy Governor, without ties to his own business elsewhere— and a man with banking experience. The man chosen was Sir Ernest Harvey, who had previously been successively Chief Cashier, Comptroller and Director. He remained Deputy Governor until 1936, when he was succeeded by another ex-Chief Cashier, B. G. Catterns.

Norman's many personal crusades—the financial rehabilitation of Europe, the establishment of other central banks and the regeneration of British industry—meant that he needed further assistance, and in 1926, with some reluctance, Court had agreed to the institution of a new post, that of Adviser. A growing band of Advisers, including Harry Siepmann, the American economist Walter Stewart, and Sir Otto Niemeyer, all men of outstanding ability, formed a ring of close associates on whom Norman could rely absolutely to further his most cherished schemes.

Harvey's appointment as Deputy Governor brought to a head the question of adequate recompense for a member of the Court giving full-time service to the Bank. In September 1932 the General Court approved an addition to the By-Law concerning the remuneration of Directors, which sanctioned the Court to engage the exclusive services of any of its members as from the preceding 1 March, and to pay them an appropriate annual sum.[24]

Further changes were introduced as a direct result of an investigation into the management of the Bank carried out under the chairmanship of Edward Peacock between 1931 and 1932. The report of this Special Committee on Organisation made recommendations of considerable significance as to the departmental structure of the Bank, as described below. Its impact on the Directorship was also significant, as it recommended the appointment of two Executive Directors, one with responsibility for the money markets and one for the staff. William Clegg was appointed Staff Director immediately on approval of the Report. Between 1932 and 1938 seven of the twelve elections were for Executive Directors, most of whom came from outside the Bank. Edward Holland-Martin from his family bank, Martins, seems to have been the first member of a clearing bank appointed to Court; others included Bunbury and Martin from the metals and mining industries. Weir, Cadbury, and Hanbury-Williams, who were

[23] Sayers, *Bank*, ii, 600–1.   [24] Ibid. ii, 622–3, 620–1; Giuseppi, *Bank*, 167–8.

all non-executive, came from various branches of industry. Even so, the 'man with practical City experience' continued to be predominant, which was what the Peacock Committee recommended.

The Committee also changed the process of selection. A list had long been kept on which any Director could note suitable candidates, who, since 1918, had been appraised by a Committee of Directors reporting to the Committee of Treasury. Post-Peacock the task was undertaken by the Committee of Treasury alone, although Norman's personal wishes obviously played a considerable part: Cameron Cobbold, for example, whom he almost certainly saw as a future Governor, was brought in by Norman as an Adviser on the overseas side in 1933 and became an Executive Director in 1938.[25]

The alteration in the type of man elected to Court was echoed by a change in the age distribution. While some of the new Executive Directors were as young as, or even younger than, the traditional youngish man from a City house who had been elected for over 200 years, some, such as Clegg, were much older (he was already 65 when he became Staff Director), and in general men coming to Court were older. Sayers notes that of those elected between 1918 and 1944 the average age at election was 47, nearly ten years older than in the pre-war generation.[26]

Norman, the longest-serving Governor to date, remained in office until illness forced his retirement in 1944. Although the question of a successor was frequently debated in the 1930s, no candidate ever quite measured up to him, and his Governorship of nearly a quarter of a century is unlikely ever to be equalled.[27] His successor, Lord Catto, came from the Treasury: he had served a brief spell as a Director in 1940. Catto's main achievement was seeing the Bank safely through nationalization.

Changes to the Court after Nationalization

The nationalization of the Bank by the Act of 1946 introduced a new regime. Governor, Deputy, and Directors became Crown appointments, and the Court was reduced from twenty-four in number to sixteen. Four of the initial sixteen were to retire after the first year, four after the second, and so on, but Directors would be eligible for re-election. The terms of office for both Governors would be five years: they too could be re-elected.

The reduction in numbers had been considered desirable for some time and would almost certainly have been carried out in any case. The Governor and Deputy Governor (Cobbold, since 1945) remained unchanged in 1946, and a further twelve of the Directors of the previous

---

[25] Elizabeth Hennessy, *A Domestic History of the Bank of England, 1930–1960* (Cambridge, 1992), 325–6.

[26] Sayers, *Bank*, ii, 600.

[27] Ibid. ii, 651–2.

Court also remained in office. Four Directors were required: Lord Piercy, the Chairman of ICFC, George Gibson, a trades union leader, Robin Brook, who had reached the rank of Brigadier during the Second World War and was now starting on a City career, and George Wansbrough, a socialist who had worked for Bensons in the field of industrial finance.[28] From that date there was a trades union leader on the Court until the retirement of Gavin Laird in 1994.

A section of the new Charter laid down the form of declaration to be made by the Directors on appointment to Court: this was in the wording established in 1694, and like their many predecessors, Directors of the nationalized Bank still undertake to be 'indifferent and equal to all manner of persons' and that they will 'faithfully and honestly demean themselves according to their skill and understanding'.

The 1946 Act caused almost no disturbance of the Bank's internal management and organization, nor did it change the tasks and duties of Directors. These have never been a sinecure. For modest pay (the stipend was fixed at the time of nationalization as £500 and has remained at this figure since then) they had not only to attend the weekly Court—an obligation which took precedence over almost any other—but to take part in the work of both standing and *ad hoc* committees. Of the former, the Committee of Treasury was both the most prestigious and the most time-consuming. Until 1914 the Committee of Daily Waiting, also dating back to the foundation of the Bank, required the presence of three Directors every day except Saturday, when only two were necessary, to carry out tedious tasks such as holding and checking keys, auditing securities held by the Bank or held against advances, and so on. These duties were gradually scaled down until the Committee was abolished by the Peacock Committee and its duties undertaken by Executive Directors or other Bank officials. New Directors from Norman's time were expected to serve several years on the Staff Committee, which in the 1930s absorbed the work of six other standing committees including the House Committee; it was itself abolished in 1993. Special or *ad hoc* committees, especially those dealing with the Branches (which necessitate a fair amount of travelling) and the Printing Works, also make considerable demands on the time and efforts of Directors, the majority of whom have full-time and demanding work of their own. This was increasingly recognized in the early 1990s, when in addition to the Committee of Treasury and the Staff Committee, the Debden Committee (which oversaw the Printing Works), the Registrar's Committee, and the Securities Committee were also wound up. The meetings of Court were shortened and attendance at every sitting was no longer obligatory.[29]

---

[28] John Fforde, *The Bank of England and Public Policy, 1941–1958* (Cambridge, 1992), 28.
[29] Information from Bank of England, June 1994.

One seemingly small, but significant erosion of the powers of the Court of the nationalized Bank occurred in 1957. Two non-executive Directors were accused of having benefited from a premature leak of a change in the Bank rate. Such changes had by tradition been discussed with members of the Court before they took place; the Parker Tribunal which enquired into the incident completely exonerated both men concerned—Lord Kindersley and Sir William Keswick—but recommended that the Bank's confidential deliberations on Bank rate should no longer be shared with members of the Court. The Bank resisted for a while, and the matter was eventually referred to the Radcliffe Committee, which reported in favour of a change in procedure. This was effected in 1959, when prior consultation ceased.[30]

The debate of the last few years over the advisability and possibility of the independence of the Bank from government, perhaps on the Bundesbank model, has led to various theories on what part the Court might play in the future, with particular emphasis on the way in which interest rates should be fixed. There are two main directions in which it might conceivably develop. It could act as a joint decision-maker with the Governor, or effectively function in a public relations capacity, allowing him to make most of the judgements but backing up the Bank in its operations and attempting to shield the Governor from external criticism of his actions. To some extent the latter is already happening, but the joint decision-making model seems to be gaining favour with those who urge the greater independence of the Bank. It is not so very long ago that the Court existed merely to rubber stamp the Governor's opinions—Directors had to stand up when they spoke, which daunted all but the bravest, and, earlier but still in this century, minutes of the current meeting of Court are said to have been read out by the Secretary *before* the meeting took place. The considerably greater freedom for individual opinion which evidently obtains in today's Court (meetings are highly confidential and minutes released in full only 100 years later) could be developed further. One idea for increasing accountability that has been suggested is for Court members of an independent Bank to testify regularly in front of a parliamentary committee. Alternatively, as in the Bundesbank and the Bank of France, different people could be brought into the decision-making process about interest rates. Sir Peter Middleton, chairman of BZW, told the Treasury and Civil Service Committee in October 1993 that he favoured the election to the Court of people who had a greater commitment than the current Directors to keeping prices down.[31]

The newly independent Bank of France pointed one way forward in this respect, when in January 1994 it announced the formation of a nine-strong committee which would in future set monetary policy—three full-time bank

[30] Fforde, *Bank*, 700–3.
[31] Treasury and Civil Service Committee: The Role of the Bank of England, *Minutes of Evidence* (1993–4, HC 98–II), q 464.

officials, two industrialists, an ex-government minister, a journalist, a financier, and a former adviser to the Treasury. This method has the advantages of removing political interference and ensuring the transparency of a decision-making process involving a relatively large number of people.

The Occupations of Directors

There has been surprisingly little serious analysis of the occupations of those chosen as Directors of the Bank. A look at the Directors' files in the Archive swiftly confirms that for the first 200 years or so they were predominantly 'merchants' of the City of London, just like the majority of the very first Directors. The report of the Revelstoke Committee spoke of 'the historic names familiar from generation to generation on the rolls of the Court', and from early on there was a natural predisposition to elect men related to current or previous Directors.

They were drawn from a wide range of commercial City concerns, representing the countries and types of trade with which Britain was engaged at any one time—the West Indies, the Baltic, China, Turkey; silk merchants, lace merchants, wine merchants and so on. In the eighteenth century there was usually at least one Alderman and many of these later became Lord Mayor.[32] Anthony Howe has published a detailed study of three groups of Directors, totalling eighty-two, effectively covering the Court from 1833 to 1873. Fifty-six of them were described as 'merchants', thirteen as merchant bankers, three from insurance or shipping, five from mining and engineering, three were 'industrial', plus two others. The majority thus comprised what Bagehot, at the very end of the period of Howe's review, characterized as 'plain, sensible, prosperous English merchants', with a rising proportion of the 'new breed' of nineteenth-century merchant bankers. A variety of other interests, Howe demonstrates, both metropolitan and (less frequently) provincial, were also represented, above all insurance. (A note in the Bank's files shows that there were twelve directors of the London Assurance on the Court between 1720 and 1920, three of whom became Governors.) Nor was the Bank as isolated from the interests of the Industrial Revolution as has sometimes been claimed—metal, mining and copper were all represented on the Court in the middle years of the nineteenth century. Family connection and personal recommendation continued to play a significant role: 'selection was therefore very much from among a group of tightly knit City families, often interrelated by marriage or linked by friendship and business interests.' They were a 'highly political business class', with 28 per cent acting as MPs at some point in their career.[33] Some 60 years after the end of Howe's

---

[32] Bank of England Archive, ADM 30/1.
[33] Anthony Howe, 'From "Old Corruption" to "New Probity": The Bank of England and its Directors in the Age of Reform', *Financial History Review*, 1 (1994), *passim*.

period, the Peacock Committee laid down that no Director should be an MP except for the City of London, which had four members until 1885 and then two until the end of the Second World War. Sayers' brief review of the Directors in the period covered by his history (1891 to 1944) points out that in the last fifty years before the First World War 'there was usually a Baring, a Goschen, a Hubbard, a Grenfell; someone from Antony Gibbs, and from Brown Shipley.' Other family names were Lubbock, Hambro, Hoare and Currie. But at no time did these names comprise a majority of the Court, and the balance of the twenty-four Directors was drawn from ship-owners, wine merchants, brewers, East India merchants, and textile merchants. 'Nor was any firm allowed to suppose that it had a prescriptive right to a place at Court, and there was usually a gap of at least a year, often longer, between members. The best known of all City names, such as Lloyd and Barclay, were absent because of the unwritten but long-established rule that the clearing banks should not be represented'.[34]

The nineteenth-century Directors have been called 'an undistinguished lot',[35] and it is true that until Cunliffe's time, few Directors and indeed Governors made any individual impression. Many of the more able and ambitious City men were probably dissuaded from becoming Directors by the amount of time that would have to be taken away from their own firms when in due course their turn came round to occupy the 'chairs', and certainly, apart from status, there was little commercial advantage to be had from being a Director. One or two Governors before 1914, such as William Lidderdale, rose to prominence because of their successful handling of external events. Humphrey Morice MP, Governor from 1727 to 1729, perpetrated an extensive fraud on the Bank involving fictitious bills, which was undiscovered until after his death in 1731—an event, as one of its historians piously remarks, fortunately unique in the annals of the Bank[36]—and certainly scandal has rarely touched the Court, apart from the bankruptcies of several Governors in the mid-nineteenth century. George Joachim Goschen, who was elected a Director in 1858 at the age of 26, became Chancellor of the Exchequer—the only ex-Director ever to do so—in 1887 in Lord Salisbury's government. But these men are only a handful of the hundreds who held office in the first 200 years of the Bank's history. Hardly any were known outside the City, far less outside Britain, and it was not until Norman's day that Governors and Directors began to travel regularly overseas, when the business of the BIS and of the growing number of newly established central banks took them around the world. Relatively few before his time had a university education, and there were hardly any Jews other than Alfred de Rothschild, despite the strong and influential Jewish presence in the City in the nineteenth century.[37]

From Norman onwards Governors have played a major role in Britain's

[34] Sayers, *Bank*, ii, 596–7.   [35] Kynaston, *City*, 84.
[36] Acres, *Bank*, i, 154.   [37] Bank of England Archive, ADM 30/1.

financial and monetary affairs, and have been in office for periods long enough to stamp their personalities on the functioning of the Bank and of the City. Most Deputy Governors, Directors, and Executive Directors have come from a much wider range of backgrounds; even so, there has never been a non-white Director, and it was not until 1993 that the first woman, Frances Heaton, was elected to Court.

The Management of the Bank

Just as the first Directors of the Bank established a pattern which was closely followed for 200 years or more, the early structure of organization and management endured for a similar period of time. Business began on 1 August 1694 with a staff of nineteen, the three senior officials being the 'First Cashier', the 'First Accomptant', and the 'Secretary and Sollicitor'. The Court took administrative decisions which were subsequently dealt with by these three, who constituted the professional managers under the wholly amateur and part-time Court. Until the 1930s, the Bank continued to be divided into the same three main areas, administered by a Secretary (the first incumbent, John Ince, was the only one holding the post to be a 'Sollicitor'), a First, later Chief Cashier and a First, later Chief Accountant. In 1694 the Chief Cashier was responsible for the banking business and the note issue. The Chief Accountant kept the Bank's own accounts and acted as the registrar of Bank stock; to these duties was soon added a function that was to grow enormously in importance and was largely responsible for the steady growth of staff numbers, that of managing the government securities, plus some others, that were registered at the Bank. The Secretary looked after the Court and the various Committees, as he does today, including keeping their minutes, and was also responsible for everything to do with premises and staff.[38] Fig. 7.1 shows the increase in staff numbers during the Bank's 300-year history.

The Chief Cashier lived on the premises, and until 1914 most of his successors did so. The Chief Accountant lived in the Bank at various times between 1699 and 1894, and the Secretary, or one of his deputies, did so between 1809 and 1867. (Abraham Newland, Chief Cashier from 1778 to 1807, was famous for never sleeping a night away from the Bank during his period in office, although he did regularly go home to Highbury for tea, returning afterwards to Threadneedle Street). Many of the staff stayed for what nowadays seem enormous lengths of service—it was not until 1870 that retirement became compulsory at the age of 65, which enforced the departure of several very aged men, including the Senior Cashier, D. Hyett, who was 79 and had served for 61 years, and the Chief Accountant, who

---

[38] Hennessy, *Domestic History*, 1–2.

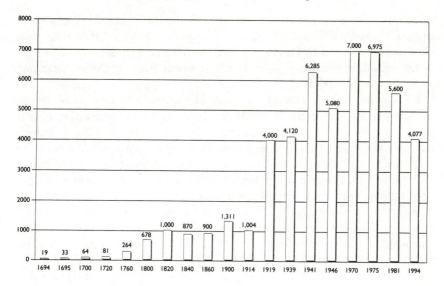

Fig. 7.1 *Staff Numbers in the Bank of England*
Source: Bank of England House List

had been in the Bank for 62 years. According to Acres the longest serving of all was J. Richards, who entered the Bank in December 1758 and worked there until his death in March 1825.[39]

In the early days, the departmental structure was far from rigid: it was not until 1851 that the House List, which shows all the staff of the Bank and their positions, was formally divided into three Departments. The senior officials had their offices in the Parlours, close to the Governors, with whom they were able to hold frequent and informal meetings. The day-to-day administration of the Bank rested on these three people, while the Directors exercised their influence by means of their membership of committees, especially the Committee of Treasury and the Committee of Daily Waiting.

The Country Bankers Act of 1826 established the right of the Bank to set up branches in any part of England or Wales—eight were in existence by the end of the following year, and more were soon added. There were no new Departments until the irregularities of a Chief Cashier, Frank May, came to light in 1893 and it was decided in the following year to institute a new post of Auditor, who with his Department was and has remained autonomous, reporting directly to the Governors. A further innovation in 1894, 200 years after foundation, was the arrival of women clerks. They were few in number at first, and were recruited to carry out the dreary task

[39] Acres, *Bank*, ii, 559.

of counting the used bank notes returned to the Bank; in 1898 a small typing pool was established. Women were rigidly segregated from the male clerks and subjected to Draconian rules as to dress and deportment which lasted with little relaxation until they were swept away by clothes rationing in the Second World War.[40]

Bank-note printing, carried out originally on behalf of the Bank by an outside printer, was brought inside the Bank in 1791; the printing operation was moved to separate premises in Old Street in 1920 but remained part of the Cashier's Department until 1922, when it was made a separate department. In 1956 it was moved to new, purpose-built premises at Debden in Essex, where it functions very much as an autonomous unit.[41]

A largely unchanging managerial style, characterized by Sayers as a 'comfortable jog-trot', continued until the 1890s, when to external financial pressures, including low interest rates, was added the upset caused by the irregularities of the Chief Cashier in 1893. The Court then initiated its series of reviews of the functions of the senior officials and of departmental working, which culminated in the wholesale reform not only of security and disciplinary standards but also of what had by this time become an almost impossibly tangled remuneration structure. These reviews also included consideration of a quite large non-clerical staff of porters, messengers, and 'manual' workers.[42] The cost of running the Bank was satisfactorily if not spectacularly trimmed; flexibility of movement between departments slightly increased, and merit began to play a marginally more important role in the question of promotion, but little else changed until 1914, when women began to assume some of the responsibilities previously the preserve of the male clerks.

Post-war pressure for increases in salaries and wages in a period of a sharp rise in the cost of living was reluctantly acceded to by the Court and a period of unprecedented upheaval resulted in the establishment of an Advisory Council of Directors and Staff in 1919, heralding a more modern attitude to labour relations.[43]

The sharp post-war rise in the amount of work undertaken for the government resulted in a correspondingly large intake in the years 1919–27, giving rise to a bulge in the age profile of employees referred to by the graphic if unlovely term of the Hump. This group of men of much the same age and seniority, rising together up the ranks, was to present grave problems within a few years, as it became evident that their chances of promotion were severely limited and their pay and pension requirements put pressure on the Bank's finances.[44]

With the advent of Norman as Governor in 1920, the Bank's inclination towards self-questioning, first evidenced in the latter years of the previous

[40] Acres, *Bank*, ii, 560–1; Hennessy, *Domestic History*, 32–3.
[41] Hennessy, *Domestic History*, 166–87.   [42] Sayers, *Bank*, ii, 607–9.
[43] Ibid. ii, 612–13.   [44] Hennessy, *Domestic History*, 332.

century, took a new and more rigorous turn. The Peacock Committee, as well as carrying out the various reforms of the Court, was given a brief to look into the whole range of the Bank's functions and the efficiency with which it operated as the public institution which it had virtually been since the 1890s.

Each Department had traditionally been responsible for the recruitment, training, and promotion of its own clerks, but as staff numbers swelled after the First World War the Secretary's Department had come to play an increasingly important role in aspects of staff administration which could be centralized, such as recruitment, wage and salary payments, income tax and so on. By the 1930s this personnel work was taking up around 75 per cent of the time of the Secretary's small staff, and Peacock saw one of his main tasks to be that of relieving the Secretary of the bulk of this work and implementing an up-to-date staff organization akin to that of the contemporary Civil Service.

Peacock recommended that a new Establishment Department should take over 'the whole domestic organisation of the Bank, other than St Luke's Printing Works', including the Branches and everything to do with buildings, staff and welfare work. Another innovation was an Overseas and Foreign Department, to take over the rapidly increasing work arising from the Bank's relationships with other central banks; under various names and organizational structures, this department was to grow both large and influential in the 1950s and 1960s, absorbing many of the Bank's most able and ambitious recruits. It was abolished in the July 1994 reorganization.[45]

At the outbreak of the Second World War the Establishment Department was in charge of a total staff of 4,120 men and women, clerical and non-clerical. During the war the Department's main sphere of operations was in Hampshire, where several hundred Bank staff from the Accountant's Department and the Printing Works were evacuated for nearly six years.

The war brought a new and unwelcome addition to the Bank's responsibilities in the form of exchange control. The Bank had operated the Exchange Equalisation Account on behalf of the government since 1932, in the wake of Britain's departure from the gold standard the previous year, and from the end of 1936 the senior officials of the Bank were convinced that some form of exchange control would be necessary in the event of war. The Treasury was slowly and reluctantly brought to agree. Outline controls were drawn up in conjunction with the Treasury, and plans were made for them to be put into operation, which included the recruitment of many of the foreign exchange staff from various London firms. The Bank made it clear that its own role was to be limited to the technical and financial sphere, and that it would operate the control not as principal but purely as

---

[45] Ibid. 325.

agent on behalf of the government. The unwillingness with which the work was undertaken was not allowed to impair the efficiency with which it was carried out, and during the 40 years of its life—the last controls were not abolished until 1979—there were several searching examinations to ensure that it was operating fairly and safeguarding the interests of the public as well as of the government. No major changes were found to be necessary. It brought several incidental benefits: the pressure and volume of the work meant that promotion within the department was on merit rather than seniority, and it also opened a window through which the outside world could look into the Bank—and through which the clerks, most of whom had spent their working days isolated from the public, got sight of the world of commerce.[46]

In the Second World War as in the First, women took over much work previously done exclusively by men. Inevitably much of their new responsibility was eroded as men returned from the Services, but the Bank was now forced into taking a close look at the career structure for women, and began to give them an increasing measure of responsibility. Nevertheless, for many years after the war the more ambitious women tended to leave because of a rigid enforcement of the rule that they should spend their first two years in the Bank on the tedious drudgery of sorting and listing used notes. There was much careful planning, during the war itself, for post-war operations, involving estimates for future staff requirements both male and female, and salary structures. The question of women's work was intimately bound up with the question of the 'Hump': the Bank was determined not to repeat that particular mistake. Women could do much of the routine work just as efficiently as men and they also cost less: their salaries were lower and many of them left before becoming eligible for a pension. Despite the Royal Commission on Equal Pay, which sat in 1942, and the realization that if the Civil Service paid equal money for equal work, the Bank would be hard put not to follow suit, it was in fact 1958 before the first steps were taken towards complete integration of the pay scales of both sexes.[47]

Departmental Establishment Officers (DEOs) were another war-time innovation, on the lines of the Civil Service where they had been created as a result of the Haldane and Bradbury Committees after the First World War. They immediately began to play an important part in post-war planning.[48] Training was also considered. Until 1939 it had been frankly inadequate, with no standardized system in place and each department responsible for its own personnel—training was 'often desultory and rarely intelligent'. Various new schemes improved matters slightly after the war, but it was the advent of graduates—cautiously recruited from 1946 onwards, at first only eight per year, all men, and known as Special

---

[46] Hennessy, *Domestic History*, 83–123.   [47] Ibid. 330.   [48] Ibid. 331.

Entrants—which ultimately precipitated a more radical approach. Many of the first graduates left within a year or two, thoroughly disillusioned and dispirited by having to serve their time in lowly routine clerking jobs and with no hope of even a modicum of responsibility for about ten years. Cobbold, who although not himself a graduate had come into the Bank at the comparatively late age of 31, was particularly concerned with this question; once he had become Governor he ensured that graduates were accorded special treatment which considerably reduced their time in routine jobs. Even as Governor, he did not find this an easy task—senior officials who had themselves survived the stultifying routines endured by junior clerks put many obstacles in the way of his desire to abolish or curtail them for the young graduates, whose lot, like that of the women, improved only slowly.[49]

A new Department, the Central Banking Information Department (CBID), was started in 1959, partly in response to the strictures of the Radcliffe Committee, which in its report of that year had commented unfavourably on the limited statistical ability of the Bank and a failure to make the fruits of its research more accessible to the outside world. The new arrangement did not prove very satisfactory, however, and in 1964 CBID was split into an Overseas Department (the third in the Bank's history) and a new Economic Intelligence Department.[50] From 1960 onwards, the Bank communicated with the outside world more openly than before by means of a slightly more informative Annual Report and the publication of the *Bank of England Quarterly Bulletin*.[51]

The organogram of the Bank in the 1960s looked, in outline, just as it would have done at any time since 1694. It was in the shape of a cottage loaf, with the main part of the loaf formed by the staff under the various departmental heads: on top of that was the smaller 'knob' composed of the three senior officials—Chief Cashier, Chief Accountant and Secretary—a small group of Executive Directors with no specific responsibilities, the Governors, and the Court of Directors (see Fig. 7.2). The departmental heads, who were responsible for the day-to-day activities of the Bank, reported to the Chief Cashier, himself a departmental head but indisputably *primus inter pares* and reporting only to the Governor. No memorandum went to the Governors without his signature, and any letter expressing any facet of the Bank's policy had to be signed by him.

The report in 1970 of McKinsey & Co., a firm of US management consultants hired, unprecedentedly, by Governor O'Brien to examine the workings of the Bank for the first time ever with an external eye, suggested no change to this 'loaf' shape. In fact their only organizational recommendation of any substance was that as computers (first introduced in the Bank in the 1960s in the Accountant's Department) were likely to be used

---

[49] Ibid. 350–1.   [50] Ibid. 320–3.   [51] Ibid. 214–15, 320–3.

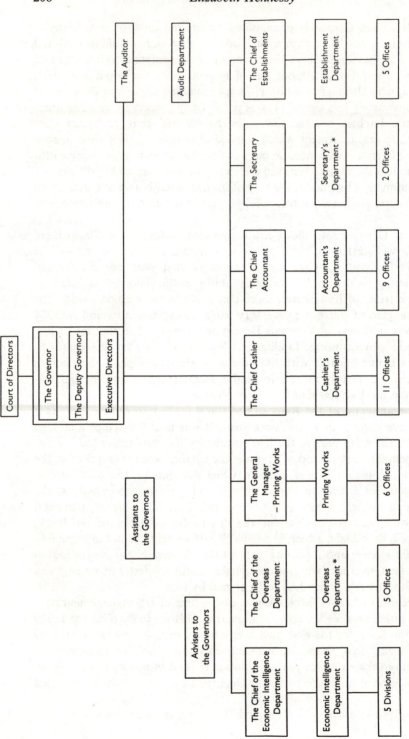

*Advisers are attached to these departments.

Fig. 7.2 *The Organization of the Bank of England, September 1966*
Source: Bank of England

increasingly, they should have their own department. This was duly established as the Manpower Services Department in June 1970 and given the task of administering and developing both computer services and the whole range of management service activities. McKinsey also recommended the introduction of a system of budgetary control which has been the key to cost control ever since.

In the autumn of 1974, as a result of the secondary banking crisis, a new Banking Supervision Division was set up by Governor Richardson under George Blunden, to expand the work done for many years by the Discount Office. The Bank and the clearing banks had joined forces and funds to ameliorate the worst effects of the crisis, and the status of the new division as well as its staff numbers began to increase rapidly.[52]

As the question of supervision was debated in the years before the passing of the 1979 Banking Act, other changes were radically altering the Bank's organization. Computerization had affected many of its traditional activities, especially with regard to government stock, principally registering owners and paying dividends, and staff numbers in the Accountant's Department therefore began to fall significantly.[53] But it was the examination of the Bank by the parliamentary Select Committee on the Nationalised Industries in 1969–70 which proved the catalyst for a period of upheaval unlike any in its previous history.

In its final assessment of the Bank's efficiency, the 1970 report of the Committee noted that

it is clear from the evidence that the Treasury do not *know* whether or not the Bank, in the conduct of its own affairs, is efficient. The Chancellor *thought* that the Bank maintained very high standards of efficiency and was anxious to maintain those standards. But the Treasury do not know what the Bank's internal investment policy is ... and they do not know what return it gets on its money.[54]

Subsequent moves by the Treasury ensured significant changes in the methods of calculating the fees paid by government to the Bank for the management of government stock, the Exchange Equalisation Account, exchange control and the note issue. The tradition of private accounting had to come to an end, to enable the Treasury to see for itself whether or not the Bank was efficient by examining its costs. It was also agreed (after over a decade of discussion) that the Bank's profits after tax, instead of being used principally to build up reserves, would be shared with the Treasury, currently on a 50/50 basis with the Treasury receiving their half as a dividend.[55]

Public expenditure cuts in the wake of the Select Committee's report

[52] Stephen Fay, *Portrait of an Old Lady: Turmoil at the Bank of England* (1987), 86.
[53] Hennessy, *Domestic History*, 80–2; Fay, *Portrait*, 101–2.
[54] Select Committee on Nationalised Industries: Bank of England, *First Report* (1969–70, vi), ch. 17.
[55] Information from Bank of England, June 1994.

intensified efforts being made internally by Blunden and the Deputy Governor, Sir Jasper Hollom, to make the Bank more efficient. This was achieved not only by the introduction of tighter budgetary controls, but also by planned reductions in the still generous staff numbers—a reduction which was assisted by the Conservative Party's sudden abolition, in October 1979, of the entire apparatus of exchange control. This effectively meant that about 675 people in the Bank had their work abolished overnight: the surplus was dealt with by a new voluntary redundancy scheme (there had been other, more limited redundancy offers in the 1950s), which was accepted by over 10 per cent of the staff, and by a temporary ban on recruitment.[56]

A few months later, in January 1980, Governor Richardson announced a reshaping of the management structure. This had been in his mind for some while, and had been accelerated by the reactions of various 'outsiders' whom he had brought in as Executive Directors. These men, mostly economists and including Kit McMahon, John Fforde, and Christopher Dow, found the old, hierarchical system an almost insurmountable hindrance to getting anything done. Richardson asked a retired Permanent Secretary to the Treasury, Lord Croham (previously Sir Douglas Allen) to undertake a review of the whole organization of the Bank. Croham identified as one of the chief sources of difficulty the gulf between the Heads of Department and the Directors, and the fact that the number of paid executives, the Executive Directors, had been limited to four—at first by the wish of the Court, perhaps anxious lest they might one day be outnumbered, and since nationalization by statute. Despite their title, they had virtually no executive power, and Croham's recommendations were firstly that their number should be enlarged, by the simple expedient of giving any extra ones the title of Associate Director but not giving them a seat on the Court, and secondly that all the Executive Directors should be given actual executive responsibilities.

The cottage loaf was flattened. The Bank was reorganized into three main areas: financial services and supervision, policy and markets, and operations and services. Within the first two, the existing departmental structure was replaced by a number of divisions, each headed by an Assistant Director or a Chief Adviser; the traditional departmental structure was retained only in Operations and Services. The aim of the reorganization was to bring the management of the Bank into line with the recent developments in its functions (see Fig. 7.3). It reinforced the arrangements for the Bank's responsibilities in the field of domestic and external monetary policy by grouping more closely together those divisions chiefly concerned, and created a new area to carry out what had become an extended supervisory role. The support services were brought together and 'any over-

---

[56] Information from Bank of England, June 1994.

lap or ambiguity' between the roles of the Executive Directors and those of senior officials was eliminated. The staff of the divisions, around 450 strong, formed a definite élite, headed by the Executive Directors and the new Associate Directors, who had a much more 'hands-on' role in terms of management.

These changes removed at a stroke virtually all the power and status from the traditional 'big three' positions. The title of Chief Cashier remained in use for statutory reasons, and was held by the new Chief of the Banking Department, but his role was significantly less important than that of all previous Chief Cashiers.[57] In 1987 there was another innovation which attracted less attention at the time but which was to prove of equal significance: the division of the Bank into officials and officers—effectively graduates and non-graduates.

Further manpower cuts soon became necessary under the cash-limits policy on public institutions announced by the Treasury in 1980, and the brunt of these were borne by the Banking and Registrar's Departments and the Printing Works, both now in the Operations and Services Division. By the beginning of 1983 the full-time staff numbered 5,300, or nearly 25 per cent less than the 1970 figure.

In the spring of 1994, the Governor, Eddie George (who was one of the younger Assistant Directors in the Policy and Markets Division at the time of the 1980 restructuring), and his Deputy Governor, Rupert Pennant-Rea, announced a further change. George and Pennant-Rea were appointed in July 1993; in December of that year the Governors and Executive and Associate Directors held a weekend think-tank session on the subject of the organization of the Bank at Ashridge Management College in Hertfordshire. This followed extensive discussion at Court of the Bank's functions. After five months of planning carried out by three working groups, and a considerable amount of consultation within the Bank, the first details were announced in May 1994 in the staff newspaper. They came after an eventful two years in which the Bank had recovered from Britain's humiliating exit from the European Exchange Rate Mechanism in September 1992 and had been able to exert a new and considerably greater influence over monetary and economic policy.

The new organization—which came into effect on 4 July 1994—groups the Bank's activities into two broad wings, one concerned with monetary stability, the other concerned with financial stability, plus a group of central service functions (see Fig. 7.4). The former wing includes analysis for and implementation of monetary policy. The latter combines the supervision of banks and financial markets in Britain, the monitoring of banking conditions and regulations abroad, and efforts to increase the competitiveness of British financial centres. Perhaps the most controversial aspect is the closure

---

[57] *Bank of England Quarterly Bulletin*, 20 (Sept. 1980), 19–22.

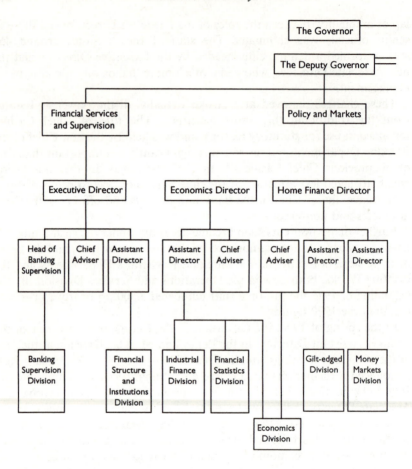

Fig. 7.3 *The Organization of the Bank of England, March 1980*
Source: Bank of England

of the International Divisions (which has also been done by the Netherlands Bank), and the allocation of their members to the two new wings—a step which the Deputy Governor believes to be essential to ensure that all international work is closely allied to the dual monetary and financial objectives, and which underlines the view that Europe is no longer seen and treated as an overseas territory but as part of the domestic sphere in which the Bank is now operating. Within a few weeks of the announcement of these changes came notification of the first wave of redundancies: seven of the forty senior

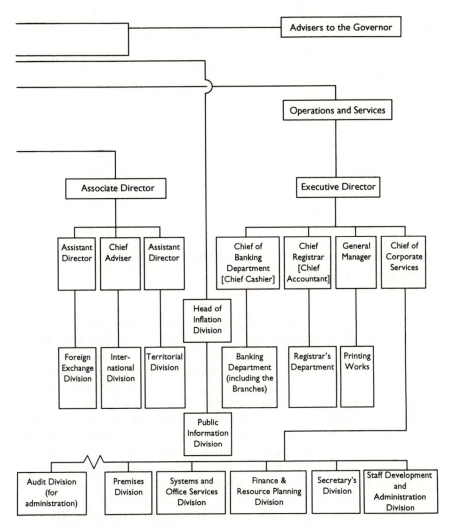

managers whose jobs did not fit into the new structure. A dozen or so managerial jobs at lower levels were also surplus.[58]

An Effective Organization?

For something under the first 200 years of its existence the Bank could be considered as a private institution; in principle it remained so until the Act of 1946 transferred it to public ownership, but by the 1890s the fact of private ownership had become largely irrelevant to what it was actually doing. In the eighteenth century it had gained status by becoming the

[58] Information from Bank of England, June 1994.

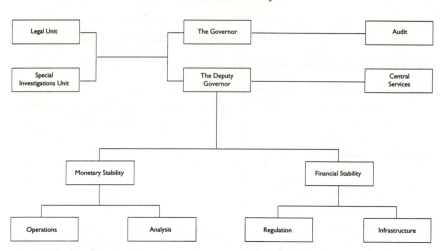

Fig. 7.4 *The Organization of the Bank of England, July 1994*
Source: Bank of England

banker to the government and registrar of government stocks, and by the
middle of the nineteenth century it was becoming to an increasing extent
the bankers' bank, and gradually coming to be regarded as the lender of
last resort. It was still an open and acknowledged competitor with the private banking firms and the new City-based joint-stock banks, the first of
which, the London and Westminster, was opened in 1834. Once the age of
joint-stock banking began, the Bank started its long, sometimes painful
journey towards the status of a nationally owned central bank; by the end
of the century it was no longer seen as appropriate that the Bank should
compete for ordinary banking business, which was gradually abandoned.

For 200 years or so, then, the efficiency and management of the Bank
was to be judged by its efficacy in two respects: as agent for the government and manager of the national debt, and as a private banker. Its operations in the first sphere could rarely be criticized. From the start it
practised the new Italian double-entry system of accounting, which was far
more efficient than the single-entry method used by the Exchequer at that
date. Its standards of accuracy and probity were, and remained, of the
highest. Gladstone, when Chancellor of the Exchequer in the middle of
the nineteenth century, had one or two brushes with the Bank about the
method of payment of dividends on the various securities inscribed there
which formed the funded part of the national debt, and demanded a reduction in the allowance which the Bank received for managing the debt, in
both of which he was ultimately successful, but the efficiency of the Bank
was never in question. Similarly its later management of the Exchange
Equalisation Account, exchange control and the note issue have been the

subject of frequent inquiries both internal and external and have rarely needed more than minor adjustments. The Bank's style of management and organization was faithfully copied by many of the central banks which were established during the Governorships of Norman and Cobbold. The Bank of England lent them personnel and provided advice. The methods worked well in Britain and, with necessary adjustments, they worked well overseas.

This effectiveness as an agent of the government, though, was until comparatively recently dependent on an over-lavish staffing policy—in effect, three people were recruited for two jobs so that any sudden demand from the Treasury for some special task to be carried out would not cause problems. This gave rise to internal difficulties with bored and under-employed clerks, with good standards of education, for whom the lack of activity meant that the most ambitious and capable often left—especially when graduates were first regularly recruited. Absenteeism, drunkenness and rowdy behaviour, particularly on the 'stock' side, were prevalent to what today seems an astonishing degree until well into the twentieth century. The position of women was often even more unsatisfactory, but the Bank was little different in this respect from most other companies and institutions. Once there was a serious effort to prune staff numbers, and when the sphere of 'women's work' was extended, such problems lessened significantly.

The management style, however, did not change as rapidly. One of the most highly regarded management theorists, the US social psychologist Douglas McGregor, identified in 1960 two distinct management styles: Theory X representing authoritarian management, and Theory Y representing participative management. X assumes that people have an inherent dislike of work, and need a mixture of carrot and stick to get them to perform it; most are immature and incapable of taking responsibility. Y assumes the opposite, that people have a psychological need to work, and a deep need for both responsibility and achievement. The outstanding practitioners of Theory X are the Japanese, who shun the idea of picking an élite early on and giving it special training and more responsible jobs. They believe in recruiting a large general pool of labour, and choosing the best when you have seen them in action over at least a decade. This is reinforced by the belief that you do not actually know what you will want, in the way of numbers or capabilities, fifteen or twenty years ahead. For most of its existence the Bank practised Theory X, with a strong tendency to a now unfashionable paternalism—working conditions, salaries, and pensions were for many years significantly higher than in comparable banking jobs, although this is no longer true. It is only in the past few years, since the advent of the flatter organizational pyramid achieved by Richardson's 1980 reforms, that there has been a move towards Theory Y, with a degree of empowerment and an attempt to push responsibility downwards. These ideas form the basis of the current (1994) review of personnel policies covering the officials' cadre.[59]

As a private bank, the criterion for efficiency was whether or not it made a profit. That it did so was unquestionable, although until 1971, when it first published accounts, the actual amounts were shrouded in mystery. The Bank Charter Act of 1844 laid down the formal separation, for accounting purposes, of the Issue and the Banking Departments, and required the profits of the Issue Department to be paid directly to HM Treasury, as they have been ever since. Banking Department profits, on the other hand, were until the early 1980s for the Bank to do with as the Bank wished: they comprised the excess of investment income and charges for services over running expenses and amortized capital expenditure, and their level has always varied markedly from year to year, only periodically giving rise to anxiety. Sometimes, there were even anxieties that profits were too large, for example in the 1930s, when they were running at a level of between £250,000 and £300,000 per year.

Once the Bank had passed into public ownership, it could only be a matter of time—as many at the top realized—before its finances and organizational structure would become subject to external scrutiny. The institution and gradual extension of the Annual Report was designed to pre-empt this for a while, but the report of the parliamentary Select Committee in 1969–70 heralded a new era. The days of mystique were over: the Bank had not only to be efficient, but had to be seen to be so. Since 1971 it has published accounts just like any commercial institution, tightened its budgetary processes, and twice drastically overhauled its organization in order to keep pace with a rapidly changing monetary and financial world.

---

[59] Douglas McGregor, *The Human Side of Enterprise* (New York, 1960), *passim*; information from Bank of England, June 1994.

8 The Bank of England: Yesterday, Today, Tomorrow

RUPERT PENNANT-REA

THE Bank's yesterdays have been covered thoroughly in the other papers. That is one reason why this paper will not dwell on the past. The other is that I have been in the Deputy Governor's chair for little more than a year, so my first-hand knowledge of the past is inevitably limited. Anyway, most of my work has been concerned with current events, whether they be the stance of monetary policy or the shape of the Bank's own budget. So this paper will concentrate on today's Bank, and on how it might evolve tomorrow.

It would be foolish, though, to ignore the links that bind today's Bank to the 300 years that have gone before it. All of us stand on the shoulders of our fathers, and that is usually even more true of institutions than it is of individuals. It is particularly true of an institution like a central bank, where continuity—of policy and of culture—ought to matter a great deal.

Nobody who works in the Bank of England can fail to appreciate the contemporary value of its history. It is not a question of detailed knowledge; more a matter of sensing that any institution that has survived for 300 years must have some enduring *raison d'être*, as good for the future as it has been for the past. The Bank was there, and is here; it is bigger than any of the individuals in it, and always has been. These are rather elementary points, to be sure, but they are confirmed by a close examination of the Bank's history. They are part of the Bank's cement, holding it together across the decades. With that brief bow to history, let me move on to give some feel of the Bank today.

Structure

The Bank is changing, and more at the moment than it has done for the past fourteen years. This is because there was a formal reorganization in 1980, and another is happening in 1994. For the purposes of this paper, the details of the current changes do not matter much. But their essence is a valuable guide to how today's Bank is preparing for the challenges of tomorrow, in philosophical as much as organizational terms.

The new structure divides most of the Bank into two wings. One is concerned with monetary stability, the other with financial stability. These notions need defining a bit further, but they are (or ought to be) the fundamental objectives of every central bank. Monetary stability means the goal of stable prices, which is achieved by adopting the right type of monetary policy and then ensuring that it is properly executed through operations in the gilt-edged, money, and foreign exchange markets. As for financial stability, it means the goal of a sound financial system; but that deserves a full paragraph of elaboration.

Given the massive and world-wide changes in finance in the past twenty years or so, the 'financial system' must be broadly defined. It means more than just banks, for which the Bank of England has statutory supervisory responsibilities. Other institutions and activities have the potential to destabilize financial systems: think of the stock-market falls of October 1987, or the closure of Drexel Burnham (an American securities house) in 1990. In both cases, central banks were involved in patrolling the pressure-points of the financial system, stopping the damage from spreading, and restoring confidence. To do that job, and to be able to anticipate problems and head them off, a central bank today must be close to markets and financial institutions of all kinds.

This is particularly true of the Bank of England, because it sits in the middle of the most international of all the world's financial centres. The City of London is host to the branches or subsidiaries of more than 500 foreign banks. It conducts almost two-thirds of all trading of overseas securities. More than half of all the international issues of Eurobonds are written in London; and three-quarters of them are traded here. The list could go on, but the point is already clear: in the much-discussed globalizing of finance, it is London that sets the trend, and London where the nature of the financial system is being continuously redefined.

So both the new wings have broad spans. They are, by their very nature, international in scope, which is why the Bank has been able to disband its International Divisions and incorporate their work into the new structure. This change is not in any sense a downgrading of the importance the Bank attaches to the wider world. On the contrary, there is no longer a risk that the international dimension will be regarded as peripheral to the formulation of policy; it is now plugged in at every point in the Bank's work.

The new wings now encompass the vital tasks of central banking, and they are natural complements to each other. The pursuit of monetary stability depends on having a financial system that provides reliable channels through which policy can take effect. The chances of achieving financial stability are strongly affected by the macroeconomic background; a boom–bust economy is one where financial institutions typically make expensive mistakes and come under heavy strain. The Bank needs both wings to do its job, and values them equally.

There is one last point to make about the new structure. The financial stability wing ranges across a spectrum that at one end covers soundness and at the other, efficiency. At the latter end, the Bank has two interests that go beyond stability *per se*. It wants to ensure that Britain's financial firms are providing competitive and wide-ranging services to the rest of the British economy. And it wants to ensure that the City of London is equipped with all the ingredients of a leading financial centre. Both come under the internal organizational heading of Financial Infrastructure. Both have been the Bank's concerns for many years. To mix the metaphors, they are the Bank as paterfamilias to the City.

Style

This leads me to a few thoughts about how the Bank approaches its work. History shows that the Bank began as a bank, in the heart of the City; quickly evolved as *primus inter pares*; acquired, often at the request of government, more and more non-banking activities; and assumed a leading role in international financial affairs. That diversity makes it impossible to pigeon-hole the Bank. It stands somewhere between government and the private sector. Many of its staff have to know markets as well as they know statutes. It needs to understand financial innovations so well that it can quickly distinguish between the malign and the benign. And it needs to understand the wider real economy of output and jobs and growth, in Britain and abroad.

Much of what the Bank does is routine work, clerical work: the jobs of printing millions of banknotes, of keeping a register of thousands of holders of government stock, of being bank manager for the government's myriad transactions—these are not glamorous jobs, but they are essential. For that reason, they need to be done thoroughly, and accurately, and scrupulously. The Bank ought to be judged by those standards for its routine jobs as much as it is judged by the quality of the more cerebral aspects of its work.

But this raises an obvious and awkward question: how to judge any institution by the quality of things that it does in private? That is particularly difficult to answer in the area of banking supervision. By its nature, supervision is done away from the public gaze. Its success is measured by the absence of publicity, for it is only when something goes wrong that the Bank's supervisors get the headlines. This does not make the supervisory task any less real or worthwhile, but it does make it difficult to gauge.

That difficulty is enhanced by the absence of easy measures of how much to spend on supervision. It is always possible to spend more: if three analysts are working on a group of banks, why not four? That would almost certainly reduce the chances of a mistake going through unnoticed. But it would increase the cost of supervision, and it is the banks themselves—and therefore their customers—that have to bear the costs. Ultimately it is a matter of judgement. The Bank has very few profit centres in the sense that commercial firms do. All that can be said with confidence is that it has an annual budget of around £230m. and a staff of 4,300. Does that mean it gives value for money? The combination of privacy and few profit centres makes the Bank a difficult institution to measure.

The Role of Monetary Policy

Thankfully, some of the obfuscation is dispersing, and particularly in the field of monetary policy. Until recently, the nature of the Bank's monetary advice could only be guessed at. Its senior staff gave speeches, and occasionally appeared before parliamentary committees. But these were often seen as opportunities to reinforce confidence in the policies of the government of the day. Journalists hankered after divisions between Treasury and Bank, and were tempted to exaggerate every nuance to turn it into something much more dramatic. Most of the time, there were no real differences of view. When disagreements happened, they occasionally came out into the open. But by and large the impression that the public—and the markets—received was confusing: official unanimity, but mixed with dark hints from the media that all was not what it seemed. In retrospect, more openness—and more independent-mindedness—would have helped.

By independent-mindedness, I do not mean formal independence: that is an issue for later in this paper. What I do mean is something very like the arrangements that are now taking shape in British monetary policy, and which began after sterling's departure from the Exchange Rate Mechanism (ERM) in September 1992. The government then found itself having to implement a new monetary policy—without delay and with credibility. Rightly, it saw the essence of the task as being counter-inflation, so it set itself a formal target: to hold the annual rise in the retail price index (excluding mortgage-interest payments) within a range of 1–4 per cent, and to get down into the lower half of this range 'by the end of the Parliament'—in other words, by May 1997 at the latest.

Crucially for the Bank, ministers decided to give it a formal role in this new approach to controlling inflation. In doing so, they were seeking both the substance and the perception of a united front, which is always a valuable element in building up credibility. On its own, a statement of a new counter-inflationary objective—particularly one that was silent on the means to achieving that objective—would have cut no ice in the markets. Thus began a series of steps that, taken together, have undoubtedly given the Bank a clearer role in monetary policy than it has had since it was nationalized in 1946.

The first of these steps was the Chancellor's request that the Bank publish a quarterly *Inflation Report*. It aims to assess, thoroughly and openly, the prospects for inflation over the succeeding 18–24 months. The *Report* is the watchdog; its valuable charge is the inflation target. If it reckons the target is under threat, its duty is to bark, and loudly. Since even the softest of growls would be heard in the financial markets, this new combination undoubtedly helps to concentrate minds. For the Bank, the new opportunity brings a new and difficult prominence. Its advice is open, and therefore open to criticism and to being proved wrong by subsequent events. Anybody who thinks that the *Inflation Report* has given the Bank more power should reflect that it is not the power of the harlot; it carries responsibility as well.

The first few issues of the *Inflation Report* established a reputation for thoroughness and high-grade analysis. The sincerest praise has come from abroad, where two countries (Sweden and New Zealand) have already introduced similar reports of their own, and others are thinking of doing so. However, it also quickly became clear that the *Inflation Report*'s most valued quality—its independent judgement—could not be assumed by markets so long as the Bank was showing drafts to the Treasury. Again, the danger came from a lack of clarity: what did the Bank really think? Again, the government was bold enough to put an end to any possible confusion. In September 1993 the Chancellor announced that henceforth the *Report* would go out from the Bank alone, unseen by the Treasury. The only commonsensical caveat to this new arrangement was that the Report should not contain any views or projections which the Bank had not already told the Treasury about in private.

Another change in the policy regime came a few months later. In November 1993 interest rates were reduced by half a percentage point. The Chancellor took the opportunity to announce a division of labour. The decisions on whether to change rates, and by how much, would continue to be taken by him, after listening to the Bank's advice. The decision on when to change rates would then be left to the Bank, the clear implication being that the change would be made before the next monthly meeting between Chancellor and Governor.

It is easy to exaggerate the significance of this change, and many people did so. In practice, it was a useful way of reducing a particular type of suspicion about the motives for monetary policy. Over the years, even the unobservant could hardly have failed to notice that cuts in interest rates sometimes coincided with occasions such as party conferences. The timing of rate changes thus came to be seen as a political matter, and it was only a short step from there to thinking that politics was also driving the substantive decision to change rates. Suspicions like that are corrosive. Among other things, they result in long-term interest rates being higher than they would have been if the markets had believed that economic considerations alone determined monetary policy. By giving the Bank discretion over the 'precise timing' of interest rate changes, the Chancellor was removing one unnecessary source of suspicion. But he was doing no more than that. Despite some of the press comment at the time, this was not a move to give the Bank real power over monetary policy.

Much more significant was the change announced in April 1993, to publish the minutes of the monthly meetings between the Chancellor and the Governor. The initiative for this came from the Treasury during 1993. At the end of the year, it was given added weight by the report from the Treasury and Civil Service Committee (TCSC) on the role of the Bank of England. The TCSC recommended publication, and it called in aid the long-established practice in the United States, where minutes of the Federal Reserve's Open Market Committee are published some weeks after the event—almost immediately after the subsequent meeting.

During 1993 the Treasury and the Bank had experimented with the idea of publication, preparing minutes after each meeting and then reviewing them later as though they were just about to be published. It took some time to find the right format: too short, and the minutes would merely invite speculation; too long, and they would be dull and convey no sense of the priorities that tend to drive any discussion of monetary policy. Eventually, the formula was right, everybody was content with the principle of publication, and the Chancellor took the decision to go ahead.

It was a brave decision, and in my view a thoroughly desirable one. It makes monetary policy more grown-up; instead of the furtive and unproductive business of guessing who said what, the markets now have a proper explanation of what determines policy. As an outsider coming in to the policy circle, I was struck by the thoroughness with which both Bank and Treasury prepare and review their judgement on monetary policy. It seemed useful, as a minimum, for the outside world to know that too. Policy is not a seat-of-the-pants affair, conducted in a rush. It is considered and thorough, and as rational as it can be. Once the markets see all this, and get used to it, their responses ought to become more considered and rational too. Since markets work best when they are well informed, the move is undoubtedly a step towards better and more efficient market behaviour.

All these changes constitute a qualitative shift in the Bank's role and responsibilities in the conduct of monetary policy. But are they any more than that? Specifically, are they way-stations on the road to independence? This is clearly the most topical of the questions about the Bank tomorrow, so the next section of this paper will concentrate on it.

Independence, and What it Means

In a moment I shall define what I mean by 'independence'. But let me start by saying that there is an impressive body of evidence that economies with independent central banks perform differently from those where monetary policy is clearly in the hands of politicians. Not only does the first group tend to have lower inflation, but it does not have to sacrifice growth to achieve this goal.

Over time, with more countries shifting towards central-bank independence, the more familiar the issues become, then the more persuasive they are. That is not just a wishful belief in the power of rational thought. It is what has actually happened in this country in the recent past. In 1993 both the TCSC report, and another by a study group from the Centre for Economic Policy Research (CEPR), came down firmly in favour of independence. I do not know precisely what the initial views of the various members were, but it is reasonable to assume that some were sceptical and a few even instinctively hostile. Once they had immersed themselves in the subject, however, all but one of the combined membership of the two groups were ready to endorse the principle of independence.

That is a microcosm of what might happen on a broader scale. Indeed it is crucial that the same process of conviction based on immersion should be followed, because a sudden change in the Bank's status would not be welcome on its own. The seed must not fall on shallow ground, because the results would be as predictable in the secular world of central banking as they were in the parable. The equivalent of the well-tilled field would be a large body of all-party support, and that is what is most needed.

It is now time to define what I mean by independence, that convenient but misleading shorthand. Terms like 'statutory accountability' and 'operational autonomy' are not so catchy, but they are much more accurate. They emphasize the vital link between a future Bank and the political system: the first would be the servant of the second, which is a long way from what is usually meant by the word independence.

The first step in this process would be a new statute, a new Bank of England Act. The central part of this Act would be a clause defining a broad objective for the Bank—'to achieve and maintain price stability', or something similar. This would serve perfectly well as a strategic goal; but, for operational purposes, it would need to be specified in more detail. You could therefore imagine the government of the day stipulating three things: a target range for inflation; a particular measure of inflation; and a timetable. These are the same three ingredients as in the current inflation target (1–4 per cent, for the RPI excluding mortgage-interest payments, with the intention of reaching the bottom half of the range by the end of the parliament).

The crucial political choice—the inflation objective—would therefore rest with the politicians. They would be delegating to the Bank the essentially technical task of achieving it. If the Bank failed in its task, the senior management would expect to be judged accordingly.

The Bank would be scrutinized in other ways too. Its Governors and

Directors would be questioned by a parliamentary committee, probably in a more systematic way than happens at the moment. The Bank could publish an annual report that parliament would debate. In addition, an active mix of articles and speeches could allow the Bank to explain what it was doing and why. In all these ways, an independent Bank would be a more open Bank. This is not a paradox. It is already the case that the Bundesbank, the most formally independent of them all, also offers a model of explanation and clarity at the highest level of its staff.

A Final Thought

I hope I have described at least some of the many changes taking place at the moment. They form a powerful combination of internal reorganization and greater external clarity about the Bank's policy role; arguably, they constitute more change for the Bank than at any time since nationalization. This is a big challenge to a 300-year-old institution. The twin tests of any organization are how it responds to outside demands, and whether it has the qualities needed for self-improvement and self-renewal. In 1994, the Bank is facing both these tests. Happily, I can report that it shows every sign of passing them.

Appendix 1: Chronology

1689	England enters the Nine Years War (1688–97) against France; growing crisis in government finances.
1691	William Paterson (*c*.1658–1719), a Scottish promoter and financier, first proposes the establishment of a national bank.
1693	Paterson, backed by a group of City businessmen, puts forward a scheme for a 'Bank of England' under which £1,200,000 is to be raised and lent to the Government at 8 per cent interest; the scheme is taken up by Charles Montagu (later Earl of Halifax), a Commissioner of the Treasury, who secures government support.
1694	
25 Apr.	Act of Parliament establishing the Bank of England receives Royal Assent.
21 June–2 July	The Bank's £1,200,000 capital is raised in twelve days by 1,520 separate subscriptions ranging from £25 to £10,000 (a total of 1,268 individual subscribers).
10–11 July	Election of Court (or board) of Directors: Sir John Houblon (1632–1712) becomes the first Bank Governor; Michael Godfrey (1658–1695) Deputy Governor; and William Paterson one of the twenty-four Directors.
27 July	Royal Charter issued to the Bank (until 1705) and sealed at Powis House, Lincoln's Inn Fields. Bank opens for business in rented premises at Mercers' Hall, Cheapside, with a staff of seventeen clerks and two gatekeepers. Britannia adopted as the symbol of the Bank. First banknotes bearing the name of the Bank of England appear very shortly after its foundation.
1 Aug.	Bank makes first payment (£112,000) to the government; the entire £1,200,000 capital is transferred by the deadline of 1 January 1695.

Oct.	Bank undertakes management of remittances to Army in Flanders; opens agency in Antwerp.
29 Dec.	Bank moves to larger premises in Grocers' Hall, Princes Street, with a staff of 36; remains there until 1734.
1695	
27 Feb.	Paterson resigns from Court of Directors.
17 July	Michael Godfrey killed (decapitated by a cannon-ball) in the trenches at the siege of Namur while on a visit to the King.
	Bank of Scotland founded.
1696	Major recoinage instituted; first serious run on the Bank forces suspension of cash payments; Bank of England notes at 20 per cent discount.
	Failure of rival Land Bank.
1696–9	Partly printed banknotes first issued by the Bank; the earlier notes had been entirely handwritten.
1697	Act of Parliament prohibits the setting up of any other bank by charter during the continuance of the Bank of England.
	Bank Charter extended to 1711.
	Death penalty imposed for forgery of the Bank's notes.
	Exchequer bills first issued (reputedly the invention of Charles Montagu, Earl of Halifax).
	Treaty of Ryswick ends Nine Years War; national debt reaches £14.5m.
1702	England enters War of the Spanish Succession (1701–13).
	National debt stands at £12.75m.
1707	Act of Union with Scotland (Paterson involved in financial arrangements).
1708	Act of Parliament forbids associations of more than six persons for the purpose of banking (specifically from issuing banknotes) other than the Bank of England.
1709	Renewal of Bank Charter until 1733.
	Bank's authorized capital doubled.
1711	South Sea Company formed.
1713	Treaty of Utrecht ends the War of the Spanish Succession.
	Bank Charter extended to 1742.
1714	National debt reaches £36m.

1715	Bank takes over from the Exchequer the management of all new issues of government stock; subscriptions for government loans first received at the Bank.
	First Jacobite Rebellion.
1720	
Oct.–Dec.	South Sea Bubble crisis; Bank emerges relatively unscathed.
	Total of Bank's notes in circulation reaches *c*.£3m.
1724	Bank purchases estate in Threadneedle Street, including the house of the first Governor, Sir John Houblon.
	Agreement between the Bank and the firm of Henry Portal in Whitchurch, Hampshire, for supply of banknote paper (continues to the present day).
	Daniel Defoe writes of the Bank at Grocers' Hall: 'no place in the world has so much business done, with so much ease'.
1725	Bank of England notes issued in printed denominations for the first time (in a range from £20 up to £1,000).
1731	Death of Humphrey Morice, Governor 1727–9, reveals massive fraud involving £29,000 in fictitious bills discounted by him at the Bank.
1732	
Jan.	Bank rejects option of renewing lease of Grocers' Hall; decision taken to build new offices on the Bank's estate in Threadneedle Street; George Sampson appointed architect.
Thurs. 3 Aug. 1.00 pm	Foundation stone of new building in Threadneedle Street laid by Sir Edward Bellamy, Governor.
1734	
Thurs. 5 June	Business first transacted at Threadneedle Street; staff of 96; Sampson's Bank arguably the first purpose-built bank in the world.
1739–48	War of the Austrian Succession.
1739	National debt reaches £46m.
1742	Renewal of Bank Charter to 1764.
1745	Second Jacobite Rebellion causes run on the Bank; notes paid in small silver (sixpences) to conserve stock of bullion.

1748	National debt reaches £75m.
1752	Existing issues of 3 per cent government stock consolidated into a single fund, the 3 per cent Consols; 4 per cent stocks later converted to 3 per cent.
	Change from Julian to Gregorian Calendar involving 'loss' of eleven calendar days (thus 2 Sept. 1752 was followed by 14 Sept. 1752); beginning of the year changed from 25 Mar. to 1 Jan.
1756	Outbreak of Seven Years War.
1759	Bank issues £10 notes for the first time.
1760	Number of Bank staff reaches 264.
1763	End of Seven Years War; national debt reaches £132m.; financial crisis in which Bank acts as lender of last resort.
1764	Robert Taylor (knighted 1782) succeeds Sampson as architect to the Bank.
	Renewal of Bank Charter to 1786.
1765–70	Construction of new East Wing.
1772	
8 June	Panic in the City following the failure of bankers Heale & Co.
1774	Completion of Taylor's Court Room, which survives to the present day in reconstructed form.
1775	Outbreak of American War of Independence.
1776	Publication of Adam Smith's *Inquiry into the Nature and Causes of the Wealth of Nations*.
1780	
June	Gordon Riots; attack on the Bank repulsed on the night of 7–8 June; Bank henceforth protected every night by a military guard—the Bank Picquet—until its abolition in 1973.
1781	Legal decision that the Bank is not liable to pay forged notes.
	Lord North (Prime Minister) describes the Bank as 'from long habit and usage of many years . . . a part of the Constitution'.
	Bank Charter extended to 1812.
	National debt reaches £188m.
1782–8	Construction of new West Wing by Taylor following the demolition of St Christopher-le-Stocks Church.

1783	Treaty of Versailles ends American War of Independence.
	Special Committee of Inquiry set up by Court of Directors to look into the Bank's 'antiquated' methods of business.
	Bank of Ireland established.
1786	National debt reaches £243m.
1788	John Soane (knighted 1831) succeeds Taylor as architect to the Bank; commences major rebuilding and enlargement of the Bank to cover the whole of the present 3.5 acre 'island' site at a total cost of around £1m.
	Number of staff at the Bank reaches 373.
1791	Printing of Bank of England notes first carried on at Threadneedle Street though still, as before (and until 1808), by a private contractor.
1792–3	Construction of Soane's Bank Stock Office.
1792	Outbreak of war against Revolutionary France; Great Britain involved from 1793; beginning of pressure on the Bank's gold reserve.
1793	Bank issues £5 notes for the first time.
1795	Bank of England note circulation reaches £13.5m.
1797	
Mon. 27 Feb.	Bank suspends cash payments following sharp fall in bullion reserves as a result of heavy government borrowing to pay for the war; the so-called 'Restriction' lasts until 1821.
2 Mar.	Bank issues £1 and £2 notes for the first time; leads to big increase in the number of notes in circulation and in the incidence of forgeries; the new notes are soon nicknamed 'Newlands' after Abraham Newland, the Chief Cashier (1778–1807), whose name appeared in the payee clause.
9 Mar.	Spanish silver dollars put into circulation to meet shortage of small change; these were over-stamped with the head of George III in a small oval on the neck of the Spanish King.
22 May	Earliest known appearance in print of the expression 'The Old Lady of Threadneedle Street' in the caption to a cartoon by James Gillray.
1798	Formation of Corps of Bank Volunteers for the

	defence of the Bank; colours presented to Regiment at Lord's Cricket Ground (the first one, in Dorset Square) on 2 Sept. 1799.
1800	Renewal of Bank Charter to 1833.
1801	Foundation of the modern Stock Exchange.
1802	Bank Volunteers disbanded following Treaty of Amiens; re-formed one year later after renewed outbreak of hostilities.
	National debt reaches £523m.
1803	Aslett fraud trial: Bank defrauded of nearly half a million pounds by Robert Aslett, Deputy Chief Cashier.
	Bank of France established.
1804	Second issue of Spanish dollars (octagonal countermark).
21 May	Bank of England Five Shilling Dollars issued.
1805	Victory at Trafalgar (21 Oct.) dispels invasion threat.
	Bank of England note production running at *c.*30,000 notes per day (all denominations) compared with *c.*2,000 notes per day in around 1790.
1809	Bank adopts Joseph Bramah's banknote numbering and dating press.
1810	Bullion Committee of House of Commons anticipating return to gold.
1811–16	Issue of silver Bank Tokens for 3*s.* and 1*s.* 6*d.* to alleviate shortage of silver coin.
1814	Bank Volunteers disbanded.
1815	Defeat of Napoleon at Waterloo (18 June).
	National debt reaches £834m.
	Bank of England note circulation reaches *c.*£26m.; falls back to £17m. by 1822.
	Number of Bank staff increases to over 900.
1816	Gold standard officially adopted; pound sterling statutorily defined in terms of a fixed quantity of gold; a new coin, the gold sovereign (worth 20 shillings and containing 123.27 grains of gold) was put into circulation in the following year.
	Mint moves out of the Tower of London to new premises on Tower Hill and commences major recoinage.
1817	Temporary partial resumption of cash payments.

1821	
1 May	Full resumption of cash payments; issue of £1 and £2 notes ceases.
1824	Trial and execution of Fauntleroy, the forger.
1825–6	Financial crisis results in panic run on the Bank which is almost forced to suspend cash payments again; widespread bankruptcies among note-issuing banks.
1826	Country Bankers Act restricts Bank's monopoly of joint-stock banking to within a radius of 65 miles from London and allows joint-stock banks to set up outside that limit and issue their own notes.
	Act also authorizes the Bank to set up country branches which could issue their own notes; first branch opened at Gloucester (on 19 July 1826), followed by branches at Manchester and Swansea in that year.
1827	Bank opens branches at Birmingham, Liverpool, Bristol, Leeds, and Exeter.
1828	Bank opens branch at Newcastle.
	Rebuilding work completed by Soane; Bank remains virtually unaltered, architecturally, for almost a century.
	National debt reaches £800m.
1829	Bank opens branches at Hull and Norwich.
1830	Introduction of cheque 'books', replacing the single pieces of 'cheque paper' used hitherto.
1832	Death penalty for forgery abolished.
1833	Renewal of Bank Charter to 1855; Act also permits establishment of joint-stock banks in London and within the 65-mile radius laid down in 1826, provided they did not issue their own notes.
1834	Bank opens branches at Plymouth and Portsmouth; closure of Exeter Branch.
1837	Financial crisis; Bank does not rescue three large Anglo-American houses.
1839	Bank compelled to borrow heavily from Bank of France.
1844	Bank Charter Act provides for separation of Bank's note issue from its banking business; note issue effectively tied to the size of the gold reserve except for a fiduciary issue of £14m.;

	Act marks decisive stage in the gradual elimi-
	nation from circulation in England and Wales
	of all notes other than the Bank's own (not
	finally achieved until 1928).
	Bank opens branch at Leicester.
1845	Railway Mania.
1846	Repeal of the Corn Laws.
1847	Financial crisis; failure of the Governor's own firm (W. R. Robinson & Co.); first suspension of Bank Charter Act.
1848	Chartist Agitation: demonstration outside heavily fortified Bank (10 Apr.). Princes Street entrance bricked up until 1882.
	Gold discovered in California.
1849	Closure of Gloucester Branch.
1851	Gold discovered in Australia.
1852	Closure of Norwich Branch.
1853	Bank of England note becomes a wholly printed instrument.
	National debt reaches £812m.
1853–6	Crimean War.
1855	Bank opens Western Branch at Uxbridge House, Burlington Street, in West End.
	Change of design on Bank of England notes to a form which remains unchanged (on denominations of £5 and above) until 1957.
1857	Financial crisis; Bank rate goes up to 10 per cent; Bank Charter Act again suspended.
1859	Closure of Swansea Branch.
1860	National debt reaches £822m.
1861	Post Office Savings Banks set up.
1861–5	American Civil War.
1866	Financial crisis precipitated by collapse of the discount house Overend Gurney (11 May, 'Black Friday'); Bank Charter Act suspended for third time; Bank rate stands at 10 per cent for three months.
	Bank Volunteer corps enrolled as 'K' Company of the Civil Service Rifle Volunteers.
1870	Postal payment of dividends introduced.
	Printed signature of Chief Cashier appears on all Bank of England notes.
1871	Bank Holiday Act.
	Germany adopts gold standard.

1872	Closure of Leicester Branch.
1873	Publication of Walter Bagehot's *Lombard Street*, which includes criticism of the Bank.
	Economic crisis in Europe and America—beginning of Great Depression (1873–96).
	USA adopts gold standard (reintroduces silver standard in 1878).
1875	German Reichsbank founded.
1880	National debt stands at £770m.
1886	Gold discovered in Transvaal.
1888	Bank opens Law Courts Branch in Fleet Street; designed by Sir Arthur Blomfield, architect to the Bank 1883–99.
1889–92	William Lidderdale, Governor.
1890	Baring Crisis; Bank's intervention successfully averts threat to banking system and confirms its role as lender of last resort.
1891	Reissue of £1 notes suggested by Chancellor of the Exchequer, G. J. Goschen, in order to enable the Bank to maintain a larger stock of gold; Goschen is the only Chancellor to have been a Director of the Bank (1858–65).
1892	Gold standard adopted in Austria-Hungary.
1893	Resignation of Chief Cashier, Frank May, following revelation of financial irregularities; results in setting up of Audit Department at the Bank.
1894	Bank becomes first major City house to employ women clerks.
Feb. 1894–Sept. 1896	Bank rate unchanged at the nineteenth-century low of 2 per cent.
1897	Discovery of Klondike goldfield. Gold standard adopted in Japan.
1898–1908	Kenneth Grahame, author of *The Wind in the Willows*, *The Golden Age*, *Dream Days*, and other children's books, employed as Secretary of the Bank.
1898	Gold standard adopted in Russia.
1899–1902	Boer War; Bank closely involved in a series of major British Government issues to fund the war.
1900	United States adopts an exclusive gold standard.
1902	National debt reaches £745m. due to the cost of the Boer War.

1907	Montagu Norman becomes a Director.
	US banking crisis; Bank rate goes up to 7 per cent, the highest level between 1873 and 1914.
1913	Beginning of Walter Cunliffe's term as Governor.
	Commonwealth Bank of Australia opens.
	National debt stands at £650m.
1914	Number of staff at the Bank reaches 1,004 (including 65 women clerks).
	Closure of Portsmouth Branch.
Sun. 28 June	Assassination of Archduke Franz Ferdinand at Sarajevo.
28 July	Austria-Hungary declares war on Serbia.
30 July	Stock Exchange closes (until 4 Jan. 1915).
31 July	Bank rate raised from 4 to 8 per cent.
Sat. 1 Aug.	Germany declares war on Russia. Bank rate raised to 10 per cent; large crowds queue outside the Bank to exchange notes for gold.
3 Aug.	Germany declares war on France and invades Belgium.
Tues. 4 Aug.	Great Britain declares war on Germany.
6 Aug.	Currency and Bank Notes Act authorizes the issue of £1 and 10-shilling notes by the Treasury (following the rejection of a proposed Bank of England £1 note); soon nicknamed 'Bradburys' because of the signature of Sir John Bradbury, Permanent Secretary to the Treasury; gold coin soon begins to disappear from circulation.
Nov.	Issue of 3½ per cent War Stock raises £350m.
1915	
Apr.	Cunliffe's normal two-year term as Governor extended for a further year (and again in 1916 and 1917); Cunliffe's five-year Governorship longer than any of his 107 predecessors.
25 May	Reginald McKenna replaces Lloyd George as Chancellor of the Exchequer.
June	Issue of 4½ per cent War Stock raises £592m.
	National debt reaches £1,105m.
1916	
Aug.	Calais Agreement on inter-Allied finance.
6 Dec.	Lloyd George replaces Asquith as Prime Minister.
10 Dec.	Bonar Law replaces McKenna as Chancellor.

1917	
Jan.	Issue of 5 per cent War Loan raises £950m.
Apr.	United States enters the War.
July	Cunliffe-Bonar Law quarrel.
7 Nov.	Russian (Bolshevik) Revolution.
	National debt reaches £4,011m.
1918	
Apr.	Cunliffe succeeded as Governor by Cokayne; becomes Chairman of [Cunliffe] Committee on Currency and Foreign Exchange.
Aug.	Cunliffe Committee, first interim report.
11 Nov.	Armistice.
	National debt reaches £5,872m.
1919	
Mar.	Britain formally goes off the gold standard (*de facto* since 1914).
28 June	Treaty of Versailles signed.
Dec.	Cunliffe Committee, final report.
	National debt reaches £7,435m.
	Number of Bank staff reaches post-First World War peak of just under 4,000.
	Bank of England note circulation (*c.*£28m. in 1913) over £70m.; Treasury note circulation *c.*£300m.
1920	Montagu Norman succeeds Cokayne as Governor.
Apr.	Bank rate 7 per cent (to April 1921).
	Rebuilding Committee set up.
	Printing Department moves out of Head Office to converted premises at St Luke's, Old Street.
	National debt reaches post-First World War peak of £7,832m. (not exceeded until 1938).
1921	Closure of last private note-issuing bank in England and Wales (Fox, Fowler & Co. of Wellington, Somerset)
	Herbert Baker (knighted 1926) invited to draw up plans for a new Bank and subsequently appointed architect.
	Bank sets up Economic Section.
	South African Reserve Bank opens.
1923	
Feb.	Anglo-American War Debt Agreement.
1924	
Jan.–Oct.	First Labour Government; Chancellor is Snowden.

Sept.	Dawes Plan reducing German reparations comes into effect.
Nov.	Churchill succeeds Snowden as Chancellor.
1925	
6 Apr.	Demolition work at the Bank begins.
28 Apr.	Churchill announces return to the gold standard in his Budget speech.
13 May	Gold Standard Act restores modified version of pre-1914 gold standard: Bank obliged to sell gold in bars of not less than 400 ounces at £3 17s. 10½d. an ounce, but no domestic circulation of gold coin; sterling exchange rate fixed at pre-war level of $4.86.
	National debt stands at £7,646m.
1926	
(3–12 May)	General Strike.
1928	Vickers-Armstrong formed with Bank support.
	Agricultural Mortgage Corporation established.
	Currency and Bank Notes Act amalgamates Treasury and Bank note issues; Bank issues coloured banknotes for the first time.
	Bank of England note circulation reaches c.£350m.
1929	Lancashire Cotton Corporation formed with Bank support.
June	Second Labour Government under Ramsay MacDonald; Snowden returns as Chancellor.
24 Oct.	Wall Street Crash begins.
	Securities Management Trust (SMT) established.
1930	Young Plan—further scaling down German reparations—comes into force.
	National Shipbuilders Security Ltd. formed.
Apr.	Bankers Industrial Development Company established.
17 May	Bank for International Settlements (BIS) established in Basle.
	Lancashire Steel Corporation formed.
	Sale of Western Branch to the Royal Bank of Scotland.
1931	
11 May	Failure of Credit Anstalt Bank in Vienna precipitates Central European financial crisis.

20 June	Hoover Moratorium for one year on reparations and war debts.
13 July	Financial crisis spreads to London. Publication, coincidentally, of the Macmillan Committee report on the financing of British Industry.
25 July	Publication of the May Committee report on government finances.
23 Aug.	Labour Government falls.
24 Aug.	National Government formed under Ramsay MacDonald; Snowden remains Chancellor.
10 Sept.	Snowden's emergency Budget.
17 Sept.	Standstill Agreement.
Sat. 19 Sept.	Gold standard suspended.
21 Sept.	Gold Standard (Amendment) Act; sterling floated.
27 Oct.	General Election: National Government returned.
5 Nov.	Neville Chamberlain replaces Snowden as Chancellor of the Exchequer.
1932	5 per cent War Loan Conversion. Exchange Equalisation Account (EEA) established.
June	Bank rate 2 per cent (until Aug. 1939); beginning of 'cheap money' policy.
June	Report of the Peacock Committee, recommending introduction of executive directors.
Nov.	Sterling reaches low point of $3.145.
1933	Anglo-American war debt final payment. Banking crisis in USA, which abandons gold standard.
June–July	World Economic Conference held in London.
16 Nov.	Sterling reaches high point of $5.50 during floating period.
1934	Reserve Bank of New Zealand opens.
1935	Pepper scandal: Bank intervenes to calm agitation in commodity markets. Bank of Canada opens. Reserve Bank of India opens.
1936	
Sept.–Oct.	Tripartite Agreement. Publication of J. M. Keynes's *The General Theory of Employment, Interest and Money*.
1939	Rebuilding of the Bank completed at a cost of £5.3m. Closure of Hull Branch.

	National debt reaches pre-war peak of £8,418m.
26 Aug.	London clearing system moves to Staffordshire.
1 Sept.	Germany invades Poland.
Sun. 3 Sept.	Great Britain and France declare war on Germany.
4 Sept.	Treasury imposes control of foreign exchange; Exchange Control Department set up at the Bank (lasts until 1979).
	Sterling exchange rate fixed at $4.03 for the duration of the war.
	Accountant's Department and most banknote production moved to Hampshire for the duration of the War.
Oct.	Bank rate reduced to 2 per cent (remains at this level until Nov. 1951).
1940	Bank opens branch in Southampton and agency in Glasgow.
	Women first outnumber men at the Bank.
10 May	Churchill forms National Government.
9–10 Sept.	Direct hit on the Bank during an air-raid; work mostly carried on underground for remainder of war.
1941	National debt reaches £11,666m.
1943	Withdrawal of all Bank of England denominations above £5 to combat tax evasion and forgery.
	National debt reaches £17,117m.
1944	
Apr.	Norman retires as Governor due to ill health; Lord Catto succeeds.
27 July	Bank celebrates 250th anniversary.
	Publication of Sir John Clapham's two-volume official history of the Bank.
	Bank of England note circulation reaches £1bn.
	Bretton Woods agreement.
1945	
May	End of European War.
July	Establishment of Industrial and Commercial Finance Corporation (ICFC, the modern 3i) with Bank support.
	Labour Government under Attlee takes office.
	National debt reaches £22,648m.

1946	
1 Jan.	Bank of France nationalized.
14 Feb.	Bank of England Act.
1 Mar.	Bank of England nationalized.
21 Apr.	Death of Lord Keynes (a Director of the Bank from October 1941).
June	International Bank for Reconstruction and Development (IBRD) begins operations.
1947	
Mar.	International Monetary Fund (IMF) comes into operation.
July	Exchange Control Act.
	Unsuccessful return to sterling convertibility following Washington Agreement.
1949	
Feb.	Cobbold succeeds Catto as Governor.
18 Sept.	Sterling devalued from $4.03 to $2.80.
	Closure of Plymouth Branch.
1950	Establishment of European Payments Union.
4 Feb.	Death of Lord Norman.
1951	
Oct.	Conservative Government under Churchill takes office.
7 Nov.	Bank rate raised for the first time since 1939.
1954	National debt reaches £26,672m.
1956	Purpose-built Bank of England Printing Works opened at Debden in Essex.
1957	
May	Setting-up of Radcliffe Committee on the working of the UK monetary system.
19 Sept.	Bank rate raised to 7 per cent. Subsequent inquiry (Parker Tribunal) into alleged 'leak' establishes that there was no leak.
	Treaty of Rome establishes the European Economic Community.
	White fiver discontinued.
1958	Registrar's Department (formerly Accountant's) moves to New Change near St Paul's.
Dec.	Convertibility of sterling.
1959	
Aug.	Publication of Radcliffe Committee Report.
1960	
17 Mar.	Monarch's portrait appears on Bank of England notes for the first time.

Dec.	First issue of the Bank's *Quarterly Bulletin*.
1961	
June	Cromer succeeds Cobbold as Governor.
1964	
Feb.	Issue of £10 notes resumed.
Oct.	Labour Government under Harold Wilson takes office; Chancellor of the Exchequer is James Callaghan.
	National debt reaches £30,226m.
1966	O'Brien succeeds Cromer as Governor.
1967	
20 Nov.	Sterling devalued by 14 per cent from $2.80 to $2.40.
	Roy Jenkins replaces Callaghan as Chancellor.
1968	Gold market breaks down: old fixed price survives only for international finance, with separate price for free-market gold.
	Merger of Westminster and National Provincial Banks to form National Westminster Bank.
1969	
13 Oct.	Issue of 10-shilling notes ceases; demonetized 22 Nov. 1970.
1970	Introduction of Special Drawing Rights (SDRs) at the IMF.
	National debt reaches £33,079m.
June	Conservative Government under Edward Heath takes office.
July	Issue of £20 notes resumed.
1971	
15 Feb.	UK changes to a decimal currency.
15 Aug.	USA suspends dollar convertibility into gold; collapse of system of fixed exchange rates.
16 Sept.	New system of credit control introduced; direct controls on bank lending removed.
Dec.	Smithsonian Agreement on exchange rate parities.
	Bank's accounts first published in annual report.
1972	
22 June	Sterling floated.
20 Nov.	Minimum Lending Rate (MLR) replaces Bank rate.
	Equal pay for women introduced at the Bank.

1973	
1 Jan.	UK becomes a member of the EEC.
July	Richardson succeeds O'Brien as Governor.
	Bank Picquet abolished (mounted for the last time on 31 July 1973).
	Huge rise in crude oil prices.
Dec.	Beginning of secondary banking crisis; Bank sets up Central Committee or 'lifeboat'.
1974	
Feb./Mar.	Election defeat for Conservatives; Labour Government takes office under Harold Wilson; Chancellor of the Exchequer is Denis Healey.
	National debt reaches £40,125m.
1975	Bank rescues Slater Walker.
Aug.	Inflation reaches post-war peak of 26.9 per cent.
12 Dec.	Closure of Law Courts Branch.
1976	
5 Mar.	Sterling goes below $2.00 for the first time.
May	Setting up of Equity Capital for Industry (ECI) by City institutions under Bank sponsorship.
Autumn	Sterling crisis; $3,900m. loan from IMF.
	Number of staff at the Bank reaches all-time peak of just over 7,900.
1979	National debt reaches £86,885m.
13 Mar.	European Monetary System (EMS) starts to operate.
3 May	General election defeat for Labour; Conservative Government takes office under Margaret Thatcher; Chancellor of the Exchequer is Sir Geoffrey Howe.
	Exchange Controls abolished.
	Banking Act gives the Bank statutory licensing and supervisory powers over all deposit-taking institutions in the UK for the first time.
15 Nov.	MLR 17 per cent (to 3 July 1980), the highest ever level.
1980	Major internal reorganization; introduction of associate directors.
1981	
Mar.	Issue of £50 notes resumed.
20 Aug.	MLR scrapped (reintroduced for one day on 14 Dec. 1985).

1982	Mexican Debt Crisis.
	Bank of England note circulation reaches £10bn.
1983	National debt reaches £127,927m.
11 June	Nigel Lawson replaces Howe as Chancellor.
July	Leigh-Pemberton succeeds Richardson as Governor.
1984	Collapse of Johnson Matthey Bankers.
31 Dec.	Issue of £1 notes ceases (£1 note demonetized on 11 March 1988); £1 coin introduced the previous year.
1985	
6 Mar.	Sterling reaches all-time low of $1.04 against the dollar.
1986	
27 Oct.	'Big Bang' on the London Stock Exchange.
1987	Banking Act strengthens the Bank's supervisory powers.
1988	HM The Queen opens the Bank of England Museum.
1989	National debt reaches £197,320m.
	Relocation of Registrar's Department to Gloucester.
	Number of Bank staff falls to 5,155.
26 Oct.	John Major replaces Lawson as Chancellor.
1990	
7 June	Series E £5 note issued.
8 Oct.	UK joins Exchange Rate Mechanism (ERM) of European Monetary System.
28 Nov.	John Major succeeds Thatcher as Prime Minister.
29 Nov.	Norman Lamont becomes Chancellor.
	National debt stands at £192,545m.
	Bank of England note circulation reaches £15bn.
1991	
July	Collapse of Bank of Credit and Commerce International (BCCI).
1992	National debt reaches £214,528m.
16 Sept.	UK leaves Exchange Rate Mechanism.
1993	National debt reaches £248,644m.
Feb.	First issue of Bank's quarterly *Inflation Report*.
27 May	Kenneth Clarke replaces Lamont as Chancellor.

July	George succeeds Leigh-Pemberton as Governor.
Nov.	Power returned to Bank to determine timing of interest-rate changes.
	First female Director appointed.
	Bank staff total 4,570.
1994	
Apr.	Publication of the minutes of the monthly meetings between the Chancellor and the Governor to set monetary policy.
4 July	Major internal reorganization: Bank divided into two 'wings', responsible for monetary stability and financial stability.
27 July	Bank's Tercentenary.

Appendix 2: Governors, Directors, and Senior Officials

1   GOVERNORS
2   DEPUTY GOVERNORS
3   DIRECTORS INCLUDING ASSOCIATE DIRECTORS AND NEW DEPUTY DIRECTORS
4   COMPTROLLERS
5   ASSISTANTS TO THE GOVERNORS
6   ADVISERS TO THE GOVERNORS
7   ASSISTANT DIRECTORS
8   CHIEF ADVISERS
9   CHIEF CASHIERS
10   CHIEF ACCOUNTANTS
11   SECRETARIES
12   AUDITORS
13   PRINCIPAL SUPERVISORS/GENERAL MANAGERS OF PRINTING WORKS
14   CHIEFS/HEADS OF DEPARTMENTS AND AREAS OF SUPERVISION
15   HEADS OF DIVISION OR FUNCTION
16   ORGANOGRAM OF ORGANIZATION OF THE BANK, JULY 1994

The following lists of Governors, Directors, and Senior Officials reflect the internal changes in the Bank from 1694 to 1994. The major reorganization which took place on 4 July 1994 is shown in the organogram on page 297. Brackets with titles such as Kt. or Bt. or decorations denote titles or decorations received during or after the period of office.

Information has been obtained from Bank histories, House Lists, Annual Reports, the *Old Lady* magazine, and telephone directories.

Governors*

Sir John Houblon	1694–7
Sir William Scawen	1697–9

* Titles of Governors are at time of taking office.

Nathaniel Tench	1699–1701
John Ward	1701–3
Abraham Houblon	1703–5
Sir James Bateman	1705–7
Francis Eyles	1707–9
Sir Gilbert Heathcote	1709–11
Nathaniel Gould	1711–13
John Rudge	1713–15
Sir Peter Delmé	1715–17
Sir Gerard Conyers	1717–19
John Hanger	1719–21
Sir Thomas Scawen	1721–3
Sir Gilbert Heathcote	1723–5
William Thompson	1725–7
Humphry Morice	1727–9
Samuel Holden	1729–31
Sir Edward Bellamy	1731–3
The Hon. Horatio Townshend	1733–5
Bryan Benson	1735–7
Thomas Cooke	1737–40
Delillers Carbonnel	1740–1
Stamp Brooksbank	1741–3
William Fawkener	1743–5
Charles Savage	1745–7
Benjamin Longuet	1747–9
William Hunt	1749–52
Alexander Sheafe	1752–4
Charles Palmer	1754–6
Matthews Beachcroft	1756–8
Merrik Burrell	1758–60
Bartholomew Burton	1760–2
Robert Marsh	1762–4
John Weyland	1764–6
Matthew Clarmont	1766–9
William Cooper	1769–71
Edward Payne	1771–3
James Sperling	1773–5
Samuel Beachcroft	1775–7
Peter Gaussen	1777–9
Daniel Booth	1779–81
William Ewer	1781–3
Richard Neave	1783–5
George Peters	1785–7
Edward Darell	1787–9

Mark Weyland	1789–91
Samuel Bosanquet	1791–3
Godfrey Thornton	1793–5
Daniel Giles	1795–7
Thomas Raikes	1797–9
Samuel Thornton	1799–1801
Job Mathew	1801–2
Joseph Nutt	1802–4
Benjamin Winthrop	1804–6
Beeston Long	1806–8
John Whitmore	1808–10
John Pearse	1810–12
William Manning	1812–14
William Mellish	1814–16
Jeremiah Harman	1816–18
George Dorrien	1818–20
Charles Pole	1820–2
John Bowden	1822–4
Cornelius Buller	1824–6
John Baker Richards	1826–8
Samuel Drewe	1828–30
John Horsley Palmer	1830–3
Richard Mee Raikes	1833–4
James Pattison	1834–7
Timothy Abraham Curtis	1837–9
Sir John Rae Reid, Bt.	1839–41
Sir John Henry Pelly, Bt.	1841–2
William Cotton	1842–5
John Benjamin Heath	1845–7
William Robinson Robinson	1847 (Apr.–Aug.)
James Morris	1847–9
Henry James Prescott	1849–51
Thomson Hankey	1851–3
John Gellibrand Hubbard	1853–5
Thomas Matthias Weguelin	1855–7
Sheffield Neave	1857–9
Bonamy Dobree	1859–61
Alfred Latham	1861–3
Kirkman Daniel Hodgson	1863–5
Henry Lancelot Holland	1865–7
Thomas Newman Hunt	1867–9
Robert Wigram Crawford	1869–71
George Lyall	1871–3
Benjamin Buck Greene	1873–5

Henry Hucks Gibbs	1875–7
Edward Howley Palmer	1877–9
John William Birch	1879–81
Henry Riversdale Grenfell	1881–3
John Saunders Gilliat	1883–5
James Pattison Currie	1885–7
Mark Wilks Collet (Bt. 1888)	1887–9
William Lidderdale (PC 1891)	1889–92
David Powell	1892–5
Albert George Sandeman	1895–7
Hugh Colin Smith	1897–9
Samuel Steuart Gladstone	1899–1901
Augustus Prevost (Bt. 1902)	1901–3
Samuel Hope Morley	1903–5
Alexander Falconer Wallace (OBE)	1905–7
William Middleton Campbell	1907–9
Reginald Eden Johnston	1909–11
Alfred Clayton Cole	1911–13
Walter Cunliffe (GBE 1917) (Baron Cunliffe 1914)	1913–18
Sir Brien Ibrican Cokayne (Baron Cullen of Ashbourne 1920)	1918–20
Montagu Collet Norman DSO (PC 1923) (Baron Norman of St Clere 1944)	1920–44
Lord Catto of Cairncatto CBE (PC 1947)	1944–9
Cameron Fromanteel Cobbold (PC 1959) (Baron Cobbold of Knebworth 1960)	1949–61
The Earl of Cromer MBE (PC 1966)	1961–6
Leslie Kenneth O'Brien (GBE 1967, PC 1970) (Baron O'Brien of Lothbury 1973)	1966–73
Gordon William Humphreys Richardson MBE (TD 1979, PC 1976) (Baron Richardson of Duntisbourne 1983)	1973–83
Robert (Robin) Leigh-Pemberton (KG 1994, PC 1987) (Baron Kingsdown 1993)	1983–93
Edward Alan John George	1993–

Deputy Governors*

Michael Godrey	1694–5
Sir William Scawen	1695–7

* Titles of Deputy Governors are at time of taking office.

Nathaniel Tench	1697–9
John Ward	1699–1701
Abraham Houblon	1701–3
Sir James Bateman	1703–5
Francis Eyles	1705–7
William Des Bouverie	1707–9
Nathaniel Gould	1709–11
John Rudge	1711–13
Peter Delmé (Kt. 1714)	1713–15
Sir Gerard Conyers	1715–17
John Hanger	1717–19
Sir Thomas Scawen	1719–21
Josiah Diston	1721–3
William Thompson	1723–5
Humphry Morice	1725–7
Samuel Holden	1727–9
Sir Edward Bellamy	1729–31
John Olmius	1731
The Hon. Horatio Townshend	1732–3
Bryan Benson	1733–5
Thomas Cooke	1735–7
Nathaniel Gould	1737–8
Delillers Carbonnel	1738–40
Stamp Brooksbank	1740–1
William Fawkener	1741–3
Charles Savage	1743–5
Benjamin Longuet	1745–7
William Hunt	1747–9
Benjamin Lethieullier	1749–50
Alexander Sheafe	1750–2
Charles Palmer	1752–4
Matthews Beachcroft	1754–6
Merrik Burrell	1756–8
Bartholomew Burton	1758–60
Robert Marsh	1760–2
John Weyland	1762–4
Matthew Clarmont	1764–6
Sir Samuel Fludyer, Bt.	1766–8
William Cooper	1768–9
Edward Payne	1769–71
James Sperling	1771–3
Samuel Beachcroft	1773–5
James Haughton Langston	1775–6
Peter Gaussen	1776–7

Daniel Booth	1777–9
William Ewer	1779–81
Richard Neave	1781–3
George Peters	1783–5
Edward Darell	1785–7
Mark Weyland	1787–9
Samuel Bosanquet	1789–91
Godfrey Thornton	1791–3
Daniel Giles	1793–5
Thomas Raikes	1795–7
Samuel Thornton	1797–9
Job Mathew	1799–1801
Joseph Nutt	1801–2
Benjamin Winthrop	1802–4
Beeston Long	1804–6
Sir Brook Watson, Bt.	1806–7
John Whitmore	1807–8
John Pearse	1808–10
William Manning	1810–12
William Mellish	1812–14
Jeremiah Harman	1814–16
George Dorrien	1816–18
Charles Pole	1818–20
John Bowden	1820–2
Cornelius Buller	1822–4
John Baker Richards	1824–6
Samuel Drewe	1826–8
John Horsley Palmer	1828–30
Andrew Henry Thomson	1830–2
Richard Mee Raikes	1832–3
James Pattison	1833–4
Timothy Abraham Curtis	1834–7
Sir John Rae Reid, Bt.	1837–9
John Henry Pelly (Bt. 1840)	1839–41
William Cotton	1841–2
John Benjamin Heath	1842–5
William Robinson Robinson	1845–7
James Morris	1847
Henry James Prescott	1847–9
Thomson Hankey	1849–51
John Gellibrand Hubbard	1851–3
Thomas Matthias Weguelin	1853–5
Sheffield Neave	1855–7
Bonamy Dobree	1857–9

Alfred Latham	1859–61
Kirkman Daniel Hodgson	1861–3
Henry Lancelot Holland	1863–5
Thomas Newman Hunt	1865–7
Robert Wigram Crawford	1867–9
George Lyall	1869–71
Benjamin Buck Greene	1871–3
Henry Hucks Gibbs	1873–5
Edward Howley Palmer	1875–7
John William Birch	1877–9
Henry Riversdale Grenfell	1879–81
John Saunders Gilliat	1881–3
James Pattison Currie	1883–5
Mark Wilks Collet	1885–7
William Lidderdale	1887–9
David Powell	1889–92
Clifford Wigram	1892–4
Albert George Sandeman	1894–5
Hugh Colin Smith	1895–7
Samuel Steuart Gladstone	1897–9
Augustus Prevost	1899–1901
Samuel Hope Morley	1901–3
Alexander Falconer Wallace (OBE)	1903–5
William Middleton Campbell	1905–7
Edgar Lubbock	1907
Reginald Eden Johnston	1907–9
Alfred Clayton Cole	1909–11
Walter Cunliffe	1911–13
Robert Lydston Newman	1913–15
Brien Ibrican Cokayne (KBE 1917)	1915–18
Montagu Collet Norman DSO	1918–20
Henry Alexander Trotter	1920–3
Cecil Lubbock	1923–5
Sir Alan Garrett Anderson KBE	1925–6
Henry Alexander Trotter	1926–7
Cecil Lubbock	1927–9
Sir Ernest Musgrave Harvey KBE (Bt. 1933)	1929–36
Basil Gage Catterns	1936–45
Cameron Fromanteel Cobbold	1945–9
Dallas Gerald Mercer Bernard (Bt. 1954)	1949–54
Humphrey Charles Baskerville Mynors (Bt. 1964)	1954–64
Leslie Kenneth O'Brien	1964–6
Sir Maurice Henry Parsons (KCMG 1970)	1966–70
Jasper Quintus Hollom (KBE 1975)	1970–80

Christopher William McMahon (Kt. 1986)   1980–6
George Blunden (Kt. 1987)   1986–90
Edward Alan John George   1990–3
Rupert Lascelles Pennant-Rea   1993–

Directors

Directors	*Period of Office*
Sir John Houblon (Governor 1694–7)	1697–9, 1700–12
Sir John Huband, Bt.	1694–7
Sir James Houblon	1694–1700
Sir William Gore	1694–7, 1698–9, 1701–6
Sir William Scawen (Deputy Governor 1695–7) (Governor 1697–9)	1694–5, 1699–1718, 1719–22
Sir Henry Furnese (Bt. 1707)	1694–7, 1699–1702
Sir Thomas Abney	1694–1700, 1703–5, 1706–9, 1710–14, 1715–18, 1719–22
Sir William Hedges	1694–1700
Brook Bridges	1694–1702, 1703–5, 1706–8
James Bateman (Kt. 1698) (Deputy Governor 1703–5) (Governor 1705–7)	1694–7, 1698–9, 1700–3, 1707–11
George Bodington or Boddington	1694–5
James Denew	1694–9, 1700–2
Thomas Goddard	1694–8, 1700
Abraham Houblon (Deputy Governor 1701–3) (Governor 1703–5)	1694–1701, 1705–8
Gilbert Heathcote (Kt. 1702, Bt. 1733) (Governor 1709–11, 1723–5)	1694–1702, 1704–9, 1711–23, 1726–33
Theodore Janssen (Bt. 1715)	1694–9, 1700–1, 1707–11, 1718–19
John Lordell	1694–8, 1700–2, 1703–5, 1706–9, 1710–14, 1715–17, 1718–20, 1721–4, 1725–6
Samuel Lethieullier	1694–1710

Directors	*Period of Office*
William Paterson	1694–5
Robert Raworth	1694–1701, 1704–6, 1707
John Smith	1694–9, 1703–5, 1706–10, 1711–13
Obadiah Sedgwick	1694–1707
Nathaniel Tench (Deputy Governor 1697–9) (Governor 1699–1701)	1694–7, 1701–9
John Ward (Kt. 1714) (Deputy Governor 1699–1701) (Governor 1701–3)	1694–7, 1698–9, 1703–11, 1712–26
John Knight	1694–7
Anthony Stevens	1695
Peter Godfrey	1695–8
Sir John Cope, Bt.	1695–8, 1700–2
Henry Cornish	1695–7, 1699–1700
Sir William Ashurst	1697–1700, 1701–3, 1704–6, 1707–9, 1710–14
Robert Bristow	1697–1700, 1701–4, 1705–7
Francis Eyles (Bt. 1714) (Deputy Governor 1705–7) (Governor 1707–9)	1697–1703, 1704–5, 1709–15
Nathaniel Gould (Kt. 1721) (Deputy Governor 1709–11) (Governor 1711–13)	1697–1701, 1704–5, 1707–8, 1713–14, 1715–21, 1722–3, 1724-8
Samuel Lock	1697–8
John Page	1697–8, 1700–2, 1710–11
Charles Chambrelan	1703–5
John Shipman	1697–8, 1702–4, 1706–8, 1709–12, 1713–16, 1717–19, 1720–2
Samuel Bulteele	1697–8, 1699–1701, 1702–5, 1706–8
William Dawsonne	1698–1701, 1702–4, 1705–6, 1707–8, 1709–11, 1714–15, 1718–19

Directors	Period of Office
Peter Delmé (Kt. 1714) (Deputy Governor 1713–15) (Governor 1715–17)	1698–1703, 1709–13, 1717–28
Peter Gott	1698–1700
Sir Richard Levett	1698–1700
Francis Stratford	1698–9
John Devink	1699–1701, 1702–4, 1705–7, 1708–10
Richard Perry	1699–1701
John Rudge (Deputy Governor 1711–13) (Governor 1713–15)	1699–1702, 1703–6, 1707–11, 1715–21, 1730–40
Jacob Reynardson	1699–1703, 1704–6, 1707–9
Charles Thorold (Kt. 1704)	1699
William Des Bouverie (Bt. 1714) (Deputy Governor 1707–9)	1700–7, 1709–11
Josiah Diston (Deputy Governor 1721–3)	1701–3, 1704–6, 1708–12, 1713–18, 1719–21
John Gould	1701–4, 1705–7, 1708–10, 1714–15, 1719–20, 1724–5, 1729–30
John Hanger (Deputy Governor 1717–19) (Governor 1719–21)	1701–3, 1704–6, 1709–12, 1713–17, 1721–33
Humphry South	1701–3
Sir Robert Clayton	1702–7
Gerard Conyers (Kt. 1714) (Deputy Governor 1715–17) (Governor 1717–19)	1702–4, 1705–7, 1708–10, 1711–15, 1719–37
Abraham Hill	1702–4
Samuel Heathcote	1702–4, 1706–8
Sir William Hodges, Bt.	1703–7, 1708–12, 1713–14
Charles Peers (Kt. 1707)	1705–7, 1708–12
Thomas Scawen (Kt. 1714) (Deputy Governor 1719–21) (Governor 1721–3)	1705–8, 1709–10, 1711–14, 1715–19, 1723–6, 1727–9

Directors	*Period of Office*
Sir John Cope (succeeded father as Bt. 1721)	1706–9, 1710–13, 1714–17, 1718–21
James Dolliffe (Kt. 1714)	1708–10
John Emilie	1708–10
William Gore	1709–12
Justus Beck (Bt. 1714)	1710–13, 1715–17
William Henry Cornelison	1710–13
John Dolben	1710
Jeremiah Powell	1710–15
John Ward	1711–12, 1716–18
Sir George Thorold, Bt.	1711–16, 1717–21
Dennis Dutry (Bt. 1716)	1711–14
Philip Jackson (Kt. 1714)	1711–14, 1715–18, 1719–22, 1723–4
Heneage Fetherston	1711
Robert Atwood	1712–15, 1716–18, 1719–22, 1723–6, 1727–30, 1731–4, 1735–7
Richard Cary	1712–15, 1716–18, 1720–2
Sir Joseph Hodges	1712–13
Sir Randolph Knipe	1712–16, 1717–20, 1721–4, 1725–8
Christopher Lethieullier	1712–16, 1717–20, 1721–4, 1725–7, 1728–31, 1732–4
Matthew Raper	1712–13
Robert Bristow	1713–16, 1718–20
John Edmonds	1713–16, 1717–19
Richard Houblon (Kt. 1715)	1713–14, 1716–17, 1718–20
Richard Chiswell	1714–16, 1717–19, 1720–1
William Jolliff (Kt. 1715)	1714–17, 1718–20, 1721–4, 1725–8, 1729–32, 1733–6, 1737–42
Henry Lyell	1714–15
William Thompson (Deputy Governor 1723–5) (Governor 1725–7)	1714–17, 1718–23, 1727–8
John Eyles (succeeded his father as Bt. 1716)	1715–17

Directors	Period of Office
Barrington Eaton	1716–18, 1720–2, 1723–6, 1727–9, 1730–2
John Francis Fauquier	1716–20, 1721–4, 1725–6
Humphry Morice (Deputy Governor 1725–7) (Governor 1727–9)	1716–19, 1720–3, 1724–5, 1729–31
Moses Raper	1716–19, 1720–3, 1724–6, 1727–30, 1731–4, 1735–8, 1739–42
Joseph Eyles (Kt. 1724)	1717–21, 1730–3
Sir William Humfreys, Bt.	1719–21, 1722–5, 1726–7, 1728–30
Richard Du Cane	1720–2, 1723–5, 1726–7, 1728–30
Samuel Holden (Deputy Governor 1727–9) (Governor 1729–31)	1720–3, 1724–7, 1731–40
Bryan Benson (Deputy Governor 1733–5) (Governor 1735–7)	1721–3, 1724–7, 1728–31, 1732–3, 1737–58
Thomas Cooke (Deputy Governor 1735–7) (Governor 1737–40)	1721–4, 1725–8, 1729–32, 1733–5, 1740–52
Delillers Carbonnel (Deputy Governor 1738–40) (Governor 1740–1)	1722–5, 1726–9, 1730–4, 1735–8, 1741–7
Nathaniel Gould (Deputy Governor 1737–8)	1722–4, 1725–9, 1730–3, 1734–7
Henry Herring	1722–5, 1726–8, 1729–32, 1733–6, 1737–40, 1741–4, 1745–8, 1749–51, 1752
The Hon. Horatio Townshend (Deputy Governor 1732–3) (Governor 1733–5)	1722–5, 1726–30, 1731–2, 1735–6
Edward Bellamy (Kt. 1727) (Deputy Governor 1729–31) (Governor 1731–3)	1723–6, 1727–9, 1733–49
Matthew Howard	1723–5, 1726–8, 1729–32, 1733–6, 1737–8

Directors	*Period of Office*
John Olmius (Deputy Governor 1731)	1723–6, 1727–31
Sir Francis Forbes	1724–7
William Fawkener (Deputy Governor 1741–3) (Governor 1743–5)	1724–7, 1728–31, 1732–5, 1736–9, 1740–1, 1745–52
John Heathcote (succeeded his father as Bt. 1733)	1725–8, 1733–5
John Nicoll	1726–8, 1729–31
Sir Francis Porten	1726–7
Stamp Brooksbank (Deputy Governor 1740–1) (Governor 1741–3)	1728–31, 1732–5, 1736–9, 1743–55
James Gaultier	1728–31, 1732–5, 1736–9, 1740–8
William Hunt (Deputy Governor 1747–9) (Governor 1749–52)	1728–30, 1731–3, 1734–6, 1737–9, 1740–3, 1744–7, 1752–63
William Snelling	1728–30, 1731–4, 1735–8, 1739–40
Clement Boehm	1729–31, 1732–4
Joseph Paice	1730–3, 1734–7
Matthew Raper	1730–3, 1734–6, 1737–40, 1741–4, 1745–6, 1747–8
James Spilman	1730–2, 1733–5, 1736–9, 1740–2, 1743–5, 1746–8, 1749–51, 1752–4, 1755–7, 1758–60, 1761–2
Robert Alsop	1731–4, 1735–7
John Bance	1731–4, 1735–8, 1739–41, 1742–5, 1746–9, 1750–3, 1754–5
Henry Neale	1732–5, 1736–9, 1740–3, 1744–7
Robert Thornton	1732–4, 1735–7, 1738–42, 1743–6, 1747–8
Charles Savage (Deputy Governor 1743–5) (Governor 1745–7)	1733–5, 1736–9, 1740–3, 1747–60

Directors	*Period of Office*
Benjamin Lethieullier (Deputy Governor 1749–50)	1734–6, 1737–40, 1741–4, 1745–7, 1748–9, 1751–60
Benjamin Longuet (Deputy Governor 1745–7) (Governor 1747–9)	1734–7, 1738–42, 1743–5, 1749–61
Sir John Thompson	1734–7, 1738–42, 1743–5, 1746–9
Christopher Tower	1734–6, 1739–40
John Eaton Dodsworth	1734–7, 1738–41, 1742–5, 1746–8, 1749–51, 1752–4, 1755–7
Frederick Frankland	1736–8
Samuel Trench	1736–8, 1739–41
Alexander Sheafe (Deputy Governor 1750–2) (Governor 1752–4)	1737–9, 1740–3, 1744–6, 1747–50, 1754–65
Richard Chiswell	1738–40, 1741–4, 1745–7, 1748–51, 1752–4
Sir John Lequesne	1738–41
Benjamin Mee	1738–41, 1742–5
Mark Weyland	1738–41, 1742
Claude Fonnereau	1739–40
Charles Palmer (Deputy Governor 1752–4) (Governor 1754–6)	1739–42, 1743–5, 1746–9, 1750–2, 1756–63
John South	1739–41, 1742–4, 1745–7, 1748–50, 1751–4, 1755–8, 1759–62
Matthews Beachcroft (Deputy Governor 1754–6) (Governor 1756–8)	1741–3, 1744–6, 1747–50, 1751–4, 1758–9
Robert Nettleton	1741–3, 1744–6, 1747–50, 1751–3, 1754–5
Thomas Whately	1741–3, 1744–6, 1747–50, 1751–4, 1755–7, 1758–60, 1761–4
Merrik Burrell (Bt. 1766) (Deputy Governor 1756–8) (Governor 1758–60)	1742–4, 1745–7, 1748–51, 1752–5, 1760–4

Directors	*Period of Office*
James Lever	1742–4, 1745–7, 1748–9
Theophilus Salwey	1742–4, 1745–7, 1748–51, 1752–5, 1756–60
Robert Marsh (Deputy Governor 1760–2) (Governor 1762–4)	1743–5, 1746–8, 1749–52, 1753–6, 1757–60, 1764–73
James Theobald	1743–5, 1746–8, 1749–51, 1752–4, 1755–6
Robert Salusbury	1744–6, 1747–9, 1750–3, 1754–7, 1758–61, 1762–6
Peter Thomas	1744–6, 1747–50, 1751–3, 1754–7, 1758–60
Bartholomew Burton (Deputy Governor 1758–60) (Governor 1760–2)	1746–8, 1749–51, 1752–4, 1755–8, 1762–70
Godfrey Thornton	1748–50, 1751–2
John Weyland (Deputy Governor 1762–4) (Governor 1764–6)	1748–50, 1751–3, 1754–7, 1758–62, 1766–7
Thomas Winterbottom	1749–52
Charles Boehm	1750–2, 1753–5, 1756–8, 1759–62, 1763–9
Matthew Clarmont (Deputy Governor 1764–6) (Governor 1766–9)	1750–2, 1753–6, 1757–9, 1760–4, 1769–72
Samuel Handley	1750–2, 1753–6
Richard Stratton	1750–2, 1753–6, 1757–8
Harry Thompson	1750–2, 1753–6, 1757–9, 1760–5
Samuel Fludyer (Kt. 1755, Bt. 1759) (Deputy Governor 1766–8)	1753–5, 1756–8, 1759–62, 1763–6
John Sargent	1753–5, 1756–8, 1759–62, 1763–5, 1766–7
William Cooper (Deputy Governor 1768–9) (Governor 1769–71)	1754–6, 1757–9, 1760–3, 1764–8, 1771–4
Philip de la Haize	1754–6, 1757–9, 1760–3, 1764–7, 1768–9
Thomas Chitty (Kt. 1759)	1755–7, 1758–61, 1762

Directors	Period of Office
Peter Du Cane	1755–7, 1758–61, 1762–5, 1766–9, 1770–3, 1774–7, 1778–80, 1781–3
Edward Payne (Deputy Governor 1769–71) (Governor 1771–3)	1756–8, 1759–61, 1762–5, 1766–9, 1773–94
Thomas Plumer	1756–8, 1759–61, 1762–5, 1767–70, 1771–3, 1774–6
Peter Theobald	1756–8, 1759–61, 1762–5, 1766–8
Robert Dingley	1757–9, 1760–3, 1764–7
James Sperling (Deputy Governor 1771–3) (Governor 1773–5)	1757–9, 1760–2, 1763–71, 1775–80
Henry Plant	1759–61, 1762–4, 1765–8, 1769–72, 1773–6, 1777–80, 1781–4
Samuel Beachcroft (Deputy Governor 1773–5) (Governor 1775–7)	1760–2, 1763–6, 1767–73, 1777–96
Gustavus Brander	1761–4, 1765–8, 1769–72, 1773–9
Daniel Booth (Deputy Governor 1777–9) (Governor 1779–81)	1761–3, 1764–7, 1768–71, 1772–7, 1781–8
John Cornwall	1761–4, 1765–8, 1769–75
Peter Gaussen (Deputy Governor 1776–7) (Governor 1777–9)	1761–4, 1765–8, 1769–76, 1779–88
James Haughton Langston (Deputy Governor 1775–6)	1761–4, 1765–8, 1769–75
Edmund Wilcox	1761–3, 1764–7
William Bowden	1763–5, 1766–9, 1770–2, 1773–6, 1777–80
William Ewer (Deputy Governor 1779–81) (Governor 1781–3)	1763–6, 1767–70, 1771–9, 1783–9
Richard Neave (Bt. 1795) (Deputy Governor 1781–3) (Governor 1783–5)	1763–5, 1766–9, 1770–3, 1774–81, 1785–1811

Directors	*Period of Office*
John Fisher	1764–6, 1767–70, 1771–4
Christopher Hake	1764–6, 1767–70, 1771–4, 1775–8, 1779–81
Benjamin Hopkins	1765–7, 1768–71, 1772–5, 1776–9
Lyonel Lyde	1765–7
Thomas Thomas	1765–7, 1768–71, 1772–5, 1776–9, 1780–1
George Peters (Deputy Governor 1783–5) (Governor 1785–7)	1766–9, 1770–2, 1773–6, 1777–80, 1781–3, 1787–97
Edward Darell (Deputy Governor 1785–7) (Governor 1787–9)	1767–9, 1770–2, 1773–5, 1776–9, 1780–5, 1789–1804
William Halhed	1767–9, 1770–2, 1773–5, 1776–8, 1779–82, 1783–6
Lyde Browne	1768–71, 1772–4, 1775–6, 1777–80, 1781–4, 1785–7
George Drake	1768–71, 1772–4, 1775–8, 1779–82, 1783–4
George Hayter	1768–70, 1771–3, 1774–7, 1778–81, 1782–4
Mark Weyland (Deputy Governor 1787–9) (Governor 1789–91)	1768–71, 1772–4, 1775–8, 1779–82, 1783–7, 1791–7
Roger Boehm	1769–71, 1772–4, 1775–7, 1778–81, 1782–5, 1786–9, 1790–3, 1794–7, 1798–1801, 1802–3
Matthew Howard	1769–70
Benjamin Branfill	1770–2, 1773–5, 1776–8, 1779–80
William Snell	1770–2, 1773–5, 1776–8, 1779–82, 1783–6, 1787–9
Samuel Bosanquet (Deputy Governor 1789–91) (Governor 1791–3)	1771–3, 1774–7, 1778–81, 1782–5, 1786–9, 1793–1806
Martyn Fonnereau	1771–3, 1774–7, 1778–9, 1780–3

Directors	*Period of Office*
Godfrey Thornton (Deputy Governor 1791–3) (Governor 1793–5)	1772–4, 1775–7, 1778–81, 1782–5, 1786–8, 1789–90, 1795–1801
Daniel Giles (Deputy Governor 1793–5) (Governor 1795–7)	1774–6, 1777–80, 1781–4, 1785–8, 1789–93, 1797–1800
Christopher Puller	1774–6, 1777–9, 1780–3, 1784–7, 1788–9
Thomas Dea	1775–7, 1778–81, 1782–4, 1785–7, 1788–91, 1792–5, 1796–9
Richard Clay	1776–8, 1779–82, 1783–5, 1786–8, 1789–91
Thomas Raikes (Deputy Governor 1795–7) (Governor 1797–9)	1776–8, 1779–81, 1782–4, 1785–7, 1788–91, 1792–5, 1799–1810
Benjamin Mee	1777–9, 1780–3
John Sargent	1778–9
William Cooke	1780–2, 1783–5, 1786–8, 1789–92
Thomas Scott Jackson	1780–2, 1783–5, 1786–8, 1789–91
Samuel Thornton (Deputy Governor 1797–9) (Governor 1799–1801)	1780–3, 1784–7, 1788–91, 1792–4, 1795–7, 1801–36
Job Mathew (Deputy Governor 1799–1801) (Governor 1801–2)	1781–3, 1784–6, 1787–90, 1791–4, 1795–9
Joseph Nutt (Deputy Governor 1801–2) (Governor 1802–4)	1781–3, 1784–6, 1787–90, 1791–4, 1795–8, 1799–1801, 1804–5
Thomas Boddington	1782–4, 1785–7, 1788–90, 1792–4, 1795–8, 1799–1805, 1806–9
Benjamin Winthrop (Deputy Governor 1802–4) (Governor 1804–6)	1782–4, 1785–7, 1788–90, 1791–3, 1794–7, 1798–1801, 1806–9
Beeston Long (Deputy Governor 1804–6) (Governor 1806–8)	1784–6, 1787–9, 1790–2, 1793–6, 1797–1800, 1801–4, 1808–20

Directors	*Period of Office*
James Maude	1784–5
Isaac Osborne	1784–6, 1787–90, 1791–3, 1794–6
Brook Watson (Bt. 1803) (Deputy Governor 1806–7)	1784–6, 1787–9, 1790–3, 1796–8, 1799–1801, 1802–4, 1805–6
John Harrison	1785–7, 1788–90, 1791–3, 1794
Bicknell Coney	1786–8, 1789–91, 1792–4, 1795–7, 1798–1801, 1802–7, 1808–11
John Whitmore (Deputy Governor 1807–8) (Governor 1808–10)	1786–8, 1789–92, 1793–6, 1797–9, 1800–2, 1803–7, 1810–23
Peter Isaac Thellusson (Baron Rendlesham 1806)	1787–9, 1790–2, 1793–6, 1797–1800, 1801–2, 1803–6
Moses Yeldham	1788–90, 1791–3
William Manning (Deputy Governor 1810–12) (Governor 1812–14)	1790–2, 1793–5, 1796–8, 1799–1802, 1803–6, 1807–10, 1814–31
John Pearse (Deputy Governor 1808–10) (Governor 1810–12)	1790–1, 1793–5, 1796–8, 1799–1802, 1803–6, 1807–8, 1812–28
John Puget	1790–2, 1793–5, 1796–9, 1800–3, 1804–5
James Reed	1790–2, 1793–5, 1796–9, 1800–1
Thomas Lewis	1791–3, 1794–6, 1797–1800, 1801–4, 1805–8, 1809–12, 1813–16
Peter Cazalet	1792–4
William Mellish (Deputy Governor 1812–14) (Governor 1814–16)	1792–4, 1795–7, 1798–1800, 1801–3, 1804–7, 1808–12, 1816–38
Edward Simeon	1792–4, 1795–7, 1798–1800, 1801–4, 1805–8, 1809–11
Alexander Champion	1794–6, 1797–9, 1800–3, 1804–7, 1808–9
George Dorrien (Deputy Governor 1816–18) (Governor 1818–20)	1794–6, 1797–9, 1800–2, 1803–6, 1807–10, 1811–14, 1815–16, 1820–35

Directors	*Period of Office*
Jeremiah Harman (Deputy Governor 1814–16) (Governor 1816–18)	1794–6, 1797–9, 1800–3, 1804–11, 1812–14, 1818–27
Nathaniel Bogle French	1796–8, 1799–1801, 1802–4, 1805–7
Charles Pole (Deputy Governor 1818–20) (Governor 1820–2)	1796–8, 1799–1801, 1802–5, 1806–9, 1810–13, 1814–18, 1822–43
Thomas Amyand	1798–1800, 1801–3, 1804–5
Thomas Langley	1798–1800, 1801–3, 1804–10, 1811–14, 1815–18, 1819–22, 1823–5
Ebenezer Maitland	1798–1800, 1801–3, 1804–6, 1807–10, 1811–14, 1815–17, 1818–21
Peter Free	1800–3
Jeremiah Olive	1800–2, 1803–6, 1807–13, 1814–17, 1818–19
Henry Smith	1802–4, 1805–8, 1809–12, 1813–16, 1817–20, 1821–4, 1825–6
Stephen Thornton	1802–5, 1806–9, 1810–13, 1814–17, 1818–20
John Bowden (Deputy Governor 1820–2) (Governor 1822–4)	1803–5, 1806–8, 1809–12, 1813–15, 1816–19, 1824–41
Cornelius Buller (Deputy Governor 1822–4) (Governor 1824–6)	1803–5, 1806–8, 1809–12, 1813–16, 1817–22, 1826–31
Alexander Baring (PC 1834) (Baron Ashburton 1835)	1805–7, 1808–10, 1811–14, 1815–17
John Josiah Holford	1805–7, 1808–11, 1812–14, 1815–17, 1818–20
John Baker Richards (Deputy Governor 1824–6) (Governor 1826–8)	1805–7, 1808–10, 1811–14, 1815–17, 1818–20, 1821–4, 1828–33
Samuel Drewe (Deputy Governor 1826–8) (Governor 1828–30)	1806–8, 1809–11, 1812–15, 1816–18, 1819–21, 1822–6, 1830–7

Directors	*Period of Office*
Samuel Turner	1806–8, 1809–11, 1812–15, 1816–19, 1820–2
Henry Davidson	1807–9, 1810–13, 1814–16, 1817–20
John Staniforth	1807–9, 1810–13, 1814–16, 1817–19
Robert Wigram (Kt. 1818; succeeded his father as Baronet in 1830; assumed name of Fitzwygram in 1832)	1807–9, 1810–12, 1813–15, 1816–18, 1819–21
James Campbell	1808–10, 1811–13, 1814–16, 1817–19, 1820–2, 1823–5, 1826–8
William Haldimand	1809–11, 1812–15, 1816–18, 1819–21, 1822–4
George Blackman	1810–12, 1813–15, 1816–18, 1819–21
William Tierney Robarts	1810–12, 1813–15, 1816–18, 1819–20
John Horsley Palmer (Deputy Governor 1828–30) (Governor 1830–3)	1811–13, 1814–16, 1817–19, 1820–2, 1823–5, 1826–8, 1833–45, 1846–57
Andrew Henry Thomson (Deputy Governor 1830–2)	1811–13, 1814–16, 1817–19, 1820–3, 1824–6, 1827–9
Thomas Neave (Bt. 1814)	1812–14, 1815–17, 1818–20, 1821–3, 1824–7
Richard Mee Raikes (Deputy Governor 1832–3) (Governor 1833–4)	1812–14, 1815–17, 1818–20, 1821–3, 1824–6, 1827–30, 1831–2
James Pattison (Deputy Governor 1833–4) (Governor 1834–7)	1813–15, 1816–18, 1819–21, 1822–4, 1825–8, 1829–33, 1837–49
William Ward	1817–19, 1820–2, 1823–5, 1826–9, 1830–1, 1832–3, 1834–6
Samuel Hibbert	1819–21, 1822–4, 1825–7, 1828–30, 1831–4, 1836–7
Timothy Abraham Curtis (Deputy Governor 1834–7) (Governor 1837–9)	1820–2, 1823–5, 1826–8, 1829–31, 1832–4, 1839–41

Directors	Period of Office
John Rae Reid (succeeded his father as Baronet in 1824) (Deputy Governor 1837–9) (Governor 1839–41)	1820–2, 1823–5, 1826–8, 1829–31, 1832–5, 1836–7, 1841–7
David Barclay	1821–3, 1824–6
John Cockerell	1821–3, 1824–6, 1827–30, 1831–7
George Warde Norman	1821–3, 1824–6, 1827–9, 1830–3, 1834–7, 1838–72
Henry Porcher	1821–3, 1824–6, 1827–9, 1830–2, 1833–6, 1837–9
William Cotton (Deputy Governor 1841–2) (Governor 1842–5)	1822–4, 1825–7, 1828–30, 1831–3, 1834–41, 1845–66
John Henry Pelly (Bt. 1840) (Deputy Governor 1839–41) (Governor 1841–2)	1822–4, 1825–7, 1828–30, 1831–2, 1833–5, 1836–9, 1843–52
Thomas Warre	1822–4, 1825–7, 1828–30, 1831–3, 1834–6, 1837–8
John Benjamin Heath (Deputy Governor 1842–5) (Governor 1845–7)	1823–5, 1826–8, 1829–31, 1832–4, 1835–9, 1840–2, 1847–72
Money Wigram	1823–5, 1826–8, 1829–31, 1832–4, 1835–7
William Mitchell	1825–7, 1828
William Robinson Robinson (Deputy Governor 1845–7) (Governor 1847)	1825–7, 1828–30, 1831–3, 1834–6, 1837–40, 1841–5
James Morris (Deputy Governor 1847) (Governor 1847–9)	1827–9, 1831–3, 1834–6, 1837–40, 1841–7, 1849–80
Simon Taylor	1827–8
William Thompson	1827–9, 1830–2, 1833–5, 1836–9, 1840–3, 1844–51, 1852–4
Humphrey St. John Mildmay	1828–30, 1831–3, 1834–6, 1837–9, 1840–1, 1842–5, 1846–9
John Oliver Hanson	1829–31, 1832–4, 1835–8, 1839–42, 1843–6, 1847–52, 1853–5, 1856–9

Directors	*Period of Office*
Stephen Edward Thornton	1829–31, 1832–4
Melvil Wilson	1829–31, 1832–4, 1835–7
Charles Pascoe Grenfell	1830–2, 1833–5, 1836–8, 1839–40, 1841–4, 1845–8, 1849–51, 1852–4, 1855–8, 1859–61, 1862–4
Abel Lewes Gower	1830–2, 1833–5, 1836–9, 1840–2, 1843–6, 1847
Sheffield Neave (Deputy Governor 1855–7) (Governor 1857–9)	1830–2, 1833–5, 1836–8, 1839–42, 1843–5, 1846–8, 1849–51, 1852–4, 1859–68
Rowland Mitchell	1833–5, 1836–8, 1839–41
Christopher Pearse	1834–6, 1837–9, 1840–3, 1844–8
Henry Davidson	1835–7, 1838–40, 1841–2
Bonamy Dobree (Deputy Governor 1857–9) (Governor 1859–61)	1835–8, 1839–41, 1842–5, 1846–8, 1849–51, 1852–4, 1855–7, 1861–3
Thomson Hankey (Deputy Governor 1849–51) (Governor 1851–3)	1835–7, 1838–42, 1843–5, 1846–8, 1853–93
Henry James Prescott (Deputy Governor 1847–9) (Governor 1849–51)	1835–8, 1839–42, 1843–5, 1846–7, 1851–6
Robert Barclay	1837–9, 1840–3
James Malcolmson	1837–40, 1841–4, 1845–8, 1849–51, 1852–4, 1855–7, 1858–61
John Gellibrand Hubbard (PC 1874) (raised to the Peerage as Baron Addington in 1887) (Deputy Governor 1851–3) (Governor 1853–5)	1838–41, 1842–4, 1845–51, 1855–89
Charles Frederick Huth	1838–40, 1841–3, 1844–6, 1847–9, 1850–3, 1854–7, 1858–61, 1862–4, 1865–8, 1869–71, 1872–6, 1877–80, 1881–5
Alfred Latham (Deputy Governor 1859–61) (Governor 1861–3)	1838–40, 1841–3, 1844–6, 1847–9, 1850–2, 1853–9, 1863–78

Directors	*Period of Office*
Thomas Charles Smith	1838–41, 1842–4, 1845–7, 1848–50, 1851–3, 1854–6, 1857–63
Thomas Matthias Weguelin (Deputy Governor 1853–5) (Governor 1855–7)	1838–41, 1842–4, 1845–7, 1848–50, 1851–3, 1857–8
William Unwin Sims	1839
Edward Henry Chapman	1840–3, 1844–6, 1847–9, 1850–2, 1853–5, 1856–8, 1859–61, 1863–4, 1865–7, 1868–9
Kirkman Daniel Hodgson (Deputy Governor 1861–3) (Governor 1863–5)	1840–3, 1844–6, 1847–9, 1850–2, 1853–5, 1856–8, 1859–61, 1865–78
William Little	1842–4, 1845–7
David Powell	1842–4, 1845–7
Francis Wilson	1842–4, 1845–7, 1848–50, 1851–3, 1854–6
Arthur Edward Campbell	1843–5, 1846–8, 1849–51, 1852–4, 1855–7, 1858–60, 1861–3, 1864–7, 1868–70, 1871–4, 1875–8, 1879–81
Thomas Tooke	1843–5, 1846–8, 1849–51, 1852–4, 1855–7
Henry Lancelot Holland (Deputy Governor 1863–5) (Governor 1865–7)	1844–6, 1847–9, 1850–2, 1853–5, 1856–8, 1859–61, 1862–3, 1867–93
Thomas Newman Hunt (Deputy Governor 1865–7) (Governor 1867–9)	1844–6, 1847–9, 1850–2, 1853–5, 1856–8, 1859–61, 1862–3, 1864–5, 1869–84
Thomas Baring	1848–50, 1851–3, 1854–6, 1857–9, 1860–2, 1863–7
Thomas Masterman	1848–50, 1851–3, 1854–6, 1857–9, 1860–2, 1863–6, 1867–70, 1871–3, 1874–5
Alexander Matheson (Bt. 1882)	1848–50, 1851–3, 1854–6, 1857–9, 1860–2, 1863–5, 1866–8, 1869–71, 1872–5, 1876–80, 1881–4
Henry Wollaston Blake	1848–50, 1851–3, 1854–6, 1857–9, 1860–2, 1863–5, 1866–8,

Directors	*Period of Office*
Henry Wollaston Blake *cont.*	1869–71, 1872–5, 1876–9, 1880–4, 1885–93
George Lyall (Deputy Governor 1869–71) (Governor 1871–3)	1848–50, 1851–3, 1854–6, 1857–9, 1860–2, 1863–5, 1866–9, 1873–81
Henry Hulse Berens	1849–51, 1852–4, 1855–7, 1858–60, 1861–3, 1864–6, 1867–9, 1870–2, 1873–6, 1877–80
Robert Wigram Crawford (Deputy Governor 1867–9) (Governor 1869–71)	1850–2, 1853–5, 1856–8, 1859–61, 1862–4, 1865–7, 1871–89
Benjamin Buck Greene (Deputy Governor 1871–3) (Governor 1873–5)	1850–2, 1853–5, 1856–8, 1859–60, 1861–3, 1864–6, 1867–9, 1870–1, 1875–1900
Henry Hucks Gibbs (Baron Aldenham 1896) (Deputy Governor 1873–5) (Governor 1875–7)	1853–5, 1856–8, 1859–61, 1862–4, 1865–7, 1868–70, 1871–3, 1877–1900
James Pattison Currie (assumed the name of Currie-Blyth 1904) (Deputy Governor 1883–5) (Governor 1885–7)	1855–7, 1858–60, 1861–3, 1864–6, 1867–9, 1870–2, 1873–83, 1887–1908
Travers Buxton	1857–9, 1860–2, 1863–5, 1866–8, 1869–71
Edward Howley Palmer (Deputy Governor 1875–7) (Governor 1877–9)	1858–60, 1861–3, 1864–6, 1867–9, 1870–2, 1873–5, 1879–97
George Joachim Goschen (PC 1865) (Viscount Goschen 1900)	1858–60, 1861–3, 1864–5
James Alexander Guthrie	1858–60, 1861–3, 1864–6, 1867–9, 1870–2
Stephen Cave (Kt. 1880)	1860–2, 1863–5, 1866
John William Birch (Deputy Governor 1877–9) (Governor 1879–81)	1860–2, 1863–5, 1866–8, 1869–71, 1872–5, 1876–7, 1881–97
John Saunders Gilliat (Deputy Governor 1881–3) (Governor 1883–5)	1862–4, 1865–7, 1868–70, 1871–4, 1875–9, 1880–1, 1885–1912

Directors	*Period of Office*
Clifford Wigram (Deputy Governor 1892–4)	1862–4, 1865–7, 1868–70, 1871–4, 1875–8, 1879–83, 1884–8, 1889–92, 1894
Henry Riversdale Grenfell (Deputy Governor 1879–81) (Governor 1881–3)	1865–7, 1868–70, 1871–3, 1874–7, 1878–9, 1883–1902
Mark Wilks Collet (Bt. 1888) (Deputy Governor 1885–7) (Governor 1887–9)	1866–8, 1869–71, 1872–3, 1875–9, 1880–5, 1889–1905
Albert George Sandeman (Deputy Governor 1894–5) (Governor 1895–7)	1866–8, 1869–71, 1872–5, 1876–9, 1880–4, 1885–8, 1889–92, 1893–4, 1897–1918
Christopher Weguelin	1867–9, 1870–2, 1873–6, 1877–80
Charles Hermann Goschen	1868–70, 1871–3, 1874–7, 1878–82, 1883–7, 1888–91, 1892–8, 1899–1915
Alfred Charles de Rothschild (CVO 1902)	1868–70, 1871–3, 1874–7, 1878–82, 1883–6, 1887–9
William Lidderdale (PC 1891) (Deputy Governor 1887–9) (Governor 1889–92)	1870–2, 1873–6, 1877–85, 1886–7, 1892–1902
David Powell (Deputy Governor 1889–92) (Governor 1892–5)	1870–2, 1873–6, 1877–81, 1882–6, 1887–9, 1895–7
Herbert Brooks	1872–4, 1875–7, 1878–81, 1882–6, 1887–90, 1891–1918
Hugh Colin Smith (Deputy Governor 1895–7) (Governor 1897–9)	1876–8, 1879–83, 1884–7, 1888–91, 1892–5, 1899–1910
Edward Charles Baring (Baron Revelstoke 1885)	1879–83, 1884–7, 1888–91
Everard Alexander Hambro (KCVO 1908)	1879–82, 1883–6, 1887–92, 1893–1925
Samuel Steuart Gladstone (Deputy Governor 1897–9) (Governor 1899–1901)	1881–5, 1886–9, 1890–7, 1901–9
Augustus Prevost (Bt. 1902) (Deputy Governor 1899–1901) (Governor 1901–3)	1881–4, 1885–8, 1889–92, 1893–9, 1903–13

Directors	*Period of Office*
Samuel Hope Morley (Baron Hollenden 1912) (Deputy Governor 1901–3) (Governor 1903–5)	1882–5, 1886–9, 1890–3, 1894–1901, 1905–21
Charles George Arbuthnot	1884–7, 1888–90, 1891–5, 1896–1928
The Hon. Ronald Ruthven Leslie Melville (PC KT) (succeeded to the Earldom of Leven and Melville in 1889)	1884–7, 1888–90, 1891–4
Henry Cosmo Orme Bonsor (Bt. 1925)	1885–8, 1889–92, 1893–6, 1897–8, 1899–1929
William Middleton Campbell (Deputy Governor 1905–7) (Governor 1907–9)	1886–8, 1889–91, 1892–6, 1897–1905, 1909–19
Alexander Falconer Wallace (OBE) (Deputy Governor 1903–5) (Governor 1905–7)	1887–90, 1891–4, 1895–1903, 1907–18
The Hon Evelyn Hubbard	1890–3, 1894–9, 1900–9
Edgar Lubbock (Deputy Governor 1907)	1890–3, 1894–9, 1900–7
Frederick Huth Jackson (PC 1911)	1892–5, 1896–1921
Robert Henderson	1893–5
Reginald Eden Johnston (Deputy Governor 1907–9) (Governor 1909–11)	1893–6, 1897–1907, 1911–22
Alfred Clayton Cole (Deputy Governor 1909–11) (Governor 1911–13)	1895–1909, 1913–20
Walter Cunliffe (GBE 1917) (Baron Cunliffe 1914) (Deputy Governor 1911–13) (Governor 1913–18)	1895–1911, 1918–20
Robert Lydston Newman (Deputy Governor 1913–15)	1896–1913, 1915–36
William Douro Hoare (CBE 1920)	1898–1928
John Baring, Lord Revelstoke (GCVO 1911)	1898–1929

Directors	Period of Office
George William Henderson	1902–29
Brien Ibrican Cokayne (KBE 1917) (Baron Cullen of Ashbourne 1920) (Deputy Governor 1915–18) (Governor 1918–20)	1902–15, 1920–32
Edward Charles Grenfell (Baron St Just 1935)	1905–40
Montagu Collet Norman DSO (PC 1923) (Baron Norman of St Clere 1944) (Deputy Governor 1918–20) (Governor 1920–44)	1907–18
Col Lionel Henry Hanbury (CMG 1916)	1908–35
Henry Alexander Trotter (Deputy Governor 1920–3, 1926–7)	1909–20, 1923–6, 1927–34
Cecil Lubbock (Deputy Governor 1923–5, 1927–9)	1909–23, 1925–7, 1929–42
Vincent Cartwright Vickers	1910–19
Frank Cyril Tiarks (OBE 1919)	1912–45
Robert Molesworth Kindersley (GBE 1920, KBE 1917) (Baron Kindersley of West Hoathly 1941)	1914–46
George Macaulay Booth	1915–46
Sir Alan Garrett Anderson KBE (GBE 1934) (Deputy Governor 1925–6)	1918–25, 1926–46
Sir Charles Stewart Addis (KCMG 1921)	1918–32
Robert Wallace	1919–31
Arthur Whitworth	1919–46
Walter Kennedy Whigham	1919–46
Michael Seymour Spencer-Smith DSO, MC	1920–8
Sir Henry Babington Smith GBE, CH, KCB, CSI	1920–3

Directors	Period of Office
Edward Robert Peacock (GCVO 1934)	1921–4, 1929–46
Kenneth Goschen	1922–36
The Hon Roland Dudley Kitson DSO, MC (Baron Airedale 1944)	1923–47
The Hon Alexander Shaw (Baron Craigmyle 1937)	1923–43
Albert Charles Gladstone MBE (Baronet 1945)	1924–47
Sir John Gordon Nairne, Bt.	1925–31
Sir Josiah Charles Stamp GBE (GCB 1935) (Baron Stamp 1938)	1928–41
*Charles Jocelyn Hambro MC (KBE 1941) (Ex. Dir. 1932–3)	1928–63
Sir Ernest Musgrave Harvey KBE (Bt. 1933) (Deputy Governor 1929–36)	1928–9
Sir Basil Phillott Blackett KCB, KCSI	1929–35
Sir Andrew Rae Duncan (GBE 1938, PC 1940)	1929–40
Lord Hyndley of Meads (GBE 1939) (Viscount Hyndley 1948)	1931–45
*William Henry Clegg (Ex. Dir. 1932–5)	1932–7
Patrick Ashley Cooper (Kt. 1944)	1932–55
*Edward Holland-Martin (Ex. Dir. 1933–48)	1933–48
*Basil Gage Catterns (Ex. Dir. 1934–6) (Deputy Governor 1936–45)	1934–6, 1945–8
James George Weir CMG, CBE	1935–46
*Dallas Gerald Mercer Bernard (Bt. 1954) (Ex. Dir. 1939–49) (Deputy Governor 1949–54)	1936–49

* Denotes Executive Directors for all or part of their period of office.

Directors	Period of Office
Laurence John Cadbury OBE	1936–8, 1940–61
*John Coldbrook Hanbury-Williams (CVO 1956) (Kt. 1950) (Ex. Dir. 1940–1)	1936–63
John Martin	1937–46
*Evelyn James Bunbury MC (CBE 1952) (Ex. Dir. 1937–8)	1937–8
*Sir Otto Ernst Niemeyer GBE, KCB (Ex. Dir. 1938–49)	1938–52
*Cameron Fromanteel Cobbold (KG 1970, GCVO 1963, PC 1959) (Baron Cobbold of Knebworth 1960) (Ex. Dir. 1938–45) (Deputy Governor 1945–9) (Governor 1949–61)	1938–45
Lord Catto of Cairncatto (CBE 1918, PC 1947) (Governor 1944–9)	1940
Isaac James Pitman (KBE 1961)	1941–5
John Maynard Keynes CB (Baron Keynes of Tilton 1942)	1941–6
The Hon. Josiah Wedgwood	1942–6
Basil Sanderson MC (Baron Sanderson of Ayot 1960)	1943–65
*Henry (Harry) Arthur Siepmann (Ex. Dir. 1945–54)	1945–54
Ralph Ellis Brook OBE (Kt. 1974, CMG 1954)	1946–9
George Gibson CH	1946–8
Lord Piercy CBE	1946–56
Arthur George Wansbrough	1946–9
Charles Dukes CBE (Baron Dukeston of Warrington 1947)	1947–8
The Hon Hugh Kenyon Molesworth Kindersley CBE, MC (Baron Kindersley of West Hoathly 1954)	1947–67
Sir Valentine George Crittall (Baron Braintree 1948)	1948–55

Directors	Period of Office
*George Lewis French Bolton (KCMG 1950) (Ex. Dir. 1948–57)	1948–68
Michael James Babington Smith CBE	1949–69
Sir George Chester CBE	1949
*Sir Kenneth Oswald Peppiatt KBE, MC (Ex. Dir. 1949–57)	1949–57
*Humphrey Charles Baskerville Mynors (Bt. 1964) (Ex. Dir. 1949–52) (Deputy Governor 1954–64)	1949–54
Andrew Naesmith CBE (Kt. 1953)	1949–57
Geoffrey Cecil Ryves Eley CBE (Kt. 1964)	1949–66
Sir George Edmond Brackenbury Abell KCIE, OBE	1952–64
*Frank Cyril Hawker (Kt. 1958) (Ex. Dir. 1954–1962)	1954–62
The Hon Randal Hugh Vivian Smith (Baron Bicester of Tusmore 1956)	1954–66
William Johnston Keswick (Kt. 1972)	1955–73
Sir William Henry Pilkington (Baron Pilkington of St Helens 1968)	1955–73
Sir Alfred Roberts CBE	1956–63
*Maurice Henry Parsons (Kt. 1966 KCMG 1970) (Ex. Dir. 1957–66) (Deputy Governor 1966–70)	1957–66
*John Melior Stevens DSO, OBE (KCMG 1967) (Ex. Dir. 1957–65)	1957–65, 1968–73
George Rowland Stanley Baring, The Earl of Cromer MBE (KG 1977, GCMG 1974, PC 1966) (Governor 1961–6)	1961
The Hon. Henry George Nelson (Baron Nelson of Stafford 1962)	1961–87
*Leslie Kenneth O'Brien (GBE 1967, PC 1970)	1962–4

Directors	Period of Office
(Baron O'Brien of Lothbury 1973) (Ex. Dir. 1962–4) (Deputy Governor 1964–6) (Governor 1966–73)	
John Maurice Laing (Kt. 1965)	1963–80
Sir William John Carron (Baron Carron of Kingston-upon-Hull 1967)	1963–9
Sir Henry Wilson Smith KCB, KBE	1964–70
*William Maurice Allen (Ex. Dir. 1964–70)	1964–70
*James Vincent Bailey (Ex. Dir. 1964–9)	1964–9
*Christopher Jeremy Morse (KCMG 1974) (Ex. Dir. 1965–72)	1965–72, 1993–
Cecil Harmsworth King	1965–8
The Rt. Hon. Lord Robens of Woldingham	1966–81
Sir Ronald George Thornton	1966–70
*Jasper Quintus Hollom (KBE 1975) (Ex. Dir. 1966–70) (Deputy Governor 1970–80)	1966–70, 1980–4
Gordon William Humphreys Richardson MBE (KG 1983, TD 1979, PC 1976) (Baron Richardson of Duntisbourne 1983) (Governor 1973–83)	1967–73
Sir Eric Roll KCMG, CB (Baron Roll of Ipsden 1977)	1968–77
Sir John Norman Valette Duncan OBE	1969–75
*Jack Gale Wilmot Davies OBE (Ex. Dir. 1969–76)	1969–76
Leopold David de Rothschild (CBE 1985)	1970–83
George Adrian Hayhurst Cadbury (Kt. 1977)	1970–94

Directors	Period of Office
*John Standish Fforde (Ex. Dir. 1970–82)	1970–82
Sir Sidney Francis Greene CBE (Baron Greene of Harrow Weald 1974)	1970–8
*Christopher William McMahon (Kt. 1986) (Ex. Dir. 1970–80) (Deputy Governor 1980–5)	1970–80
The Hon. William Kenneth James Weir (succeeded as Viscount Weir 1975)	1972–84
John Martin Clay	1973–83
*John Christopher Roderick Dow (Ex. Dir. 1973–81)	1973–81
Hector Laing (Kt. 1978) (Baron Laing of Dunphail in the District of Moray 1991)	1973–91
Sir Lionel Alexander Bethune Pilkington (Sir Alastair)	1974–84
*George Blunden (Kt. 1987) (Ex. Dir. 1976–84) (Deputy Governor 1986–90)	1976–85
Sir Robert Anthony Clark DSC	1976–85
Sir David Edward Charles Steel DSO, MC, TD	1978–85
Geoffrey Ayrton Drain (CBE 1981)	1978–86
*John Brangwyn Page (Ex. Dir. 1980–2)	1980–2
*Anthony David Loehnis (CMG 1988) (Ex. Dir. 1981–9) (Associate Director 1980–1, executive position)	1981–9
David Gerald Scholey CBE (Kt. 1987)	1981–
*Edward Alan John George (Ex. Dir. 1982–90) (Deputy Governor 1990–3) (Governor 1993–)	1982–90
*David Alan Walker (Kt. 1991) (Ex. Dir. 1982–8)	1982–93

Directors	*Period of Office*
The Hon Sir John Francis Harcourt Baring CVO (KCVO 1990) (Baron Ashburton 1991)	1983–91
Alan Lord CB	1983–6
Dr David Valentine Atterton CBE	1984–92
*Rodney Desmond Galpin (Ex. Dir. 1984–8) (Associate Director 1982–4, executive position)	1984–8
Professor Brian Griffiths (Baron Griffiths of Fforestfach 1991)	1984–5
Frederick Brian Corby (Kt. 1989)	1985–93
Sir Robert Haslam (created Baron Haslam of Bolton 1990)	1985–93
Gavin Harry Laird (CBE 1988)	1986–94
Deryk Vander Weyer CBE	1986–8
Sir Leslie Clarence Young CBE	1986–90
Sir Martin Wakefield Jacomb	1986–
Sir Colin Ross Corness	1987–
*Brian Quinn (Ex. Dir. 1988–)	1988–
*John Stanton Flemming (Ex. Dir. 1988–91) (Associate Director and Chief Economist 1988, executive position)	1988–91
*Andrew Duncan Crockett (Ex. Dir. 1989–93)	1989–93
*Anthony Laurie Coleby (Ex. Dir. 1990–4)	1990–4
*Professor Mervyn Allister King (Mr King from 1991) (Ex. Dir. 1991–)	1990–
David Bryan Lees (Kt. 1991)	1991–
Professor Roland Smith (Kt. 1991)	1991–
Colin Grieve Southgate (Kt. 1992)	1991–
Sir Christopher Anthony Hogg	1992–
Mrs Frances Anne Heaton	1993–

Directors	Period of Office
Sir John Chippendale Lindley Keswick	1993–
*Pendarell Hugh Kent (Ex. Dir. 1994–) (Associate Director 1988–93, executive position)	1994–
*Ian Plenderleith (Ex. Dir. 1994–) (Associate Director 1990–4, executive position)	1994–
Sir David James Scott Cooksey	1994–
Ms Sheila Valerie Masters	1994–

Associate Directors†	Period of Office
Anthony David Loehnis	1980–1
William Peter Cooke	1982–8
Rodney Desmond Galpin	1982–4
Douglas Alfred Dawkins	1985–7
Hugh Christopher Emlyn Harris	1988–
Pendarell Hugh Kent	1988–94
John Stanton Flemming (Associate Director and Chief Economist)	1988
Ian Plenderleith	1990–4

Deputy Directors‡	Period of Office
Graham Edward Alfred Kentfield	1994–
John Coupe Townend	1994–
William Anthony Allen	1994–
Michael David Kenneth W. Foot	1994–
Thomas Alistair Clark	1994–

† In 1980 the post of Associate Director was created. Associate Directors fill jobs equivalent to those performed by Executive Directors (the number of which is limited to four by the terms of the Charter of 1946).

‡ The post of Deputy Director was created from 4 July 1994.

Other Senior Bank Officials

This list of Bank of England Officials gives the names of those holding the more significant offices, from 1694 to 1994. Until the twentieth century the number of such offices was limited and their functions relatively unchanging.

In more recent times, however, the organization has been more fluid and has changed more rapidly. It has been necessary, therefore, to exercise more subjective judgement about which offices should appear in the list. The aim has been to include the senior posts relevant to the Bank's involvement in financial and monetary matters. Only the highest appointments concerned with internal affairs have been included.

Comptrollers of the Bank

Sir John Gordon Nairne, Bt.	1918–25
Sir Ernest Musgrave Harvey KBE	1925–8
Cyril Patrick Mahon	1929–32

Assistants to the Governors

Leslie Lefeaux	1932–3
Ernest Harry Dudley Skinner	1935–45
Sir George Edmond Brackenbury KCIE	1949–52
Maurice Henry Parsons	1954–7
John Melior Stevens DSO, OBE (TD) (Acting)	1956–7
Jasper St. John Rootham	1965–7
Roy Arthur Odell Bridge (CMG)	1965–9
Jack Gale Wilmot Davies OBE	1968–9

Advisers to the Governors

Henry Arthur Siepmann (Acting Chief of the Overseas and Foreign Department 1932–5)	1926–45
Sir Otto Ernst Niemeyer GBE, KCB	1927–38
Dr Walter W. Stewart	1927–30
Francis James Rennell Rodd	1929–32

Raymond Newton Kershaw MC (CMG 1947)	1929–53
Dr Oliver Mitchell Wentworth Sprague	1930–3
Cameron Fromanteel Cobbold (Acting Deputy Chief of the Overseas and Foreign Department 1933–5)	1933–8
Professor Henry Clay	1933–44
Charles Bruce Gardner	1935–8
Gilbert Edward Jackson	1935–9
Evelyn James Bunbury	1935–7
John Arundel Caulfeild Osborne	1938–45
George Lewis French Bolton (KCMG)	1941–8
John Bernard Rickatson-Hatt	1941–58
Humphrey Charles Baskerville Mynors	1944–9
John Stewart Lithiby	1946–55
Frederic Francis Joseph Powell	1946–51
Percival Spencer Beale (acting)	1946–8
Anthony P. Grafftey Smith CBE (acting)	1947–8
Sir George Edmond Brackenbury Abell KCIE	1948–9
Lucius Perronet Thompson-McCausland (acting, 1947–9)	1949–65
John Lenox Fisher (CMG) (acting, 1946)	1950–9
Frank Cyril Hawker (Kt.)	1953–4
William Maurice Allen (acting, 1953)	1954–64
The Hon. Arthur Maxwell Stamp (acting, 1950–2; seconded for Special Duties—International Monetary Fund)	1954–8
Laurence James Menzies (Kt. 1962) (seconded to ECGD 1958–62)	1957–65
Jasper St. John Rootham	1957–63
Roy Arthur Odell Bridge	1963–5
George Rupert Raw	1963–72
Guy McOlvin Watson	1963–5
John Standish Fforde	1964–6, 1983–4

Claude Evan Loombe CMG	1964–5
Christopher Jeremy Morse	1964–5
Eric Percival Haslam	1965–72
John Barraclough Loynes CMG (name change by Deed Poll to de Loynes 1965)	1965–9
Christopher William McMahon	1966–70
Leslie Frederick Crick	1967–8
Piers Reginald William Legh	1967–70
John Arthur Kirbyshire	1970–7
Patrick James Keogh MC	1973–4
Richard Charles Henry Hallett	1973–5
William Peter Cooke	1973–6
Sir Henry Alexander Benson GBE (Baron 1981)	1975–83
Lord Douglas Albert Vivian Allen Croham GCB	1978–83
John Christopher Roderick Dow	1981–4
Sidney Procter	1986–8
John Stanton Flemming	1984–8
Anthony Laurie Coleby	1987–90
Jonathan Philip Charkham	1988–93
Sir Peter Petrie, Bt., CMG	1989–
Peter Charles Peddie	1993–
Ian Glendinning Watt	1993–

Assistant Directors

David Alan Walker	1980–2
Douglas Alfred Dawkins	1980–5
Michael John Balfour	1980–5
John Laing Sangster	1980–2
Anthony Laurie Coleby	1980–7
Edward Alan John George	1980–2
Brian Quinn	1982–8
Christopher John Farrow	1983–7
Ian Plenderleith	1986–90
Roger Anthony Barnes	1987–93

Chief Advisers

John Arthur Kirbyshire	1977–80
Michael John Balfour	1977–80
Charles Albert Eric Goodhart	1978–85
Anthony David Loehnis	1978–80
David Alan Walker	1978–80
Alberto Augusto Weissmüller	1979–81
John Stanton Flemming	1980–4
John Laing Sangster	1979–80
David George Holland (CMG)	1980–5
Jonathan Philip Charkham	1986–8
Christopher Thomas Taylor	1990–4

Chief Cashiers*

John Kendrick	1694
Thomas Speed	1694–9
Thomas Madockes	1699–1739
James Collier ⎱ jointly Daniel Race ⎰	1739–51
Daniel Race ⎱ jointly Elias Simes ⎰	1751–9
Daniel Race	1759–75
Charles Jewson	1775–7
Abraham Newland	1778–1807
Henry Hase	1807–29
Thomas Rippon	1829–35
Matthew Marshall	1835–64
William Miller	1864–6
George Forbes	1866–73
Frank May	1873–93
Horace George Bowen	1893–1902
John Gordon Nairne (Kt. 1914)	1902–18
Ernest Musgrave Harvey (KBE 1920)	1918–25

* From March 1980 the Cashier's Department was renamed the Banking Department and the Chief of the Banking Department carried the traditional title of Chief Cashier.

Cyril Patrick Mahon	1925–9
Basil Gage Catterns	1929–34
Kenneth Oswald Peppiatt MC (KBE 1941)	1934–49
Percival Spencer Beale	1949–55
Leslie Kenneth O'Brien	1955–62
Jasper Quintus Hollom	1962–6
John Standish Fforde	1966–70
John Brangwyn Page	1970–80
David Henry Fitzroy Somerset	1980–8
George Malcolm Gill	1988–91
Graham Edward Alfred Kentfield	1991–

Chief Accountants*

Thomas Mercer	1694–1717
John Monteage	1717–24
Zerubbabel Crouch	1724–42
John Harvey	1742–5
Theophilus Jones	1745–60
Nathaniel Hammond	1760–8
Samuel Jacobson	1768–73
John Stonehouse	1773–80
John Payne	1780–5
William Edwards	1785–1800
William Walton	1800–6
William Dawes	1806–31
William Smee	1831–58
George Earle Gray	1858–70
John Francis	1870–5
Henry Gerald Aylmer	1875–9
Samuel Octavus Gray	1879–88
Horace George Bowen	1888–93
George Frederick Stutchbury	1893–1905
Henry Ben Orchard	1905–10

* From March 1980 the Accountant's Department was renamed Registrar's Department and the Chief Accountant became Chief Registrar and Chief Accountant.

Charles Northcote Latter	1910–19
William Henry Clegg	1919–21
Frank Stanley Arnold	1921
Augustus Merrifield Walker	1921–39
Augustus Merrifield Walker Edward Maitland Stapley } jointly	1939–45
Edward Maitland Stapley	1945–8
Frank Cyril Hawker	1948–53
William Duncan Simpson	1953–62
James Vincent Bailey	1962–4
Lewis Henry Frederick Bardo	1964–7
Roy Ernest Heasman	1967–70
Richard Creighton Balfour MBE	1970–5
Gordon John Costello	1975–8
George Lewis Bush Morgan	1978–80
George Lewis Bush Morgan	1980–3
John Gair Drake	1983–90
Derek Andrew Bridger	1990–

Secretaries

John Ince	1694–1717
David Le Gros	1717–43
Robert Lewin	1743–86
Francis Martin	1786–97
Robert Best	1797–1829
John Knight	1829–50
John Bentley	1850–9
James Stewart	1859–64
Hammond Chubb	1864–94
George Frederick Glennie	1894–8
Kenneth Grahame	1898–1908
Charles Elliot Edlmann	1908–11
Harold Stanley Inman	1911–17
Harry Tilden	1917–27
Ronald Clement George Dale	1927–34
John Arundel Caulfeild Osborne	1934

Edward Maitland Stapley	1935–9
Humphrey Charles Baskerville Mynors	1939–44
Walter Howard Nevill	1944–9
Arthur William Charles Dascombe	1949–59
Howard Mossforth Neatby	1959–68
Peter Arthur Storey Taylor	1968–76
Geoffrey Charles Gough	1976–81
Anthony John Terrell Williams	1981–4
Peter Edward Towndrow	1984–6
Geoffrey Alan Croughton	1986–

Auditors

Ernest Edye	1894–7
Ernest Musgrave Harvey ⎫ jointly William Henry Clegg ⎭	1897–1900
William Henry Clegg	1900–2
Reginald Graham ⎫ jointly Catesby Paget ⎭	1902–6
Reginald Graham	1906–7
Frank Forrest Somers	1907–10
Reginald Henry Prideaux	1910–19
Francis Mure Whiting	1919–23
Leslie Lefeaux	1923–5
John Douglas Spencer Dean	1925–31
Walter Howard Nevill	1931–5
William Axten	1935–8
Alexander Stewart Craig	1938–41
Ronald Clapham Thomas	1941–9
Alexander Stewart Craig	1949–52
Howard Mossforth Neatby	1952–7
Stanley Lamb	1957–9
Kenneth James Stuart Andrews MBE	1959–63
Edward de Montjoie Rudolf	1963–9
John Frank Monton Smallwood (CBE)	1969–74
Brian Patrick McCarthy	1974–80
John Anthony Penny	1980–4

Leslie Geoffrey Lloyd	1984–8
John Bartlett	1988–90
Michael John William Phillips	1990–

Principal Supervisors/General Managers of Printing Works

St. Lukes in Old Street was the Printing Works from 1920 to 1956. Prior to 1920 security printing was carried out in the Bank. From 1956 the Bank of England Printing Works has been at Debden Industrial Estate, Loughton, Essex.

Herbert King, Principal Supervisor	1920–7
Herbert George de Fraine, Principal Supervisor	1927–31
Stanley Beaumont Chamberlain (CBE 1947), General Works Manager	1931–48
John Rowland Dudin MC, Works Manager	1948–9
Donald William Tilley, General Manager	1949–59
Henry Loveridge Chadder, General Manager	1959–64
Gordon Chalmers Fortin, General Manager	1964–72
Michael James Stephen Cubbage MBE, General Manager	1972–81
Geoffrey Leonard Wheatley, General Manager	1981–7
Alexander William Jarvis	1987–

Chiefs/Heads of Departments and Areas of Supervision

Chief of Administration

Peter Arthur Storey Taylor (CBE)	1976–80

Banking Supervision

George Blunden	1974–6

William Peter Cooke (also Head of Cashiers Departmental (BAMMS) 1977–9)	1976–80
John Brangwyn Page (combined with supervision of Financial Structure and Institutions Division)	1980–2
William Peter Cooke (Associate Director 1982–8)	1982–5
Rodney Desmond Galpin (Executive Director 1984–8)	1985–8
Brian Quinn (Executive Director 1988–)	1988–

Chiefs of Central Banking Information Department

Guy McOlvin Watson	1959–63
Jasper St. John Rootham	1963–4

Chiefs of Corporate Services

Rodney Desmond Galpin	1980–4
Hugh Christopher Emlyn Harris (Associate Director 1988–)	1984–

Chiefs of Economic Intelligence Department

Roy Ernest Heasman	1964–7
Michael James Thornton MC (CBE)	1967–78
David Alan Walker	1978–80

Chiefs of Establishments

Ronald Clement George Dale (Secretary and Chief of Establishments)	1932–4
John Drysdale Mackenzie	1934–43
John Drysdale Mackenzie } Eric Neale Dalton	1943–5
Eric Neale Dalton	1945–9
Michael McGrath	1949–53
Donald Murray Randell	1953–5
Howard George Askwith	1955–63

Charles Henry Hayden White	1963–8
Kenneth James Stuart Andrews MBE	1968–78
Rodney Desmond Galpin	1978–80

Exchange Control Department

Edwin Brian Bennett DSC	1972–9
Douglas Alfred Dawkins	1979–80

Financial Structure and Supervision/Finance and Industry

John Brangwyn Page (Executive Director 1980–2)	1980–2
David Alan Walker (Executive Director 1982–8)	1982–8
Pendarell Hugh Kent (Associate Director 1988–93, Executive Director 1994–)	1988–

Legal Unit

Peter Charles Peddie (Adviser to the Governors 1993–)	1993–

Chiefs of Management Services

Roy Ernest Heasman	1970–3
George Blunden	1973–4
Guy Laurence Layard de Moubray	1974–6

Operations and Services

George Blunden (Executive Director 1976–84)	1980–4
Rodney Desmond Galpin (Executive Director 1984–8)	1984–5
Douglas Alfred Dawkins (Associate Director 1985–7)	1985–7
Hugh Christopher Emlyn Harris (Associate Director 1988–)	1988–

Overseas and Foreign Department

Henry Arthur Siepmann—Acting Chief	1932–5
Cameron Fromanteel Cobbald—Acting Deputy Chief	1933–5
Frederic Francis Joseph Powell—Deputy Chief	1935–41

Exchange Control and Overseas

Frank Cyril Hawker—Deputy Chief Cashier	1944–8
John Lenox Fisher—Deputy Chief Cashier	1948–50
Anthony P. Grafftey-Smith—Deputy Chief Cashier	1948–51
Laurence James Menzies—Deputy Chief Cashier	1951–7
Maurice Henry Parsons—Deputy Chief Cashier	1952–4
Guy McOlvin Watson—Deputy Chief Cashier	1954–7
Cyril Robert Parke Hamilton—Deputy Chief Cashier	1955–7

Overseas Department

Guy McOlvin Watson	1957–9
Jasper St. John Rootham	1964–5
Roy Pentelow Fenton CMG	1965–75
Stanley Walden Payton CMG	1975–80

Policy and Markets

Economics

John Christopher Roderick Dow (Executive Director 1973–81, Adviser to the Governors 1981–4)	1980–4
John Stanton Flemming (Adviser to the Governors 1984–8, Associate Director 1988, Executive Director 1988–91)	1984–91

Mervyn Allister King   1991–
(Executive Director 1991–)

Home Finance

John Standish Fforde   1980–2
(Executive Director 1970–82)

Edward Alan John George   1982–90
(Executive Director 1982–90)

Anthony Laurie Coleby   1990–4
(Executive Director 1990–4)

Ian Plenderleith   1990–
(Associate Director 1990–4, Executive
Director 1994–)

Overseas

Anthony David Loehnis   1980–9
(Associate Director 1980–1, Executive
Director 1981–9)

Andrew Duncan Crockett   1989–93
(Executive Director 1989–93)

Special Investigations Unit

Ian Glendinning Watt   1993–
(Adviser to the Governors 1993–)

Heads of Division or Function

This list of Bank of England Officials gives the names of the Heads of Division etc. from the late 1970s. It takes no account of the major re-organization which was implemented from 4 July as a result of which certain roles disappeared and others significantly changed.

Administration

Anne Skinner   1988–92

Banking

Graham Edward Alfred Kentfield   1991
Merlyn Vivienne Lowther   1992–

Banking Supervision

George Blunden   1974–6

William Peter Cooke (Associate Director 1982–8)	1976–84
Brian Quinn (Assistant Director 1982–8)	1984–8
Roger Anthony Barnes (Assistant Director 1987–93)	1988–93
Michael David Kenneth W. Foot	1993–

Banknotes and Security

Peter George Mitchell	1991–

Director of Studies Centre for Central Banking Studies

Michael Earling Hewitt	1991–

Officials' Career Development—Advisers

David Shilson	1988–92
Timothy Patrick Sweeney	1992–

Computer Services

Guy Laurence Layard de Moubray	1976
Ronald Alfred John Middleton MBE (Deputy Chief of Administration)	1976–80

Economic Section

Leslie Arthur Dicks-Mireaux (Deputy Chief of EID) (Special Adviser 1981–4)	1970–80
Christopher Thomas Taylor	1984–90
Lionel Dennis Dixon Price	1990–

Finance and Resource Planning

John Sandford Rumins (Deputy Chief of Corporate Services)	1980–

Financial Markets and Institutions

Thomas Alistair Clark	1988–93
John Stephen Beverly	1993–

Financial Statistics

Geoffrey Kenneth Willetts	1980–7
Peter Anthony Bull	1988–

Financial Structure and Institutions

Roger Charles Stevens	1980–1

Financial Supervision General

Roger Charles Stevens (Senior Adviser)	1982
Douglas Alfred Dawkins (Assistant Director 1980–5)	1983
Michael Earling Hewitt (Senior Adviser)	1984–8
Thomas Alistair Clark	1988–9

Foreign Exchange

George Malcolm Gill	1982–8
Michael David Kenneth W. Foot	1988–90
William Anthony Allen	1990–

Chief Manager Foreign Exchange

Derrick Alfred Henry Byatt (Adviser—Foreign Exchange 1975–80)	1980–6
Terence Ross Smeeton	1986–

Chief Manager Reserves Management Foreign Exchange

Oliver Page	1988–90
Iain David Saville	1991–4
Sue Camper	1994–

Gilt-Edged/Gilt-Edged and Money Markets

Edward Alan John George	1980–2

Ian Plenderleith	1982–90
(Assistant Director 1986–90)	
William Anthony Allen	1990
John Coupe Townend	1990

Government Brokers

Nigel Frederick Althaus (Kt. 1989)	1982–9
(formerly Senior Partner Mullens & Co,	
joined Bank Staff in 1986)	
Ian Plenderleith	1989–
(Assistant Director 1986–90)	
(Associate Director 1990–4)	
(Executive Director 1994–)	

Chief Dealing Manager Gilt-Edged and Money Markets Division

John George Hill	1987–

Industrial Finance

Alan Thomas Bell	1980–3
Roger Harry Lomax	1984–6
Michael Thomas Ramsay Smith	1988–

Information

Brian Quinn	1980–1
Lionel Dennis Dixon Price	1982–3
Hugh Pendarell Kent	1984–5
Philip John Warland	1985–9
John Richard Evelegh Footman	1989–

International Division

David George Holland CMG	1980–5

International (Developing World)

Oliver Page	1990–3
Anthony Robert Latter	1993–

G10 and Europe

John Edward Weston Kirby	1986–8

International (European)

Lionel Dennis Dixon Price	1989–90
Michael David Kenneth W. Foot	1990–3
Thomas Alistair Clark	1993–

International (Financial Institutions Developing Countries)

Pendarell Hugh Kent	1986–8
John Edward Weston Kirby	1988–90

International (Financial Markets and World Economy)

Lionel Dennis Dixon Price	1986–8

International (Financial Markets, World Economy and Debt/ International Finance, Economy and Debt)

Anthony Robert Latter	1988–91

International (General)

Ronald Henry Gilchrist	1986–7

International (Industrial World)

David William Green	1990
Anthony Robert Latter	1992–3
Stephen Paul Collins	1993–

International (North America, Western Europe, and Japan)

John Edward Weston Kirby	1986–8
Lionel Dennis Dixon Price	1988–9

International (North America and Japan)

David William Green	1990–2

Territorial Division

Michael John Balfour	1980–5

Management Services

Leslie Geoffrey Lloyd	1988–91
Gordon Midgley	1992–

Money Markets

George Malcolm Gill (Chief Manager Banking and Credit Markets)	1980–2
Anthony Laurie Coleby (Assistant Director 1980–7)	1980–7

Money Markets Operations

William Anthony Allen	1987–90

Payment Systems

Peter William Allsopp	1991–

Personnel

Roger John Woodley (Divisional Chief of Corporate Services)	1984–7
David Aquila Sharp (Divisional Chief of Corporate Services)	1988–94

Premises

Hugh Christopher Emlyn Harris (Deputy Chief of Corporate Services)	1980–3
John Anthony Penny	1984
Gerald Francis John Everett (Principal 1985–8)	1988–

Staff Development and Administration/Management Development and S and PM Administration

Donald George Herbert Cook (Deputy Chief of Corporate Services)	1980–2

Systems and Office Services

Ronald Alfred John Middleton MBE (Deputy Chief of Corporate Services)	1980–3
Stuart Rodwell Chandler	1984–8

Wholesale Markets Supervision

John Coupe Townend	1987–90
John Stephen Beverly	1990–3
Oliver Page	1993–

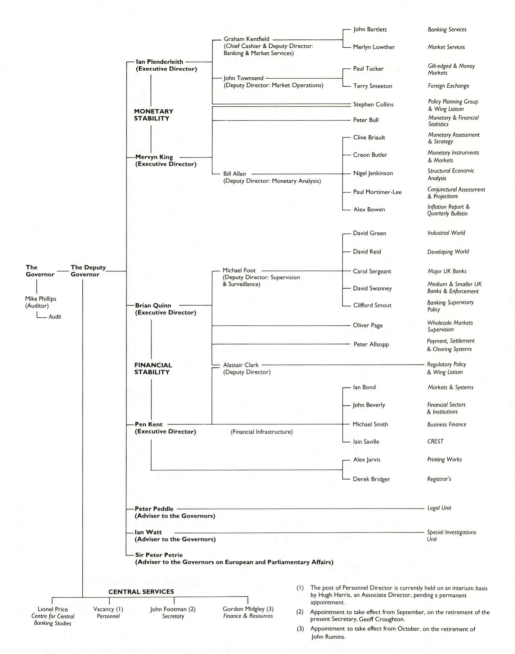

Fig. A2.1 *Organizational Diagram showing the most important officers of the Bank and their responsibilities, July 1994*

Notes:

[1] The post of Personnel Director is currently held on an interim basis by Hugh Harris, an Associate Director, pending a permanent appointment.

[2] Appointment to take effect from September 1994, on the retirement of the present Secretary, Geoff Croughton.

[3] Appointment to take effect from October, on the retirement of John Rumins.

Select Bibliography

Place of publication is London unless specified differently.

ACRES, W. M., *The Bank of England from Within, 1694–1900* (Oxford, 1931).
—— 'Directors of the Bank of England', *Notes and Queries*, 179 (20 July–21 Sept. 1940).
ALLY, R., 'War and Gold—The Bank of England, the London Gold Market and South Africa's Gold, 1914–19', *Journal of Southern African Studies*, 17 (1991).
—— *Gold and Empire: The Bank of England and South Africa's Gold Producers, 1886–1926* (Johannesburg, 1994).
—— 'The South African Pound Comes of Age: Sterling, the Bank of England and South Africa's Monetary Policy, 1914–25', *Journal of Imperial and Commonwealth History*, 22 (1994).
ANDRÉADÈS, A., *History of the Bank of England, 1640 to 1903* (1909).
ARMITAGE, D., ' "The Projecting Age": William Paterson and the Bank of England', *History Today*, 44 (June 1994).
ARTIS, M. J., *Foundations of British Monetary Policy* (Oxford, 1965).
ATKIN, J., 'Official Regulation of British Overseas Investment, 1914–1931', *Economic History Review*, 2nd ser., 23 (1970).
—— *British Overseas Investment, 1918–1931* (New York, 1977).
ATTARD, B., 'The Bank of England and the Origins of the Niemeyer Mission, 1921–1930', *Australian Economic History Review*, 32 (1992).
BAMBERG, J. H., 'The Rationalization of the British Cotton Industry in the Interwar Years', *Textile History*, 19 (1988).
BINNEY, J. E. D., *British Public Finance and Administration, 1774–92* (Oxford, 1958).
BLOOMFIELD, A. I., *Monetary Policy under the International Gold Standard, 1880–1914* (New York, 1959).
BORDO, M. D. and SCHWARTZ, A. J. (eds.), *A Retrospective on the Classical Gold Standard, 1821–1931* (Chicago, 1984).
BOWDEN, S. and COLLINS, M., 'The Bank of England, Industrial Regeneration, and Hire Purchase between the Wars', *Economic History Review*, 2nd ser., 45 (1992).
BOYCE, R. W. D., *British Capitalism at the Crossroads, 1919–1932* (Cambridge, 1987).
BOYLE, A., *Montagu Norman: A Biography* (1967).
BREWER, J., *The Sinews of Power: War, Money and the English State, 1688–1783* (1989).
BURK, K., 'The Treasury: From Impotence to Power', in K. Burk (ed.), *War and the State: The Transformation of British Government, 1914–1919* (1982).
—— *Britain, America and the Sinews of War, 1914–1918* (1985).
—— *The First Privatisation: The Politicians, The City, and the Denationalisation of Steel* (1988).

—— *Morgan Grenfell, 1838–1988: The Biography of a Merchant Bank* (Oxford, 1989).

BYATT, D., *Promises to Pay: The First Three Hundred Years of Bank of England Notes* (1994).

CAIN, P. J. and HOPKINS, A. G.,*British Imperialism: Crisis and Deconstruction, 1914–1990* (1993).

—— —— *British Imperialism: Innovation and Expansion, 1688– 1914* (1993).

CAIRNCROSS, A., 'Prelude to Radcliffe: Monetary Policy in the United Kingdom, 1948–57', *Rivista Di Storia Economica*, 2nd ser., 4 (1987).

—— 'The Bank of England: Relationships with the Government, the Civil Service, and Parliament', in G. Toniolo, *Central Banks' Independence in Historical Perspective* (Berlin, 1988).

—— (ed.), *The Robert Hall Diaries, 1947–53* (1989).

—— (ed.), *The Robert Hall Diaries, 1954–61* (1991).

—— and EICHENGREEN, B., *Sterling in Decline: The Devaluations of 1931, 1949 and 1967* (Oxford, 1983).

CAPIE, F. H. and WEBBER, A., *A Monetary History of the United Kingdom, 1870–1982*, i, *Data, Sources, Methods* (1985).

—— and WOOD, G. E. (eds.), *Financial Crises and the World Banking System* (1986).

—— —— 'Central Banks and Inflation: A Historical Perspective', *Central Banking*, 2 (Autumn/Winter 1991).

—— MILLS, T. C., and WOOD, G. E., 'Debt Management and Interest Rates: The British Stock Conversion of 1932', *Applied Economics*, 18 (1986).

—— GOODHART, C. A. E., and SCHNADT, N., *The Development of Central Banking* (1994).

CASSIS, Y., 'La Banque d'Angleterre et la position internationale de la Grande-Bretagne, 1870–1914', *Relations Internationales*, 56 (1988).

—— *City Bankers, 1890–1914* (Cambridge, 1994).

CECCO, M. DE, *Money and Empire: The International Gold Standard, 1890–1914* (Oxford, 1974).

CHEONG, W. E., 'China Houses and the Bank of England Crisis of 1825', *Business History*, 15 (1973).

CLAPHAM, J., 'The Private Business of the Bank of England, 1744–1800', *Economic History Review*, 11 (1941).

—— *The Bank of England: A History* (Cambridge, 1944).

CLARKE, P., 'Churchill's Economic Ideas, 1900–1930', in R. Blake and W. R. Louis, *Churchill* (Oxford, 1993).

CLARKE, S. V. O., *Central Bank Co-operation, 1924–1931* (New York, 1967).

—— *The Reconstruction of the International Monetary System: The Attempts of 1922 and 1933* (Princeton, NJ, 1973).

—— *Exchange Rate Stabilization in the Mid-1930s: Negotiating the Tripartite Agreement* (Princeton, NJ, 1977).

CLAVIN, P., ' "The Fetishes of So-Called International Bankers": Central Bank Co-operation for the World Economic Conference, 1932–3', *Contemporary European History*, 1 (1992).

CLAY, H., *Lord Norman* (1957).

COLLINS, M., 'The Langton Papers: Banking and Bank of England Policy in the 1830s', *Economica*, NS 39 (1972).

COLLINS, M., *Money and Banking in the UK: A History* (1988).

—— 'The Banking Crisis of 1878', *Economic History Review*, 2nd ser., 42 (1989).

—— 'The Bank of England as Lender of Last Resort', *Economic History Review*, 2nd ser., 45 (1992).

COPE, S. R., *Walter Boyd: A Merchant Banker in the Age of Napoleon* (1983).

COTTRELL, P. L., 'London, Paris and Silver, 1848–1867', in A. Slaven and D. H. Aldcroft (eds.), *Business, Banking and Urban History: Essays in Honour of S. G. Checkland* (Edinburgh, 1982).

DAUNTON, M. J., 'Inside the Bank of England', *Twentieth Century British History*, 4 (1993).

DAVENPORT-HINES, R. P. T., 'Thomas Sivewright Catto, 1st Lord Catto of Cairncatto', in D. J. Jeremy (ed.), *Dictionary of Business Biography*, i (1984).

—— 'Cameron Fromanteel Cobbold, 1st Lord Cobbold', in D. J. Jeremy (ed.), *Dictionary of Business Biography, i* (1984).

—— 'Walter Cunliffe, 1st Lord Cunliffe', in D. J. Jeremy (ed.), *Dictionary of Business Biography, i* (1984).

DAYER, R. A., *Finance and Empire: Sir Charles Addis, 1861–1945* (1988).

DICKSON, P. G. M., *The Financial Revolution in England: A Study in the Development of Public Credit, 1688–1756* (1967).

DRUMMOND, I. M., *London, Washington, and the Management of the Franc, 1936–39* (Princeton, NJ., 1979).

—— *The Floating Pound and the Sterling Area, 1931–1939* (Cambridge, 1981).

—— *The Gold Standard and the International Monetary System, 1900–1939* (Basingstoke, 1987).

EICHENGREEN, B., *Elusive Stability: Essays in the History of International Finance, 1919–1939* (Cambridge, 1990).

—— *Golden Fetters: The Gold Standard and the Great Depression, 1919–1939* (New York, 1992).

—— (ed.), *The Gold Standard in Theory and History* (1985).

FAY, S., *Portrait of an Old Lady: Turmoil at the Bank of England* (1987).

FETTER, F. W., *Development of British Monetary Orthodoxy, 1797–1875* (Cambridge, Mass., 1965).

FFORDE, J., *The Bank of England and Public Policy, 1941–1958* (Cambridge, 1992).

FLETCHER, G. A., *The Discount Houses in London: Principles, Operations and Change* (1976).

FORBES, N., 'London Banks, the German Standstill Agreements, and "Economic Appeasement" in the 1930s', *Economic History Review*, 2nd ser., 40 (1987).

FORD, A. G., 'International Financial Policy and the Gold Standard, 1870–1914', in P. Mathias and S. Pollard (eds.), *The Cambridge Economic History of Europe*, viii, *The Industrial Economies: The Development of Economic and Social Policies* (Cambridge, 1989).

FRAINE, H. G. DE, *Servant of This House: Life in the Old Bank of England* (1960).

GEDDES, P., *Inside the Bank of England* (1987).

GIUSEPPI, J., *The Bank of England: A History from its Foundation in 1694* (1966).

GOODHART, C. A. E., *The Business of Banking, 1891–1914* (1972).

—— *The Evolution of Central Banks: A Natural Development?* (1985).

GREEN, EDWIN, and MOSS, M., *A Business of National Importance: The Royal Mail Shipping Group, 1902–1937* (1982).

GREEN, E. H. H., 'The Influence of the City over British Economic Policy, c.1880–1960', in Y. Cassis (ed.), *Finance and Financiers in European History, 1880–1960* (Cambridge, 1992).

GREGORY, T., *The Present Position of Central Banks* (1955).

—— 'The "Norman Conquest" Reconsidered', *Lloyds Bank Review* (Oct. 1957).

—— 'Lord Norman: A New Interpretation', *Lloyds Bank Review* (Apr. 1968).

HARGREAVES, E. L., *The National Debt* (1930).

HAWTREY, R. G., *A Century of Bank Rate* (1938).

HEIM, C. E., 'Limits to Intervention: The Bank of England and Industrial Diversification in the Depressed Areas', *Economic History Review*, 2nd ser., 37 (1984).

HENNESSY, E., *A Domestic History of the Bank of England, 1930–1960* (Cambridge, 1992).

HILTON, B., *Corn, Cash, Commerce: The Economic Policies of the Tory Governments, 1815–1830* (Oxford, 1977).

HINDS, A. E., 'Imperial Policy and Colonial Sterling Balances, 1943–56', *Journal of Imperial and Commonwealth History*, 19 (1991).

HORSEFIELD, J. K., 'The Bank and Its Treasure', *Economica*, NS 7 (1940).

—— 'The Duties of a Banker: The Eighteenth Century View', *Economica*, NS 8 (1941).

—— 'The Duties of a Banker—II: The Effects of Inconvertibility', *Economica*, NS 11 (1944).

—— 'The Origins of the Bank Charter Act, 1844', *Economica*, NS 11 (1944).

—— 'The Bankers and the Bullionists in 1819', *Journal of Political Economy*, 57 (1949).

—— 'The Opinions of Horsley Palmer', *Economica*, NS 16 (1949).

—— *British Monetary Experiments, 1650–1710* (1960).

HOWE, A., 'From "Old Corruption" to "New Probity": The Bank of England and its Directors in the Age of Reform', *Financial History Review*, 1 (1994).

HOWSON, S. 'The Origins of Dear Money, 1919–20', *Economic History Review*, 2nd ser., 27 (1974).

—— *Domestic Monetary Management in Britain, 1919–38* (Cambridge, 1975).

—— *Sterling's Managed Float: The Operations of the Exchange Equalisation Account, 1932–39* (Princeton, NJ, 1980).

—— 'Cheap Money and Debt Management in Britain, 1932–51', in P. L. Cottrell and D. E. Moggridge (eds.), *Money and Power: Essays in Honour of L. S. Pressnell* (1988).

—— *British Monetary Policy, 1945–51* (Oxford, 1993).

KING, W. T. C., *History of the London Discount Market* (1936).

KUNZ, D. B., *The Battle for Britain's Gold Standard in 1931* (1987).

KYNASTON, D., *The Chancellor of the Exchequer* (Lavenham, 1980).

—— *The City of London*, i. *A World of Its Own, 1815–1890* (1994).

LAWSON, N., *The View from No. 11: Memoirs of a Tory Radical* (1992).

LENTIN, A., 'Walter Cunliffe, first Baron Cunliffe', in C. S. Nicholls (ed.), *The Dictionary of National Biography: Missing Persons* (Oxford, 1993).

LÉVY-LEBOYER, M., 'Central Banking and Foreign Trade: The Anglo-American Cycle in the 1830s', in C. P. Kindleberger and J.-P. Laffargue (eds.), *Financial Crises: Theory, History and Policy* (Cambridge, 1982).

LISLE-WILLIAMS, M., 'Beyond the Market: The Survival of Family Capitalism in the English Merchant Banks', *British Journal of Sociology*, 35 (1984).

LOVE, P., 'Niemeyer's Australian Diary and other English Records of his Mission', *Historical Studies*, 20 (1982).

LOVELL, M. C., 'The Role of the Bank of England as Lender of Last Resort in the Crises of the Eighteenth Century', *Explorations in Entrepreneurial History*, 10 (1957–8).

MARRINER, S., 'William Lidderdale', in D. J. Jeremy (ed.), *Dictionary of Business Biography,* iii (1985).

MEYER, R. H., *Bankers' Diplomacy: Monetary Stabilization in the Twenties* (New York, 1970).

MICHIE, R. C., 'The Myth of the Gold Standard: An Historian's Approach', *Revue internationale d'histoire de la banque*, 32–3 (1986).

MIDDLEMAS, K., *Power, Competition and the State,* i, *Britain in Search of Balance, 1940–61* (Basingstoke, 1986).

—— *Power, Competition and the State,* ii, *Threats to the Postwar Settlement: Britain, 1961–74* (Basingstoke, 1990).

—— *Power, Competition and the State,* iii, *The End of the Postwar Era: Britain since 1974* (Basingstoke, 1991).

MOGGRIDGE, D. E., *British Monetary Policy, 1924–1931: The Norman Conquest of $4.86* (Cambridge, 1972).

MORAN, M., 'Power, Policy and the City of London', in R. King (ed.), *Capital and Politics* (1983).

—— *The Politics of Banking: The Strange Case of Competition and Credit Control* (Basingstoke, 1984).

—— 'City Pressure: The City of London as a Pressure Group since 1945', *Contemporary Record*, 2 (Summer 1988).

MOREAU, E., *The Golden Franc: Memoirs of a Governor of the Bank of France: The Stabilization of the Franc, 1926–1928* (Boulder, Colo., 1991).

MORGAN, E. V., *The Theory and Practice of Central Banking, 1797–1913* (Cambridge, 1943).

—— *Studies in British Financial Policy, 1914–25* (1952).

—— and THOMAS, W. A., *The Stock Exchange: Its History and Functions* (1962).

MOSS, D. J., 'The Bank of England and the Country Banks, 1827–33', *Economic History Review*, 2nd ser., 34 (1981).

—— 'The Bank of England and the Establishment of a Branch System, 1826–1829', *Canadian Journal of History*, 27 (1992).

MOSS, M., 'Montagu Collet Norman, Lord Norman of St Clere', in D. J. Jeremy (ed.), *Dictionary of Business Biography,* iv (1985).

MOURÉ, K., 'The Limits to Central Bank Co-operation, 1916–36', *Contemporary European History*, 1 (1992).

NEAL, L., *The Rise of Financial Capitalism: International Capital Markets in the Age of Reason* (Cambridge, 1990).

NEVIN, E., *The Mechanism of Cheap Money: A Study of British Monetary Policy, 1931–1939* (Cardiff, 1955).

—— and DAVIS, E. W., *The London Clearing Banks* (1970).

OGDEN, T., 'An Analysis of Bank of England Discount and Advance Behaviour, 1870–1914', in J. Foreman-Peck (ed.), *New Perspectives on the Late Victorian*

Economy: Essays in Quantitative Economic History, 1860–1914 (Cambridge, 1990).

ORBELL, J., 'John Baring, 2nd Lord Revelstoke', in D. J. Jeremy (ed.), *Dictionary of Business Biography*, i (1984).

—— 'Sir Edward Robert Peacock', in D. J. Jeremy (ed.), *Dictionary of Business Biography*, iv (1985).

ORDE, A., *British Policy and European Reconstruction after the First World War* (Cambridge, 1990).

—— 'Baring Brothers, the Bank of England, the British Government and the Czechoslovak State Loan of 1922', *English Historical Review*, 106 (1991).

PARKER, R. A. C., 'The Pound Sterling, the American Treasury and British Preparations for War, 1938–1939', *English Historical Review*, 98 (1983).

PÉTERI, G., 'Central Bank Diplomacy: Montagu Norman and Central Europe's Monetary Reconstruction after World War I', *Contemporary European History*, 1 (1992).

PETERS, J., 'The British Government and the City-Industry Divide: The Case of the 1914 Financial Crisis', *Twentieth Century British History*, 4 (1993).

PLUMPTRE, A. F. W., *Central Banking in the British Dominions* (Toronto, 1940).

PRESSNELL, L. S., *Country Banking in the Industrial Revolution* (Oxford, 1956).

—— 'Gold Reserves, Banking Reserves, and the Baring Crisis of 1890', in C. R. Whittlesey and J. S. G. Wilson (eds.), *Essays in Money and Banking in Honour of R. S. Sayers* (Oxford, 1968).

—— '1925: The Burden of Sterling', *Economic History Review*, 2nd ser., 31 (1978).

—— *External Economic Policy since the War*, i, *The Post-War Financial Settlement* (1986).

PROCTER, S. J., 'Floating Convertibility: The Emergence of the Robot Plan, 1951–52', *Contemporary Record*, 7 (1993).

REID, M., *The Secondary Banking Crisis, 1973–75: Its Causes and Course* (1982).

—— *All-Change in the City: The Revolution in Britain's Financial Sector* (1988).

—— 'Mrs Thatcher's Impact on the City', *Contemporary Record*, 2 (Summer 1989).

RICHARDS, R. D., 'The First Fifty Years of the Bank of England (1694–1744)', in J. G. van Dillen (ed.), *History of the Principal Public Banks* (The Hague, 1934).

ROBERTS, R., 'Regulatory Responses to the Rise of the Market for Corporate Control in Britain in the 1950s', *Business History*, 34 (1992).

ROSEVEARE, H., *The Treasury: The Evolution of a British Institution* (1969).

—— *The Financial Revolution, 1660–1760* (1991).

SANTONI, G. J., 'A Private Central Bank: Some Olde English Lessons', *The Federal Reserve Bank of St Louis Economic Review*, 66 (Apr. 1984).

SAYERS, R. S., *Bank of England Operations, 1890–1914* (1936).

—— 'The Bank in the Gold Market, 1890–1914', in T. S. Ashton and R. S. Sayers (eds.), *Papers in English Monetary History* (Oxford, 1953).

—— *Financial Policy, 1939–45* (1956).

—— *Central Banking after Bagehot* (Oxford, 1957).

—— *Gilletts in the London Money Market* (Oxford, 1968).

—— *The Bank of England, 1891–1944* (Cambridge, 1976).

SAYERS, R. S., 'Bank Rate in Keynes's Century', *Proceedings of the British Academy*, 65 (1979).

SCAMMELL, W. M., *The London Discount Market* (1968).

SCHENK, C. R., 'The Origins of a Central Bank in Malaya and the Transition to Independence, 1954–59', *Journal of Imperial and Commonwealth History*, 21 (1993).

SCHUMANN-BACIA, E., *John Soane and the Bank of England* (1991).

SLINN, J., *A History of Freshfields* (1984).

STRANGE, S., *Sterling and British Policy: A Political Study of an International Currency in Decline* (1971).

TEICHOVA, A., 'Versailles and the Expansion of the Bank of England into Central Europe', in N. Horn and J. Kocka (eds.), *Law and the Formation of the Big Enterprises in the 19th and early 20th Centuries* (Göttingen, 1979).

TOLLIDAY, S., *Business, Banking, and Politics: The Case of British Steel, 1918–1939* (Cambridge, Mass., 1987).

TOMLINSON, B. R., 'Indo-British Relations in the Post-Colonial Era: The Sterling Balances Negotiations, 1947–49', *Journal of Imperial and Commonwealth History*, 13 (1985).

VAN-HELTEN, J. J., 'Empire and High Finance: South Africa and the International Gold Standard, 1890–1914', *Journal of African History*, 23 (1982).

WAINWRIGHT, D., *Government Broker: The Story of an Office and of Mullens & Co* (1990).

WHALE, P. B., 'A Retrospective View of the Bank Charter Act, 1844', in T. S. Ashton and R. S. Sayers (eds.), *Papers in English Monetary History* (Oxford, 1953).

WHITE, L. H., *Free Banking in Britain: Theory, Experience, and Debate, 1800–1845* (Cambridge, 1984).

WILLIAMSON, P., 'A "Bankers Ramp"? Financiers and the British Political Crisis of August 1931', *English Historical Review*, 99 (1984).

—— 'Financiers, the Gold Standard and British Politics, 1925–1931', in J. Turner (ed.), *Businessmen and Politics: Studies of Business Activity in British Politics, 1900–1945* (1984).

—— *National Crisis and National Government: British Politics, the Economy and Empire, 1926–1932* (Cambridge, 1992).

WORMELL, J., *The Gilt-Edged Market* (1985).

ZIEGLER, D., *Central Bank, Peripheral Industry: The Bank of England in the Provinces, 1826–1913* (Leicester, 1990).

—— 'The Banking Crisis of 1878: Some Remarks', *Economic History Review*, 2nd ser., 45 (1992).

INDEX

N.B. Page references to charts and tables are in italic. The term 'Bank', when undefined, indicates the Bank of England.